ILLINOIS CENTRAL COLLEGE
PN1995.S34
STACKS
Confessions of a cultist: on the ci

A12900 267634

W9-BCW-209

A12900 267634

PN
1995
.S34

40148

SARRIS
Confessions of a
cultist

WITHDRAWN

EGLI

Illinois Central College
Learning Resource Center

BOOKS BY ANDREW SARRIS

The Films of Josef von Sternberg (1966)
Interviews with Film Directors (1967)
The Film (1968)
The American Cinema: Directors and Directions,
    1929–1968 (1969)
Film 68/69, coeditor (1969)
Confessions of a Cultist: On the Cinema,
    1955–1969 (1970)

Andrew Sarris

CONFESSIONS
OF A CULTIST:

On the Cinema,
1955-1969

Illinois Central College
Learning Resouce Center

Simon and Schuster · New York

40448

PN
1995
. S34

All rights reserved
including the right of reproduction
in whole or in part in any form
Copyright © 1961, 1962, 1963,
  1964, 1965, 1966, 1967, 1968,
1969, 1970 by Andrew Sarris
Published by Simon and Schuster
Rockefeller Center, 630 Fifth Avenue
New York, New York 10020

First printing

SBN 671-20554-4 cloth
SBN 671-20555-2 paper
Library of Congress Catalog Card Number: 71-116499
Manufactured in the United States of America
Printed by The Murray Printing Company, Forge Village, Mass.
Bound by The Book Press, Brattleboro, Vermont

For permission to reprint articles originally appearing in their pub-
lications, the author gives grateful acknowledgment to the fol-
lowing:
Book World for "Jules and Jim Meets Psycho";
Cavalier Magazine for "Veni, Vidi, Vitti," copyright © 1963 by
Dugent Publishing Co., Inc.;
Film Culture Magazine for "Guys and Dolls," "The Rose Tat-
too," "Court-Martial," "A Face in the Crowd," "Cabiria" and
"Misfits and Misalliances";
Gentlemen's Quarterly for "Belmondo," copyright © 1966 by
Esquire, Inc.;
Movie Magazine for "What Ever Happened to Baby Jane?";
The New York Times for "Carl Dreyer, 1889-1968," "Directors,
How Personal Can You Get?" and "Marilyn Monroe: A Review
of Norma Jean," copyright © 1968, 1969 by The New York
Times Company;
N.Y. Film Bulletin for "Rossellini, Renoir and Ford" and "Dia-
logue of a Schizocritic";
and The Village Voice, in which the rest of the articles in this
book originally appeared.

To Dan Wolf and Ed Fancher for giving a Voice to my views.

To the John Simon Guggenheim Memorial Foundation, and its President, Mr. Gordon N. Ray, for granting me a year of grace.

To all the boys in the back room (and front row) for the benefit and pleasure of their perceptive comments.

CONTENTS

CONFESSIONS OF A CULTIST: A FOREWORD

My career as a cultist began unobtrusively, if not inadvertently, in a dingy railroad flat on New York's Lower East Side back in the unlamented Eisenhower era. It was there and then that I first met Jonas and Adolfas Mekas, the genially bohemian (actually Lithuanian) editors of a new magazine called *Film Culture*, an unfortunately pompous title that always made me think of microbic movies under glass. I had been taking an evening course in film appreciation at Columbia between meandering through graduate English and malingering in Teachers College. The movie mentor was Roger Tilton, a film-maker (*Jazz Dance*) himself and one of *Film Culture*'s first sponsors, whatever that meant. (Among other "sponsors" listed on a back page were James Agee, Shirley Clarke, David and Francis Flaherty, Lewis Jacobs, Arthur Knight, Helen Levitt, Len Lye, Hans Richter, Willard Van Dyke and Amos Vogel.) Tilton sent me to the Mekas brothers, and the rest is cult history.

The brothers Mekas were generally buried under a pile of manuscripts ranging from the illegible to the unreadable, and I am afraid I only added to the confusion. The entire operation seemed hopelessly impractical to a congenital pessimist like me. I took the satirical view that we were not poor because we were pure, but pure because we were poor, and our integrity was directly proportional to our obscurity. Still, I suppose we represented a new breed of film critic. The cultural rationale for our worthier predecessors—Agee, Ferguson, Levin, Murphy, Sherwood, *et al.*—was that they were too good to be reviewing movies. We, on the contrary, were not considered much good for anything else. Like one-eyed lemmings, we plunged headlong into the murky depths of specialization. No back pages of literary and political pulps for us. We may have lived in a ramshackle house, but we always came in the front door.

Somehow, the first issue of *Film Culture*—January 1955, Volume I, Number 1—had already materialized without my assistance. I was enlisted as a reviewer and editor for Number 2. I recall that I was not enchanted by the prospect of writing and editing for no money at all. It seemed almost as demeaning as paying to be published, an act of vanity I vowed never to perform even at the cost of immortality. However, my bargaining position was not enhanced by the fact that all my previous professional writing credits added up to seven movie columns in the Fort Devens *Dispatch*, within the period of my tour of duty through the Army's movie houses during the Korean war.

At the time I started writing in *Film Culture* I was not quite twenty-seven years old, a dangerously advanced age for a writer *manqué* if not *maudit*, a dreadfully uncomfortable age for a middle-class cultural guerrilla without any base, contacts, or reliable lines of supply. I was of the same generation as Norman Podhoretz, but while he had been "making it" as an undergraduate at Columbia I had drifted, like Jack Kerouac, down from Morningside Heights ever deeper into the darkness of movie houses, not so much in search of a vocation as in flight from the laborious realities of careerism. Nonetheless I agree with Podhoretz that failure is more banal and more boring than success. Indeed, I have always been impatient as a critic with characters (like Ginger Coffey) who manage to mess up every job. The trouble with failure as a subject is that it is not instructive in any way and only contributes to an audience's false sense of superiority. Unfortunately, success stories lack "charm" unless they are leavened with audience-pleasing intimations of futility. The trick of the stand-up comic and the syndicated columnist is to ingratiate himself with his audience by groveling in his own weaknesses and misfortunes, real and fabricated, while withholding all the evidence of his manipulative personality. This strategy evolves from a conspiracy of the successful to delude the unsuccessful into thinking that worldly success doesn't really matter. But as I look back upon my own failures I am appalled by my unoriginal reactions of self-hatred and mean-

spirited paranoia. Every block and hang-up known to the disen-
franchised intellect seemed at the time uniquely personal and
chock-full of anecdotal fascination. My biggest problem was focusing my general knowledge on a specific intellectual target. Novels,
short stories, plays, screenplays, poems slithered off my typewriter
in haphazard spasms of abortive creation. Far from filling up
trunks, I could barely jam up a drawer, and yet if I had been
knowledgeable enough to understand the fantastic odds against
me, I might never have invested in a typewriter. As it was, I was
not even sophisticated enough to realize what a stroke of luck my
meeting with the Mekas brothers turned out to be. I was always
looking beyond *Film Culture* (and later the *Village Voice*) for
more lucrative opportunities elsewhere. There was never a time
that I would not have given up being a cultist to be a careerist.
And then one day—I don't remember exactly when—I realized
that if I had not yet indeed succeeded, I had at least stopped failing. I had managed at long last to function in a role I had improvised with my left hand while my right hand was knocking at all
the doors of the Establishment. I had written and published a
million words under my own name, and I had made contact with
thousands of people, and in the process I had managed to locate
myself while mediating between my readers and the screen.

In the realm of role-playing, I stopped lowering my head at the
epithet "cultist" as soon as I realized that the quasi-religious connotation of the term was somewhat justified for those of us who
loved movies beyond all reason. No less a cultist than the late
André Bazin had once likened film festivals to religious revivals,
and a long sojourn in Paris in 1961 reassured me that film not only
demanded but deserved as much faith as did any other cultural
discipline. (Cultists and buffs in other areas are generally described
as scholars and specialists, but interdisciplinary intolerance seems
to be the eternal reaction of the old against the new.) As I remember that fateful year in Paris, deliriously prolonged conversations
at sidewalk cafés still assault my ears with what in Paris passed for
profundity and in New York for peculiarity. I have never really recovered from the Parisian heresy (in New York eyes) concerning
the sacred importance of the cinema. Hence I returned to New
York not merely a cultist but a subversive cultist with a foreign
ideology.

Thereafter I could see more clearly that the main difference between a cultist and a careerist is that the cultist does not require the justification of a career to pursue his passion, and the careerist does. Indeed, passion is too strong a word to apply to journalistic reviewers who would be equally happy in the Real Estate departments of their publications, or to high-brow humanists who admire the late Siegfried Kracauer's *From Caligari to Hitler* simply because they, like Kracauer, are more interested in Hitler than in *Caligari*. Of course, lacking intellectual discipline, the passion of a cultist could be perverted into mindless mysticism and infantile irrationality. (I must admit that I had qualms about the title of this book after glancing at the lurid *Daily News* headline shortly after the Sharon Tate murders: "Police Seek Cultists.") Still, film scholarship was in such a shambles by the early sixties that the risks of passion were preferable to the rigidities of professionalism.

As I look back on the past I have very mixed feelings about all the slights I have suffered and all the furors I have caused. People were always telling me that I was lucky to be attacked in print and that the only thing that really mattered was the correct spelling of my name. However, it has been my observation that no one enjoys being attacked in print or in person no matter what publicity may accrue from the aggression. Indeed, I have been struck by the inability of critics who love dishing out abuse to take the mildest reproof in return. For myself, I can't really complain in terms of any Kantian categorical imperative. He who lives by the sword of criticism must expect counterthrusts as a matter of course. All that is required of the embattled critic as a test of his courage is that he never lose faith in his own judgment. And all the slings and arrows of outraged opponents never led me to doubt the direction I had chosen as a critic. Part of my intransigence may be attributed to the relative ignorance that my generally bookish attackers displayed in the movie medium. Not that I believe (as do the maxi-McLuhanists) that books have become culturally irrelevant. On the contrary, every aspect of culture is relevant to every other aspect, and the best criticism, like the best poetry, is that which is richest in associations. Unfortunately, too many bookish film critics have perverted the notion of ecumenical erudition by snobbishly subordinating film to every other art. Whereas the late James Agee discovered cinema through his love for movies, too many of his self-proclaimed successors chose to abuse movies in the name of *Kultur*.

Hence I was the beneficiary as well as the victim of the intellectual vacuum that occurred in movie reviewing with the death of Agee in 1955. For reasons that I still do not fully understand, serious film reviewing on a steady basis had fallen into cultural disrepute when I started breaking into print. My very existence was generally ignored for almost eight years, a period in which I was occasionally quoted without credit. Then in 1963 I rose from obscurity to notoriety by being quoted out of context. Even so, I was treated as a relatively unique phenomenon, however invidious to the cultural establishment. The late New York *Herald Tribune* even listed me as one of the phrase-makers of the avant-garde, a distinction that helped keep me unemployable as far as the Establishment was concerned. I didn't realize at the time that slowly but surely I was gathering professional seniority in a discipline that was about to explode. I didn't even have to maneuver or manipulate. All I had to do was stand my ground, and suddenly I would find myself in the center of the cultural landscape, returning in triumph to Columbia University, a scholar more prodigal than prodigious.

Even at the time of my most painfully polemical agonies I realized that most controversies in the intellectual world are determined by the first principle of Euclidean egometry: *Two egos cannot occupy the same position of power at the same time*. It follows that the first inkling that I had acquired a position of power came when I was attacked by other critics. Ironically, my enemies were the first to alert me to the fact that I had followers. And with followers came increased responsibilities to clarify and develop my position as a critic and historian.

Still, I shall not pretend at this late date that my career as a cultist has followed a preconceived pattern. Nor shall I define the role of the film critic in self-congratulatory terms applicable only to me. My response to my role as a critic has generally been intuitive, and nothing is to be gained by institutionalizing my intuitions. Every would-be critic must seek his or her own role in terms of his or her own personality and outlook. I am grateful to film for allowing me to focus my intellectual insights and world views within a manageable frame. I believe the subject of film is larger than any one critic or indeed the entire corps of critics. What follows is my personal view of the films that have helped mold my consciousness. At this climactic moment of self-revelation all I can do is commend my critical soul to your mercy and understanding.

—Andrew Sarris

New York City

January 1970

i
1955-1962

■ 1. *GUYS AND DOLLS*

Stylization is the key to the success of any musical, but it is peculiarly indispensable to *Guys and Dolls*, a Broadway show that came over as a clever, tuneful musical. Hollywood's dismal past is filled with the corpses of clever, tuneful Broadway musicals. Aside from vulgarities of taste, the disastrous film versions of *Oklahoma, Brigadoon,* and *Kiss Me Kate* suffered mainly from the camera's tendency to stare coldly at the musical conceits of fanciful characters. Joseph Mankiewicz and Michael Kidd are therefore to be congratulated for demonstrating in *Guys and Dolls* that the camera can wink, as well as stare, at the improbable.

It is difficult to determine where Joseph Mankiewicz' direction leaves off and Michael Kidd's choreography begins. Theirs is a collective effort of taste, verve and pacing. The choreography is particularly brilliant in the opening scene in Times Square that sets the light-hearted, low-life tone of the entire film. Mankiewicz has wisely employed a stylized set of the Square, combining a painted backdrop with such realistic props of the city as cars, newsstands, and subway entrances. The Damon Runyon world of softhearted hoodlums and beautiful Salvation Army dolls would have been grotesque in documentary process shots of real New York.

It is possible to exaggerate Runyon's contribution to *Guys and Dolls*. The book of the musical by Jo Swerling and Abe Burrows is a creative achievement in its own right. Its authors have developed a well-motivated plot structure to a size Runyon never attempted.

They have also abstracted his most effective literary mannerisms: his oddly pseudo-grammatical insertions ("take it back to from whence it came"), his sentimental vulgarisms ("there's a right broad"), and his pretentious description of the demimonde ("the oldest established permanent floating crap game in New York"). Mankiewicz has made a mistake in naturalizing some of the dialogue: the heaviest scenes are those in which people talk like people.

Frank Loesser's score for both the Broadway musical and the film is by turns melodious and appropriately frenetic. Some of the substitutions, however, are debatable. The film has replaced "Bushel and a Peck" with the ugly burlesque-show vulgarity of "Pet Me Poppa." Gone are such crucial mood songs as "My Time of Day" and "Marry Him Today"—replaced by the less effective "Adelaide" and "A Woman in Love." An argument may be made for cutting out songs that were unsuitable for the untrained voices of Jean Simmons and Marlon Brando, and for cutting, generally, in a score that was much too long for the screen. Yet the feeling persists that a foolish attempt was made to "improve" a score that needed little improvement.

The film is well cast, with two major exceptions. On the positive side is the inspired performance of Jean Simmons as Sarah Brown, the mission doll. Her singing voice seems to get better as it goes along, but it is her exuberant ingenue performance that is the highlight of the film. Vivian Blaine repeats her excellent stage characterization of the dumb blonde, Adelaide, belting out her numbers with professional assurance. The supporting cast contains most of the unforgettable faces of the Broadway production. Stubby Kaye and B. S. Pulley are particularly effective as Nicely-Nicely and Big Julie.

The major flaws in the film are Marlon Brando and Frank Sinatra, who are simply miscast. Brando is all wrong for the role of Sky Masterson, not so much because he can't sing but because both his acting and his speaking voice are much too mannered for the modest demands of his role. For an actor who has demonstrated good voice control in the past, Brando made a big mistake in using the whining, high-pitched drawl of *The Wild One*. Sinatra goes to the other extreme of underacting in the role of Nathan Detroit, a character written with Jewish mannerisms and intonations. Sam

Levene's persuasive stage performance is a major loss to the film. Fortunately, both Brando and Sinatra retain enough personal charm to keep *Guys and Dolls* moving along as the most entertaining musical from Hollywood since *Singin' in the Rain.*

—*Film Culture*, No. 5-6, Winter 1955

■ 2. *THE ROSE TATTOO*

Anna Magnani is one of those rare actresses who can tear a dramatic scene to tatters and in the next instant turn on a brilliant comedy style. Tennessee Williams had Magnani in mind for the role of Serafina when he wrote the play from which he has adapted the film script, and it is frightening to think what this movie would have been without her. She meets every challenge of a confused production, and even when the film is steadily deteriorating into a silly farce, she maintains the integrity of her performance.

Magnani's role is that of a confused widow whose bootlegger-husband has been killed in a police chase. The rose tattoo on his chest is the symbol of her passion and a recurrent motif of the story: her daughter (Marisa Pavan) is named Rosa; her would-be lover (Burt Lancaster) simplemindedly obtains a rose tattoo for *his* chest; her late husband's mistress (Virginia Grey) flaunts her own rose tattoo in a climactic confrontation scene with Magnani. But these other people are just plot dressing, dominated completely by Magnani's wild grief and laughter.

Indeed, the main flaw in *The Rose Tattoo* is Burt Lancaster's unskilled performance as Serafina's idiot lover. It is painful to report on Lancaster's deficiencies; no actor in Hollywood has higher notions of acting. In 1948 Lancaster took a pay cut to appear in Arthur Miller's *All My Sons*; he was just adequate. He took another pay cut in 1952 for William Inge's *Come Back Little Sheba*, in which he was badly miscast. Now, with *The Rose Tattoo* of Tennessee Williams, Lancaster has acted in works by America's three leading dramatists. It is about time that he realized he is all wrong for these difficult roles. Yet, much more talented actors could use some of Lancaster's aspiration.

After Lancaster, the main trouble with *The Rose Tattoo* is the absence of any unifying tone. The line between drama and farce is always very thin in a Williams play. Williams has them separated in his mind, no doubt, but unless he has a director like Kazan to keep the line rigid, his scripts degenerate in the playing. Daniel Mann is still relatively new in the film medium, and although his direction shows some promise, he is still weak in developing a unified conception for his actors.

The other actors besides Magnani and Lancaster (and Jo Van Fleet in a minor role) are all treated with great seriousness. The insipid subplot between Rosa and her pure-minded sailor (Ben Cooper) should have been played lightly to be at all bearable. Instead, it becomes cloying in its bogus innocence. It is possible that if Mann and Williams had thrown all their cards on a comic interpretation of the theme, possibly going so far as to burlesque the *commedia dell'arte* in decadent New Orleans, *The Rose Tattoo* might have been salvaged. As it is, there is nothing to recommend in the film but the incomparable Magnani.

—Film Culture, No. 5-6, Winter 1955

■ 3. COURT-MARTIAL

Court-Martial is a typical British well-made play transcribed faithfully and unimaginatively to the screen. The cinema in Britain has always been closer to the theater than Hollywood has been to Broadway, not just in land miles but in professional attitudes. British stage actors and dramatists don't strike soul-selling postures when they make films. Nor do they renounce one medium or the other at given intervals. The main drawback to this civilized relationship is that the stage seems to dominate the screen in adaptations of plays.

Court-Martial is theatrical enough, with its courtroom scenes of Major Carrington, V.C. (David Niven), defending himself against charges of diverting military funds for his own purposes. There are all the recognizable bits of stage business to liven up the stage talk.

Anthony Asquith, a once promising director who has become less and less creative in his medium, excludes any cinematic foreshortening of theatrical effects; there is no real background music, for example. The sole power of the film is derived from the excellent readings of the dialogue.

The film's big scene occurs outside the courtroom between Major Carrington's wife (Margaret Leighton) and his mistress (Noelle Middleton). The scene almost shocks American audiences because of its sexual frankness and the sympathetic quality of the two antagonists. It is refreshing, indeed, to find a film that does not "clean up" the play from which it is adapted. It is refreshing also not to see the cold hand of the censor striking down a nice girl for admitting her affair with a married man.

—*Film Culture*, No. 5-6, Winter 1955

■ 4. A FACE IN THE CROWD

In tracing the rise and fall of a homespun television personality turned demagogue, *A Face in the Crowd* exhibits a tough-minded approach to the problems of mass culture and the facile manipulation of public opinion. Elia Kazan and Budd Schulberg employ both hilarious satire and bitter invective to dramatize their point. An orgiastic drum majorettes' contest in Arkansas ridicules the hypocritical exploitation of leg-bared adolescent girls for the nominal art of baton twirling. The absurdity of charity telethons, television weddings, soft-sell and hard-sell advertising techniques spills over into a broader indictment of susceptible audiences. If Kazan and Schulberg had been content to make their case by implication, *A Face in the Crowd* might have been a completely sophisticated piece of movie-making. Instead, every idea is completely spelled out, and the film degenerates into preposterous liberal propaganda.

Kazan and Schulberg start off by creating authentic roots for their central character, a hillbilly singer and folksy philosopher called "Lonesome Rhodes." The fly-swatting indolence of a small town in Arkansas and the country-music hysteria of Memphis are palpably real. When the action shifts to the well-upholstered advertising agencies and penthouses of New York, Lonesome Rhodes is transformed into a malignant caricature; his shows become incredibly offensive and lecherous even for television, and as a consequence, his audiences are implicitly greater idiots than ever. It is then possible for Kazan and Schulberg to present a fantastic political conspiracy.

Lonesome Rhodes attracts a reactionary cabal, whose members speak of rule by the elite, publicly oppose Social Security, and make outdated attacks on our Allies. Rhodes offers to combine his high Trendex rating with the unattractive personality of a presidential aspirant in return for an appointment as the first Secretary of National Morale.

The improbability of this situation weakens the arguments of the film. Kazan and Schulberg are attacking straw men. The trend in American politics is not toward a sugarcoating of unpalatable issues but toward a blurring of all issues. The television medium has become the refuge not of vulgar paranoiacs but of mediocre opportunists. Television ultimately destroyed Joe McCarthy, just as it may eventually advance Richard Nixon to the Presidency.

Andy Griffith's characterization of Lonesome Rhodes makes a powerful impact at first, but one soon wearies of its unmodulated loudness and intensity. Griffith, who achieved fame as the soft-spoken comic nuisance in *No Time for Sergeants*, has been obviously overdirected. According to press releases, Kazan drove his star into a perpetual frenzy to induce a Method portrayal. As compensation, Kazan has drawn a finely graded performance from Patricia Neal as the intelligent innocent who discovers Lonesome Rhodes in a country jail and finally destroys him at the pinnacle of his career. Her transition from Piggott, Arkansas, to Sardi's is skillfully reflected in her stiffening carriage and the gradual compression of her drawl.

Excellent performances are provided also by Walter Matthau, a writer with integrity, Anthony Franciosa, a cynical agent who climbs with Rhodes but retains his footing when his patron is dislodged, and Lee Remick, the pathetic drum majorette, who joins the Rhodes act through matrimony. Indeed, the quiet, intimate scenes and background effects of Miss Neal, Matthau, and Franciosa maintain a level of distinction that cancels out much of

the bombast and makes A *Face in the Crowd,* paradoxically
enough, the most interesting film from Hollywood this year.

—*Film Culture,* No. 13, Fall 1957

■ *5. CABIRIA*

Cabiria (*Le Notti di Cabiria*), with its titular evocation of D'An-
nunzio and the epic tradition of early Italian films, is the name of
a shabby prostitute in Federico Fellini's parable on the human
condition. Attired in a sleeveless, zebra-striped blouse, a moth-eaten
fur stole, and grotesquely inappropriate bobby socks, Giulietta
Masina's Cabiria impishly burlesques her ancient calling and then
poignantly transcends it in a burst of tragic irony. The film ends
on a note of high pathos, comparable to the finest moments of
Chaplin, as Miss Masina's final close-up sums up one of the most
resourceful performances in screen history.

The plot of *Cabiria* consists of five events in the heroine's life,
each event logically related to the development of her character.
The film opens with Cabiria running across a lonely field with her
lover. The camera remains distant from the apparently carefree
couple. The two figures are framed against a bleak, gray-lit landscape, its pastoral simplicity marred by telephone poles and distant
housing developments. The absence of mood music and expository
dialogue creates some of the sinister tension of the first sequences
in *Great Expectations.* The suspense heightens as Cabiria stops at
the edge of a stream and gaily swings her handbag in an ever-
widening arc while her lover furtively glances about. Suddenly
Cabiria's escort seizes her handbag, shoves her into the stream,
and runs off, never to be seen again.

This one episode establishes the pattern of Cabiria's life from
illusion to disillusion. In the early scenes the loud, vulgar, ungainly
aspects of Cabiria's personality are emphasized. She is literally
dragged from the stream and absurdly handled like a sack of soggy
potatoes. Her rescue and the inept artificial respiration that follows
deny her even the dignity of a disaster. The audience is almost invited to laugh at her plight, but the physical discomfort of the

situation—her young rescuers shivering in their bathing suits, Cabiria almost collapsing as she calls her lover and tries to escape from her nightmarish predicament—kills the laughter her appearance would normally arouse. At this point in the film it is not clear what mood Fellini is trying to achieve. His manner is cold and impersonal.

Cabiria soon resumes the nightly routine of her existence with her circle of prostitutes, dope peddlers, and procurers on the Via Borghese. Here Fellini does not glamorize Cabiria's profession. Actually, prostitutes are merely another tribe in the confederation of wanderers and outcasts, wastrels and opportunists, with whose irregular patterns of living Fellini has been concerned throughout his distinguished career. In his first film, *The White Sheik*, Fellini satirized the bumbling artisans of the Italian comic strips. (Giulietta Masina appeared briefly here as a whimsical lady of the evening.) *Vitelloni* dramatized the aimless existence of young loafers in a resort town; *Il Bidone* examined the machinations of confidence men; *La Strada* was an odyssey of itinerant circus performers. In each instance Fellini approached his untidy characters on a plane of universal meaning.

By casting the diminutive, clown-visaged, essentially sexless Giulietta Masina as his prostitute, Fellini has automatically divorced himself from the currently fashionable exploitation of lurid themes. His treatment is neither sensual nor sentimental. By depicting Cabiria's spirited recovery from her ludicrous betrayal, Fellini indicates his concern with the indestructibility of his heroine, and by implication, of the human spirit generally. We sense that Cabiria's dunking in the stream is not her first setback, and Fellini quickly insures that it shall not be her last.

Cabiria jauntily plies her wares in a more fashionable part of Rome, where she witnesses a violent argument between a famous actor (Amedeo Nazzari) and his glamorous mistress (Dorian Gray). After the mistress stalks away, the actor curtly summons Cabiria to his car. They drive to a nightclub, and from there to his palatial villa. Cabiria stands up in the actor's convertible and waves to more elegant prostitutes in the neighborhood to display her good fortune.

When they arrive at the villa, Cabiria is overwhelmed by the splendor around her. The actor solemnly plays Beethoven's Fifth Symphony on his phonograph and confides to Cabiria that he is fond of this music. The actor and Cabiria are at emotional cross-purposes in this situation, but both are equally silly in their poses. There is something unpleasant in the actor's condescension to Cabiria; he seems to have no desire to make love to her, and his reluctance to do so curiously reaffirms Cabiria's stylized, somewhat unreal personality.

The actor's disaffected mistress returns unexpectedly; the actor hastily conceals Cabiria in his sumptuous bathroom, where she spends the night while the actor and his first desire renew their relationship. Cabiria is surreptitiously released the next morning. As the actor quietly leads her through the bedroom, Cabiria looks wistfully over her shoulder at the girl sleeping contentedly. The pathos of the situation is intensified when Cabiria attempts to return the money the actor gives her. Her gesture is clearly intended to make the actor recognize her as a human being, and like every other such gesture in her life, it fails.

As it turns out, this is the funniest episode in the film. The pace is leisurely as Miss Masina runs through her bag of low-comedy tricks. She collides with glass doors, grapples with endless curtains, scales heavily carpeted stairs with the hunched-forward determination of an Alpine skier, and grimaces at every new situation with the knowingly pursed lips of a fishwife at an art gallery. Her defeat here is less of a downfall than a pratfall, and the entire sequence seems gratuitous until the total symmetry of the film is perceived.

Suddenly God enters Cabiria's life in the guise of a miracle-seeking procession to a shrine of the Virgin Mary. Here Fellini divides his attention between Cabiria, who prays for the intangible miracle of a new life, and a crippled procurer and dope peddler, who has come to have his limbs healed. In a brilliantly composed and edited passage, Cabiria and the procurer alternately struggle through a milling, hysterical crowd of penitents to reach the altar. At the edge of one overhead shot, an elaborate loudspeaker subtly mocks the spontaneity of the occasion. The forward motion of the scene accelerates until the procurer throws away his crutches and collapses, writhing and threshing briefly on the floor before Fellini tastefully fades out the scene.

Fellini's treatment of this episode is crucial to an understanding of his general position. Although he does not believe in the more obvious manifestations of the miraculous (he was the author of

Rossellini's controversial work, *The Miracle*), Fellini does not indulge in De Sica's sly anticlericalism. The problem for Fellini is
one of individual faith rather than social responsibility. The emotional power of the religious spectacle he creates suggests that God
is sanctioned by man's need for faith, possibly even that God was
created by man to supply hope for a better life. Fellini never spells
out his personal commitments, but he seems to accept the Church
as part of the furniture of his environment. There are indications
in *Cabiria* as well as in *La Strada* that Fellini is more kindly disposed to the humanistic influences within the Church than to its
authoritarian dogmas. A mendicant friar whom Cabiria meets on a
lonely road has a greater impact on her soul than all the elaborate
machinery of the miracle festival. However, like Cabiria and Gelsomina, and the nun in *La Strada*, who shares Gelsomina's sense of
rootlessness, the friar is something of an outcast in the eyes of the
Church. To accept the universality of these people as Fellini apparently does, it is necessary to consider the notion that in some
sense we are all outcasts in our moments of loneliness and in the
individual paths we follow to our salvation. In any event, by stress-
ing the pugnacity and indestructibility of Cabiria, Fellini comes
closer to creating a viable symbol of humanity than does De Sica
with his whining protagonist in *The Bicycle Thief*.

Although Fellini has a limited degree of compassion for his band
of stragglers, he never ignores the probabilities of their existence.
When Cabiria attempts to regenerate herself, Fellini rewards her
efforts with the most disastrous experience of her life. After de-
nouncing her companions for remaining unchanged after their
pious invocations to the Madonna, Cabiria temporarily abandons
her profession and visits a tawdry music hall, where a hypnotist re-
cruits her for his act. Cabiria is quickly thrust into a romantic
fantasy before a boorish audience. She gracefully dances with an
imaginary lover whom the hypnotist calls Oscar as the orchestra
plays a tinny version of "The Merry Widow Waltz." After picking
some imaginary flowers, Cabiria relives her youthful innocence,
which is symbolically evoked by her memory of her long black
hair. In a breathtaking scene of dramatic recall, Cabiria worriedly
asks Oscar if he really loves her and is not just deceiving her. She is
then snapped out of her trance to find herself an object of derision
and ridicule.

Outside, a shy young man (François Périer) tells her that he was moved by the purity of her memories, and the final movement of the film starts slowly toward its preordained conclusion. After a series of meetings, Cabiria's suspicions are lulled by the apparent guilelessness of her admirer, whose name, by what he claims to be a fateful coincidence, is Oscar. Even after Cabiria reveals her profession, he asks her to marry him. On the day they are to leave for the country to be married, he lures her to the edge of a cliff overlooking the sea. Lacking the courage to push Cabiria to her death, he leaves her clawing the ground in grief-stricken revulsion against her fate while he ignobly picks up the handbag she has dropped at his feet and runs and stumbles through the forest.

Cabiria rises eventually and slowly makes her way to the road, Fellini's perennial symbol of life. There a group of adolescents lightheartedly serenading each other include Cabiria in their merry circle. A young girl smilingly greets Cabiria, whose tears are suddenly illuminated by her smile as the camera closes in on her face, slightly turned, slowly moving forward toward an unconditional acceptance of life. At that final moment Cabiria is in a state of secular grace, innocent and inviolate despite all the deceptions that have been practiced upon her.

In *Cabiria* one sees the familiar landmarks of the anarchic subworld of Fellini's imagination. Empty fields, roads, and streets set off by solitary travelers and distant buildings convey an image of the world as a lonely desert peopled by insubstantial De Chirico figures vainly striding toward mathematically improbable intersections of humanity. In such a world, social theories are meaningless, since society itself seems to exist beyond the horizon of any given individual. Personal relationships, however tenuous, achieve an exaggerated intensity, and the mystiques of romantic illusion and religious faith become the indispensable components of existence. This would be a forbiddingly dismal view of life if Fellini did not provide compensations with a rich sense of humor and a perceptive eye for colorful detail. Fellini does not merely assert that life is worth living under the worst circumstances, he demonstrates the strange joys that flourish in the midst of loneliness and suffering. Without this demonstration *Cabiria* would be an unbearably sadistic experience.

Fellini's work since *The White Sheik* has been a continuous adventure in symbolism within the framework of unusually complex plots. Yet Fellini's technique does not lend itself to what we are accustomed to in the way of symbolic imagery. He does not give surfaces or objects any special gloss or lighting to emphasize their significance. There are never any meaningful shadows in a Fellini film, or any unusual contrasts between sunlight and darkness. His shots, day or night, fall into a neutral zone of grayness.

It might be argued that Fellini does not need to construct bizarre images, since such oddities abound in the Italian landscape. Italian religious festivals, for example, outdo Orson Welles in their addiction to grotesque shock effects. However, no matter how colorful the paraphernalia of Italian Catholicism may be, prop symbolism is only a small part of Fellini's achievement. It is in the symbolism and dreamlike quality of experience itself that Fellini excels. Here the lonely streets and fields serve their main function. What are Fellini's unforgettable images? The young men walking slowly on a deserted beach in *Vitelloni*; Gelsomina marching behind three musicians in *La Strada*; Cabiria dancing on a stage suddenly detached from the audience—these are his magical moments.

It is odd to think of Fellini following in the footsteps of the neorealists, but it would be an error to consider his work completely apart from their influence. Indeed, it is the realism in Fellini's technique that enriches his symbols. He does not prettify reality although he tends to control it somewhat more than his predecessors. He does not shrink from dirt or grime or the garish ugliness of stage make-up. Indeed, like most neorealists, Fellini seems more at ease with settings of poverty and moderate means than with citadels of luxury. His cheap, noisy music hall in *Cabiria* seems more authentic than the plush, unusually quiet nightclub. Cabiria's drab house seems less of a caricature than the actor's incredibly palatial villa. It is not a question of visual reality but one of camera treatment. Fellini looks at the poorer settings objectively, picking out their most characteristic elements. However, the luxurious settings are viewed satirically and only their most ridiculous features are emphasized.

Similarly, in *Cabiria* at least, the upper-class people—the actor and his mistress—are seen mechanically from the viewpoint of a lowly wide-eyed prostitute. Fellini's unwillingess to study a wider range of social strata does not imply an inability to do so. Still, with all its merits, *Cabiria* may represent the point at which Fellini's concern with the stragglers of society begins to yield diminishing returns. Somehow *Cabiria* does not have the feel of greatness that *Vitelloni* communicates. In *Vitelloni* every character counts for something and every incident advances toward a common truth. *Cabiria* is too much of a one-woman show, with Giulietta Masina's heroine achieving a sublime illumination while all the other characters linger in the darkness of deception and irresolution. Like *La Strada*, Fellini's other near-masterpiece, *Cabiria* has some of the limitations of an acting vehicle that sometimes loses its way on the road of life and forks out into the bypaths of a virtuoso performance.

—Film Culture, No. 16, January 1958

■ 6. ITALY'S BIG FOUR

Of the hundred and eighteen directors now involved in the industrial renaissance of Italian film-making only four—Luchino Visconti, Roberto Rossellini, Michelangelo Antonioni, and Federico Fellini—seem destined for more than the immortality of a footnote. Visconti and Rossellini have been directing feature films for twenty years, Antonioni and Fellini for ten and the significant history of the Italian cinema can be encompassed within these career spans even though Italian film-makers were producing ambitious spectacles before Griffith's *Birth of a Nation* in 1915.

Because of freakish distribution problems Visconti's *Ossessione* (1942) and Rossellini's *Open City* (1946) have been separately honored as the midwives of neorealism, an overdefined movement that in its time and place simply marked the rejection of the sanctimonious conventions of Fascism. The Italian cinema before *Ossessione* is a mountain of spaghetti, some of it reasonably tasteful, most of it too starchy for anything but home consumption. Mussolini came to power more than a decade before Hitler, and the crucially formative years of the twenties found Murnau, Lang, Pabst, and lesser German directors evolving their techniques under the relatively protective aegis of the Weimar Republic while their Italian colleagues were marking time under Il Duce's balcony.

Visconti at sixty-four, Rossellini at fifty-four, Antonioni at forty-eight, and Fellini at forty-one seem reasonably safe from the creeping standardization that has afflicted so many of their once promising colleagues. One might except the late Curzio Malaparte, whose one film, *Strange Deception*, lent the Italian cinema intellectual prestige at a crucial point in its postwar development; and on another level of deception, a special note must be devoted to the inflated reputation of Vittorio De Sica in the early fifties.

If Visconti and Rossellini invented neorealism in *Ossessione* and *Open City* and then invested it with the ultimate profundity of *La Terra Trema* and *Paisan*, De Sica milked it dry with *Shoeshine* and *The Bicycle Thief*. Lacking an insight into the real world, De Sica relied instead on tricks of pathos that he had learned too well as an actor. It is unlikely that any of the Big Four would have made *The Bicycle Thief* in the De Sica–Zavattini manner. Visconti would have catapulted his victim into the Roman underworld, where social corruption and a sense of personal dignity would transform the wronged laborer into a professional bicycle thief. Rossellini's character, heroically transfigured by God during the search, would return home with the awareness that his integrity as a human being was more important than any material object. Antonioni's hero, realizing the futility of his isolated existence in an impersonal society, would ride the recovered bicycle off an embankment in a quasi-suicidal gesture. After some bizarre experiences, Fellini's protagonist would find his bicycle only to have it stolen again the next day, but the hapless victim would come up smiling at the hope radiated by a little girl playing a harmonica.

All four directors have diverged from the literal path of neorealism, which was never anything more than the Stalinallee of social realism. In Visconti's work there has always been an unreconciled tension between a Marxian vision of society and an operatic conception of character. *Rocco and His Brothers* is comparable in its contradictions to what might have come out of a Verdi-Brecht adaptation of *The Brothers Karamazov*. The unity of the family in *Rocco* is destroyed partly because of the urban pressures of Milan on the rural mystique of the depressed South, partly because of the inhumanly Christlike sanctity of Rocco, partly because of the destructive intervention of a willful prostitute, and partly because of the fratricidal destiny of the brothers. The disturbing homosexual overtones of *Rocco* (and *Ossessione*) reflect additional conflicts with which the director must cope.

Throughout his career Visconti has been haunted by the image of the destructive woman. In the sublime cinema of Mizoguchi and Ophuls, most notably in *Ugetsu* and *Lola Montès*, woman is presented as the Redeemer of men but for Visconti she is man's Nemesis. The females in *Ossessione, Senso, White Nights, Bellissima,* and *Rocco* wreak their havoc not through spidery machinations but through a psychic force that the male can neither resist nor overcome. It follows almost logically that Visconti is the best director of actresses in the world, and the performances of Clara Calamai (*Ossessione*), Anna Magnani (*Bellissima*), Alida Valli (*Senso*), Maria Schell (*White Nights*), and Annie Girardot (*Rocco*) are among the most memorable creations of the cinema.

Roberto Rossellini had directed three obscure wartime films— *La Nave Bianca, Un Pilote Ritorna, L'Uomo Della Croce*—before he emerged on the world scene with his neorealistic classics *Open City, Paisan,* and *Germany Year Zero.* Then he went into a Magnani-Cocteau period with *The Miracle, The Human Voice,* and *The Infernal Machine* before the advent of Ingrid Bergman in *Stromboli, Europa 51 (The Greatest Love), Strangers, Joan at the Stake,* and *Fear.* During his Bergman period he also directed *Flowers of St. Francis, Dov'È La Liberta,* an episode in *The Seven Deadly Sins* ("Envy"), and *We Are the Women* (with Bergman). Except for the brilliant, scandal-provoking documentary *India,* Rossellini was off the screen for five years before making his comeback with *General Della Rovere,* a patriotic success followed by *Era Notte a Roma,* Stendhal's *Vanina Vanini,* and *Viva Italia!*

The most Catholic of all directors, Rossellini has always been obsessed by the inner miracles of human personality. In his oddly stylized treatment of the Honegger-Claudel *Joan at the Stake* Rossellini sends Ingrid Bergman awkwardly soaring into heaven, a fitting climax to his cinematic conversion of the actress into a saint. Rossellini has confronted death as a metaphysical experience with none of the histrionics of Visconti, the despair of Antonioni, the emotional causality of Fellini. The final death images of Magnani in *Open City,* the partisans in *Paisan,* the prostitute in *Europa 51*

■ 7. *L'AVVENTURA*

As long as the great foreign films continue to trickle into New York at the present snail's pace, the enthusiasm of discerning moviegoers will have to be concentrated on one phenomenon at a time: 1959 was the year of *Wild Strawberries* and *The Four Hundred Blows*; 1960 belonged to *Hiroshima, Mon Amour* and *Picnic on the Grass*. So far this year it has been all *Breathless*, but now it is time for another blast of trumpets. Beginning April 4 at the Beekman Theater, *L'Avventura* will become the one first-run film to see in New York. The sixth feature film of Italian director Michelangelo Antonioni, *L'Avventura* will probably be even more controversial than its French and Swedish predecessors, which have been conveniently misunderstood as problem tracts of old age, childhood, juvenile delinquency, miscegenation, nuclear warfare, or what have you.

With *L'Avventura* the issue cannot be muddled. Antonioni's film is an intellectual adventure or it is nothing. The plot, such as it is, will infuriate audiences who still demand plotted cinema and potted climaxes. A group of bored Italian socialites disembark from their yacht on a deserted island. After wandering about a while they discover that one of their number, a perverse girl named Anna, is missing. Up to that time Anna (Lea Massari) had been the protagonist. Not only does she never reappear, the mystery of her disappearance is never solved. Anna's fiancé (Gabriele Ferzetti) and her best friend (Monica Vitti) continue the search from one town to another, ultimately betraying the object of their search by becoming lovers. The film ends on a note of further betrayal and weary acceptance, with the two lovers facing a blank wall and a distant island, both literally and symbolically.

The film is almost over before we learn that the hero is an architect who has sacrificed his ambitions for the lucrative position of a middleman in the building industry. The other characterizations are sketched in much the same apparently incidental manner. A graduate of Screenwriting 1-2 might dismiss this method as casualness or even carelessness, but every shot and bit of business in *L'Avventura* represents calculation of the highest order. The characteristic Antonioni image consists of two or more characters within the same frame not looking at each other. They may be separated by space, mood, interest, but the point comes across, and the imposing cinematic theme of communication is brilliantly demonstrated.

If Antonioni's characters are unable to communicate with those who should be closest to them, they are also unable to avoid the intrusion of strangers. When Monica Vitti is contemplating suicide, a passerby looks up at her and jars her sense of solitude without relieving her loneliness. Is this not typical of modern society, where crowds supersede communities?

For Antonioni there is no solution to the moral problem created by the failure of contemporary behavior to meet the hypocritical standards of ancient codes. The architect observes that his predecessors built for the centuries while he would be building for the decades or less. Love, fidelity, and mourning are similarly abbreviated in the hectic chronology of our time, even though social customs still insist on concealing a shameful change of heart.

Antonioni stated in a recent interview that eroticism was the disease of our age, and the eroticism in *L'Avventura* is presented with this clinical awareness. The four sexual encounters in the film are so graphically complete in their sensual essence that it becomes quite clear that Antonioni is demonstrating the inadequacy of sexual contact as a means of moral communication. The erotic disease subordinates the person to the process, and one's specific identity is lost. It is no accident that a copy of F. Scott Fitzgerald's *Tender Is the Night* is found with the missing girl's possessions. Fitzgerald's stylistic device of replacing protagonists, Nicole for Rosemary, is repeated in *L'Avventura* with a vengeance. Later in the film, when Anna's blonde girl friend adorns herself with a dark wig, we are confronted with a breathtaking Pirandellian moment of confused identities. For the hero there is really little difference between his missing fiancée and her successor.

There is much more to this modern Odyssey for an alert audience. The travels of the characters are paralleled by the meaningfully shifting backgrounds of geography, architecture, and painting. This intellectual muscle of *L'Avventura* should appeal to anyone who seeks something more from the cinema than the finger exercises of conventional films.

—*Village Voice*, March 23, 1961

■ 8. ROSSELLINI, RENOIR, AND FORD

The Greatest Love and Strangers are probably the two most controversial films shown in the recent series "The Forgotten Film" at the New Yorker Theatre. For purposes of historical perspective it should be noted that The Greatest Love, originally titled Europa 51, was released in Europe in 1952 and in New York in 1954; for Strangers the respective years of release are 1953 and 1955. It is commonly assumed in America that these two films belong to Rossellini's off-period, between Germany Year Zero (1949) and General Della Rovere (1960). Conversely, Ingrid Bergman's admirers presume that she wasted her talents on amateurs like Rossellini and Renoir (Paris Does Strange Things) until she was rescued by Anatole Litvak and Hollywood's know-how. When the rival camps of Ingrid and Roberto converge on a screening of The Greatest Love, no one is happy with what seems to be an unsatisfactory blend of Open City and The Bells of Saint Mary's.

The fact remains that The Greatest Love and Strangers are two of the most influential films in modern cinema. Like it or not, Rossellini has strongly affected the work of Resnais, Antonioni, Fellini and the entire New Wave. (One might compare the museum sequences in Strangers and Hiroshima, Mon Amour.) Why, then, have Rossellini's Bergman films, including also Stromboli and Fear, been so lightly regarded in America? First of all, they are intensely personal works, and the notion that the personality of a director is of supreme importance has not yet taken hold in American criticism. Second, the Rossellini personality has been so closely associated with scandalous publicity that it would seem audacious and indeed sacrilegious to suggest that Rossellini is the most Catholic of all directors. Third, Rossellini's visual conceptions and rhythms were so revolutionary for their time that few Americans could suspect that what seemed like apparent ineptitude was actually a part of a transcendent order. Finally, it must be acknowledged that audiences are irritated by the bad dubbing into English of the Italian players in The Greatest Love, particularly the Bronx accent with which Giulietta Masina is afflicted. In Strangers the post-synchronization of the dialogue produces an oddly abstracted effect, as if Ingrid Bergman and George Sanders were conversing from a single loudspeaker. Also, the reading of lines and the lines in themselves are marked by a ritualistic quality, with little of the casually graded small talk that traditionally bridges the undramatized portions of the scenario.

On its most superficial level *The Greatest Love* seems to assert that the world is not ready to receive its saints. The self-indulgent existence of a wealthy American matron in Rome is rudely shattered by her son's death, a presumably suicidal attempt to gain maternal attention. Breaking with her past indifference, she aids the needy, works in a factory, and ministers to a dying prostitute. When she fails to report a fugitive from justice, she is arrested and committed to an insane asylum. After she refuses to conform to the decorum of society, she is permanently committed by her estranged husband. The film ends with Bergman tearfully smiling through the barred window of her room at her newly acquired but unfortunately powerless friends below.

These are the bare bones of the plot, the mechanical turns of the screw. A conventional analysis of the film's structure might suggest that the intrigue-caused martyrdom of the heroine is not justified by the pitiful tokenism of her social challenge. However, this is precisely the point at which modern cinema departs from the conventional norms. Rossellini is not focusing on society's persecution of its moral nemesis but on the absorption of a withered soul, first by the world and then by God. Rossellini's camera stays with Bergman continuously except for the disinterested intrigues of her captors: family, police, clergy, psychiatrists. The immanence of God is revealed to her eyes while she seeks an end to her solitude. This is the transcendent meaning of Rossellini's visual conception of a unified cosmos, undivided by the conceptual detail of montage.

When Bergman first emerges from her sybaritic enclosure to confront the world at large, she stands on the Roman horizon line, that peculiar landscape of emptiness and disconnected skyscrapers that Fellini will later exploit. She is still under the influence of a Communist lawyer who is her closest confidant. She follows a group of children who have just witnessed the recovery of a suicide's body from the river. They lead her to a hearty creature of the slums, Giulietta Masina, whose maternal vitality transforms

Bergman's numb feeling of loss into the first vestiges of Christian humility. Bergman persuades the Communist lawyer to secure employment for Masina, but when Masina is unable to work the first day because of an assignation, Bergman is thrust into the cauldron of industrial production. Rossellini's impressive montage of machinery emphasizes the inhuman, time-stretching drudgery of mechanical toil. For those who believe that style can always be separated from meaning, here is a Catholic's response to Eisenstein's dialectical montage. Whereas Eisenstein's conceptual editing extracts a truth from the collision of two mechanistic forces in history, Rossellini's relentlessly cyclical montage submerges the vital rhythms of man's God-given life to the godless ordinances of the modern world.

When Bergman seeks to communicate her horror to the rhetoric-laden Communist, she becomes alienated from a vision of earthly paradise that fails to accommodate her dead son. Freed of all commitments, she sets out for her Calvary. What is strange and modern about Rossellini here is his unwillingness to capitalize on his dramatic opportunities. He refuses to signal his audience at the moment of redemption. His camera lens does not become agitated or portentously intimate as he asks his audience to share in the unprompted discovery of God on the screen. For example, it would be inconceivable to the average American director that the day of Christ's crucifixion could be treated as any other day in the life of man without implying disrespect.

Bergman continues her planless quest by giving her love to a dying prostitute. A vulgar creature in life, the prostitute achieves in death an ethereal, two-dimensional immortality that recalls the formal death pose of the Sicilian girl in the first episode of *Paisan*. Man's life, however qualified, passes ultimately into the Grace of eternity, and the human body even in its ugliest and most degraded condition is retrieved by God. Thus, what to the conventional critic appears to be the aimless wandering of a disorganized saint becomes in the modern cinema a genuine adventure in metaphysical suspense. At what moment in man's infernal time machine and at what point in his ravaged geography will God's presence be felt? Ultimately, the precise space-time coordinates elude us. It has happened. Bergman looks out from her barred window with tears of love in her eyes, the love she has gained for a world she has lost.

The plot of *Strangers* could be summarized in an inexpensive telegram: ENGLISH COUPLE CANNOT COMMUNICATE WITH EACH OTHER ON VOYAGE IN ITALY STOP THEY PART STOP HUSBAND SOCIALIZES WITHOUT EFFECT STOP WIFE VISITS RUINS AND GALLERIES STOP SOMETHING MYSTERIOUS HAPPENS STOP COUPLE HUMBLED AND REUNITED STOP. The "something mysterious" is, of course, God in all His cinematic ramifications. However, there is more, much more to be considered. Communication is one of the major themes of cinema, particularly the modern cinema. In *Strangers*, as in *Wild Strawberries*, the failure to communicate creates a hellish existence on earth. It is interesting to note that *Strangers* is, at least tangentially, anti-Protestant and that *Wild Strawberries* is at least tangentially anti-Catholic. If *Wild Strawberries* seems more relevant to Americans, it is partly because our intellectual climate is predominantly Protestant-agnostic rather than Catholic. The Catholic couple in *Wild Strawberries* and the Protestant couple in *Strangers* are profoundly disoriented, but in different contexts. For Ingmar Bergman hell is an existential condition of religious skepticism. For Rossellini hell is the detachment of man from the natural order of the world. Both couples are surrounded by uncongenial environments. The Catholics in *Wild Strawberries* maintain an unnatural union in a climate that makes nature man's antagonist and abstracts God from the sensuousness of life. The Protestant-agnostics in *Strangers* are trapped in an atmosphere of sensual complicity shared by man and nature. Wherever Ingrid Bergman goes to seek the spiritual-aesthetic beauty of the past, she is confronted by the intransigent corporeality of human history. The sculpted figures in the museum in Naples seem to burst from their molds with a carnal vitality. The streets of Naples bear an uncommonly large percentage of pregnant women. The plaster-encased survivors of Pompeii seem to be immortalized in the eternal instant of their absorption in the mysteries of the flesh. Ultimately, Ingrid Bergman is conquered by an invisible force coexistent with the visible churnings of Vesuvius. The Scandinavian Either-Or of *Wild Strawberries* is countered in *Strangers* by the Latin summum bonum. Protestant man as a barren rock consenting to the erosion of human contacts in order to lessen the bleak solitude of a monologue to a God who may not exist after all is countered by Catholic man as a soppy sponge absorbing the juices of life from a universe that God inhabits both in the flesh and in the spirit.

Rossellini's technique is an intricate instrument of expression that cannot be categorized. It is intensely personal, and yet in a very curious sense it is utterly realistic. Every major director creates his own world, but in Rossellini's films one senses a strong affinity to the real world. He will follow his heroine up and down stairs, in and out of cars. He will listen to her speak aloud and look at her intently when she seems to be adrift in a sea of indifference. Although he knows Bergman, the woman, better than any other director, better than we know her, he never seems to exploit the Bergman we know as an actress. Bergman is not woman to Rossellini, but *a* woman. Yet, in his films we never come to know Bergman's screen character with any psychological precision. Emmanuelle Riva in *Hiroshima, Mon Amour* and Jeanne Moreau in *Les Amantes* reveal their innermost secrets and ambiguities, and we revel with them in the employment of their senses. We come to know what they think and how they feel when they make love, before they make love, and after they make love, and in the long periods of moody contemplation in between. We never come to know Bergman in this way because Rossellini disdains interior psychological analysis that would distinguish one being from another. Nor does he generalize Bergman into a universal constant. Instead, Bergman is concretized in the universe as a plastic reactor to the invisible forces of reality. By showing us everything she sees, Rossellini convinces us there must be something in the arrangement of all reality rather than in some strikingly picturesque detail that convulses her inner being. We look at her, we look at what she sees, we look at her looking at what she sees. Suddenly she changes before our eyes, and the continuity of reality persists as if we had not reached a dramatic climax that would normally transfigure the screen. This is what makes Rossellini seem dull to many people, and he *is* dull in the way that Bach is dull when he does not supply the dramatic emphases we would like to hear.

This cinematic rendering of a Catholic vision has the profundity and splendor one finds in James Joyce and Saint Augustine and reflects the peculiar genius of Catholicism through the ages in reconciling the temporality of physical reality with the Grace of eternity. However, one does not have to accept this vision to acknowledge Rossellini's genius in transforming the camera into the eye of a believer. To display the world to such a purpose is a remarkable extension of neorealism.

Jean Renoir's *French Can-Can* is an extraordinarily beautiful film, and here I record a response not to mere prettiness or decorativeness but to a classic conception of beauty as the objective of all aesthetics. Unfortunately, the aesthetic of cinematic beauty has been hopelessly muddled in our time by trivial debates on equally trivial theories of realism. Beauty has been presented as the enemy of truth, and in the ensuing confusion a French can-can dancer has become less truthful than a Bengali peasant. This distinction is particularly silly in the case of Renoir, who can extract the beautiful truths of both dancer and peasant, and in fact has done so. The art that created *French Can-Can* is the art that created *The River*, and the art that created *Picnic on the Grass* is the art that created *The Southerner*. Those who hate Renoir's recent films but lack the consistency to denounce *La Grande Illusion* comfort themselves with the notion of Renoir's decline. If anything, Renoir's work has become more impressively personal over the years, which have softened the contours of his sensuous world.

French Can-Can is an artist's tribute to art. Jean Gabin as the dedicated impresario is Renoir, the dedicated director. Gabin has his financial difficulties and his romantic entanglements, but he is sustained by the mission of his calling. As he threads his way across the pastel-colored background of an Auguste Renoir's Paris, Gabin is accompanied by the motifs of the music halls. The other characters in the film seek to find some modus vivendi between art and life. A young prince attempts futilely to realize his illusion, a belly dancer pursues pleasure, a laundry girl seeks love, but only the impresario knows that ultimately his can-can dancers will engulf their audience just as art engulfs life and that the can-can will take its place in its society just as art, drawn from life, becomes a part of it. The can-can scenes in John Huston's *Moulin Rouge* were the best scenes in the film, and the color lighting was a prodigious technical achievement, but throughout these passages one felt detached from the mood of the action and the action itself. Renoir hurls his can-can dancers at the audience and defies it to withdraw from the consuming spectacle. Renoir's conception is thus much deeper than Huston's, and the effect is ultimately more beautiful.

It can be argued that *Wagonmaster* is John Ford's greatest film. If I choose not to argue the point at this time, it is because there are too many other candidates to consider, and these do not include

The Informer and *The Grapes of Wrath*. *Wagonmaster* has only
fragments of a plot. A wagon train of Mormon settlers are led to a
promised land by a young horse trader. They encounter deserts and
mountains, Indians and outlaws, and even encompass a traveling
medicine show that provides a strange romance for the horse trader
turned wagonmaster. Well served by an unmannered cast led by
Ben Johnson, Joanne Dru and Ward Bond, Ford does not waste
any time over the subtleties of characterization and twists of plot.
He strokes boldly across the canvas of the American past as he concentrates on the evocative images of a folk tradition that no other
American director has ever been able to render. It is a tradition of
free adventure and compelling adaptability. There are no moral
shadings. His villains are evil incarnate—whining, wheedling and
uselessly destructive. The hero destroys them in the end as he
would destroy a snake, and the sophisticated medicine-show girl
smiles inscrutably as she realizes without an exchange of words
that she is destined for this virile "rube." There are the Mormon
square dances and the unforgettable circular stomp of friendly
Indians. Above all, there are the wagons themselves, those symbolic
vehicles that remind us that John Ford's *Stagecoach* initiated the
modern American cinema.

—New York Film Bulletin, March 27, 1961

■ 9. *JULES AND JIM*

François Truffaut's *Jules and Jim* is that rarity of rarities, a genuinely romantic film. I must hasten to add that what I mean by
"romantic" does not involve gypsy violins, rose-colored filters, murmurs by candlelight, and a generally soft-headed view of life. Truffaut's work contains none of this. If anything, *Jules and Jim* expresses a brutal vision of love as a private war fought apart from
the rules and regulations of society. Significantly, one of the characters invokes the experience of Apollinaire, the remarkably disengaged French poet who composed his fervent love poems in the
trenches during the First World War.

Adapted from a first novel by a seventy-three-year-old author,

Henri-Pierre Roché, *Jules and Jim* describes the rapport between a German and a Frenchman in that hopeful period before 1914 when the stream of history had not yet become a raging torrent. Both men become obsessed with an ancient statue, and subsequently with a woman who recaptures the statue's enigmatic smile. Jules and Jim share their aesthetic creation through the years that follow, but what begins as an unconventional idyll culminates in tragedy.

Truffaut has avoided the homosexual implication of the *ménage à trois* by equalizing the intensities of masculine friendship and heterosexual love. This is admittedly easier to do in France than in America, where complex or conflicting relationships are invested with Freudian overtones. Happily, Truffaut has transcended the clinical pitfalls of his material with the inspired casting of Jeanne Moreau, the glorious Galatea of the modern cinema, in the central role. I suspect that in twenty years or so Moreau will evoke the spirit of our time as Garbo, Brooks, and Dietrich now evoke the spirit of theirs.

The range of Truffaut's sympathies in *Jules and Jim* is quite impressive for a young director. Youth is generally a state of taking sides, but not in Truffaut's case. He is able to express his deep love for children without making parents seem gross and insensitive. I cannot recall another film in which a child is treated as the fruit of love and the accomplice of passion. Children are more often presented as obstacles, substitutes, or dire consequences in the love game of adults. The fact that Jules and Jim can love the same woman and the same child is the most moving demonstration of their friendship. Truffaut's generosity of spirit here shocks our inherited proprietary conceptions of emotion.

However, there is more to romanticism than an outpouring of love. In fact, romanticism is not concerned primarily with love but with a theory of character that excludes accident. *Last Year at Marienbad*, for example, is an antiromantic film because, in its materialistic universe, man is imprisoned by the accidents of time and space. It makes no difference who or what you are or where you have been. There is no causality in *Marienbad*, no pattern of character. By contrast, everything that happens in *Jules and Jim* is psychologically inevitable. At the end you understand the beginning, and even if external events had been rearranged in time and space, the outcome would have been the same. In the romantic cinema of Truffaut, Ophuls, Welles, and Stroheim, among others, man manufactures his own destiny, and he must observe the unique laws of his personality through every step of his life. *Jules and Jim* ends appropriately in death, not fatalistically but triumphantly, celebrating, as it does, the sweet pain of the impossible and the magnificent failure of an ideal.

—*Village Voice*, May 3, 1962

■ 10. DIALOGUE OF A SCHIZOCRITIC

A. Seen any movies lately?

B. Mostly odds and ends.

A. Like what?

B. Like *Loss of Innocence, The Interns, Light in the Piazza, View from the Bridge, Tales of Paris, Safari, Panic in the Year Zero, Jessica, Boys' Night Out, Woman They Almost Lynched, Walk on the Wild Side*.

A. Let's stop right there. You've made your point.

B. These are all relatively unimportant films, most of them quite vile, and only one of them with the slightest *auteur* interest.

A. You mean Lumet's *View from the Bridge*?

B. No. Dwan's *Woman They Almost Lynched*.

A. You're being perverse again.

B. I know, but there's nothing to be done about it.

A. All right. Be a martyr. What's the verdict on *Woman They Almost Lynched*?

B. The jury is still out. After all, this is Republic, 1953, with a lot of has-beens—Joan Leslie, Audrey Totter, John Lund, Brian Donlevy. The action is set in a border town, half in the Union and half in the Confederacy. The James and Younger boys are still running around with Quantrill's raiders. Joan Leslie, a refined lady from back East, inherits her brother's gambling casino after said brother is shot by John Lund, who is really a Confederate intelligence officer working as foreman in some nearby lead mines. Lund kills with admirable reluctance, because Joan's brother only wants to shoot hard-drinking, fast-living Audrey Totter, who has deserted brother to be Quantrill's woman. It would take too long to explain why Audrey Totter and Joan Leslie have a showdown on Main Street or why Miss Leslie is almost lynched when she tries to save Lund.

A. Or why you worry about the picture at all.

B. I know, but there is something refreshingly frank about Dwan's treatment of this material. I can't decide whether it's a question of vitality or vulgarity, but either way, this is not the kind of lazy or jaded film-making one usually expects in the lower depths. The trouble is it's hard to find anyone comparable to Dwan working on this naïve pulp level, and so I have to reserve judgment.

A. Some of the French critics treat Dwan as Griffith's ghost.

B. But in a very marginal conception of his career. The French always seem to be most fascinated by those directors engulfed in the damnation of necessity. If Dwan is Griffith's ghost, and Ulmer is Murnau's ghost, what to do with the total Dwan-Ulmer output, which is more often ghastly than ghostly by any conventional standards? It is on this level that the *auteur* theory is most vulnerable to the charge of idiocy. The critic is placed in a delicate position. If he recommends *Woman They Almost Lynched* to the lay audience, he creates a false expectation of eyepopping art. To fully appreciate Dwan here, one must be able to perceive what a hundred other directors on Poverty Row would have done with this silly material, and this is difficult for the average moviegoer, who tries to see only the most essential films. Thus there is little point in arguing Dwan's case too strenuously, but somewhere, sometime, a reader may stumble on a minor Dwan film and remember vaguely that Dwan was worthy of a little attention despite his low estate, and the film might then burst into the pleasurable spectrum of tarnished creation. I have "pulled" Dwan on unsuspecting friends with gratifying results.

A. I think you have a weakness for old directors.

B. And dead ones too. Ophuls, Mizoguchi, Murnau, Griffith, Stroheim, Vigo, Eisenstein, Lubitsch, Becker, Flaherty. Of the living, Renoir, Dreyer, Ford, Hitchcock, Welles, Chaplin, Rossellini, Buñuel, Hawks—and that just about makes up a twenty-name definition of the cinema; but there are others, and there will be more to come. Of the newcomers, I'd bet on Godard at this point, with reservations about a possible tendency toward self-destruction.

A. Let's get back to the other movies you've seen recently.

B. As you wish. Lumet's *View from the Bridge* indicates how much the cinema has changed in the past twenty-five years. It's not just that studio exteriors, whether from Hollywood or UFA, have just about had it, but that audiences have become optically sophisticated. Realism is now a commercial necessity even when the subject matter seems to dictate stylization.

A. Dwight Macdonald was bothered by the location quality of New York clashing with the conventions of musical comedy in *West Side Story*.

B. I know—and some critics have defended DaCosta's complete fakery in *The Music Man*. We are going through a painful period of adjustment, with every critic thrashing around for a personal aesthetic. The thin line between documentary and fiction is less visible than ever, and I don't think this is all to the good.

A. Why not?

B. If critics and audiences develop a resistance to stylistic conventions, the cinema may be shackled by the kind of pseudorealism that has virtually destroyed the theater as a creative arena.

A. This is all very abstract. How does it apply to *View from the Bridge?*

B. Well, Sidney Lumet has transformed Arthur Miller's choppy stab at Greek tragedy into a chillingly photographed slice of life, on the whole an intelligent process of draining off most of the pretentiousness into the gutter. An international cast has worked for once as an instrument of abstraction. Raf Vallone, Jean Sorel, Raymond Pellegrin, Maureen Stapleton, Carol Lawrence are so detached from any social context that they become relatively universal. Vallone is particularly inspired casting.

A. His virile force and subtle comedy style reminded me of Magnani in *The Rose Tattoo*.

B. True, but the film doesn't work, because Miller's Freudian-Stalinist determinism defrauds the street tragedy of any meaning. The idea of rationalizing Vallone's reactionary political act as the product of unconscious sexual repression is an example of muddled thinking.

A. Now, wait a minute. *Coriolanus* operates on the separate levels of Freud, Marx, and Machiavelli; Chaplin's anal ballet with a balloon in *The Great Dictator* is a Freudian interpretation of Hitler—and let's not forget Eisenstein's Ivan kissing the chosen assassin of Ivan's family.

B. For *Coriolanus, The Great Dictator,* and *Ivan The Terrible* I would invoke the richness of their ambiguities, their many views from the bridge. In Miller there is only one view. Anyway, there is a merit beyond meaning in the other works, to which Miller's bad play has no serious relevance. However, what interests me is the way Lumet has handled this stylized material in 1962, as opposed to the way Santell approached Maxwell Anderson's *Winterset* in 1936.

A. I remember that Anderson's horribly effeminate blank verse called for someone like John Garfield to tear it to pieces. Instead, we had Burgess Meredith sensitively intoning it as if it were Holy Writ.

B. But Meredith was consistent with the poetic design of the production. Everything about the film was fake and unreal, because this was serious poetry as opposed to those other gangster movies, which were just supposed to make money.

Lumet's meaty, realistic treatment is superior to Santell's fake artiness mainly because Lumet is trying to make a commercial success out of a flop play. Unfortunately, Lumet does not have a strong personality of his own, with the result that he is never quite as good as his best material and never quite as bad as his worst. Still, it's nice to have him around in this new age of package deals. At the very least, he doesn't obstruct the work of good actors.

A. How was Carol Lawrence?

B. She's properly cast here, but she seems a limited type for the movies, more on the order of Anne Bancroft and Ina Balin.

A. Was there any point in seeing *Walk on the Wild Side,* beside Saul Bass?

B. Not really, but Bass looks ready to direct a feature film. His cat titles are very ambitious in a new way. Otherwise, *Walk on the Wild Side* is one of the silliest movies in years, but not in the way you might expect. The script is a hodge-podge of compromise with a bawdy novel, but Dmytryk is such a dull director that the absurdity of the script becomes boring. Jane Fonda is the most interesting player, although most of her scenes are paralyzed by the intolerable presence of Laurence Harvey. Why the movie chose to add lesbianism to Algren's material I have no idea.

A. Sidney Skolsky claims that the cat gave a better performance than Jane Fonda.

B. That's unfair. The cat was directed by Bass while Miss Fonda was directed by Dmytryk. The *auteur* theory works with players too.

A. How about *The Interns?*

B. Well, it's supposed to gross five million domestic, and that ain't peanut brittle.

A. Is that your excuse for seeing it?

B. Pretty much. I also wanted to take a look at some of the younger players we have around.

A. How did they come out?

B. Michael Callan, Cliff Robertson, and James MacArthur are serviceable types. I was disappointed again in Suzy Parker. She looked so pretty on "Open End" recently that I thought some director might be able to get something out of her. She still can't act, but that hasn't been fatal in the past. Her hairdo was wrong, and for some reason she projected the sullen anguish of Tina Louise. I can see why *The Interns* is making money, aside from its tie-in with Television's "Ben Casey" and the revamped "Dr. Kildare." The plot has a little bit of everything and not too much of anything. David Swift is slick enough after his stint with Disney to package the corn with reasonable skill. The abortion plot line interested me particularly. Cliff Robertson steals some pills to help Suzy Parker out of her predicament. Robertson's best friend, James MacArthur, turns him in and gets him disbarred. MacArthur is the all-American boy. He is nobly motivated by a desire to bring children into the world. He meets a nurse, who wants to travel while she is young. He forces her to choose between travel and marriage and makes her give up a lifelong dream in exchange for domestic bliss. The other characters, even Robertson, end up admiring MacArthur for this integrity, and the audience hates his guts. I find this interesting.

A. He sounds like the good woman described by C. S. Lewis in *The Screwtape Letters:* "She is the sort of person who lives for others—you can always tell the others by their hunted expression." Let's tick them off now. *Jessica?*

B. In two words, Angie Dickinson. The picture is vile, as is customary with Negulesco after Cinemascope. Before Cinemascope he was interesting, with *Johnny Belinda, Road House,*

Three Strangers, Deep Valley—far superior to Delmer Daves, for example. After Cinemascope, I must admit that the bravura badness of Daves is more striking than the sagginess of Negulesco. The cast is an international mess, Maurice Chevalier and Noel Noel as Italians, Gabriele Ferzetti from Antonioni, Agnes Moorehead from Welles, Angie, of course, from Hawks, Kerima from Sir Carol Reed, and various nondescript French and Italian actresses. I'm sorry, but Angie made even this tasteless tripe worth seeing.

A. That sounds like a breach in the *auteur* theory.

B. I don't care. I only wish Hawks had used Angie instead of Elsa Martinelli in *Hatari*. And if he is looking for another French actress, I would like to recommend Alexandra Stewart. Speaking of *Hatari*, did you know that in the 1956 *Safari*, with Janet Leigh and Victor Mature, they are hunting for a lion named Hatari?

A. No, I didn't know that.

B. You should go to the movies more.

A. I prefer reading books.

B. Cultural snob!

A. Movie junkie!

B. Enough. Here is another tidbit, more down the alley of *Films in Review*. Did you know that Bessie Love appears in *Loss of Innocence* as an American tourist, stupid, of course?

A. No, I didn't know that either, but I remember some New York film critic voting for *Loss* as best picture of the year.

B. It's vile. The awakening of a young girl to the duplicity of adult life. A muted Addinsell score and never-never-land pastel colors, a delicate novel by Rumer Godden, and all you need is Lewis Gibert to direct. Adult themes. Danielle Darrieux and Claude Nollier have a lesbian relationship.

A. I'm shocked.

B. The children in the film are shocked too. That's what makes the film so sensitive, tender, poignant, straining on the brink of anticipation. In short, it stinks. The critics who love this for its delicacy undoubtedly hate the genuine lyricism of Renoir's *Picnic on the Grass*. Now, there is a film that plucks nature out by the roots and offers it to man as a token of his life. I must add that Susannah York gives a skillful performance and will probably be an interesting actress once she washes off the adolescent ruddiness from her cheeks. Interesting eyes for a fake character, and Danielle Darrieux looks much less used up than Kenneth More, although in the script it's supposed to be the other way around. As for *Light in the Piazza*, Yvette Mimieux is very pretty in another false part. She may turn out to be a replacement for May Britt. Guy Green is a clever director who almost gets by until you start thinking about him. He plays a double game with the audience, drawing them into a problem, which is then painlessly resolved. *The Mark* and *Light in the Piazza* have nasty subjects that are glossed over by making apparent victims of mental disorder and retardation idyllically identifiable to the audience. There is no reason why Stuart Whitman cannot make a good husband and Yvette Mimieux a good wife, but if their characters were straight to begin with, the audience would get bored, because, like most minor directors, Green cannot sustain interest in a character without the intrigue of a problem. A better director would have treated *Light in the Piazza* as a paradox, since what is often most endearing about adults is the remnants of their innocence.

A. Besides, you can't have problem films about photogenic people. Beautiful people transcend society to illuminate the universe. They can express the highest aspirations of Everyman, but never the pressing needs of the anonymous mass and the afflicted minority.

B. But if I must choose between beautiful people and ugly problems, I will choose the beautiful people and leave the problems to the politicians. For some people, I suppose, the biggest problem is the Bomb, and *Panic in the Year Zero* has enough anti-Bomb propaganda to choke a horse. Ray Milland directed it as a scabrous quickie, with five killings and a rape to jolly things along —just the treatment this exalted subject deserves.

A. Anything else before we close up shop?

B. Yes, I liked Roger Vadim's new discovery, Catherine Deneuve, in the last episode of *Tales of Paris*. She is an improvement on Annette and even Brigitte.

A. I'll give you just three words to sum up your conception of the cinema as reflected in all these bad movies.

B. Girls! Girls! Girls!

A. The truth is out at last.

—*New York Film Bulletin*, May 15, 1962

■ 11. HAPPY BIRTHDAY, JFK

As I was striding up Fiftieth Street—and on the New Frontier we do stride up, damn it—to attend New York's Birthday Salute to President Kennedy at Madison Square Garden, a tall youth in casual attire was passing out handbills mimeographed by something called the Greater New York Council of Young Americans for Freedom, an organization apparently agitated by events in Cuba, Berlin, Katanga, Laos, and Vietnam. Other Freedom Fighters were waving placards opposing aid to Tito and grain for Red China. On this hot, rainy Saturday night in New York I was disappointed by the absence of peace marchers mainly because my acquired French soul delights in paradoxes—and also because I am just no good at recording irrelevant journalistic impressions, like the smell of dung from the assembled Cossack horses.

JFK happened to be in town to plug some domestic legislation on what he thought were gut issues. Unfortunately the fat American middle class has drifted away from populist economics as its most articulate representatives have embraced the abstractions of "peace" on the left and "freedom" on the right. To discuss political arithmetic in these circumstances is considered the height of bad taste. While the peace movement cannot recruit one congressman to its colors, JFK is maneuvering for 250 loyal Representatives to break the conservative coalition that has been in power since 1938. This runs into millions of votes, not handfuls of pickets—and where there are millions of votes there can be no abstract morality.

Still, the hypocrisy and self-deception of politics must sicken anyone who does not treat this activity as a ritualistic game where you root for one side or the other out of some irrational loyalty to a personality, be he JFK or Yogi Berra. As a fatalistic anarchist, I celebrated JFK's birthday party in good faith, and in a strange way I was entertained by the spectacle of the President of the United States being lovingly insulted by his subjects.

The show began reverently enough with Robert Merrill singing our transcendentally unsingable national anthem at 9:10. The President was seated in a box on the 50th Street side of the Garden

—which meant that the audience on the 49th Street side had excellent rear views of the entertainers, and the spectators on the Avenue sides saw everything in profile. The Garden defeats everyone but Ethel Merman, Billy Graham, and Bob Cousy, anyway.

Ella Fitzgerald came on in these unconducive surroundings to belt out her standards into the void of Squaresville. The Jerome Robbins dancers followed with excerpts from "New York Export, Opus Jazz," enabling JFK to crack pointedly afterward that Robbins' choreography has more vitality than Ike's minuet. This youthful thrust at an old man was a bit unfair, I thought. Harry Belafonte was announced as a substitute for an ailing Danny Kaye—one member of the Peace Corps, as it were, substituting for another. Nothing is sadder than the degeneration of demonic talent into responsible citizenship.

Jack Benny breezily introduced Henry Fonda as a registered Republican and a vice-president of the John Birch Society. Laughter. It was perhaps a bit ungallant to announce that Maria Callas was born in Brooklyn. She retaliated with some standards from *Carmen* for the peasants in the royal box. Elliott Reid is a minor Fox actor who imitates the lion JFK. There is rumored to be a Washington bureaucrat who imitates Reid imitating JFK. Enough. Shirley MacLaine gushed onstage as a surprise starter. (Diahann Carroll, a program entry, was scratched.) Someone should tell Shirley that kooks are out of style. She introduced Peggy Lee, who became the first entertainer to acknowledge the long-suffering spectators in the rear balcony with artful head turns in a slow, beautifully improvised beat.

Jimmy Durante confronted JFK with the arrogance of Adenauer. Once more, to demonstrate Durante's warm heart, we were burdened with Eddie Jackson. Bobby Darin decided to milk the rear balcony and half the time he was gyrating with his rear to the royal box. Such lese majesty on the anal level is one of the privileges accorded to callow youth in our society. Mike Nichols and Elaine May shrewdly bumbled along with a clumsy telegram routine, ingratiating themselves with jabs at Adenauer and De Gaulle before hitting the solar plexus with Billie Sol Estes, the CIA, and Chiang Kai-shek, and then tapering off with Bobby Kennedy and Robert Frost. If JFK was bleeding, he certainly didn't show it.

However, the king was not to be denied on this night of nights.

Peter Lawford, the palace steward, presented Marilyn Monroe, the choicest delicacy our repressed civilization can officially provide the royal palate. Her cloak was removed, and there she was in all her lustrous glory, intimately—i.e., inaudibly—singing "Happy Birthday" to JFK. The birthday cake in the shape of a White House was paraded in and out with none of the guests tasting it. (Idea: Why not have Marilyn burst out of the cake next time? Superidea: Why not have a real orgy next time?)

JFK mounted the stage in that endearingly shambling movement that cancels out the chilling self-confidence of an intelligent politician. He had some mike trouble as he literally threw away some of his best lines. But he was in top form as he parodied the melodramatic utterances of his predecessors in office. He pleaded for the poor and yet recognized the grotesqueness of his plea. He invited us to stay over for the senior citizens' rally the next afternoon, and we laughed complacently because the joke was on him and on the senior citizens. Still, he is fighting as well as he can, and until the opposition nominates Albert Schweitzer, Bertrand Russell, Murray Kempton, or someone comparable to the FDR of erroneous legend, he is the purest liberal we are ever going to have. As for his alleged lack of passion, I submit that these are hardly the times for a man who will set the world on fire. Happy Birthday, JFK.

—Village Voice, May 24, 1962

■ 12. VIRIDIANA

When Luis Buñuel's *Viridiana* finally materialized in the dreary twilight of the 1961 Cannes Film Festival, many of those present were surprised to discover not merely a great film but, indeed, a really good movie. Some of the more modern critics still rotating around the Resnais-Antonioni axis were a bit suspicious of Buñuel's archaic technique, and the Festival jury hedged its bets by jointly honoring Buñuel's rousing entertainment in *Viridiana* and Henri Colpi's tedious coupling of amnesia and ambiguity in *Une Aussi Longue Absence*. For once the international box-office barometer has recorded the relative merits of the two works more accurately than the festival judges. Of course, every film is liked and disliked both for right and wrong reasons, and *Viridiana* is particularly susceptible to partisan critiques. Buñuel's personal triumph has been used to chastise everything from *Marienbad* to the Vatican, with the predictable counterreactions. However, when one attempts to place Buñuel in apposition or opposition to other directors, his remarkable isolation becomes apparent. On the most obvious level of identification, he is the only great Spanish-language director, and his career is one of the most bizarre in film history.

For a long time before *Viridiana* Buñuel had been treated as a victim of the world's repressions and inhibitions, variously represented by French censorship, Spanish fascism, Hollywood commercialism, and Mexican mediocrity. The Buñuel cult, at least in the Anglo-Saxon countries, had become an exercise less in cinema than in metacinema, that is, the study of cinema that might have or should have evolved under the proper social conditions. This cult assumed the mannerisms of privileged scholarship by exploiting the director's underground reputation as the creator of *Un Chien Andalou* (1928) and *L'Age d'Or* (1930), banned works carrying the cultural prestige of surrealism but generally unavailable to the lay public. Buñuel himself was gradually fossilized in the swamp of his legend by the reluctance of his defenders to confront the uneven quality of his career as a whole. Consequently, many of us at Cannes had to readjust to a new conception of Buñuel as a master instead of a martyr. Realizing that he had become a creature of festivals and film societies, and that his efforts held no interest for the distributors with the big cigars, most of us were quite willing to go along with the Buñuel claque in awarding him another sympathy prize, as for *The Young One*. Then, almost miraculously, the old surrealist crossed everyone up with a resounding commercial success.

Viridiana has a plot that is almost too lurid to synopsize even in these enlightened times. The heroine is summoned from a convent by her uncle, Don Jaime, an old Spanish *hidalgo* living on a neglected estate (Spain?) in obsessive mourning for his dead wife (the republic?). The novice arrives on the thirtieth anniversary of Don Jaime's marriage. Viridiana's resemblance to the *hidalgo*'s wife introduces the theme of substitution so dear to Hitchcock, but

Buñuel is less concerned with the illusion of the substitution than with the sexual drives aroused by it. Failing to persuade his niece to marry him, Don Jaime orders a compliant maid to drug her. He carries her upstairs to the accompaniment of *The Messiah* while Buñuel intensifies the outrageous eroticism of the situation by photographing the choreography of abduction through the prying eyes of the maid's little girl. Almost inexplicably, Don Jaime desists from the attempted rape. The morning after, in progressive stages of desperation, he tells his outraged niece that she has been violated, then denies the violation, outraging her even more with his mendacity, and after watching her departure, hangs himself. Viridiana returns to atone for her guilt, and the second movement of the film begins with the maid's little girl skipping with the rope that has been the instrument of the *hidalgo*'s deliverance.

The incestuous texture of the film is maintained with the entrance of the novice's virile cousin, Jorge, a pragmatist of the most ruthless kind. He discards his mistress to pursue Viridiana more efficiently, but willingly seduces the adoring maid in the interim. While Jorge is patching up the estate in slapdash Spanish fashion, Viridiana is pursuing the Franciscan ethic by adopting the most revolting beggars in the area. Buñuel intercuts the Angelus recited by Viridiana and her scabrous flock with detail shots of Jorge's rebuilding. Buñuel's despair for Spain leads him to dismiss reform as a possibility; Jorge is moved by humane feelings to purchase a dog that is chained under a cart and forced to trot along at a horse's pace. No sooner is the "liberal" purchase consummated than another dog comes trotting by under another cart going in the opposite direction on the same Spanish road, reversing the pattern of futility. The demolition of Viridiana's principles is reserved for the film's remarkable climax.

The beggar's orgy is set up dramatically by the departure of Viridiana, Jorge, the maid and her little girl on business in the town. For the first time the beggars move into the house itself, and they assault every sacred feeling of property that any audience could be presumed to possess. Wine and food smear fancy tapestries, antique furniture is smashed, ornate dishes and glasses are broken. But unlike their colleagues in depravity from *La Dolce Vita*, the beggars enjoy themselves, and suddenly, with *The Messiah* blaring on the phonograph, the screen reverberates with a hymn to liberation. These vile creatures (and Buñuel leaves no doubt of their vileness, their cruelty, even their mean hypocrisy), these blind, halt, leprous, syphilitic dregs become gloriously human.

When Viridiana and Jorge return, they are assaulted, and Viridiana's slowly vanishing purity is saved only when her cousin bribes one of the beggars to murder the would-be rapist. Deciding that two lives are too high a price to pay for her chastity, Viridiana casts her cross and her crown of thorns into the flames and prepares to surrender to Jorge. The production's government supervisor, who must have been dozing until this point, finally intervened. Viridiana and Jorge must not be left alone in a room after this, he ordered. Buñuel dutifully complied with a *ménage-à-trois* ending in which Jorge, Viridiana, and the maid play cards together in the long Spanish evening while the camera recedes on the hellish tableau to the accompaniment of some appropriate American juke-box slop.

How Buñuel managed to realize *Viridiana* at all under the Spanish censor may never be fully explained. The intangibles of national prestige may have played a part. Also, the myopic vision of the bureaucratic mind may not have fully grasped the almost magical transformation of images into ideas between shooting and screening. It would be naïve to think that Buñuel was without guile in this undertaking. The deviousness of his subsequent interviews was worthy of Hitchcock, and there is enough ambiguity in the film itself to confound the most perverse critics. For example, there seems to be some controversy about the fate of the beleaguered heroine. To put it bluntly, is Viridiana, the chaste novice in the film, actually raped by the syphilitic beggar who murders her first attacker? If so, does she then renounce her vows of chastity as result of a D. H. Lawrence awakening? The argument for this interpretation depends upon the time gap assumed in the editing of the action. The fact that Buñuel compels normally fastidious critics to ponder such lurid questions reflects the dark humor that rescues him from the absurdities of Ichikawa.

Whether or not Buñuel has circumvented the censor with suggestive elisions, the plot of *Viridiana* gives one pause. The modern cinema, such as it is presumed to be, is supposed to have supplanted plot with mood. Then suddenly Buñuel bursts in like a resurrected Victorian novelist steeped in violent depravity and unashamedly flourishing the most obvious symbols. The spectacle of a contemporary director cutting away metaphorically from a brutal seduction to a cat pouncing on a mouse jolts the critic who has finally adjusted to the languorous introspection of an Antonioni. Then, too, the flagrant display of eroticism, sadism, and fetishism reveals the director's personality with the embarrassing Krafft-Ebing frankness one recalls in the films of Stroheim and Lang. Buñuel may have been more shocking in the past, but never before have his shock effects seemed so much the warp and woof of his philosophy. *Un Chien Andalou* and *L'Age d'Or* have their moments, of course, but audiences are usually cushioned for "avant-garde" cinema, where anything goes. *Las Hurdes* (*Land Without Bread*) and *Los Olvidados* (*The Young and the Damned*) mask details of horror with a socially conscious narration. Even though it is hard to imagine any other director conceiving of a mountain goat falling off a mountain or a legless beggar being rolled down a hill, the spectator can console himself with the thought that this is not the best of all possible worlds and the next election or the next revolution may improve conditions. There is no such consolation in *Viridiana*, Buñuel's despairing allegory of the Spanish condition. For the first time in his career Buñuel ends his action in an existential enclosure in which hell, in Sartre's phrase, is other people.

If every director must be assigned a political station, Buñuel is unmistakably a man of the left. He actively supported the Spanish Republic against Franco's insurgents, and he has been highly critical of the Establishments in Mexico, America, and France. A story is told about Buñuel, perhaps apocryphal but still relevant. It seems that Jean Epstein, with whom Buñuel began his career in 1926, once offered his Spanish assistant an opportunity to work with Abel Gance. Buñuel reportedly refused because of what he considered Gance's fascist leanings. Epstein, a Gallic product of apolitical *amitié*, was outraged, but Buñuel stood his ground. Later Buñuel had a falling out with Salvador Dali over the sacrilegious treatment of *L'Age d'Or*.

The point is that Buñuel has been more intransigent over the years than most of his colleagues, and he has had more than his share of problems, but whereas one sometimes suspects the temptation of martyrdom in a Stroheim or a Welles, one is struck mainly by Buñuel's tenacity. During the long drought between

1932 and 1947, without any directorial opportunities, he remained on the fringes of the industry in New York and Hollywood. Despite several canceled projects in Mexico and France since 1947, he has managed to direct twenty films, about half of which are meaningful projections of his ideas and personality. Even in a potboiler like *Susana*, released in 1950, the year of *The Young and the Damned*, there are one or two passages that foreshadow *Viridiana*.

There is a danger in attaching an explicitly political moral to Buñuel's career. For a director of the left, Buñuel has evidenced almost no interest in the mechanics of reform or revolution. The superimposed narrations in *Land Without Bread* and *The Young and the Damned* suggest amelioration, but the images of the films operate autonomously in terms of a fatalistic Spanish temperament. Even in his Mexican films there is no trace of the theory of progress through technology, and one could never imagine his making a tractor film behind the Iron Curtain. He has never concerned himself with the mystiques of peasant and worker; nor has he dramatized the injustices of economic exploitation in any detail. As the late André Bazin observed, Buñuel lacks the Manichean tendencies of a propagandist. As cruel as his world may be, its characters are never divided into villains and victims. His obsession with mental and physical deformities generally deprives his plots of any sociological plausibility. Even his handling of the racial issue in *Robinson Crusoe* and *The Young One* is too perverse to serve as a respectably liberal blueprint.

Ado Kyrou's recently published book on Buñuel sheds some new light on the paradoxes of the director's personality. Particularly interesting is some of the director's own film criticism in the late twenties, when, like many critics today, he tried to establish polar relationships. Whereas Truffaut has invented the Lumière-Delluc and Sagan-Queneau games, Buñuel pioneered in the Keaton-Jannings game. Buñuel preferred Keaton, with all the hostility to German expressionism such a preference implies. He frankly admired the American cinema for its empty-headed grace and rhythm, qualities that he attributed to a Jungian sense of racial instinct. Conversely, he understood his own limitations, and his perceptive humility is still one of his greatest virtues. Buñuel is not and never has been a stylist of the first rank. He would have been lost in the Hollywood shuffle on commissioned projects, even though he functioned creditably and efficiently on impossible Mexican assignments. To Buñuel the cinema is simply a vehicle for his ideas. Once these ideas have taken the appropriately plastic form, he shoots very quickly, and any additional values are either incidental or accidental. One of his Mexican producers has reported that Buñuel seems bored by the actual shooting of a film.

Even though one may treat Dali's accusations of atheism as malicious slander designed to get Buñuel fired from the Museum of Modern Art in New York, Buñuel's films are clearly not intended to win friends and influence people for the Church. As a director who began his career by throwing live priests and dead jackasses out the window, and then compounded his sacrilege by confusing Christ with the Marquis de Sade, he has been almost exclusively identified in terms of these and subsequent impieties. Because he titillates anticlerical audiences with glimpses of forbidden frankness, Buñuel has found it difficult to convey the full dimensions of his metaphysical rebellion. As soon as he introduces the theme of sexual liberation into the argument, the latent puritanism of the organized left reacts against the degeneration of protest into anarchy. Yet even Buñuel's anarchy is unusually individualistic. Whereas Vigo is concerned with the disavowal and destruction of social institutions, Buñuel invokes the biological anarchy of nature to reconstruct humanity. Buñuel finds it quite natural for the protagonist of *El* to notice the legs of a pretty girl while he is washing a priest's feet for a Catholic ceremony. Buñuel's defiance of the Church for excluding nature from the altar thus takes on a mystical quality. The pleasure Buñuel takes in the beggar's orgy in *Viridiana* is almost indistinguishable from the religious ecstasy of self-denial one finds in Bresson. It is perhaps appropriate that Buñuel lacks Bresson's sensibility while Bresson lacks Buñuel's force.

The odd circumstances of Buñuel's career preclude an analysis of periods and stylistic progression. More than most other directors of comparable stature, the man is inseparable from his art. His camera has always viewed his characters from a middle distance, too close for cosmic groupings and too far away for self-identification. Normally this would make his films cold and his point of view detached, but by focusing on the abnormality of life, Buñuel forces his audience to accept man unconditionally. When we look at the monstrous long enough and hard enough, we realize, in Truffaut's phrase, that there are no monsters. The drawback to Buñuel's choice of distance is that he creates horror without terror, and pity without catharsis. In short, he lacks the sense of tragedy his ideas demand.

How a director who seems so disconcertingly obvious can turn out to be so complex is one of the mysteries of the cinema. For example, it seems too symmetrically ironic to synchronize a beggar's orgy with Handel's *Messiah*. However, Buñuel has never been a champion of background music. He simply does not care enough about his score to seek something more subtle. Yet his indifference to details that more clever directors have mastered only reminds us that ingenuity is no substitute for genius. Buñuel's blend of the real and the surreal, the grotesque and the erotic, the scabrous and the sublime never quite fits into any critical theory. The triumph of *Viridiana* leaves us just about where we were before, but henceforth we shall have to allow Buñuel to tailor his own straitjacket.

—*Movie*, No. 1, June 1962

■ 13. *LOLITA*

Most of the reviews of Stanley Kubrick's cinematic treatment of Vladimir Nabokov's *Lolita* emphasized the novel's awesome difficulties rather than its glorious opportunities. *Lolita* is, after all, a "road" novel. A director with a flair for cars and roadside Americana could have taken off with this material. As it is, Nabokov's literary wit has not been translated into visual wit, with the result that the film is leaden where it should be light. Kubrick has a fatal weakness for long scenes in which everything is explained and then explained again. Yet Nabokov's reverse-Jamesian conception of the European intellectual corrupted by American vitality is never adequately realized, and the sex is so discreetly handled that an unsophisticated spectator may be completely mystified.

To compound the felony, the acting never meshes. Shelley Winters is hilarious as the voracious matron drinking and lusting her way out of her slightly Europeanized shell. When her character is killed off, the film dies with her. James Mason, a serious actor with no flair for comedy, cannot take up the slack. In at least two of Mason's most deliciously written scenes, one longs for the dark humor of an Olivier. Peter Sellers is an accurate mimic without physical presence or discernible personality. Sue Lyon almost justifies her being "discovered" for Lolita, but not quite. Her sullen presence is effective at first, but increasing demands on her acting ability eventually destroy the illusion. In short, Lolita is a film that runs steadily downhill at too slow a pace for a needless two and a half hours.

There is something to be said for the director's accepting Lionel Trilling's interpretation of Lolita as a love story concerned, like all great love stories, with forbidden love. However, I suspect that Kubrick lost his nerve and wound up underestimating his audience. People are not so easily shocked nowadays as they used to be. Anyway, there are far more shocking perversions of propriety than falling in love with a twelve-year-old girl or a twelve-year-old what-have-you, as the French would say. I suppose almost every male has momentarily lost his heart to a nymphet devouring a banana split at Howard Johnson's, and there is nothing new about nymphet-worship on the screen. Mary Pickford's appeal was that of a pseudonymphet, and Shirley Temple's, even more shockingly, that of a prenymphet. (Adults always liked Shirley more than children did, anyway.) Ginger Rogers charmingly impersonated a wartime Lolita in The Major and the Minor, and Brigitte Bardot first exploded on the American scene as a daughter-substitute for repressed fathers.

What Lolita needed more than anything else was a director in tune with Nabokov's delirious approach to his subject. We are never shown the inspiringly unconscious gestures and movements that transform the most emotionally impoverished nymphet into a creature of fantasy and desire. Kubrick goes through the motions with a hula hoop and the munching of potato chips, but there is nothing intuitive or abandoned about the man-nymphet relationship. The director's heart is apparently elsewhere. Consequently, we face the problem without the passion, the badness without the beauty, the agony without the ecstasy.

—Village Voice, July 5, 1962

■ 14. *SHOOT THE PIANO PLAYER*

François Truffaut's *Shoot the Piano Player* is a movie most readers of this column should enjoy without any further critical rationalization. Just for the record, this relaxed piece of film-making is
Truffaut's second feature-length opus, released in France in 1960,
a year before *Jules and Jim.* The director's apparent casualness has
disconcerted some of our more solemn critics, who would rather
suffer along with Antonioni than sing along with Truffaut. The
notion that great art can be great fun, and vice versa, has always
offended spokesmen for moral sensibility. The argument against
humor in what should be serious art has been disguised as an argument over purity of form, the argument advanced for Racine
against Shakespeare, Richardson against Fielding, and Mann
against Proust. I suppose that Antonioni is purer than Truffaut,
but I suspect that cinema, like water, obtains its flavor from its
impurities. And what impurities there are in *Shoot the Piano
Player!*

To begin with, *Shoot the Piano Player* is adapted from a wildly
melodramatic novel, *Down There,* by the relatively unknown
American novelist David Goodis. Everyone knows that melodrama
is not the stuff of great art. Everyone knows you can't make an
important film about a small, homely piano player with a tragic
past as a concert pianist even when the piano player is admirably
played by Charles Aznavour. You can't have gangsters, chases, kid-
nappings, murders, and a suicide littering the pristine art-house
screen, particularly when you are not indicting society in the
process. Furthermore, why is this sad-eyed piano player so irresistible to lovely girls like Marie Dubois, Nicole Berger, and Michèle Mercier? How can you have pathos that way, and since when
does a serious film spend so much time in bed? However, if this is
not a serious film, how do you explain that strange opening in
which a stranger passing down the street talks briefly about the
love he feels for his wife and then disappears into the vast conjugal
sea of middle-class humanity? What are we supposed to understand
when a brutal bartender declares before his death that for him
woman was always supreme? Why did Truffaut say in 1960 that

Welles has added a fluent tracking style with the visual controls of remembered meaning. For example, the vertical camera movement down a tower after Arkadin's death supersedes the script and quite naturally escapes the attention of our literary film critics. Similarly, to express any enthusiasm for the prodigality of Welles's lateral tracks is to violate the guild rules of the exalted criticism that insists that after *Citizen Kane* Orson Welles was obliged to deal with Big Themes, at least as big as Hearst, perhaps "Citizen Schiff" or "Citizen Sulzberger." Fortunately Welles has gone his own way, and what a dazzling spectacle he provides here for those discerning moviegoers who have outgrown the tedious affections of realism. For the others I can think of nothing more fitting than to be shipwrecked on *The Island*, that Japanese regression to the anachronistic anonymity of silent-screen characters.

—*Village Voice*, October 18, 1962

■ 16. *LAWRENCE OF ARABIA*

If there had been no newspaper strike, and mine were a lonely voice instead of an only voice, *Lawrence of Arabia* might now be festooned with the superlatives accorded such previous superproductions as *The Best Years of Our Lives, Around the World in 80 Days, The Bridge on the River Kwai,* and *Ben Hur.* But like its almost forgotten predecessors, *Lawrence* is simply another expensive mirage, dull, overlong, and coldly impersonal. Its objective is less to entertain or enlighten than to impress and intimidate. It is not as stupid as *The Longest Day* or as silly as *Mutiny on the Bounty.* Some of its acting and technical effects are interesting. But on the whole I find it hatefully calculating and condescending.

What baffles me about the promotion of the film is the assumption that everyone is passionately interested in T. E. Lawrence. Perhaps there is a cultural gap between generations. Lawrence was born in 1888 and died in 1935. Lowell Thomas popularized the legend of Lawrence of Arabia between 1918 and 1920. Those of us in America who grew up during the Depression had little reason to cultivate a champion of Arab nationalism as a personal idol. In my cultural adolescence I associated the name Lawrence with the initials D. H. rather than T. E. I even wondered whether my earliest literary hero had been involved in Arabia. Then I learned that this was another Lawrence and that there was something disreputable about him, something that inspired veiled queer jokes. Somehow I failed to pursue the subject until quite recently—and I must concede that is one of the film's fringe benefits. The main trouble with this four-hour ordeal, two years and $13 million in the making, is that it grossly oversimplifies the murky politics of the Middle East without coming to grips with the man himself.

The film begins with a short prologue re-enacting Lawrence's fatal motorcycle accident and the dedication of his bust in the crypt of St. Paul's Cathedral in London. After several of his acquaintances—some historical, some fictional-historical—have been briefly interviewed the plot flashes back to Lawrence in 1916 as a junior officer in the Maps Division of British General Headquarters in Cairo. This reverse opening suggests a possible "Kane" approach to the mystery of the hero—that is, a depiction of Lawrence as others saw him. However, David Lean's meticulously bloated direction and Robert Bolt's limply epigrammatic dialogue quickly dispel that notion.

The strange thing about this movie is that people look smaller in rooms than they do on the desert. I am sure that Lean was trying for some bizarre caricature of officialdom to the advantage of the wild Bedouin existence, but this stylistic trick never comes off because it is both too obvious and too unpleasant. As Lawrence, Peter O'Toole gives a nervous, hysterical, and at times effeminate performance that is not entirely wrong for the part but that somewhat distorts the historical magnitude of the character. For example, Lawrence's remarkable skill as a diplomat among the warring Arab factions is only vaguely suggested. Too often his image on horseback or camelback is allowed to prevail over his insight in the conference tent. His first great victory, the capture of Aqaba, is described from a towering crane as an exciting charge. The real Lawrence astutely persuaded the Turks to surrender without firing a shot. Of course a charge is generally considered more "cinematic."

Lean's interpretation of Lawrence's capture by the Turks is a further "cinematic" exploitation. Lawrence himself records that he was flogged and sodomized on that occasion. Biographers differ on

40448

the comparative traumatic effects of the torture and the perversion. B. H. Liddell Hart emphasized the awakening homosexuality, Anthony Nutting the discovery of a raging masochism. There appears to be no evidence that Lawrence was ever an overt homosexual. Terence Rattigan's Ross suggests that the Turks, with their Byzantine cunning, detected a latent homosexuality in Lawrence and brought it to the surface to destroy their prisoner as an Arab hero. This silly interpretation defies all logical, psychological, and historical probability, but it is an interpretation. Again Lean and Bolt try to have it both ways in the film. José Ferrer plays a coughing Turkish pederast to the hilt as he literally unveils his blond captive and fondles his breast. We see the hero striking his tormentor and being flogged for his pains, and then we see nothing more until Lawrence is cast out of the barracks. We never find out what happened, and an incredibly naïve spectator might even assume that Lawrence was disheartened by his inability to endure torture.

I find the treatment of this episode thoroughly distasteful. For one thing, it seems to be the big sales gimmick of the film. If a beautiful girl were stripped and then flogged for her resistance, the censors would be up in arms demanding an end to this immorality, and the critics would chortle about such outrageous Arabian Nights commercialism. But let a man be stripped and flogged, and we are supposed to be impressed with the seriousness of the theme. Perhaps Lawrence of Arabia is one brutal queer film too many. Perhaps I am a little weary of people telling me about the silliness of the heterosexual action in The Lovers and about the profundity of the sadism in Billy Budd. Perhaps I am just plain tired of all these "serious" moral films with no women in the cast. There is a calculating sickness at work here, an Anglo-American syndrome of abstract morality for men only that sickens me as a recurringly acclaimed theme of the cinema. By all means, let's bring on the girls.

—Village Voice, December 20, 1962

ii

1963

■ 1. VENI, VIDI, VITTI

In the flesh Monica Vitti bears little resemblance to the usual image of an Italian screen star. Not only does she lack the sculptured majesty of such compatriots as Sophia Loren, Gina Lollobrigida and Claudia Cardinale, but also, in terms of the high-I. Q. sex appeal projected in person, she is inaccessible to the greater part of the mass audience. Her mischievously expressive eyes are generally too intelligently focused on matters beyond biological attraction, and despite her genial mannerisms of playful femininity, there is little of the coquette and less of the *cocotte* in her complex personality.

The would-be superior male is forewarned. This is a girl who not only reads books—Stendhal, Camus, Beckett, press handouts tell us—she apparently understands them as well. This supposedly means something more than the late Marilyn Monroe's touching affection for Dostoyevsky and much more than Kim Novak's carrying Plutarch under her arm to the Cannes Film Festival. Dare we say it out loud? Monica Vitti is an intellectual actress, the visible flowering of what has come to be known as the modern cinema. As Greta Garbo and Emmanuelle Riva have been the pin-up girls of the soul, and Marlene Dietrich and Jeanne Moreau the pin-up girls of the senses, perhaps Monica Vitti will go down in film history as the first pin-up girl of the intellect.

The beauties of her mind aside, Miss Vitti is a remarkable phenomenon in an industry that virtually manufactures symmetrical features. The unusual extension of her sensual lips, the prominence of her slightly misshapen nose, the authentication of her unruly blond hair by intransigently blond freckles testify to an individuality gained at the expense of universality. If hers is not the face to launch a thousand ships or the body to set the world on fire, there is still something to be said for the so easily identified face and figure as the exclusive and ancestral property of Monica Vitti, born Maria Luise Ceciarelle. This is undoubtedly a decisive consideration for an actress who claims that she is groping through her art for the meaning of her life. At present, however, even the casual observer cannot consider the art and life of Monica Vitti apart from the art and life of her director, Michelangelo Antonioni. Under the terms of their mutual destiny, the director and the actress will probably rise or fall together.

"Doing a film with him," Miss Vitti says of Antonioni, "is like arguing about everything: my career, my life, my love for him. I ask myself when I'll be able to do a part where I can abandon myself to precise sentiments: hatred, passion, jealousy. That's what they taught me at the Academy of Dramatic Art. With Michelangelo, roles are more difficult. Everything is lost in subtleties, and I don't have the intuitions that he has. But I am not able to do a film with anyone else. I have refused offers from Hollywood. I don't want to leave him."

From the day in 1957 when Antonioni interviewed Miss Vitti for a dubbing assignment in his fifth film, *Il Grido* (*The Cry*), the nature of their relationship has never been discreetly masked. Antonioni was then and still is separated from his wife; Miss Vitti was engaged to be married. They have been inseparable ever since. Short of a divorce, Italian style, it is unlikely that their liaison will ever be regularized. Curiously, this state of affairs has never provoked a scandalized reaction, possibly because the obsessive intensity of their joined existences seems to transcend mere conjugal vows.

Indeed, Miss Vitti's possessive feeling for Antonioni assumed legendary proportions during the filming of *La Notte*, when the presence of the French temptress Jeanne Moreau created a fantastic atmosphere of sexual rivalry on the set. Miss Vitti insisted at one point on watching Miss Moreau's nude scene, a spectacle that, some observers report, could have made a choice film in itself.

As it turned out, Miss Moreau parted from the Antonioni-Vitti maze of complexes with relief and bad feelings.

For his part, Antonioni has been ungallant enough to suggest that Jeanne Moreau was hired in the first place only for commercial reasons; and Miss Vitti, now that the disruptive sensuality of the French invader no longer threatens Monica's ménage, has been discreetly silent about the episode. Although Antonioni at fifty is more than twenty years older than his protégée, the union seems about as permanent as anything can be in this volatile world of illusion and reality. One is almost tempted to predict, in the spirit of a typical Antonioni film, that they will suffer happily ever after.

However, the classic parallels of Pygmalion and Galatea, Svengali and Trilby do not exactly apply here. Nor can one invoke the cinematic precedents of Mauritz Stiller and Greta Garbo, Josef von Sternberg and Marlene Dietrich, Ingmar Bergman and Harriet Andersson any more appropriately.

For one thing, Monica Vitti was already a relatively polished artist when she met Antonioni. That she started in the dub-happy Italian film industry with her own voice is a refreshing switch from the voluptuous starlet who is usually hired to be seen and not heard. Having acted with distinction on both the Italian and French stage, Miss Vitti had no need for a mentor to teach her how to talk and walk. Consequently the fluid eroticism of her movements, fore and aft, cannot be chalked up entirely to the magic of Antonioni's camera. Finally, her mind and spirit had been formed against a middle-class intellectual background similar to, but separate from, Antonioni's. What makes the Antonioni-Vitti relationship modern—one might say almost pathologically modern—is a subtle reversal of roles. This reversal has taken the form, on film and in fact, of feminizing the masculine role and masculinizing the feminine.

"Before knowing Monica," Antonioni recalls, "nothing ever went right for me. I was two years without work, mainly because I wouldn't direct films I didn't like. There was even a time when I didn't have money to buy proper food. That was when I sold my tennis trophies for cigarettes. *The Cry* was doing badly, not making a lira. When I proposed *L'Avventura*, no one would finance it. The story was strange, they said, and who was Monica Vitti?"

Now, this is hardly the presumptuously domineering attitude of a Pygmalion or a Svengali, or even a Rossellini. It has been reported, for example, that Miss Vitti carried the script of *L'Avventura* from producer to producer for months on end. The point here is not her loyalty but her assumption of what has long been considered a male prerogative, at least on the ideal level. Antonioni's implied passivity toward the management of his career is reflected in the weakness of his male characters on the screen.

Strangely enough, Antonioni is considered one of the most fearsome tyrants on the set in the history of the cinema. He once denied a report that he had slapped an actress by explaining that he had merely slapped a nonactress. (He was not, of course, referring to Monica Vitti.) However, what is at issue here is not the professional methods of a meticulous director who believes in annihilating the personalities of his players to achieve the moody fatalism of a despairing world but rather the vision of life and the conception of the sexes embodied in the Antonioni-Vitti union.

Even the couple's living arrangements indicate a partnership of equals. Their apartment takes up the two top floors of a new building in a Roman suburb. The lower floor is occupied by Miss Vitti, but although the two can maintain the appearance of living apart from each other, an interior circular stairway connects the two apartments. (What a cinematic symbol that stairway would make!) They reportedly split the rent, share the same maid and secretary, dine at the same table, and have access to the same telephone.

This peculiarly post-Ibsen arrangement of the sexes is not too unusual in our time, since Monica Vitti clearly represents a certain type of modern woman found at almost any intellectual cocktail party. She is usually searching for something, and as she strives to communicate what that something is, the unwary male becomes enmeshed in a hopeless guessing game. It is not marriage exactly, not money exactly, not security exactly, not sex exactly, not companionship exactly, not a career exactly—in fact, not anything exactly. Ultimately, inexactitude becomes the modern woman's secret weapon. By making the terms of agreement vague and baiting the trap with tantalizing visions of sexual experimentation, the woman feminizes man's instincts and sensibilities. Because man, the eternal wanderer and truth-seeker, is biologically incapable of woman's constancy, he is doomed to appear, at least in Antonioni's films, as a pitiable weakling in terms of woman's character. This, ultimately, is the cinematic psychology of Michelangelo Antonioni.

In *L'Avventura* Monica Vitti is involved with an architect, in *La Notte* with a novelist, and in *Eclipse* with a stockbroker. In each instance the man spiritually disintegrates under the probing gaze of Miss Vitti. It can and should be argued that a man's value does not depend entirely on how well he communicates with a woman; how well a man performs his work is at least equally important. But Antonioni, like Ingmar Bergman, Tennessee Williams, and Paddy Chayefsky before him, cannot grasp this elemental premise of masculine psychology.

Yet what else is one to expect of a director capable of the following flowery recollection: "You see, I like women very much. I admire their strength and their closeness to nature. I've always been surrounded by women. When I was a boy in Ferrara, our country home, we were constantly visited by my cousins and aunts. I listened to them for hours . . . their talk of veils, flowers, etc. . . . fascinated me."

The obsolete notion of men engaged in the world's action while women wait at home has been so completely eroded by the dynamic intervention of the modern woman that even fundamental sexual relationships have been affected. Emasculation inevitably breeds perversion, and it is not surprising that Antonioni's films are noted for the director's vicious treatment of sexual experience. What is most depressing is that Antonioni may represent the wave of the future, and Monica Vitti the final triumph of the feminine principle in the western world. We doomed playboys of that western world could do a lot worse.

—*Cavalier*, February 1963

■ *2. THE ELUSIVE CORPORAL*

Jean Renoir's *The Elusive Corporal* is the kind of movie that separates the men from the boys. As in all great films, the plot is less important than the theme, and the theme is less important than the director's personal vision. Renoir has returned to the subject of prisoners of war and their desire to escape, a subject that he treated so memorably in *Grand Illusion*. That was in 1936. By 1939, as Renoir has ruefully observed, the world was at war again.

The Elusive Corporal begins with the fall of France in 1940. For Renoir this is a new war and these are new times. Interspersed newsreel footage of monumental battles and bombings expresses the dissolution of a world to which the prisoners still cling. Led by an idealistic corporal (Jean-Pierre Cassel), five of the prisoners become involved in escape plans ranging from the obvious to the ludicrous. Renoir is clearly not interested in how prisoners escape, but why. Whereas *Grand Illusion* was concerned with the idea of fraternity, *The Elusive Corporal* is concerned with the idea of liberty. Whereas the earlier film suggested that class differences were more decisive than national differences, the later one suggests that liberty means something different for each man. To one prisoner liberty means returning to his farm, to another regaining his civilian job, to still another retaining the military camaraderie that ignores class distinctions, and so on through the spectrum of fantasies and memories of the status quo.

When the elusive corporal finally does escape, he and his comrade encounter a French prisoner near the border working a farm with a German war widow. "You've never made a run for it?" asks the corporal. "You've never wanted to escape to the land of your fathers?" "I worked others' land," is the simple and eloquent reply. For Renoir everyone has his reasons. The tone of the film is serio-comic, and the camera keeps man in the foreground at all times. No jazzy montage, no meaningless swoops and tracks. Just the apparently effortless achievement not of an old man but of an old master.

Welcome also is the current revival of *The Earrings of Madame De* and *Le Plaisir*, two classic films of the late Max Ophuls. Below the glittering surfaces, the lush decor, the sensuous fabrics, there is the cruel sensibility of an artist mourning the death of this world and all other worlds to come. Inside the beautiful ladies and lovers of romance lurk the grinning skeletons of tragedy. If the cinema had produced no other artists except Ophuls and Renoir, it would still be an art form of profundity and splendor.

—*Village Voice*, February 21, 1963

■ 3. *TO KILL A MOCKINGBIRD*

To Kill a Mockingbird relates the Cult of Childhood to the Negro Problem with disastrous results. Before the intellectual confusion of the project is considered, it should be noted that this is not much of a movie even by purely formal standards. Horton Foote's script is a fuzzy digest of Harper Lee's Pulitzer Prize best seller, while Robert Mulligan's direction is slavishly faithful to the elliptical style of Miss Lee's action sequences. For example, Miss Lee describes the shadow of a spooky neighbor creeping up on a young boy. So Mulligan compliantly photographs the shadow of a spooky neighbor creeping up on a young boy. What could be more cinematic? Unfortunately, a director who manipulates a shadow without delivering its substance is only cheating his audience. Mulligan flubs the violent climax by the same misapplication of a literary effect to the cinema. A reader can always catch up on a mystifying action a page or two later, but a moviegoer wants to see what is happening while it is happening. All the talk in the world afterward cannot redeem a lost image.

What fools too many critics about a project like this is the trick of the child's point of view. The camera drops a foot, then darts and swoops with the child's erratic movements. The world opens up, and everything looks more profound and inventive. It is just too easy for a bad director to look good when the adult world can be reduced to homespun parables like: "Mockingbirds don't do one thing but make music for us to enjoy. They don't eat up people's gardens, don't nest in corncribs, they don't do one thing but sing their hearts out for us. That's why it's a sin to kill a mockingbird."

The movie begins innocently enough, trailing after a little girl who is even more adorable than the moppet in *Sundays and Cybèle,* another overrated trick film. The setting is Maycomb, Alabama, in the early thirties. The novel teems with relatives, neighbors, and assorted gargoyles arranged in an intricate network of political and social alliances, but the movie Maycomb comes out looking deserted and underpopulated, and lacking spatial unity besides. When Gregory Peck is assigned to defend a Negro sharecropper falsely accused of raping a white woman, Peck's adorable children help deter the obligatory lynch mob and then watch the courtroom spectacle from the balcony segregated for Negroes. (I daresay the Maycomb courtroom is still segregated thirty years yater, and so much for Miss Lee's cleverly masked argument for gradualism.)

As usual, the Negro is less a rounded character than a liberal construct, a projection of the moral superiority Negroes supposedly attain through their suffering and degradation. He is not only innocent of the charge and infinitely nobler than his white-trash accusers, father and daughter; he is also incredibly pure of heart. Brock Peters tries hard to break through the layers of moral whitewash, but he is finally smothered by Peck's unctuous nobility. When the Negro is convicted on evidence flimsy enough to acquit Trotsky in a Stalinist court, Peck offers the glowing hope of an appeal. (This is in the days of the Nine-Old-Men Court.) When the Negro is shot (off screen) for attempting to escape, Peck is so upset that, by some inverted logic understood only by liberal southerners, he deplores the Negro's unwarranted impetuosity. Here the movie tries to placate Dixie audiences by departing from the sacred text of the novel to omit a reference to fourteen bullets fired into the escapee's body. It never seems to occur to Miss Lee, Mr. Foote, or Mr. Mulligan, as it occurred to someone sitting behind me, that the Negro's reported escape is as malodorous as his unjust conviction. Aside from doubting the word of the local constabulary on a matter concerning the rape of white womanhood, the disinterested spectator is aesthetically justified in questioning the truth of something not shown on the screen.

The plot takes a retributive turn of sorts with the red-neck who started all the fuss getting his just deserts while attempting to murder Peck's children. The sheriff decides to shelter the red-neck's murderer so that the dead can bury the dead and all accounts can be squared.

This is a heartwarming resolution of the novel and the film. Yet somehow the moral arithmetic fails to come out even. One innocent Negro and one murderous red-neck hardly cancel each other out. How neat and painless it is for the good people of Maycomb to find a bothersome victim in one grave and a convenient scapegoat in the other. When all is said and done, southerners are People Like Us, some good and some bad. So what? No one who has read the last letters of the German troops trapped in Stalingrad can easily believe in a nation of monsters, but the millions of corpses are an objective fact. At some point a social system is too evil and too unjust for personal ethics to carry any weight. Perhaps the Negro and the red-neck are brothers under the skin, both victims of the same system. Perhaps they are the nucleus of a new political coalition. It is too early to tell, but it is too late for the Negro to act as moral litmus paper for the white conscience. The Negro is not a mockingbird.

—*Village Voice*, March 7, 1963

■ 4. *WHAT EVER HAPPENED TO BABY JANE?*

What Ever Happened to Baby Jane? is shaping up in America as an unpremeditated commercial success on the scale of *Psycho*. That is to say, it is not one of those publicity inflated extravaganzas that allegedly grosses ten million dollars without anyone you know having seen it. Everyone seems to have seen *Baby Jane*, mostly in the casual surroundings of the neighborhood movie house. No nonsense about reserved seats and advanced prices. Just a regular movie, shot in four weeks for under seven hundred thousand dollars with the assured professionalism that now passes for prodigious virtuosity. But like *Psycho*, *Baby Jane* seems destined to be seen and not honored. The adverse reviews far outnumber the favorable ones, and the very size of the audience works against the film's reputation. For one reason or another *Baby Jane* has attracted such dissident types as the Bette Davis and Joan Crawford camp followers, jaded teen-agers out for kicks, elderly movie fans back for a reprise, and even the fashionable attuned patrons of the art circuits. Since these groups barely tolerate each other on the streets, it is hardly surprising that they resent each other in the audience at the expense of the film.

The workaday reviewer is additionally handicapped by the problem of not giving away too much of the melodramatic plot and still finding something to say about a film that has no apparent theme or moral, no particular relevance to "real life," and no implied social problem. Although *Baby Jane* is reasonably consistent with Robert Aldrich's career, it is a relatively isolated phenomenon, a technical exercise to the *n*th power, a Pirandellian conceit violating that most fundamental of realistic conventions, the immersion of the player in the part. The thought of immersing Bette Davis and Joan Crawford at any time is formidable enough, but here the plot itself is immersed in the presences and pasts of these two ageless stars. In fact, if *Baby Jane* is about anything at all, it is about Bette Davis and Joan Crawford.

The biographical premises of the action are established in three curious precredit sequences spanning twenty years in approximately ten minutes. The film opens on a tearful little girl clutching a crying doll. After a series of establishing shots we find ourselves in a 1915 vaudeville theater where Baby Jane Hudson is entertaining a packed house of children and adults with a tap dance. The tinny band accompaniment switches from minstrel to ragtime, and Aldrich cut-cut-cutting along, picks up the period floral headgear and rustling taffeta in the savagely innocent audience. The context has been established, but that first shot of the unidentified little girl with the crying doll sets the mood for the extended infantile wail to come.

For an encore Baby Jane Hudson renders a stridently mawkish song that begins: "I'm writing a letter to Daddy/The address is Heaven Above . . ." Aldrich's editing slashes the spectacle on stage into bits and pieces of arrested development. The traditional long, medium, and close-up montage sequence is broken up by obliquely angled shots from the side of the theater. Aldrich never moves his camera to unify the discordant spatial images. The visual disruption expressed by this analytical style precedes the dramatization of the elementary conflicts in the Hudson family—Baby Jane and her father in the spotlight versus Sister Blanche and her mother in the wings.

The Hudson *ménage* is a far cry from the affectionate June Havoc–Gypsy Rose Lee sibling rivalry in *Gypsy*. Mervyn Leroy's admirably appropriate long-take treatment of the *Gypsy* numbers emphasizes the emotional cohesion of show people on-stage. Aldrich's montage of antagonisms expresses the disintegration of a show family offstage. The teeth-grinding meanness of the Hudson relationships suggests less the development of characters than the evolution of monsters. Meanwhile the Daddy song and a strangely lifelike Baby Jane doll are planted for future reference as lyrical echoes.

The next precredit sequence whisks the audience to a 1935 studio projection room where a bored producer and a nervous agent are inspecting the "rushes" of a Baby Jane movie. These actually consist of clips from two 1933 Bette Davis efforts, *Parachute Jumper* and *Ex-Lady*. These deservedly forgotten films belong to the period before Miss Davis hit it big with *Of Human Bondage* (1934), but she projected a striking personality even then. Not as Baby Jane, however. The producer snorts at her bogus southern accent, her heavy drinking, and her box-office poison. We are told that Blanche Hudson is such a big Hollywood star that her contract forces the studio to grind out a Baby Jane vehicle for every Blanche Hudson vehicle. The producer wants Blanche's agent to get the studio off the hook with Baby Jane. Aldrich's camera crowds in on the desultory conversation between producer and agent without any humanizing close-ups. This stifling treatment conveys unpleasantness without intimacy. Again in the far-cry department, the Hudson rivalry hardly parallels the equal footing on which Joan Fontaine and Olivia de Havilland waged their celebrated feud.

In the course of the conversation Blanche is described ambiguously as magnanimous toward her slipping, if not fallen, sister and arrogant toward the rest of the world. Walking up to Blanche's ornate car, the producer asks: "Why do they build monsters like this?" The agent almost tosses away the reply, "For Blanche Hudson." That night the "monster" glides down a Los Angeles street and up the driveway of a house we have been told the Hudsons share. No faces are revealed, only legs draped in party dresses. One of the sisters gets out of the car to open the gate. The other presses down on the gas pedal, and in a mystery montage sequence of legs, gleaming hood, smoking exhaust pipe, and glaring searchlights the car hurtles forward. A scream and a broken Baby Jane doll freeze the action as the titles come on the screen.

This flat-footed exposition is justified in *Baby Jane* only because of the peculiarly ambivalent demands of the project. For example,

we do not see the faces of the sisters during the "accident" because
(a) it would be fatal to the illusion if Davis-Crawford 1962 were
impersonating Jane-Blanche 1935, and (b) because the faces would
be withheld anyway for the sake of a future plot twist. Thus does
necessity make a virtue of mystery, and mystery a virtue of necessity. Similarly, a flashback treatment of the precredit sequences
would not work, because once the stars have been introduced, their
pasts as characters are no longer objectively convincing.

Even after the story begins formally in the present tense, the
stars are withheld long enough to show the Hudsons' next-door
neighbors enjoying a televised revival of an old Blanche Hudson
movie, actually Joan Crawford's 1934 vehicle, *Sadie McKee.* The
neighbors, mother and daughter, played with hysterical normality
by Anna Lee and Bette Davis' daughter, reveal that it was Baby
Jane who drove into Blanche. When the television program is
switched to Blanche Hudson's second-floor bedroom, where she is
confined in a wheelchair, a faithfully preserved, benignly smiling
Joan Crawford immediately projects an image of gallant suffering.
(Applause.) Cut to Bette Davis swigging Scotch in a messy kitchen.
(Laughter.) With a fright wig of Baby Jane curls, Betty Boop lips,
darkly popped eyes outlining otherwise cadaverous features, Miss
Davis seems to be auditioning for the *Bride of Frankenstein.* Before the issues of the melodrama have been resolved, this most
obvious of monsters will run the gamut of nastiness from serving
a dead rat on a silver platter to murdering the only sensible character in the whole film.

The casting is inspired. Poor Joan Crawford trapped upstairs in
her wheelchair and menaced by crazy Bette Davis downstairs—the
screen's eternal masochist confronting the screen's eternal sadist.
What could be more fitting for what most reviewers have dismissed as an old-fashioned gaslight melodrama? However, *Baby
Jane* has many deficiencies as a chiller of the *Angel Street* school.
The violence, such as it is, is wildly improvised by a madwoman
between lyrical passages of nostalgic fantasy. There is also a fatal
slackness in the terrorized relationship of victim to villainess. Not
only does Joan Crawford seem to enjoy her suffering as always but
her efforts to escape seem unusually feeble. Aldrich throws in some
zoom shots on a crucial rescue note and the inevitable telephone
downstairs, but the will to escape is never made plausible. We all

know, of course, that only Hitchcock would have the temerity to kill off Miss Crawford prematurely, but that does not entirely explain the inadequacy of the suspense. Most "lady in distress" thrillers feed on a repressed sexual menace. In the Anglo-Saxon countries murder has long served as a polite substitute for rape, and it hardly requires the services of a canny erotologist like Lo Duca to detect the substitution in the classic Hitchcockian assaults on Laura Elliott (*Strangers on a Train*) and Grace Kelly (*Dial M for Murder*). As the veneer of the genre is scraped off, the murder-rape relationship becomes muddled in *Experiment in Terror* and insanely dislocated in Buñuel's *The Criminal Life of Archibaldo de la Cruz*. No matter. This line of inquiry would lead nowhere in *Baby Jane*, one of the most arid films ever made in Hollywood. Not only are the stars made up for some grotesquely sexless masquerade. The sun-bleached world around them seems relentlessly asexual. The neighbors next door, mother and daughter, apparently lack any kind of man on the premises. The Hudsons' housekeeper is explicitly unmarried, and aside from a bloated capon of a pianist and his gnomelike Cockney mother, there are no other organic characters. Such functionaries as routine-ridden policemen, a bored psychiatrist and his receptionist, beach peddlers, advertising clerks, bank tellers and remarkably lifeless extras drift through the film without the slightest trace of sensual complicity. The sisters themselves operate on a pre-Freudian, or perhaps post-Freudian, level of unabashed nastiness, more Grimm than grim. Even the bone-crunching sadism for which Aldrich has been noted in the past is lacking here. Physical violence is indicated instead by wide-eyed reaction shots, first Bette, then Joan, then Bette, etc.

Lacking genuine suspense or horror, *Baby Jane* is sustained instead by outrageous humor, curiously self-enclosed lyricism, and above all, intelligent professionalism. Aldrich had a job to do and he did it. He realized that Bette Davis was a more gifted actress than Joan Crawford. So he allowed Bette to shock everyone with ludicrous make-up and then break through with a performance of emotional intensity. Knowing that Joan could not carry her big scenes, he enhanced her hysterics with jazzy overhead shots and a tilted staircase. In a situation fraught with the peril of cross-cutting, Aldrich falls back on the natural planes of the action—Bette standing, Joan sitting, Bette downstairs and outside, Joan upstairs and inside. The diagonals are derived from the plot and décor. Consequently the vertical detachment of the director from his addled protagonists never lapses into Gothic vertigo.

Choice and necessity, method and meaning are delicately balanced. Bette renders three devastatingly accurate impersonations of Joan, once on the telephone to take an order of liquor, once to taunt Joan, and once, in the direst moment of her personal melodrama, to prevent help from reaching Joan. Aldrich's first sustained camera movement is a malignant expression of the Oedipal *ménage* of the pianist (Victor Buono) and his possessive mother (Marjorie Bennett), proving that the director is not asleep at the switch, particularly when he is about to introduce a hilarious parody of the soul-searing Gloria Swanson-William Holden arrangement in *Sunset Boulevard*. What finally happens to Baby Jane constitutes a reversal of sorts, and the film ends as it should, in the form of an irresponsible circle. The world, you see, has not made the Hudson sisters what they are. They did it all to themselves by themselves, with little help or hindrance from the rest of sun-baked Southern California.

—*Movie*, March–April 1963

■ 5. THE FOUR DAYS OF NAPLES

The Four Days of Naples is such a resounding bore that comparisons with Rossellini's *Open City* and *Paisan* become grotesque. Director Nanni Loy (no relation to Myrna) is a competent second-unit technician with the knack of keeping hordes of extras on the move. It is this superficially "epic" quality that has undoubtedly caused American critics to drool over a slice of Neapolitan bologna as if it were the caviar of the cinema. Loy certainly had more technical equipment at his disposal than Rossellini ever dreamed of back in the Forties. Whereas Rossellini had to convey his Odysseys via artful camera placements and deliberate panning shots, Loy mounted his camera on a crane and swept down the streets, around the corners, and over the rooftops of Naples without breaking the continuity of movement. If the cinema were indeed a machine art, as some critics have alleged, Loy's superior technology should have it all over Rossellini's primitive apparatus. What *Four Days* proves instead is that a crane is no match for a conception, and that machinery is no substitute for inspiration.

Loy's vulgar sentimentality makes *The Alamo* look like an austere military document. A dying partisan asks to be taken back to Sorrento, a street urchin charges a German tank and inspires all the adults to follow after his corpse; the head of a reform school leads his adolescent charges into martial manhood; a frustrated civilian on a bread line gleefully kicks a German captive for comedy relief. Ultimately, mass hysteria is idealized into a spurious patriotism and a footnote to history is inflated into grand opera. Not even opera, really, but operetta. What the picture really needs is a score by Rudolf Friml or Sigmund Romberg and the bowdlerized verses of François Villon. Even the battle sequences are absurdly choreographed with the kind of dying-swan entrechats that went out with high-button shoes. Undiscriminating champions of foreign films against Hollywood movies might profitably inspect the crisp authority of Samuel Fuller's *Merrill's Marauders* and Don Siegel's *Hell Is for Heroes*.

Postwar Italian film-makers have never been candid about fascism. Even Rossellini misrepresented historical reality by focusing on random heroism, but the intensity and profundity of his vision justified the distortion of his point of view. Whereas Rossellini sacrificed external facts to inner truths, Loy burlesques facts into fantasies. Loy's Italians become lions pitted against Germans reduced to sheep in wolves' clothing. The undistinguished military history of modern Italy is actually a mark of that nation's refined civilization, but the disease of nationalism infects Italians like everyone else. One suspects that many Italians in high places would gladly trade Dante, Verdi, and a good left-handed pitcher for Napoleon. The fact remains that the Warsaw uprising claimed the lives of half a million people, that the Prague uprising involved several armored divisions, and that the French partisans captured the German garrison in Paris. All the Neapolitans achieved was the harassment of a few German units that had to leave the city anyway in the path of the American advance. There was no lack of individual bravery in Naples for four days, but the politics of Naples has always been opportunism, and there is nothing wrong with opportunism except when it passes itself off as unalloyed idealism.

—*Village Voice*, March 28, 1963

■ 6. *THE BIRDS*

The Birds is here, and what a joy to behold a self-contained movie that does not feed parasitically on outside cultural references— Chekhov, Synge, O'Neill, Genet, Behan, Melville, or what have you. Drawing from the relatively invisible literary talents of Daphne du Maurier and Evan Hunter, Alfred Hitchcock has fashioned a major work of cinematic art, and "cinematic" is the operative term here, not "literary" or "sociological." There is one sequence, for example, where the heroine is in an outboard motorboat churning across the bay while the hero's car is racing around the shore road to intercept her on the other side. This race, in itself pure cinema, is seen entirely from the girl's point of view. We see only what she can see from the boat. Suddenly, near shore, the camera picks up a sea gull swooping down on our heroine. For just a second the point of view is shifted and we are permitted to see the bird before its victim does. The director has apparently broken an aesthetic rule for the sake of a shock effect—gull pecks girl. Yet this momentary incursion of the objective on the subjective is remarkably consistent with the meaning of the film.

The theme, after all, is complacency, as the director has stated on innumerable occasions. When we first meet the major characters their infinite capacity for self-absorption is emphasized. Tippi Hedren's bored socialite is addicted to elaborately time-consuming practical jokes. Rod Taylor's self-righteous lawyer flaunts his arrogant sensuality, Suzanne Pleshette, his ex-fiancée, wallows in self-pity, and Jessica Tandy, his possessive mother, cringes in her fear of loneliness. With such complex, unsympathetic characters to contend with, the audience quite naturally begins to identify with the point of view of the birds, actually the inhuman point of view. As in *Psycho*, Hitchcock succeeds in engaging his audience to such an extent that the much-criticized, apparently anticlimactic ending of the film finds the audience more bloodthirsty than the birds. Although three people are killed and many others assaulted by man's fine-feathered friends, critics and spectators have demanded more gore and more victims.

In *Psycho*, if you recall, there is a moment after Tony Perkins has run Janet Leigh's car into a swamp when the car stops sinking. One could almost hear the audience holding its breath until the car resumed its descent below the surface. At that first intake of breath the audience became implicated in the fantasy of the perfect crime. In *The Birds* the audience is similarly implicated but this time in the fantasy of annihilation. The point Hitchcock seems to be making is that morality is not a function of sympathy but a rigorous test of principles. If we can become even momentarily indifferent to the fate of a promiscuous blonde (Janet Leigh in *Psycho*) or a spoiled playgirl (Tippi Hedren in *The Birds*), we have clearly failed the test.

As symbols of evil and disorder, Hitchcock's winged bipeds lend themselves to many possible interpretations—Freudian, Thomistic, existential, among others—but the imaginative spectator may draw his own analogies. What is beyond speculation is the strikingly visual potential of the subject. One penultimate shot of a row of blackbirds perched magisterially above the fearfully departing humans is worth a thousand words on man's unworthiness. Hitchcock's dark humor is as impressive as ever on both human and ornithological planes. There is something indescribably funny in the familiar gesture of a man winding up to throw a rock at some crows before being deterred by his prudent girl friend. Her "let sleeping birds perch" philosophy explodes its grotesque context into half-fragmented memories of human presumption.

Yet in the midst of all the human guilt the idea of innocence survives. When the survivors of the bird-attacks venture past thousands of their erstwhile enemies, now ominously passive, the hero's eleven-year-old sister asks him to return to the house for her caged love birds. "They did no harm," she insists. The audience fears and anticipates the worst, but nothing happens. The caged love birds do not arouse the free hordes of the species. Instead, these two guiltless creatures seem to clear the path to the car as if the rediscovery of innocence were yet the only hope of the world.

The Birds finds Hitchcock at the summit of his artistic powers.

His is the only contemporary style that unites the divergent classical traditions of Murnau (camera movement) and Eisenstein (montage). (Welles, for example, owes more to Murnau, while Resnais is closer to Eisenstein.) If formal excellence is still a valid criterion for film criticism—and there are those who will argue that it is not—then *The Birds* is probably the picture of the year.

—Village Voice April 4, 1963

■ 7. *LANDRU*

Claude Chabrol's *Landru* is the eighth feature film of this "New Wave" director, but only the fourth to reach our shores. Landru was apparently a Parisian lonelyhearts operator who murdered anywhere between eleven and two hundred smitten females during the First World War. I say "apparently" because Chabrol declines to explore Landru's career with any biographical precision. In fact, the director's treatment is so stylized that suspension of disbelief and of moral judgment is encouraged in every scene, particularly toward the end, when Landru's downfall suggests Jack the Ripper being apprehended by the Keystone Kops, convicted in a Gilbert & Sullivan courtroom, and guillotined in a Stendhalian courtyard. Nor is Chabrol particularly concerned with the ingenuity of Landru's modus operandi. After placing an ad in the Personals column, he meets all his prospective victims on the same bench in the same park, purchases two railway tickets—one return and one one-way—to his rented villa with furnace in the country, and all with a blithe disregard for witnesses and appearances, even to the stench from his chimney. Anyway, Landru as interpreted by music-hall comedian Charles Denner is such a recognizably ugly, bald, bearded, Toulouse-Lautrec figure that the inevitability of his detection is never at issue. Chabrol and his script writer, Françoise Sagan, have something else in mind, and with the aid of François Rabier's dazzling color photography, they almost succeed in achieving it.

Landru was undoubtedly inspired in part by Chaplin's *Monsieur Verdoux* and the idea that if war, in Clausewitz's phrase, is the logical extension of diplomacy, then murder, in Chaplin's phrase, is the logical extension of business. Chabrol inserts silent footage of the war to suggest the absurdity of condemning a "mass murderer" in a world where millions of men are being systematically butchered, but here, too, Chabrol's social rationalization is perfunctory. Verdoux, after all, was commenting on all war, but Landru is concerned only with the conditions arising from a particular war. Even though both men are essentially tired businessmen attempting to support their families in difficult times, Verdoux is a Brechtian character, while Landru is more Baudelairean. It follows that Verdoux is more the deceiver and Landru more the seducer, and that deception can be treated as an idea, while seduction must be viewed as an experience.

Chabrol's most seductive effects bear the imprint of directors he admires. One can discern Renoir's sensuousness, Hitchcock's vertiginous camera movements, and Stroheim's preoccupation with bric-a-brac. When Landru takes on a faithful mistress who sings operatic arias off-key, the parallel with *Citizen Kane* is unmistakable. Even Chabrol's actresses, who all act badly, reflect his attitudes toward the cinema. Michèle Morgan and Danielle Darrieux, two mainstays of the Old Guard French cinema, are cruelly photographed in bright sunlight that emphasizes every wrinkle and coarsening feature. Curiously, Chabrol is kinder to Catherine Rouvel, Renoir's discovery in *Picnic on the Grass*, than to Juliette Mayniel, his own find for *The Cousins*.

Yet beneath the brilliant surface of his film Chabrol expresses the point of view not of a moralist or of an amoral aesthete but of an uncompromising satirist of human behavior. What is most striking about all his characters in all his films is their infinite stupidity, and in this respect Landru seldom has much of an edge on his victims. What Chabrol proves once again is that stupidity when viewed honestly and sympathetically is the stuff of poetry.

—*Village Voice*, April 18, 1963

■ 8. *THE UGLY AMERICAN*

The Ugly American was photographed in curiously subdued pastel colors in Thailand, but a foreword to the film cautions us not to

interpret the plot as a comment on the politics and history of
Thailand. The action is set in a fictitious country of the Southeast
Asian Buddhist Belt—Sarkand, Napalm, Sagan, or something like
that. Presumably it doesn't matter where, but even with allegories,
nowhere in particular usually turns out to be nowhere in general.
With an allegory about the Cold War it becomes especially important to specify the historical and geographical coordinates.
Graham Greene's *The Quiet American* may have reached out into
left field for its attack on American liberal activists and their
fantasies about a magical third force led by a shadowy figure of
virtuous moderation, revolutionary but not red, egalitarian but not
class-conscious, firm but not cruel, popular but not demagogic,
someone halfway between Mao and Chiang, Ho and Diem, Castro
and Batista. Yet Greene, for all his anti-American contrivance, did
sketch in the actual background of the Indo-Chinese War, and
when he took off after a hard-boiled American correspondent willing to fight to the last drop of French blood, the reader could smell
Joseph Alsop. There are no such links in *The Ugly American*, a
film dedicated to the platitudinous proposition that we had all
better buckle down to win the Cold War. That is like saying the
Mets will need better hitting, pitching, and fielding to win the National League pennant. Of course, there are those who argue that
victory would be equally disastrous for America and the Mets—
but that is another story.

What links the Quiet American to the Ugly American is the
same mystical belief in a third force. All the trouble in *The Ugly
American* can be traced to that fatal moment when the American
ambassador (Marlon Brando) jumps to the conclusion that his
dearest friend among the natives (Eiji Okada) has turned Communist. Our Ugly Innocent Abroad then persuades the rightist
Premier to reroute an unwanted Freedom Road as an offensive
gesture against Red China. This farfetched objective correlative
triggers a revolution, which the Communists attempt to divert to
their own nefarious purposes. The Ugly American finally sees the
error of treating every foreigner who screams about Little Rock as
a Communist. At worst, these alien critics might be carefully sub-
sidized into the nasty neutralism of Nehru, Nasser, Sukarno.

Ultimately *The Ugly American* is less interesting for its insights
on Southeast Asia than for its illumination of the politics of Lower

Brandovia. The power center of Lower Brandovia is Marlon Brando, and no one else. There have been temperamental performers before, of course, and I suppose Electra was already upstaging Orestes in the time of Sophocles. The egocentricities of Hollywood alone would take up volumes and volumes of confessional gush, but Brando, I submit, is something new and revolutionary in the motion picture industry. *The Ugly American* is designed to make Brando the center of attention at all times. Sandra Church (*Gypsy*) comes out on the screen in the colorless tradition of Julie Adams and Virginia Leith. Brando could steal a scene from her by simply breathing, but no, he has to practice a few additional gestures to render her more invisible. Arthur Hill reads lines beautifully in *Who's Afraid of Virginia Woolf?*, therefore his part must be cut down to three lines so as not to conflict with Brando's. Eiji Okada (*Hiroshima, Mon Amour*) has all the best non-Brando lines, but he can barely speak English well enough to be understood even intermittently, and the audience must look at Brando's reactions for an emotional translation.

When Brando has been forced to appear with comparable talents like the incomparable Magnani (*The Fugitive Kind*), Trevor Howard, and Richard Harris (*Mutiny on the Bounty*) he kills their performances by going up on his lines, take after take. More often he manages to keep big names out of his pictures, even though they would profit him commercially. Elizabeth Taylor, for example, is shrewd enough to appear with skilled actors like Richard Burton and Rex Harrison as guarantors of her investment, and Chaplin, for whom solipsism is a style, glorified his supporting players—Claire Bloom (*Limelight*), Martha Raye (*Monsieur Verdoux*), Jack Oakie (*The Great Dictator*). By contrast, Brando seeks out the most obscure and most unattractive actresses as his costars. The strange part of this situation is that Brando is still a remarkably talented actor. His reflexes are still sharp, his instincts sound, and he could hold his own with any player in the English-speaking world. Yet he persists in obliterating all possible competition as if he were a frightened starlet suddenly called upon to play *Camille*. Why? I suppose that is just one of the many mysteries of Lower Brandovia.

—*Village Voice*, June 6, 1963

■ 9. *HUD*

Hud features a title character with what has been advertised as a "barbed-wire soul"—whatever that means. As played by Paul Newman, directed by Martin Ritt, and written by Irving Ravetch and Harriet Frank, Jr. (sic), Hud swaggers across the screen like Evil Incarnate, but his assorted peccadilloes barely fill the quota of a Peck's Bad Boy of the Prairie. Even before Hud appears the audience is alerted to his wicked reputation. Hud's doe-eyed nephew (Brandon de Wilde) wanders innocently through a sleepy Texas cattle town, expertly photographed by James Wong Howe by the dawn's ugly light. The whole film, in fact, displays that hungover look that is almost invariably confused with honest realism. Here the visual correlative of decadence is dust, even though Texas was dusty long before the Alamo.

We see a broken café window, and we are told by the angry proprietor in the midst of his morning sweeping that Hud perpetrated this outrage the night before. This rhetorical cheating of effects is typical of this kind of rhetorical movie-making. Denied a glimpse of the Saturday-night brawl, we must sit patiently in our pews for the Sunday-morning sermon. When de Wilde finally locates Hud's pink Cadillac outside a married woman's cottage, he honks the horn, and our surly hero comes out buttoning his shirt. We don't see the woman, just one of her gaily abandoned spike-heeled shoes on the path outside. The rest is left to our imagination. The husband chooses this congested occasion to drive up in a station wagon apparently designed for long business trips and is understandably piqued to see two grown men camped on his wife's doorstep. Hud craftily shifts the blame to his nephew before zooming off in his evil Cadillac, a curiously dated symbol of arrogance in its postdorsal evolution. Hud drives too fast, smirking with equal contempt at the bedside morals and speed limits of the middle-class critics who find him so malignantly expressive of "modern" life. When Hud brings his Cadillac to a screeching halt right in the middle of the housekeeper's zinnia bed, that is the last straw—or should we say the last zinnia?

The rest of the film dissolves predictably into anti-Hud oratory that seems a trifle sanctimonious. The housekeeper (Patricia Neal) lashes out at Hud for being a "cold-blooded bastard." (It is ironic that when the tigerish Miss Neal was vibrantly sensual in Kazan's *Face in the Crowd* back in 1957, most critics ignored her performance, but now that she has been reduced to playing a faded slattern she is suddenly appreciated.) Hud's aging and agonizingly slow-spoken father (Melvyn Douglas) solemnly announces that he has always hated Hud for "not giving a damn." There is an attempted rape for the ad-copy boys and the theater stills, but it is as dishonestly presented as all the other "action." A subplot about diseased cattle makes no sense at all. Hud wants to sell off the herd before the government inspectors can intervene, but Hud's Old Frontier father dutifully complies with federal regulations. The cattle are all herded into a depressed enclosure, and after the humane societies have been appeased and the audience cheated through the fakery of cross-cutting, the gallant old man shoots his two prized Longhorns off screen. This whole cattle-shooting plot sounds like the work of greenhorns. Since when have ranchers of any era been noted for their sense of public duty? Hud's father is utterly false as a character because he refers back to a legend in which the authors of *Hud* have never believed. Directors like Ford and Ophuls, who genuinely mourn the past, never malign the present, whereas a dude director like Martin Ritt would have deplored the Old West in much the same obvious terms he deplores the New. After all, cigarettes, whiskey, and wild, wild women were no strangers to the frontier, and sharp business practices antedate even the predorsal period of the Cadillac. Too many critics seem to be too easily impressed these days by any intimation of decadence, however obvious. Yet, on balance, the world is probably in better moral shape today than it has ever been in the past, and a character like Hud belongs more properly to the mustachio melodramas of another age. One only wonders if Hud would have seemed so meaningfully villainous to our socially conscious critics if he had been a churchgoing, Bible-thumping man like Billy Sol Estes—or is the notion of a Texas Tartuffe somewhat too complex for our naïve conception of evil? Frankly, I thought the real villain of *Hud* was the self-righteous father, possibly because Melvyn Douglas gave the worst performance.

■ 10. *THE LEOPARD*

The version of Luchino Visconti's *The Leopard* now on display
may come to be referred to derisively as the "American," or more
precisely, "North American" form of the species. It was this striped
tabby cat that opened the Fourth Montreal International Film
Festival to no great acclaim.

It is necessary to criticize the dubbing into English, if only because Burt Lancaster would probably gain authority and plausibility if his overenunciated Americanese were dubbed into Italian.
After all, Fellini did wonders for Anthony Quinn (*La Strada*) and
Broderick Crawford (*Il Bidone*). The advantage of Italian (or
Swahili, for that matter) over English—dubbed or otherwise—for
most of us North American "art film" addicts consists of our sus-
pending judgment on the reading of lines to concentrate better on
the visual component. If more of our snobbishly subtitular critics
would stop and look at American films instead of just listening to
the familiar noises on the sound track, they might discover a new
world of visual glories. Still, snob values being what they are, I
think it would have been wiser to open the original Italian-lan-
guage version of *The Leopard* in New York for prestige purposes
and then circulate the dubbed print in the hinterlands. (If you hear
shots in the distance, that is just the hinterlanders retaliating
against big-city condescension.)

I think another mistake was the shortening of the film for American consumption. A bad film can never be improved by cutting
simply for length, and a good film can only be harmed. Careless
scissors only increase tedium, because the meaningful links are
severed and the plot dribbles out in all directions.

This is particularly true of Visconti's ambitious and reasonably
tasteful treatment of the late Prince Giuseppe di Lampedusa's
surprise best seller on the lethargy of the Sicilian nobility during
the earth-shaking decades between 1860 and 1910. Lampedusa's
novel expresses some of that temporal resonance one finds in Chateaubriand, that sense of history which defines the beginning in
terms of the end, birth in terms of death, revolution in terms of
restoration. "Nothing could be decently hated," Lampedusa's

prince observes, "except eternity." It is this conception of eternity rather than the slight action of the novel which dictated Visconti's long running time, and even American distributors should think twice before trifling with eternity. The whole theme of *The Leopard* is, in fact, eternity fashioned after the intransigent Sicilian landscape, climate, and temperament, draining history of its vitality and momentum.

Curiously, Visconti fails to avail himself of some of Lampedusa's most striking symbols, most obviously the leopard on the frayed coat of arms, and the incredibly tenacious dog-being Benedico, the great Dane, who (in the second paragraph of the novel), "grieved at exclusion, came wagging its tail, through the door by which the servants had left." Fifty years and the rest of the book later we come upon the stuffed form of Benedico "flung into a corner of the courtyard visited every day by the dustman. During the flight down from the window his form recomposed itself for an instant; in the air one could have seen dancing a quadruped with long whiskers, and its right foreleg seemed to be raised in imprecation. Then all found peace in a little heap of livid dust." The only comparable image I can recall is Chateaubriand's simultaneous recollection of Marie Antoinette at court and his identification of her skeleton many years later from the smile she had flashed for an ephemeral instant.

Where Visconti poured most of his talent and feeling was into his stunning decors, particularly those embellishing his climactically anticlimactic ballroom sequence, where history executes an ironic quadrille with death, dung, decay, and disgust to the mocking strains of a hitherto undiscovered Verdi waltz. The dream and the specter of Garibaldi have dissolved in the morning mists. Revolution and reform have disintegrated into bourgeois idiocies.

Visconti's conception is impressive even without the breadth of Lampedusa's symbolic tapestry. Visconti, the shrewd Marxist-aristocrat, the exquisite decorator, lacks that final spark of the mystic so necessary to a unified vision of life. On screen *The Leopard* is an admirable film of parts, fully revealing the virtues and limitations of its director. What for Lampedusa is an expression of vanity of vanities is reduced by Visconti to the more familiar dimensions of a victory of reactionaries.

—*Village Voice*, August 22, 1963

■ 11. *SHOCK CORRIDOR*

Samuel Fuller's *Shock Corridor* is about the most interesting entry
in the current loony cycle. Why American film-makers should become so obsessed with the clinical details of lunacy at this late date
I have no idea. Perhaps the commercial success shared by such
perverse but otherwise diverse case histories as *Psycho* and *David
and Lisa* finally set the long-dormant Hollywood rubber stamps
into motion. A popular television series like "The Eleventh Hour"
and the more psychosomatic episodes in "Ben Casey" and "Dr.
Kildare" may have contributed to the trend. But who knows? Perhaps Dr. Knock and Dr. Rose Franzblau are closer to the mark in
suggesting that we are all sick to some extent in devious ways we
never seem to understand.

Shock Corridor is at least free of the cant and hypocrisy of a
pseudoconstructive tract like *The Caretakers*. Far from assuming a
responsible tone, Fuller's surface plot bears the earmarks of the
transparent trashiness that characterizes the last Hollywood films
of Orson Welles (*Touch of Evil*) and Fritz Lang (*Beyond a Reasonable Doubt*). Fuller would have us believe, or at least not dis-
believe, that an ace reporter bucking for the Pulitzer Prize would
have himself committed to a mental institution in order to solve a
murder. To accomplish this he persuades his sweetheart, a stripper,
to pretend that she is his sister and that he has been molesting her.
The girl is opposed to the project because it is morbid, cynical,
and senseless. After all, she argues, Shakespeare and Dickens didn't
need Freud to create great art. At this point one has the heady
feeling of hearing flowery silent film titles verbalized for the first
time. The dialogue is so intense, so compressed, so lacking in all
the shadings of wit and verisimilitude that it is impossible to escape
the impression of a primitive artist at work.

Primitive, that is, only in the literary sense. Fuller's camera style
is fluid enough to lend at least visual conviction to his rhetorical
characters. Once the hero is committed to the asylum, the movie
erupts with a manic force. He is looking for three witnesses to the
alleged murder: the first, an ex-veteran brainwashed in Korea and

then returned in disgrace to his southern family; the second, a Negro student from a southern university, the victim of a nervous breakdown that has left him believing himself a white bigot and a member of the Klan; and the third, a nuclear scientist who has retreated into infancy. The three major hysterias of America—the Cold War in Asia, race relations at home, the Bomb—are evoked with startling audacity. Along the way Johnny is more ravaged than ravished by a band of apparently carnivorous nymphomaniacs. Finally he cracks the case and then is cracked himself. "What a tragic irony," the doctor observes in the penultimate scene, "the winner of this year's Pulitzer Prize is a catatonic deaf-mute"—sort of a last line to end last lines.

Fuller's style furnishes an interesting contrast to that of more realistic directors. Whereas Fuller creates outrageous situations and then plays them out quietly, Lindsay Anderson will charge up a normal situation into hysteria. Fuller's close-ups are even more intense than Anderson's, but Fuller's characters invariably talk more softly. At one point the hero is screaming through one of his hallucinations. As the hallucination dissolves back into objective reality, a homosexual opera singer turns slowly toward the protagonist and remarks quietly that the protagonist's singing is off-key.

Samuel Fuller has never received particularly serious reviews in America. Only British and French cultists have saved him from complete anonymity. Consequently it is amazing to find him recapitulating the themes from all his neglected films of the past fifteen years—*I Shot Jesse James, The Baron of Arizona, The Steel Helmet, Fixed Bayonets, Park Row, Pickup on South Street, Hell and High Water, House of Bamboo, China Gate, Run of the Arrow, Forty Guns, The Crimson Kimono, Verboten!, Underworld USA, Merrill's Marauders.* Hardly the most prestigious list of films, but an interesting list nevertheless for the true connoisseur of individuality.

Shock Corridor is ultimately an allegory of America today, not so much surreal as subreal in its hallucinatory view of history that can be perceived only beneath a littered surface of plot intrigue. There are no extras in the film, and no establishment of the commonplace that marked the matter-of-fact approach to horror of the late Tod Browning and Val Lewton. Nevertheless *Shock Corridor* emerges as a distinguished addition to that art form in which Hollywood has always excelled—the baroque B-picture.

—*Village Voice*, September 12, 1963

■ 12. MY LIFE TO LIVE

My Life to Live is the fourth feature film of Jean-Luc Godard but only the second to be released in America. Consequently Godard's local reputation, such as it is, is based almost entirely on his first feature film, *Breathless*. Except for an episode ("Sloth") in the omnibus package of *The Seven Capital Sins*, Godard has been unrepresented on American screens for more than two years. During this period he has turned out five full-length movies—*Le Petit Soldat*, *A Woman Is a Woman*, *My Life to Live*, *Les Carabiniers*, *Contempt*—and one of the four sketches in *RoGoPaG*. Godard's sketch was the one most violently hissed by the Lincoln Center audience in this year's New York Film Festival. This reaction only goes to prove that waiting for Godard can be a very lonely pastime for his admirers, particularly when his works are released perforce in piecemeal fashion.

My Life to Live consists of twelve tableaux depicting the adventures of a Parisian salesgirl who drifts into a life of prostitution. Each tableau is introduced with the moralistic narratage of the eighteenth-century novel with just a soupçon of the naïve refinement of the D. W. Griffith silent title. On the surface at least, Godard's style is radically different here from the synthesis of kinetic shock cuts and expressive camera movements that made *Breathless* such a disturbing experience. By contrast, *My Life to Live* is more precise in its framing, more discreet in its camera movements, more conventional in its editing. Paris, so airy in *Breathless*, is almost Bressonian in its oppressiveness here. The gay gray of *Breathless* has been supplanted by the starkly black and white.

Whereas *Breathless* achieves the suspense of poetic gratuitousness, *My Life to Live* is dictated by the logic of poetic necessity.

Godard's heroine is destroyed by the very terms with which she is defined. Her Zolaesque screen name is Nana, and she wears the Louise Brooks hairdo of the Pabst-Wedekind Lulu. The paradox in Nana's profession is derived from Max Ophuls' Lola Montès, the famous courtesan who, according to the Ophulsian camera filters, surrendered her body without losing her soul. Nana's soul is defined in turn as she watches a performance of Dreyer's *Passion of Joan of Arc* on the screen within the screen. Nana is played by Godard's Danish wife, Anna Karina, and conversely, Dreyer's Joan is played by the French actress Falconetti. In the resultant transubstantiation the tears of Joan and Nana—Falconetti and Karina—flow into the single stream of that agony expressing all the tortured paradoxes of womanhood.

After passing through the grimly documented and anti-erotic world of the prostitute, Nana-Karina finds a brief interlude of romantic emotion with a young man who reads Poe's *Oval Portrait* (in Godard's voice). Godard breaks into his own reading to proclaim, "This is our own story, an artist painting the portrait of his wife." Again the crossover is staggering—Poe and Baudelaire, Faulkner's *The Wild Palms* and Valéry's *Monsieur Teste*, America and France, artist and model, the director and his inspiration, the dream and the reality. Yet on the whole Godard's treatment of this sequence is disconcertingly clumsy.

Elsewhere the peculiar mixture of fact and truth, Rouch and Rossellini, never quite jells for the audience. One can respect the artistic integrity of Godard's ending. Karina is murdered with awkward abruptness. The end. Death be not proud nor poetic—but can the audience take it? Not at the moment, I suppose, but probably much later in retrospect. I recall that *Breathless* seemed at first much slighter and much colder than either *Hiroshima, Mon Amour* or *The 400 Blows*. Today *Breathless* is acknowledged not only as the most important of the New Wave films but also as the most passionate. Time seems to work for Godard, and in time the apparent coldness of *My Life to Live* will be perceived more clearly as admirably formal control of the wildest romanticism in the cinema today. *My Life to Live*, by the very violence of the reactions it evokes, is the most profoundly modern film of the year.

—*Village Voice*, September 26, 1963

■ 13. *TOM JONES*

I

Tom Jones is more a parody of Henry Fielding's classic novel than an adaptation. For some reason best known to director Tony Richardson, scenarist John Osborne, and the seven wise New York daily reviewers, the film opens with a mock–silent movie episode spoofing the discovery of the foundling Tom Jones in Squire Allworthy's bed. At this juncture the camera is unusually jittery and the color agonizingly murky even for a parody of Edwin S. Porter, but little does the unwary spectator suspect how much the whole film is going to resemble the dream of a rarebit fiend.

One detail will suffice to convey the alien spirit of the sequence. Basic situation: Man in nightshirt shocks spinsterish servant. Here is Fielding's version:

> She therefore no sooner opened the door, and saw her master standing by the bedside in his shirt, with a candle in his hand, than she started back in a most terrible fright, and might perhaps have swooned away, had he not now recollected his being undressed, and put an end to her terrors by desiring her to stay without the door till he had thrown some clothes over his back, and was become incapable of shocking the pure eyes of Mrs. Deborah Wilkins, who, though in the fifty-second year of her age, vowed she had never beheld a man without his coat. Sneerers and profane wits may perhaps laugh at her first fright; yet my graver reader, when he considers the time of night, the situation in which she found her summons from her bed, and the master, will highly justify and applaud her conduct unless the prudence which must be supposed to attend maidens at that period of life at which Mrs. Deborah had arrived, should a little lessen his admiration.

Richardson and Osborne, like the astute vaudevillians they are, have streamlined this commentary into one guffaw-provoking image (on the anal level) of Allworthy's posterior. Not that they had much leeway in compressing an 824-page novel into a two-and-a-quarter-hour movie. Granted. But the Osborne-Richardson perversion of Fielding goes beyond mere compression. One of the most admired scenes in the film concerns the sensual first supper of Tom Jones and Mrs. Waters. For once Walter Lassally's epileptic camera is steady as Richardson cross-cuts between Albert Finney and Joyce Redman as they devour fish, fowl, and crustacean with voluptuous slurps. The scene is well acted and reasonably effective for what it conveys—a cliché of Merrie Olde Elizabethan England indulging the twin appetites of gluttony and lust. This is a cliché derived not from Elizabethan drama, which is quite neurotic about sex, but from old Charles Laughton impersonations of Henry VIII eating with his hands while leering at the ladies of the court. The main point, however, is that the scene is derived not from the moral serenity of Fielding's world but from the yowling nursery of Osborne's anger. Eat, drink, and be merry before the Establishment gets you. That's Osborne, not Fielding. The way Fielding does the scene, Mrs. Waters waits until Tom has finished slobbering his food and then seduces him, not with her saliva but with her luminous eyes. As James Thurber once remarked, you can look it up.

II

I had not intended originally to belabor *Tom Jones* two weeks running, but as so often happens in this imperfect world, the demons of disorder intervened. Somewhere between the typewriter and the typesetter half of my scintillating review mysteriously disappeared. Unfortunately, last week's abridged blast failed to do full justice to Tony Richardson's strenuous misdirection, and it seldom happens that a film is at once so popular and so instructively inept.

Last week, if I recall correctly, we established that *Tom Jones* is not particularly faithful to the novel of the same title by an eighteenth-century novelist named Henry Fielding. I would be the last to argue that infidelity, in and of itself, is a capital crime as far as film adaptations of novels are concerned. Yet it should be noted that Fielding is at least a few notches above the novels-for-filming syndicate of Braine, Wain, Sillitoe, and Waterhouse, and even above such titans of the dishpan-and-desire theater as John Osborne and Shelagh Delaney. Tony Richardson can jazz up and distort his contemporaries to his eclectic heart's desire even if it means making bad movies out of such effective theater pieces as *Look Back in Anger, The Entertainer,* and *Taste of Honey,* but poor Henry Fielding lacks even an agent to protect his artistic interests. Hence my objections.

The basic Fielding plot is undoubtedly a refreshing change of pace for audiences weary of the dreary ennui (not to mention Antoniennui) of much of today's plotless film-making. Why, then, does Richardson feel it necessary to apologize coyly at every opportunity for the contrivances and coincidences that have delighted readers for more than two centuries? (Was it only fifteen years ago that appreciative audiences at Radio City Music Hall applauded David Lean's "straight" treatment of Dickens' equally outrageous *Great Expectations?*) I suspect that Richardson has shrewdly gauged current audience psychology, torn between an emotional longing for direct storytelling and the intellectual guilt fostered by that longing. To satisfy the longing, Richardson vulgarizes Fielding down to the level of a road company production of *The Drunkard* until even Dame Edith Evans begins to sound like Marjorie Main essaying *The Importance of Being Earnest* for the Sioux Falls Stock Company. To placate the guilt Richardson fragments his footage into jiggling bits and pieces and then splices it all together with the kind of ornamental wipes, iris dissolves, and flip-page transitions that would be considered excessive on the opening credits of a Jerry Lewis movie. Thus, as the film's content becomes more synthetic, the form becomes more analytical. The simplicity of the what is redeemed by the complexity of the how, and with the plot safely nailed down, the reviewer is free to rave over Richardson's "cinematic" style.

An interesting example of overcompensation is involved here. It is always literary people who seem most concerned about what is and what is not "cinematic." Yet excessive technical flourishes very often signal the director's condescension to a genre or to the medium itself. Robert Wise's Gothic mannerisms make *The Haunting* just about the silliest movie of the year. Wise is a dully realistic director on subjects he considers "serious," but throw in a few ghosts and he becomes a gibbering stylist. John Huston's characteristically sour direction of *The List of Adrian Messenger* is a more complex example of stylistic corruption resulting from lack of conviction.

Similarly, Richardson, who has spent his directorial career thinking up tricks to conceal the fatal indecisiveness of his characters, suddenly goes berserk when he is confronted by a full-bodied plot. All the outdated *nouvelle vague* stunts in *Tom Jones* only emphasize Richardson's pathetic inability to tell a story with his camera, to describe a place with the slightest degree of spatial unity, or to move from shot to shot without making a separate production out of each time lapse.

Richardson could be forgiven a great deal if he had at least managed to be funny, and I am talking now about comedy/ha-ha rather than comedy/chuckle-chuckle. Even if Richardson were better with players than he is, his cutting and jiggling never permit them to establish any style or rhythm. When one thinks of Chaplin, Keaton, Lloyd, Mae West, W. C. Fields, and the Marx Brothers, one thinks invariably of relatively simple single-take techniques emphasizing the rhythms and movements not of the cutter or the cameraman but of the comedian. In itself montage is not very funny unless your taste runs to the Kerensky-Napoleon "jokes" in Eisenstein's *October*.

Where Richardson goes most wrong, however, is in forgetting that in this cowardly old world, if not in the brave new one, the motion picture is at most a spectacle, however sublime, and not a sublimation, however ridiculous. The frenzied agitato of Lassally's camera becomes monotonous after more than two hours of unrelieved eyestrain, and no valid aesthetic purpose is served by this optical torture. In fact, the agitato only emphasizes itself, and there is consequently little contrast between one character and another, between one mode of existence and another, even between one locale and another. For example, one of Fielding's most inspired bursts of humor involves the hot-tempered Squire Western, who interrupts his pursuit of his errant daughter to join in a hunt along the way. This is a joke of character, a monstrously funny joke based on the rupture of a paternal obligation by an atavistic impulse. Richardson loses the joke completely because he has created such a zany atmosphere that Squire Western's action seems entirely normal. As for the editing of the action on film, a process the French call *découpage*, Richardson displays a clumsiness that would be beyond mere technique if it were not so obviously beneath it.

—*Village Voice*, October 17 and 24, 1963

■ 14. MURIEL

I

Alain Resnais' *Muriel* is the kind of cultural event that encourages the worst excesses of critical one-upmanship. The word is out. "They" like *Muriel*, and "we" all know who "they" are. Even when "they" like the same things "we" do, "they" manage to be so pretentious about what is "in" and what is "out." As if "we" could be swayed by such petty snobbery. Bertrand Russell invented the game of irregular verbs some years ago to cover situations like *Muriel*. For example, I am firm, you are rigid, he is dogmatic. Or, I have exquisite taste, you are a bit arty, he is slavishly cult-ridden. These self-congratulatory conjugations are available to any self-righteous film critic—Crowther, Crist, or Phyllis Steen herself. The only trouble with this puttering (and Pottering) around is that Resnais gets lost in the shuffle of critical egos.

Alain Resnais was born on June 3, 1922, in Vannes, France. From 1945 through 1958 he worked on about twenty short films, some little more than technical exercises. His *Van Gogh* won an Academy Award in 1949 despite its being rendered in black and white. (I have always remembered Resnais' final tracking shot across a Van Gogh canvas into the blackness of death.) *Gauguin* and *Guernica* were equally distinguished examples of the art film, strictly speaking. *Guernica* was particularly notable for the violent tonal contrasts of its editing. Resnais collaborated with Chris Marker on *Les Statues Meurent Aussi*, an aesthetic indictment of French colonial policy in Africa. Banned by the government in 1954, this work was only recently released in a cut version for showings in Paris.

Night and Fog (1955) is a harrowing vision of the Nazi concentration-camp universe. The narration was written by Jean Cayrol, formerly an inmate of the Hitlerian hell and subsequently the author of the memory-ridden *Muriel*. Resnais shifts back and forth between color footage of the innocently vegetating camps of the tourist-trap present and the black-and-white documentary pictures, still and moving, of the past. Hans Eisler contributed a score that lent itself to emotional synchronization with Resnais' parallel tracks. Penultimately, *Le Chant du Styrene* is one of the most beautiful industrial documentaries ever filmed, a poem in plastics, a testament to the director's abiding materialism, graced with an appropriately witty commentary by linguistic stylist Raymond Queneau. This brings us up to date to what is now a formal trilogy of memory and desire—*Hiroshima, Mon Amour, Last Year at Marienbad*, and *Muriel*.

There is no particular reason for a critic aware of Resnais' over-all career to treat *Muriel* as if it had dropped from Mars. So much that seems confused, contrived, and chaotic at first glance falls into place once the aesthetic and political coordinates are charted on the director's graph. To begin with, *Muriel* is at least partly concerned with the consequences of the Algerian war. Muriel is the name of an Arab girl tortured to death before the film begins by Bernard Aughain, stepson of Hélène Aughain, a widow in her late thirties. Bernard suppresses his guilt by inventing fantasies about his engagement to an imaginary French girl named Muriel. In the course of the film he hears the name Muriel called at random. Bernard tells his story to a virtual stranger, a mysteriously philosophical proprietor of a stable where the hero rents a horse in order to ride along the grassy cliffs of Boulogne-sur-Mer.

The revelation about Muriel comes about an hour after the picture has begun, and it is narrated to the visual accompaniment of grainy color footage of crudely photographed French soldiers cavorting grotesquely in Algeria. The sustained harshness of this film within a film suggests the resistance of the French subconscious to the truth about Algeria. Later we are introduced to Robert, Bernard's comrade in torture, now a member of the OAS, which is dedicated to an extension of the Algerian terror to the French mainland. Bernard finally shoots Robert, an act so convulsively gratuitous that Bernard's perfect aim takes on Orphic overtones. Bernard flees Boulogne after his room is demolished by a plastic bomb. These overt political incidents constitute a relatively minor subplot in *Muriel* and yet are the key to the maddeningly elliptical way the rest of the story is told on the screen.

Any coherent synopsis of *Muriel* would be misleading because many of the details are presented out of logical and chronological sequence. If anything, Resnais and Cayrol tell us too much about each of the major characters. Hélène Aughain, about whom all the other characters rotate in erratic orbits, is a compulsive gambler and was once a drug addict. Although she operates an antique business in her own apartment, she is more a creature of impulse than a calculating businesswoman. She owes a great deal of money to a manicurist friend and frequently accepts assistance from her devoted lover, De Smoke, an affable wrecker and scavenger of old buildings for high profits. Hélène married the late Monsieur Aughain more for security than for love, but she has always been unusually close to Bernard. She writes to her first lover, Alphonse, from whom she was separated by the war, and he arrives in Boulogne with Françoise, a young mistress he passes off as his niece. What with Alphonse's lies and Bernard's fantasies, one must assume the relative candor of Hélène and Françoise if *Muriel* is not to succumb to Marienbadism.

Alphonse is an accomplished liar. Although his white hair makes us want to believe him, he has never owned a bar in Algiers as he claims, nor has he fought in the underground, visited Buckingham Palace, spied in Cairo, worked in films. All he has to show for his life is a bankrupt restaurant in Paris and a deserted wife, Simone. Simone's brother, Ernest, comes to Boulogne to take Alphonse back to Paris, but Ernest does not know that Alphonse has come to see Hélène, whom Ernest once loved. If anything, there is too much plot. The four basic characters—Hélène, Alphonse, Bernard, Françoise—manage to crisscross not only each other but sixteen other beings plucked from out of the ambience of Boulogne.

II

My review of *Muriel* was abruptly interrupted in midpassage last week for lack of space. To make matters worse, the dastardly distributors withdrew *Muriel* from the Plaza in the dead of night with no advance warning. I have little to contribute in the way of a post-mortem except possibly the suggestion that favorably disposed critics should refrain from trumpeting the obscurantist fallacy that some movies should be seen twice or not at all. If I felt that my readers could get nothing out of one viewing of *Muriel*, I would not consider the film worth recommending. A critic should see any worthy film from *Birth of a Nation* on more than once, but a spectator should derive pleasure and/or edification from only one viewing. After all, anyone who hates a film the first time is hardly likely to be adequately motivated for a second try, particularly at today's first-run prices. If for nothing else, *Muriel* deserves to be seen for Sacha (*Marienbad*) Vierny's superb color photography of Boulogne. Color specialists might note the curious blend of Bernard's cool blue sweater with a bloody sunset-red elevator door as one of the key tonal contrasts between Hélène's plot and Bernard's.

The point Resnais makes with a plot Hélène herself describes as banal is the futility of lives lacking a common purpose. Boulogne is a beehive of activity devoid of accomplishment because each character is consumed by his or her own obsession and has nothing left over for anyone else. *Muriel* is as much about things as about people. There are innumerable shots of food and other consumer goods, and unlike the immaculate patrons of Marienbad, who never contemplated an action as vulgar as eating, the characters in *Muriel* spend a sinful amount of time at the dinner table. Although *Muriel* is not as intransigently mysterious as *Marienbad*, Resnais does manage to antagonize audiences with his accumulation of irrelevant details. The breathtaking revelation that De Smoke possesses the staircase of a hotel in which Hélène spent a weekend with Alphonse nearly twenty years before is almost buried in a casual conversation about De Smoke's other possessions.

Resnais is back to his old tricks of introducing shots of people and places as mental images before identifying their dramatic contexts. We see De Smoke and Ernest, for example, long before these characters have been properly introduced. Resnais indulges also in asynchronous conversations in which one set of characters will be talking about another, and we see those spoken about rather than those speaking. Resnais' choice of Hans Werner Henze to supply the music indicates that he is not ready to make a complete break with the classical cinema. Henze is a modernist of the atonal school, but like Berg and Webern, more of a personality than the indistinguishable disciples of the Cologne cabal. Resnais has long been attracted to Germanic music, but he still clings to the more popular movie composers like Fusco and Delerue and Eisler, and he will probably never succumb to the metallic temptations of electronic music.

Although the rhythm of Resnais' editing is subtler than it has ever been in the past, one can appreciate his visual rhymes and echoes after several viewings. He introduces three skyscraper apartments out of context in the first five minutes of the film, and then reintroduces these same impersonal edifices from more dramatic angles in the last five minutes. Two of the more poetic characters—a mussel digger seeking a mate for his nanny goat, and the proprietor of the table—make their exits via identical sequences of three shock-cuts. The average spectator does not have to be aware of this formal symmetry to appreciate the effect of a film that finally resolves its harmonic tensions in terms of a thematic dominant.

Muriel opens with about 30 cuts in the first 90 seconds simply to establish that Hélène Aughain sells antique furniture in an apartment she shares with her stepson. In the next 50 minutes the four major characters are introduced in a leisurely but straightforward manner. Then for 10 minutes everyone goes ricocheting in all directions. Then comes the story about Muriel, followed by longer and longer visual phrases drawing out to the last-minute introduction of Simone wandering through the empty Aughain apartment in one sustained camera movement that allows us to see the apartment in its spatial entirety for the first time. With Resnais, as with Eisenstein, one sees the affinity of montage to music.

Not that *Muriel* is beyond criticism or necessarily every aesthete's cup of tea. Resnais' cinema has always been longer on reflection than on action, and now it is quite clear that the director is at his worst when any form of action is required dramatically. His characters always talk about the past, but Resnais lacks Hollywood's gumption when it comes to reliving it. If Resnais had made *The Birth of a Nation*, for example, he would have intercut shots of old veterans reminiscing about the war with unimpeachable Brady photographs. His camera is chained more than ever to the eternal present. In *Hiroshima, Mon Amour* Resnais did recreate Nevers and a German soldier-lover, but without any accompanying sound. Nevers and the German were not actually reconstructions of the past, but mental images in the heroine's mind. The sound track remained in Hiroshima throughout. The one ground rule of *Marienbad* was that everything took place in the present, mentally or physically. Resnais goes far beyond the surface mannerisms of realism into a chillingly materialistic vision of the universe without precedent in the history of the cinema. For Resnais history is defined by memory. The guilt of Algeria will remain only so long as Bernard remembers Muriel. No longer.

The acting is uneven even when one makes allowances for the fragmentation of the editing. Resnais has a weakness for picking strange-looking types for strange roles, thus overloading the audience with eccentricity. Nevertheless Delphine Seyrig creates an unusually rounded portrait of a woman captured in unguarded moments, an infinitely more interesting characterization and performance, for example, than Monica Vitti's in *Eclipse*, where every gesture is fraught with significance. Curiously, Miss Seyrig's eyes, like Michael Redgrave's, seem to be afflicted with an unfocused beyondness when confronted with other characters. It is as if she were looking past her visible companion to some ideal replica lurking in the shadows beyond, perhaps to some memory of what was or might have been. For Miss Seyrig, as for Resnais, the remembrance of things past is a solitary occupation.

—*Village Voice*, November 21 and 28, 1963

■ 15. *THERESE*

Thérèse has just completed a whirlwind engagement at the Paris Theatre, but do make a note to see this faithful adaptation of François Mauriac's 1927 novel, *Thérèse Desqueyroux*, sometime in its second run. *Thérèse* is the fourth feature film of Georges Franju, a director I described earlier in the year as too old for the New Wave and too new for the Old Guard. At that time I was calling attention to *The Horror Chamber of Dr. Faustus*, a dubbed, truncated version of Franju's second feature, *Les Yeux sans Visage*. It might be noted in passing that Franju made his debut in 1949 with *The Blood of the Beasts*, a documentary study of a slaughterhouse as part of the unseen and unfelt horror of our daily lives.

His other famous short film, *Hôtel des Invalides*, is a scathing indictment of the military mystique. Quite by accident I happened to
catch a curious lament (*Mon Chien*) Franju had devoted to a lost
dog who winds up inexorably and "mercifully" in a gas chamber.
(I know you refer to a dog as "that" and not "who," but with
Franju all animals and birds are "who.") Franju's first feature film,
La Tête Contre les Murs, not yet released in America, is a strangely
one-sided attack on mental institutions and psychoanalysis as totalitarian devices. Most memorable is Charles Aznavour's poignant
depiction of an epileptic and ultimate suicide. *Les Yeux sans
Visage* is a heartfelt, if at times deranged, wail against the inhu-
manity of modern science. *Plein Feux sur l'Assassin* is a routine
potboiler spoofing the French "lumière et son" exhibits in a gruesome way. Consequently *Thérèse* with its literary languidness is
something of a change of pace for the hitherto horrific Franju,
almost comparable to Hitchcock tackling Henry James.

Thérèse Desqueyroux is the kind of novel that years ago both
smirking producers and sniveling aesthetes would agree could not
be made into a movie. Not only is there not enough plot but there
is hardly any adequate motivation. The heroine does manage to
forget her boredom long enough to poison her husband—but why?
He recovers, but does not press charges. Why? She suffers for a
time in passive captivity, but before we can get up a good hate
against her husband, he acts with fantastic kindness. Yet there is
no moving reconciliation, no comfortable philosophical summa-
tion. Husband and wife will remain strangers to each other to the
end.

The whole first hour of the film is expended on a flashback that
sets out to explain why Thérèse poisoned her husband but only succeeds in describing where. American audiences cannot fully appreciate the hatred French intellectuals feel for the provinces. Louis
Malle's *The Lovers* made little sense to most Americans largely
because Jeanne Moreau's provincial home and marriage seem almost
idyllic by American standards. Then again, Thérèse is particularly
hateful because all her actions are apparently gratuitous. Emmanuelle Riva's skillful performance makes of Thérèse a somnolent
Hedda Gabler trapped in a provincial atmosphere so oppressive
she cannot understand her own feelings. We are more accustomed
to the dramatic calculations of a Bette Davis in a similar situation.

Our Bette would poison a boring husband with such relish that we would applaud her emotional directness, but existential Emmanuelle Riva can find no release in mere action. Her piercing eyes are pools of skepticism in which familiar motives sink without a trace. We never find out exactly why she acted as she did, but we do come to understand what it was she was always seeking, albeit unconsciously. The truth of Thérèse is embodied in one final metaphor so profound as to validate all that has preceded it. As she walks through the streets of Paris in a forest of humanity she suddenly realizes that what she always loved about the pines on her husband's estate were the human noises made by the wind. *Thérèse* is the first film I have ever seen advance the mystique of the city over the country for those of us who can breathe only by submerging ourselves in a sea of humanity. It is perhaps some consolation that even this endless night of the assassin can be illuminated however fitfully by an idea.

—*Village Voice*, November 28, 1963

■ 16. *THE CARDINAL*

The Cardinal is probably the twenty-eighth film directed by Otto Preminger in a stormy career that began forty years ago in the Vienna of Max Reinhardt. I say "probably" because Mr. Preminger disclaims all responsibility for any of his film credits before *Laura* in 1944. More than most contemporary American directors, Preminger has taken it upon himself to embody the conception (some would say presumption) of the director as the sole author of a film. If the personality he exudes, with the help of a corps of press agents, is more that of a blustering impresario than of a brooding artist, the fact remains that the cinema, at its most introspective, has never been a fruitful calling for asthmatic aesthetes. As for Preminger's blatant commercialism, even the older and more respectable art forms have been infested with shrewd businessmen like Shakespeare, Dürer, Ibsen, Shaw, Brahms, and Picasso.

The point is that there is no such thing as an "artistic" personality except for purposes of parody. I would certainly never cast

Preminger in *La Bohème*, except possibly as the landlord, but that is no reason to deny his talents when they are so visible on the screen. The literary establishment might insist that the screenplay of *The Cardinal* was adapted by Robert Dozier from a novel by Henry Morton Robinson, but it would be difficult to argue that anyone but Preminger is the author of the film—and that goes for better or worse. *Exodus, Advise and Consent,* and *The Cardinal* all bear the signature of one man in their cinematic renderings, despite their varied and invariably dubious literary antecedents.

The big merit of *The Cardinal* is the sheer size and audacity of its conception. It has become fashionable in America to overlook the grandeur of Preminger's design so as to carp at the gaffes of his detail. There is much to carp at in *The Cardinal.* The acting is singularly uneven, the plot excessively melodramatic, and many of the arguments nakedly didactic. If I totted up the film, minute by minute, the bad would just about equal the good; and yet, because I value design over detail and form over fact, I tend to praise *The Cardinal* rather than seek to bury it.

Like most of Preminger's films, *The Cardinal* is better seen than heard. As his camera sweeps across the ecclesiastical canvas represented by Rome, New England, Georgia, and Vienna, Preminger's meaning comes through more strongly in his feeling for architecture than in his feeling for drama. It is significant that the opening credit sequence depicting Father Stephen Fermoyle ascending an endless series of steps lingers in the mind long after the same character's final speech has been completely forgotten. One visual ascension is not necessarily worth a thousand verbal summations. It is just that Preminger is much better with images than with actors. Of some thirty-odd players in the cast only four—Romy Schneider, John Huston, Burgess Meredith, and Jill Haworth—emerge with any distinction, and even these admirable cameo performances are allowed to fizzle out in anticlimax. None of the other players rises above dull competence, if that high. Tom Tryon is so devoid of personality in the central role that he seems almost properly cast for self-abnegation through much of the film. It is perhaps part of Preminger's visual perverseness that Tryon's impassive face comes to resemble a death mask.

Carol Lynley has been afflicted with what is probably the most thankless role of the year. In an otherwise dignified production, poor Carol has to go to the dogs as a priest's sister hopelessly in love with an irritatingly irreverent Jewish boy who not only resists conversion but chooses to be offended by the genial anti-Semitism of the Boston Irish. She falls in with an unsavory tango dancer known on television as Juan Valdez of coffee-commercial fame, and becomes so disreputably pregnant that her personal cataclysm becomes her brother's odious catechism. Forced to choose between mother and baby, the clerical hero sacrifices his own sister and then compounds the improbability by applying extreme unction with extreme unctuousness. Preminger rounds out the tastelessness of this episode by recasting Carol Lynley as her own daughter. This bit of casual metempsychosis so common in the movies is grotesque in this context. Preminger is almost as unconvincing in his treatment of the KKK on the rampage in Georgia, but he is surprisingly tactful in his treatment of the abortive Tryon-Schneider courtship in Vienna.

The Cardinal is an uneven film, whatever one's frame of reference. The primarily visual critics will hail it, and the primarily literary critics will deplore it. This is as it should be with a director whose talent is more expansive than incisive. If I side with the visual critics on Preminger, it is because I believe we are in the midst of a visual revolution, which the literary establishment is apparently ignoring if not actively resisting. Yet I cannot help feeling that literary accounts of the Kennedy funeral have seemed so pitifully inadequate largely because the image of a riderless black horse possesses a visual power far beyond any literary meaning. On the one great state occasion of our time a group of anonymous television photographers transcended all the poets, novelists, and assorted wordmongers of Western Civilization. At long last the Image had made the Word superfluous.

—*Village Voice*, December 12, 1963

■ 17. *BILLY LIAR*

Billy Liar, in the film of that name, is a cross between Walter Mitty and Andy Hardy. John Schlesinger's comic-strip direction is so bad it is almost nostalgic. This is only Schlesinger's second film, but the vulgarity of his first—A *Kind of Loving*— has been almost effortlessly surpassed. Schlesinger is obviously a man to watch for future awards. Everything he does is so wrong that the accumulation of errors resembles a personal style. Yet even if Schlesinger had more talent, the central theme of *Billy Liar* would remain a dubious one for the movies. Here we have the eponymous hero, expertly played by Tom Courtenay, pretending that he is the benevolent dictator of an imaginary country when, in so-called reality, Billy is merely an undertaker's clerk with vaguely literary aspirations. The trouble with the reality-fantasy plot—and neither Don Quixote nor Walter Mitty has ever been successfully transferred to the screen—is that the reality of the screen is itself a kind of fantasy. Fantasy piled upon fantasy yields only banality. When Norman Mailer announced that he was serving secretly as President, he had no way of knowing that I was rounding out my sixth term in an era of tranquillity and that I had long since curbed the excesses of the Rules Committee. Of course, Mailer is fascinating not because his fantasies are original but because he has transformed them into an entertaining vaudeville act. Billy Liar lacks the assured style of Mitty or Mailer, and his imagination is even sloppier than his environment. The one touch of beauty in his life is a poetic apparition professionally known as Julie Christie, and she is supposed to be real. Yet she is the film's only genuine creature of fantasy and desire, the only felicitous touch in a saga of perpetual humiliation.

—*Village Voice*, December 19, 1963

iii

1964

■ 1. CHARADE; THE VICTORS; KUDOS FOR CRITICS

Charade is consistently better than ordinary without ever being extraordinary, but in this blighted season we moviegoing beggars can't be choosers. The inevitably invidious comparisons with Hitchcock do not really apply here, although I would hate to bet that director Stanley Donen and writer Peter Stone have not seen the master's *To Catch a Thief, The Trouble with Harry, North by Northwest,* and both versions of *The Man Who Knew Too Much.*

Despite the surface borrowings, *Charade* has an original quality of its own as it displays the sick elegance of a fashion show in a funeral parlor. With a plot that smells of red herrings, the picture is memorable for its irrelevant eccentricities—Audrey Hepburn, exquisitely emaciated in her Givenchy wardrobe; Cary Grant, more elfin than dolphin, taking a shower in his drip-dry suit; Walter Matthau doing setting-up exercises with the camera when he is not burping realistically as counterpoint to the ethereal Hepburn-Grant charade on sex.

Before the game is up, the audience is treated to five corpses without moral charge or remorse. Even at the violent chase denouement, when Audrey herself is in danger, the audience remains detached. This lack of concern is appropriate for the amoral world depicted in *Charade,* a world where one can tell right from gauche but not from wrong. Without that old bore morality tagging along, Donen and Stone have had to settle for mystification without mystery and suspicion without suspense. The saddest news of the year is that Cary Dorian Grant is finally beginning to look his age.

The Victors is Carl Foreman's belated vision of World War II, and a film so destitute of merit as to qualify for emergency critical pity. The victors, according to Foreman, lose as much as the vanquished. This is true up to a point, although the victors seem to be losing intangible things like honor, integrity, self-respect, and other banal abstractions, while the vanquished are losing tangible things like food, clothing, shelter, and in hack movies like *The Victors*, privacy in bed. How bad can war be when it enables American dogfaces to crawl into the sack with such continental booty as Romy Schneider and Jeanne Moreau? Civilians should have it so good. Of course, people get killed now and then, and no one is truly happy with all the beastly fighting, but that only goes to prove that war is heck.

While the ten-best season is still with us I would like to honor the ten critics who have contributed most to elevating the tone and extending the boundaries of film criticism in 1963. They are as follows: Ado Couvert, editor of the Paris monthly *Mise-en-Scène*, author of *Ulmer et Utrillo* and *L'Aspect Corneillean des Cowboys*; Gino Aristotle, Italian critic, author of *Who Killed Neo-Realism?*; H. G. Fabian, curator of the Satyajit Ray Institute of Advanced Humanism in London, film critic for *Masses and Classes*, author of *Stand Up Before You're Blown Up*; Wolfgang Krockhaus, author of *From Kuleshov to Khrushchev* and *From Lumière to Laval*; Sylvester J. Caligari, author of *The Infernal Soundtrack*, *To Hell with Technicolor*, and *No Wide Screens for Me*; Irving J. Lecher, film critic and caption editor for *Libertine* magazine; Prescott Styler, aesthete at large, author of *Double Meanings in Double Features*; Drat McNulty, film critic of *Exquisite* magazine, author of *How to Succeed in Movie Reviewing Without Really Seeing Movies*; Pauline Kafka, film critic of the *Rocky Mountain Review* and the *Sierra Madre Sentinel*, author of *All Male Critics Are Cockroaches*; and Phyllis Steen, entertainment editor of the *Herald Angel*, author of *The Earth Is Square* and *Block That Cult*. Keep up the good work, gang.

—*Village Voice*, January 2, 1964

■ 2. AMERICA AMERICA

America America is undoubtedly the most personal work of Elia Kazan's long and violent career, which has embraced on screen sixteen films in almost twenty years and ranged on stage from the maverick days of Odetsian cab drivers in the Group Theatre and mumbling Methodists in the Actors Studio to the now resoundingly hollow Golden Age of Thornton Wilder and Tennessee Williams, Arthur Miller and Archibald MacLeish—or *The Death of a Salesman Named JB on a Streetcar Named Desire Suspended by the Skin of Our Teeth* down to the Establishment-tainted twilight of Lincoln Center and the fawning foundations.

Kazan's voice invades the sound track of *America America* with Wellesian presumption to introduce the director himself as a Greek by blood, a Turk by birth, and an American by adoption. The story Kazan tells is that of a legendary uncle who journeyed in 1894 from an Anatolian village across the mountains to Ankara, across the Bosporus to Constantinople, and across the sea to America.

Despite his personal involvement in his material, Kazan is hardly the ideal chronicler of an odyssey. The director's deepest instincts are less epic than dramatic, with the result that he gets sidetracked more often than his errant hero. The picturesque is gained too often at the expense of the picaresque, and the contour of a legend is obscured time and again by the pointless intimacy of a close-up.

In the past Kazan has attempted to restrain his instinctive theatricality with the classicism of an Eisenstein (*Viva Zapata!*) or a Ford (*Wild River*), but sooner or later he feels the compulsion to hit his audience in the stomach. It follows that Kazan is generally better with individual scenes than with a whole scenario, and that his players are remembered long after the import of their playing has been forgotten. Barbara Bel Geddes, Vivien Leigh, Kim Hunter, Dorothy McGuire, Julie Harris, Patricia Neal, Ethel Waters, Marlon Brando, James Dean, Burl Ives, *et al.* comprise a gallery of no mean proportions, but they are as much voices as faces. *America America* is afflicted with the kind of distractingly dubbed sound track that would negate Duse herself. Drama, after all, is more a province of the ear than of the eye, and a bad sound track is particularly fatal to a dramatic director like Kazan. To make matters worse, Kazan's dialogue is composed of all the stagy clichés of formal peasant rhetoric, and the accents of his players are more off-Broadway than off-Bosporus. It might be noted that bad dubbing has marred also such otherwise distinguished films as Visconti's *The Leopard* and Welles's *The Trial*.

Kazan has gone to great lengths to conceal the lumpiness of his plot by adopting old *nouvelle vague* mannerisms now devoid of their original meaning. He reaches into Truffaut's *Les Mistons* to render a remembered embrace in slow motion. Previously he has resorted to Godardian jump-cuts out of *Breathless* to abridge an obligatory explanatory scene in Constantinople, where the hero must confess that all his money has been stolen. The parallel tracks in Resnais' *Hiroshima, Mon Amour* are not forgotten in the bizarre climax aboard ship in which a tubercular Christ-figure goes over the side to give the hero a new identity. Elsewhere Kazan experiments with tonal contrasts for shock effect out of Murnau and Eisenstein via Marienbad.

Where Kazan is most himself is in his curious absorption in the spectacle of the unwanted woman being sexually humiliated by the beautiful male. In the instance, the Inge-Williams trauma is enacted by a Greek Warren Beatty called Stathis Giallelis and a masochistic American actress called Linda Marsh and adorned for the occasion with a light mustache.

Still, Kazan is to be commended for not glossing over the motivations of his protagonist. The Land of Opportunity has attracted more than its share of opportunists, and men more often than not have been economic animals. Kazan stresses the idea that a man can maintain his honor internally despite all his external compromises. This notion of honor as subjective rather than objective bears more than a passing resemblance to the Salinger line for Ivy League conformists who may be copywriters on the outside but are really poets on the inside.

—*Village Voice*, January 9, 1964

■ 3. *POINT OF ORDER!*

Point of Order! is a fascinating slice of remembered history. Producers Emile de Antonio and Daniel Talbot have edited miles and miles of the 1954 Army-McCarthy kinescopes into a compact 97-minute Punch-and-Judy political spectacle ending in the pratfall of a demagogue. The Messrs. De Antonio and Talbot may be criticized by the Right for liberal bias and by the *cinéma vérité* people for a lack of objectivity. Neither criticism is particularly well taken. Bias, frankly avowed, is always preferable to a spurious objectivity. Then again, it is difficult to see how cinema can ever be genuinely objective—live television, perhaps, but nothing that can be edited before exhibition. Not that the live television cameraman himself can ever be completely objective. If he prefers—even on allegedly technical grounds—to study Senator Mundt in repose rather than to capture Senator Symington in action, our supposedly candid cameraman might alter the ideological orientation of the spectacle with no one watching ever being the wiser. The only safeguard against such manipulation is an awareness of all spectacle as representing a deliberate point of view. If, in a very limited sense, the camera never lies, the cameraman can lie to his heart's content. Fortunately there is enough ambiguity in spectacle to confound the most systematic propagandist. Who could have known back in 1954 that in 1964 the most electrifying image in the Army-McCarthy kinescopes would be that of a minor spear-carrier called Robert Kennedy?

The strange ironies of history aside, the star of the show is still the late Joe McCarthy—and what a performer he was! One can recall his jowly menace and five-o'clock shadow, but it is shocking to rediscover his nervous giggle and his showbiz personality. There was a strangely populist appeal working for McCarthy as the last apostle of direct democracy unsullied by all the confidential "arrangements" of the well born and well educated. When Ike plugged up his keyhole after throwing Stevens to the wolves outside the door, McCarthy was finished. Even the Trotskyists, who had toyed with the idea of using McCarthy as their golem against the Stalinists, were soon bored by Joe's ludicrous inexactitude. Curiously, Joe's medium was neither television nor radio, and he was hardly a Huey Long out on the stump. With succinctness as his forte and fear as his gospel, McCarthy may have been the first and last demagogue of the wire services.

—*Village Voice*, January 16, 1964

■ 4. *THE GUEST*

The Guest comes off so well as a cinematic rendering of Harold Pinter's *The Caretaker* that Clive Donner's creative direction may be lost in the shuffle of superlatives. Certainly the ensemble acting of Donald Pleasance, Robert Shaw, and Alan Bates is not likely to be topped in many a moon, although "ensemble" may seem a strange word to apply to characters as disconnected from each other as the fixtures in that cluttered attic where the exchange of soliloquies passes for conversation. How, then, do you show disconnectedness on the screen? Donner has chosen to compromise between the real and the abstract, between the banal and the bizarre. He has neither overloaded with allegory by emphasizing the attic as some cosmic enclosure of Sartrean dimensions and pretensions nor implicated the world at large by moving outside his characters when he has gone out of doors.

With the director's choice of inconsistency as a lesser risk than incoherence, the Pinter plot unfolds much of the time like a conventional suspense drama. Will the old vagrant be able to play off one brother against the other? Can an instinct for survival prevail over an obsession? What do the brothers really want? Tune in next week to the BBC Third Programme and find out. Of course, since Pinter is not Rattigan, we never do find out, but Donner's resourceful direction keeps up our hopes to the very end. Although Donner gets his richest comic effects when he keeps two actors in the same frame, he frequently resorts to the kind of gratuitous crosscutting that suggests missing links between Pinter's elliptical phrases.

Although Pinter is generally linked, albeit loosely, to the Theater of the Absurd, he clearly lacks Beckett's poetic vision and Ionesco's comic invention. If Beckett is truly absurd in his conception of an empty world—a conception, incidentally, opposed to the mystique of the cinema—and Ionesco relatively grotesque, Pinter is more in the eccentric tradition of Wilde, Gilbert, Carroll, and Lear. The most hilarious moments in *The Guest* are embellished by the excessively factual essence of Algernon's cucumber sandwiches; and if Bunbury were alive today, he would probably live in Pinter's Sidcup.

Where Donner (and Pinter) have miscalculated most grievously is with Aston's long lobotomy speech, broken up on the screen into three distinct sequences of camera movement, but to no avail. Once the message has been so crudely delivered in a phlegmatically British echo of *Suddenly Last Summer*, the game is up with the characters. Someone Out There is the scapegoat—not Up There, as in Beckett's more majestic conception, but Out There. Not Him, but Them. Not the universe, but society. Not man, but a trio of misfits. Still, despite his structural weaknesses, Pinter exhibits a talent for small talk that approaches genius, and Donner, restricted to British quickies for the past few years, may be ready to vault over the Richardson-Reisz-Anderson-Schlesinger class of socially conscious butterflies. The acting has always been there. Only the direction has been confused.

—*Village Voice*, January 30, 1964

■ 5. DR. STRANGELOVE

The great merit of *Dr. Strangelove* is its bad taste. It is silly to argue that we have the right to say anything we want but that to exercise this right is the height of irresponsibility. Responsible art is dead art, and a sane (no pun intended) film on the Bomb would have been a deadly bore.

Given the basic premise of nuclear annihilation, the zany conception of Stanley Kubrick, Terry Southern, and Peter George has much to commend it. Where my critical fall out with most of my colleagues occurs is in the realm of execution. Aided by the tightest scenario since *Rashomon*, and the most deceptive as far as directorial exercises go, Kubrick has been hailed in many quarters as the greatest director since D. W. Griffith. This despite a career that has consisted of six near and far misses.

Why not? *Dr. Strangelove* seems so audacious at first glance that even its faults have been rationalized into virtues. To take a crucial example, no one to my knowledge has commented on the fact that Peter Sellers was supposed to play the pivotal role of Major King Kong, commander of the ill-fated bomber (named *Leper Colony*) that destroys the world. Because of an injury, Sellers was replaced at the last moment by Slim Pickens. Sellers was already involved in three roles—President Merkin Muffley, RAF Group Captain Lionel Mandrake, Dr. Strangelove alias Merkwürdigichliebe, formerly one of Hitler's V-2 rocket researchers at Peenemunde—so that almost everywhere you turn there is some version of Peter Sellers holding the fate of the world in his hands. The satiric symmetry of this mass casting, cribbed from *Kind Hearts and Coronets*, makes comic sense only if Sellers closes every escape hatch with his mimicry. By dropping Sellers out of the Kong role, Kubrick creates a fatal gap in his scenario between the War Room–Air Force Base sequences, where everyone is horsing around, and the bomber sequences, where an antistereotype Negro bombardier (James Earl Jones) evokes a Hawksian nobility that reminds us that "our boys" once destroyed Hitler with the same courage and professionalism now deemed ridiculous. Kubrick does his best to hoke up the actual bombing with anticowboy whoops and hollers, but the bomber has long since eluded him as it has the combined surveillance of the Pentagon and the Kremlin. Sellers playing three out of the four parts originally assigned to him is comparable to Guinness' having interpreted only six of the eight D'Ascoynes in *Kind Hearts*. Not that Sellers is any Guinness. More a mimic than an actor, Sellers starts brilliantly with President Muffley but ends badly; starts badly with Strangelove but ends brilliantly; and just muddles through with Mandrake despite some of the choicest lines in the script.

I suspect that most of the clever touches in the script can be credited to Terry Southern, author of such "underground" classics as *Flash and Filigree* and *Candy*. The nomenclature is particularly ambitious in its unrelenting expressiveness. Mandrake and Jack D. Ripper make a particularly mythic pair of misfits. Turgidson and DeSedeski read better than they sound, while Dimitri Kissoff and Bat Guano sound better than they read. Merkin Muffley is about perfect as a representation of a Stevensonian cipher.

Since Kubrick's major shortcoming, like Kurosawa's, is in structuring (or rather in failing to structure) his films with a consistent camera viewpoint, a scenario like *Dr. Strangelove* comes as a godsend. All the action is divided neatly and plausibly into three main sections, separate in space and concurrent in time. With the fate of the world riding on every twist and turn of the plot, suspense is virtually built into the theme of the film. Kubrick could sit back and let the clock tick away without reducing the tension in the audience. In this context the feeblest jokes gain added vibrations from the nervous relief they provide. Still, Kubrick's direction is, on the whole, efficient without ever being inspired. Where I think he has miscalculated most grievously is in directing George C. Scott's Air Force Chief of Staff, General Turgidson, like a saber-rattling hillbilly. Scott, who can play very quietly given half the chance, is encouraged to chew up his lines and any spare scenery lying around the War Room. By contrast, Sterling Hayden's General Ripper comes over as a tortured, psychotic, but never unintelligent fanatic. Whereas Scott masquerades as a general as if there were nothing sillier than exercising authority, Hayden captures the pathos of the man of action perverted by the contradictions of his calling. With the pathos, Hayden captures more of the comedy as well.

Kubrick can be faulted occasionally for blatant overstatement. The sign reading "Peace Is Our Business" has an ironic kick, however obvious, the first time it is shown in a strife-torn Air Force base, but when repeated a half dozen times more, the effect crosses the thin line between satire and propaganda. It is also hardly necessary to have General Turgidson lead the War Room dignitaries in prayer when all seems saved. This is even bad propaganda, since it confuses the argument. If the Pentagon is ruled by monstrous hypocrites, the audience can assume that a more reasonable set of chieftains might avert such a disaster.

Some of Kubrick's most admired effects are not quite as original as they may seem to the unschooled eye. The aerial copulation-fueling introduction is hardly a patch on the rampant jet-propelled sexuality of Josef von Sternberg's *Jet Pilot* some seven years ago. (Of course, an anti-Communist farce with John Wayne could never hope to be taken as seriously as an anti-American farce with Peter Sellers.) The trick of using popular songs as an ironic counterpoint to monstrous images may be relatively new in feature films, but people like Stan Vanderbeek have been turning out shorts like this for years. The Hiroshima and Christmas Island explosions constitute the most dog-eared footage for "peace" movies on both sides of the Iron Curtain. Consequently it is never clear whether Kubrick's "doomsday" ending is actually representational or merely rhetorical in the time-honored symbolism of anti-Bomb movies.

Dr. Strangelove is more effective, if less consistent, when it probes the irregular sexual motivations of its crazy generals. It is hilariously unfair to ridicule one officer for keeping a tootsie on the side and then ridicule the other for conserving his precious fluids from hordes of women seeking his depletion.

Ultimately, *Dr. Strangelove* is not a bad movie by any standards, and I would feel much more kindly toward it if it were not so grossly overrated. Yet aside from questions of critical perspective, I think the whole subject is about a year out of date. It is just Kubrick's bad luck that he instituted this project before the signing of the test-ban treaty and the Kennedy assassination. The agitated apocalyptic mood of the Cuban confrontation is long gone. Today we read about natives with bows and arrows shooting down American helicopters flying under an alleged nuclear umbrella that is becoming more and more nebulous. What Walter Lippmann calls polycentrism is infecting both hitherto monolithic concentrations of power in the Cold War. Each day local satraps taunt the moguls in the Kremlin and the Pentagon with greater and greater impunity. Indeed, as I write, a Russian negotiator at Geneva has apparently defected to the West with all the secret Soviet strategy for conducting disarmament negotiations. Maybe Kubrick, Southern, and George can now turn their talents to a satire on all those people who were subconsciously disappointed when the world was not obliterated at the time President Kennedy had the impudence to affirm America's interests in the world. As it is, *Dr. Strangelove* can serve as a comic testament to the death wish of many American intellectuals. The world may still come to an end, of course, but the current odds are not with a bang but a whimper.

—*Village Voice*, February 13, 1964

■ *6. THE FIRE WITHIN*

Louis Malle's *The Fire Within* is based very loosely on *Le Feu Follet*, a work of the late Drieu La Rochelle, a precious symbolist of the twenties and thirties. If memory serves me correctly, La Rochelle either committed suicide or was executed as a collaborationist in 1945. By merely updating *Le Feu Follet* to the fifties and sixties, Malle has transformed the novelist's personal statement into his own, with the result that the plot now unfolds on a double level of signification.

Alain Leroy, a jaded playboy-alcoholic turned thirty, has set a date for his suicide. The time of the film consists of the last forty-eight hours of his life, time spent in a rendezvous with his American wife's best friend, a return to the Versailles sanitarium where he was taking a cure from alcoholism at his wife's expense, a pilgrimage to his former haunts in Paris, where his friends, like puppets in a philosophical allegory on the Will Durant level, explain why life is worth living. Some have found the animal warmth of a bourgeois marriage, others the consolation of a career or political action, however futile, and the distracting games of love and money, however dangerous. Alain is unconvinced; he returns to the sanitarium a second time and shoots himself very decorously in his disengaged heart.

For Malle, as for Antonioni, the legend of F. Scott Fitzgerald is loosened from its context to furnish an alibi for the director's own ennui. Antonioni had already used up *Tender Is the Night* in *L'Avventura,* and so Malle countered with an early shot of *Babylon Revisited* on the hero's bookshelf before the fateful visit (or "revisit") to Paris and a climactic shot of *The Great Gatsby,* the last book the hero reads before pulling the trigger. Another Malle touch is the mythic collage of the late Marilyn Monroe rendered through the pictures published at the time of her death.

Yet when all is said and done, and all the cultural cross-references have been endlessly sifted, *The Fire Within* remains a very trivial film by a very presumptuous director. Malle's self-pity here is even more boring than Fellini's in *8½* and his personal confession equally unsolicited. And make no mistake about it. The real protagonist of *The Fire Within* is not Alain Leroy or Drieu La Rochelle but Louis Malle himself. His first film, *Frantic,* with Maurice Ronet and Jeanne Moreau, was made when the director was twenty-four. Then came great commercial success and artistic respect with *The Lovers;* a commercial setback, not entirely deserved, with *Zazie;* and penultimately an artistic and commercial disaster with *A Very Private Life,* despite the box-office insurance of Brigitte Bardot and Marcello Mastroianni. Barely past thirty, Malle was practically washed up in the French film industry. What to do?

The Fire Within constitutes a rationalization for self-exploitation and, like Goethe's Werther, enables Malle to commit suicide by proxy.

Unfortunately Malle has failed to avoid the various fallacies inherent in a suicide plot. If you justify the suicide, you tend to make the world too drab and dreary a place for serious contemplation; but if you make the world genuinely interesting and livable-in, you make the suicidal protagonist a complete fool. Malle chooses to make the world drab and dreary, and he reaches his low point with some kind of vague opium den presided over by spiritually ravaged Jeanne Moreau. Yet Malle's protagonist, played with genial despair by Maurice Ronet, fails to rise above his surroundings even when he is tricked up with supplementary motivations. At one point Malle seems to have dipped into Henry James's *The Beast in the Jungle* for a speech in which the protagonist explains that he had always been waiting for something to happen and then one day realized that nothing would. Malle is closer to La Rochelle when he suggests a conscious decision not to surrender his youth, a decision only death—physical or, in Cocteau's sense, poetic—can make. Finally, there is the invariable equation of women and art. Alain complains again and again that although he has touched many women, he has been unable to hold any. This, in short, is Malle's verdict on his own art. Frequently touching, but never gripping.

—*Village Voice*, February 27, 1964

■ 7. *THE GREAT DICTATOR*

I

The Great Dictator is a genuinely great film, perhaps Chaplin's greatest, though not necessarily his most nearly perfect or even his most personal. His earlier work, centered on the Tramp, is less flawed by excessive ambition. His later work, gradually darkening into the melancholy twilight of reflective old age, is more direct in its expression of a personal vision. What makes *The Great Dictator* relatively unique in Chaplin's career is the heavy historical anchor holding it in place and time.

Originally released in 1940, Chaplin's satiric assault on Adolf Hitler, alias Adenoid Hynkel, had already lost much of its context, if none of its conviction, with the outbreak of World War II. After the war German audiences reportedly resisted Chaplin's rendering of Hitler, and Italian audiences, I have been told, were similarly unimpressed with Jack Oakie's imitation of Mussolini. Actually, Oakie's performance, with its Chico Marx dialect readings, now seems too broad by even so-called Brechtian standards. The Chaplin-Oakie sequences also suffer from Chaplin's complete misrepresentation of the Hitler-Mussolini power relationship in the era between Dollfuss and *Anschluss*. Events proved only too quickly that Hitler's war machine was hardly the paper tiger of Chaplin's imagination, but Chaplin was hardly a paper tiger himself in challenging the authority of irrational power at a time when many intellectuals were dazzled by the muscular sex appeal of totalitarianism.

Yet viewed purely as a historical document, *The Great Dictator* abounds with perplexing incongruities and inconsistencies. Lacking the benefit of Hannah Arendt's hindsight, Chaplin may be forgiven for overlooking the transition from the crudely bullying Brownshirts of the S.A. to the calculatingly brutal Blackshirts of the S.S. Still, there is something disconcertingly naïve in Chaplin's view of a concentration camp as a spacious enclosure within which the prisoners goose-step all day long. More than hindsight is involved here. Fritz Lang, long before Chaplin, described organized terror with prophetic accuracy, but, then, Lang had actually seen the inside of a Gestapo headquarters, and Chaplin had not.

What is stranger still is that Chaplin looks at Germany from a distinctly Jewish point of view, and yet he is never particularly anti-German. The Nazi officials, including Hynkel, never bother to affect German accents. Chaplin does render Hynkel's speeches in ranting "mit sauerkraut" gibberish, but only to parody Hitler's hysterical radio delivery with its incongruously moderate English translation. (This was an "inside" touch of the time worthy of that Man from Mars, Orson Welles.) It might be noted that two years later Ernst Lubitsch's *To Be or Not To Be* would reflect the civilized temperament of a Viennese director at war with the brutishness of German character. By contrast, *The Great Dictator* represents the emotional though somewhat abstract identification of an immigrant from London's East End with the sufferings of his fellow Jews.

The two worlds of film are Hynkel's palace and the ghetto, and the ghetto is peopled largely by actors with Yiddish dialects in contradistinction to the neutrally accented Germans. Even the conception of the ghetto applies more to eastern Europe than to Germany, where assimilation had long been trumpeted as a cure for anti-Semitism. Chaplin simply could not conceive of Nazi persecution as anything more than a gigantic pogrom of limited function and duration. With a smattering of Marxist theory naïvely applied to the German (or Ptomanian) state, Chaplin concluded erroneously that the Jews were serving in their familiar roles as scapegoats for economic failures of the regime. Once the German people realized that they were being swindled by their leaders, they would overthrow these leaders and help build a brave new world. In a sense, the thirties ended with the betrayal of Chaplin's faith in *The Great Dictator* and the confirmation of Renoir's despair in *The Rules of the Game*.

II

Although nearly a quarter of a century has elapsed between the original release of *The Great Dictator* and its current revival at the Plaza, Hynkel's high jinks with a globular balloon have lost none of their breathtaking boldness and delicacy. Children in the audience still giggle slightly when Chaplin bounces the aery globe off his baggy posterior in a literal demonstration of the anal level of humor, but the giggles gradually die out when this slightly obscene maneuver is ritualized by repetition, and the camera persistently follows the slow ascent of the balloon into the lofty realms of fantasy.

The extraordinary beauty and power of this entire sequence can be attributed to the paradoxes of Chaplin's personality. Within moments Chaplin can glide from the ridiculous to the sublime and back to the ridiculous. This talent for the tragicomic is seldom appreciated in America. You're either funny or you're serious, and that's that. Consequently there has been a tendency in Chaplin's American critics to measure his art by the number of laughs he provokes per minute.

By this standard *The Great Dictator* represents Chaplin in decline. There are whole sequences with no laughs at all and more than a few sequences with no intrinsic merit. Critics who measure a film frame by frame, second by second, could write volumes on Chaplin's directorial deficiencies. He even manages to kill a gag—Napoloni's unexpected entrance behind Hynkel's desk—by bad cutting and camera placement. The inconsistent texture of the match-ups between studio and newsreel footage cannot be rationalized away by modern theories of stylization. Nor can the glaring process shots and cardboard sets. Back in 1940, Chaplin was not making a "Look-Ma-I'm-Arty" atrocity like *The Balcony*. He was turning out a movie for mass audiences, and all his unsatisfactory subterfuges served the cheap illusionism of the time. Today's audiences, more sophisticated optically and yet more tolerant stylistically, tend to assume a greater unity of visual design than was actually intended. An audience that can spot the artifice of La Shelle's exquisite color photography in the otherwise excruciating *Irma La Douce* may find it hard to believe that other audiences once enjoyed *The Great Dictator* as a realistic parody of Hitler. But they did.

What, then, is great about *The Great Dictator?* Simply the remarkable duality of Chaplin as the Dictator and the Barber. Not simply as one or the other, but as both in one. There is no trick photography here beyond the occasional dissolution of the Barber's image into the Dictator's or the Dictator's into the Barber's. The two characters never share the same frame, or even the same scene, and yet they inhabit each other, somehow as Chaplin and Hitler inhabited each other. This is what keeps *The Great Dictator* from leaving the sour aftertaste of *Dr. Strangelove*. In parodying Hitler with consummate technique as actor and mime, Chaplin breaks through the shell of his model with his own artistic personality. The clever artists involved with *Dr. Strangelove* always seem outside of their targets, as if none of the evil could ever be shared. The attitude toward the Strangelove menagerie is cold, smug, pitiless. Chaplin's relationship to Hitler is unavoidably intimate. After all, it takes a megalomaniac to know one, and there is not all that much difference between a man who wants to save the world and a man who wants to destroy it. Even Chaplin's beloved Paulette Goddard is pressed into service as his emotional correlative for all humanity. "Look up, Hannah," he cries hysterically at the end.

He might just as well have added that he wished to encompass the world with his love as Hynkel encompassed the globe with his hate and destroyed it. Chaplin reads his last speech not for its simplistic ideas but for its powerful emotions. He calls for an end to greed, and as a Marxist of sorts, he should have been less naïve; but when he declares that only the "unloved and the unnatural hate," he strikes a more personal chord. Twenty-five years later, hearing this strange diagnosis of Hitler in terms of vaguely Freudian symptoms, I am suddenly struck by the image of a frustrated student in Vienna walking the streets with a big dog and a big stick to cover up his sexual inferiority complex. It is part of the liberal heritage to reach out to the "unloved and the unnatural" with love and understanding, not to condemn them out of hand. It is now too late to speculate whether a healthier sex life for Hitler could have aborted the Nazi movement. Yet even with Hitler the price of understanding is compassion, and the genius of Chaplin is measured by his profound understanding of those attributes that place the most monstrous of men within the confines of the human condition.

—*Village Voice*, March 5 and 12, 1964

■ 8. *MAN'S FAVORITE SPORT?*

Man's Favorite Sport? is just another movie in the preeminently commercial career of producer-director Howard Hawks, and the operative word here is "movie." For discriminating connoisseurs of the cinema as an art form—that is to say, for people with tastes too fastidious for exposure to more than a dozen films a year—*Man's Favorite Sport?* is a complete waste of time. After all, how much profundity can be derived in these perilous times from a plot concerning an Abercrombie & Fitch salesman trapped by an aggressive female into entering a fishing contest for which he is qualified more by literary reputation than by direct experience?

Somehow our woefully incompleat angler muddles through to victory despite his nearly drowning on those occasions when he is not about to be devoured by the nearest bear or woman. On the first viewing, this one basic joke of the phony painfully unmasked wears dangerously thin for a two-hour movie. Hawks's deadpan documentation of a physical gag is as effective as ever, but the over-all pace of his direction is curiously contemplative, as if he were savoring all his past jokes for the last time.

It seems unfortunate, at least on first viewing, that Rock Hudson and Paula Prentiss clearly lack a light touch for comedy, a fact of casting Hawks accepted gallantly and exploited skillfully when he was unable to land Cary Grant and Audrey Hepburn for his leads. The very clumsiness of the Hudson-Prentiss coupling is deftly integrated with the central parody of professionalism. Call it classic or archaic, but *Man's Favorite Sport?* harks back to the golden age of Cary Grant and Katharine Hepburn in *Bringing Up Baby.* The bitter spectacle of a man divested of his dignity, and the humor derived thereby, seem to apply to some pre-Feiffer species of male with dignity to spare. The only question in this age of anxiety is whether such a heroic creature has become extinct, like the dodo, or was always as mythical as the unicorn.

—*Village Voice,* March 19, 1964

■ 9. *THE SERVANT*

The Servant is the first work in Joseph Losey's tortured career to bear his personal signature from the first frame to the last. Since Losey has always displayed a tendency to invest his most conventional projects with personal and social overtones of a perverse nature, it is hard to believe that he would collaborate with Harold Pinter on a trivial melodrama patterned after *Kind Lady* or *The Green Bay Tree.* Yet some critics have objected to the slackening of tension in the second half of the film as if they were back on Angel Street. Part of the confusion may be caused by the preciseness and fluidity of Losey's camera style. It's too beautiful to be anything but melodrama, our dreary realists would argue. But it must be remembered that Losey was an admirer of Brecht long before such admiration was either fashionable or feasible, and that if he is any kind of realist at all, he is a symbolic realist. Still, no matter how symbolic you get, if the psychology is false, the sociology is equally false. Where many critics have gone wrong is in assuming a psychology for the Losey-Pinter characters in accordance with the preconceptions of a genre. If Dirk Bogarde's Servant is immediately identified as half Mephistopheles and half Machiavelli out to corrupt James Fox's innocent Master, half Faust and half Dorian Gray, then we are no longer in the realm of the why but of the how. Intellectual irony gives way to formal allegory, and the turns of the plot transcend the turns of the screw.

Now let's stop and think a moment. Why would a Brechtian-Marxist like Losey be unduly concerned over the possible corruption of an upper-class Englishman by his servant? The answer is that Losey is not particularly interested in this aspect of the plot. What must have interested Losey from the beginning was the opportunity provided by Robin Maugham's conventional novel of decadence to dissect British class society within a controlled frame. By concentrating on four characters—master, servant, master's fiancée, servant's mistress—Losey could establish all the necessary lines of communication between classes and then snarl them up with insolence and ignoblesse oblige. One critic has asked why the servant undertakes to undermine his master. The servant's references are in order. He doesn't do this as a hobby. What's his motivation? Well, "motivation" is a kind of Sammy Glick script-conference word left over from Hollywood's traumatic experience with the talkies. What is Hamlet's motivation? If we knew for sure, perhaps *Hamlet* would not fail so dismally as a straightforward revenge play. Too much slackness in the second half, you know.

There is one staggering episode in *The Servant* that provides the key to all the motivations. It is the famous restaurant scene with the snatches of bullying conversations from three unrelated couples. This is not an extraneous sample of Pinter's virtuosity for comedy relief. It is the evocation of power as the dominant passion of a collapsing class society. Why, then, does the servant take over his master? Simply because someone has to take over someone else. Every relationship—indeed, every conversation—is a power struggle. Lacking a plan, the servant has to improvise. Each nastiness, like Hitler's, leads to unexpected gains, and the process continues until the servant is as corrupted by power as the master is corrupted by sloth. The servant goes too far. He is fired, then rehired. Chaos.

Utter perversion. Then, finally, a fine house where everyone once knew his place has been converted into a seedy brothel where everyone now knows his vice—in short, Losey's vision of contemporary England.

The ensemble acting is extraordinary. Dirk Bogarde gives the performance of his life with a skillful blend of charm, rascality, and uncertainty. Sarah Miles exudes sex as a rousing stimulus rather than a rhetorical symbol, and no one since the early days of Joan Greenwood has been more delectably suspicious of her own sensuality. Wendy Craig is uncommonly expert in the difficult role of the upper-class character with too much character and not enough façade to play the chess game to the bitter end. In the most difficult part, James Fox manages his upper but not higher role without a trace of caricature or condescension.

The Servant is undeniably the most exciting movie of the year so far. There is some overelaboration of Losey's circular camera movements that trace the shape of his deterministic conceptions, and there is also some leakage of meaning through hysteria. It must be acknowledged, if only on the most sublime level of movie-making, that Losey lacks the unified vision of a Renoir in *The Rules of the Game*. Nevertheless *The Servant* is a genuinely shocking experience for audiences with the imagination to understand the dimensions of the shock. In years to come *The Servant* may be cited as a prophetic work making the decline and fall of our last cherished illusions about ourselves and our alleged civilization.

—*Village Voice*, March 26, 1964

■ 10. *THE CRIME OF MONSIEUR LANGE*

The world's greatest living director is not Akira Kurosawa or Stanley Kubrick or Tony Richardson or even Martin Ritt. If it is any one person at all, it is Jean Renoir, the true heir of Auguste Renoir and the true father of neorealism and the *nouvelle vague*. Renoir's career over forty years is a river of personal expression. The waters may vary here and there in turbulence and depth, but the flow of personality is consistently directed to its final outlet in the sea of

life. Which brings us to the belated New York openings of Renoir's
The Crime of Monsieur Lange (1935) and Robert Bresson's *Les
Dames du Bois de Boulogne* (1944). To read the daily reviewers
on vintage Renoir and Bresson, one would think that Brandon
films had tried to open two nudist movies in St. Patrick's Cathedral. My first response to this Philistinish idiocy is an urgent SOS
to all my readers to rush to see the two films before they fade back
to the oblivion whence they came.

The conventional American line on Renoir is that everything he
made before *Grand Illusion* in 1937 is primitive and everything he
made after it is decadent. Ironically, Renoir has turned out at least
a dozen films with more force and insight, but *Grand Illusion* continues to be preeminent in its obviousness. *The Crime of Monsieur
Lange* is the product of Renoir's communard period, when there
was still hope that fascism could be defeated. As was often the
case with Renoir, the film was made on a shoestring, with the result that the sound recording, editing, and lab work are not all they
should be. This was part of the price Renoir paid to make personal
films, and I would say in retrospect that it was worth it. Through
Monsieur Lange, the day-dreaming author of *Arizona Jim*, Renoir
expresses the comic yet poignant plight of the artist coping with
commerce. Batala, the evil yet charming publisher, probably represents many of the conniving producers Renoir encountered in
that epoch. Even when Jacques Prevert's pretentious dialogue tends
to inflate Batala into a Don Juanish Hitler, Renoir's relentless humanism preserves the ambiguity of the characterization. When
Lange shoots Batala, there is no ideological jubilation, no orgasmic
fantasy release. Renoir's camera lingers on the dying man in his
incongruous priest's robes.

Renoir's greatness as a director is not so much the consequences
of his warmth and humanism as it is the evidence of an integral
camera style fully expressive of warmth and humanism. What Renoir had already achieved in *La Chienne, Boudu,* and *Toni,* and
consolidated in *The Crime of Monsieur Lange* was nothing less
than the overthrow of the tyranny of the camera set-up. Where
even Bresson, for example, frames characters, Renoir follows them.
Life is always spilling over a Renoir frame as if the screen were not
big enough to encompass all humanity. By emphasizing the flow of
his players, Renoir creates the illusion, at least for the unwary

reviewer, of a lazy camera and a sloppy style. Actually, Renoir's camera movements are fantastically complex. One of the high points of film history is René Lefèvre's one-take walk from his upstairs office, past walls and windows as seen from the outside of the building, downstairs to the courtyard, where the fatal rendezvous with Jules Berry is to take place. This one meaningfully sustained camera movement makes most of the new movies in town look like mush.

—Village Voice, April 9, 1964

■ 11. *LES DAMES DU BOIS DE BOULOGNE*

Robert Bresson's *Les Dames du Bois de Boulogne* deserves a few explanatory notes, if only because this brilliant work has been so widely and wildly vilified by so-called realistic criticism. Realism, as Harold Rosenberg has so sagely remarked, is but one of the 57 varieties of decoration. Yet, particularly where movies are concerned, the absurdly limited realism of the script girl and the shop girl is too often invoked at the expense of the artist's meaning. Why, oh why, whines one local reviewer, does Maria Casarès wear long dresses in the afternoon? (This same reviewer is unperturbed by the transparent contrivance through which East German nuns are dumped pathetically in Arizona, where they can be saved with topical miraculousness by a Negro deus-ex-machina machinist out of *Robinson Crusoe* via *Going My Way*—but that is another story.)

Admittedly, long dresses in the afternoon had been "out" even back in 1944 when Bresson made *Les Dames du Bois de Boulogne*. Why then did Bresson flout such an obvious canon of realism as the appropriateness of attire around the clock? Mere carelessness? The most superficial consideration of Bresson's fantastically controlled career makes such a suggestion unthinkable.

Bresson could have saved himself a great deal of criticism by distancing his material in time. We are generally more tolerant of the past than of the present. Jeanne Moreau is forgiven her indiscretions more readily in *Jules and Jim* than in *The Lovers*, and

Scarlett O'Hara is always given better odds than Blanche Dubois. Actually, *Les Dames* is adapted from an interpolated episode in Denis Diderot's philosophic dialogue *Jacques le Fataliste* (1773). Bresson could have retreated to the allegorical past in which the Jacques Prevert-Marcel Carné team flourished during the German occupation through such elegant escapism as *The Devil's Envoys* and *Children of Paradise*. Instead of lingering in the more permissive world of carriages, Bresson thrusts his intrigue into the more urgent world of cars. In a sense, Bresson suspends his characters in that dead present Camus commemorated in *The Plague* at about the same time. Yet his characters retain a Racinean purity of feeling in a century that demands a more detailed documentation of social relevance.

Even a bare outline of the plot suggests unconscionable self-indulgence for any period after 1929. Hélène (Maria Casarès), rebuffed by Jean (Paul Bernard), gains revenge by maneuvering her ertswhile lover into a marriage with Agnes (Elina Labourdette), a prostitute masquerading, at Hélène's bidding and financing, as a provincial virgin. The implied class structure that might legitimize such an involved deployment of desires is shunted so far into the background that it virtually ceases to exist. Jean Cocteau's dialogue serves Bresson well in its laconic indirection and improbability. The preciseness of Bresson's framing is designed to emphasize the internal drama, and what there is of the external world is more often heard than seen. The rigor of Bresson's style reduces geography to the shortest distance between two rooms, and architecture to the contrasting lightness and darkness of enclosures.

It is not surprising that a baroque figure like Orson Welles should hate Bresson's films. Release, so crucial to Welles's art, is conspicuously absent in Bresson's. Jean and Agnes ultimately triumph over Hélène's hate with their love, but their grace is internal. No dramatic cut or camera movement has heralded the moment of recognition. Agnes, enmeshed in her bridal gown, regains her purity through the sheer intensity of the camera's gaze on the Manichean whiteness. The black-silk-coat-and-top-hat dancing costume, reminiscent of similar costumes worn virginally by Ginger Rogers and Ann Miller in Gregory La Cava's *Stage Door*, is further sensualized and degraded by the addition of silk stockings, the most electrifyingly symbolic reverse striptease in the history of the cinema and an index of Bresson's giddy notions of sinfulness. From these depths of depravity our heroine rises on the moral scale to the relative purity of a white trench coat to the absolute purity of the bridal gown. Meanwhile Maria Casarès has remained throughout in her magisterially black gown like a modern Medea.

Why, then, does Maria Casarès wear long dresses in the afternoon? Well, let us say that in classical tragedy the actors' masks were uninflected in counterpoint to the inflected poetry. (Karl Marx makes the distinction in Diderot's dialogues between the honest consciousness of static values and the disintegrated consciousness of universal flux.) With Bresson the costumes are uninflected, if you will, in counterpoint to the inflected faces of his players. Bresson's counterpoint can be translated visually into the conflicting notions of determinism and free will. It is as inevitable in terms of the chromatic roles of the costumes that Maria Casarès will execute her revenge as it is that Elina Labourdette will attain Grace. Yet the faces falter humanly in their superhuman roles. Hélène sheds real tears when she realizes that her lover is lost to her irrevocably, and Agnes gallantly seeks her own ruination through a perverse desire for liberty.

—*Village Voice*, April 16, 1964

■ 12. *THE COOL WORLD*

The Cool World is at its best when it reflects upon that strange world north of Central Park and east of Morningside Drive. Baird Bryant's location photography renders Harlem with heartbreaking authenticity as a colorful place to visit on location but no place to live *in extremis*. This is the outer shell of the "Negro problem." What of the inner voice?

Shirley Clarke, Warren Miller, Carl Lee, and their associates have tried earnestly and sincerely to penetrate the superficial objectivity of the documentary method. Miss Clarke flings wet-mop close-ups of eloquently questioning black faces at her white audiences as if these audiences had never really seen a Negro before—and, in a sense, they never have, we never have. At times Miss

Clarke seems to succumb to an inverted racism, particularly with a Negro gangster's white-blonde floozie, a racist status symbol at first glance, but ultimately a Pyrrhic victory. No matter. By the end of *The Cool World* the white race has been reduced to an alien presence from another planet, and the Negro, at long last, has become the norm. No nonsense about a "dialogue" between the races here.

Still, despite her sympathetic intentions, Shirley Clarke has repeated all the artistic mistakes that defeated her first feature, *The Connection*. Her camera still sweeps and swoops excessively, suggesting nothing so much as visual hysteria blotting out intellectual contemplation. She never quite meshes the materials of stylized melodrama into the network of realistic cross-references, and she goes so soppy over her protagonists that she is unable to make any moral distinctions between what they are and what they do. The end result is that a gang rumble becomes a painless ballet involving graceful animals, and white audiences can return smugly to a conception of the Negro as exotic entertainer, Mau Mau instead of minstrel, Stepin Fetchit with a switchblade.

—*Village Voice*, April 23, 1964

■ 13. THE NIGHT WATCH; OHARU

The Night Watch is the thirteenth and last feature film signed by the late French stylist Jacques Becker (1906–60). Becker had served all through the thirties as Jean Renoir's assistant, shared Renoir's Popular Front politics, and even made a cameo appearance in *La Grande Illusion* as a British officer. To my knowledge, at least nine of Becker's films have been released in America, but their over-all style is apparently too subtle to register on the crude seismographs of American criticism. Becker's name has had little currency outside the special film magazines, and even *Casque d'Or*, probably his most popular export to the States, is generally regarded as a vehicle for Simone Signoret's distinctive brand of sensuality.

Becker's tragedy, so far as his American reputation is concerned, is the tragedy of the honest craftsman in the marketplace of pretense. *The Night Watch*, particularly, is so well wrought that it makes the feeble frenetics of a *Tom Jones* look like a kindergarten exercise. It is as if Becker had left as his last will and testament a documentation of unself-conscious film-making in the service of pleasurable entertainment. But, then, Becker had always liked American movies and had never affected Pagnol's grainy crudity for the edification of the cliff-dwelling aesthetes of the art circuits— which is another way of saying that Becker's movies are always easier on sybaritic eyes than on angst-seeking souls. Not even Warners has ever turned out a more luminous prison-escape movie than *The Night Watch*.

As a stylist who valued entertainment above edification, Becker projected his personality not so much in his choice of plots, which are often ultraconventional, as in the dreamlike quality of his decor, itself an expression of the fatalistically closed world of the studio movie. By integrating character and setting, Becker generally succeeds in persuading his audience that his plots can end only one way, the way of emotional logic.

In *The Night Watch* five prisoners in a maximum-security prison in Paris attempt to escape. But we have not been with these men very long before we realize that Becker's theme is not liberty, as in Bresson's *A Man Escapes*, but fraternity. There is a moment of breathtaking aeriness when two of the prisoners finally come up through a manhole on a Paris street early and empty in the morning. One of the men, hitherto presented as the genteel, self-indulgent outsider, mentions half-jokingly the possibility of hailing a passing taxi. The other man, a proletarian superhero out of Dovzhenko's *Arsenal*, calmly reminds his companion that their comrades are waiting back in their cell for deliverance. The strongest proof of collective heroism is returning to hell from Paradise to pick up your buddy. One man passes the test; the other flunks. The final sellout to the authorities is superfluous. The poor little rich boy will soon be out, if not truly free, and his comrades will be locked up in solitary, their solidarity unimpaired. "Pauvre Gaspard," says one of the "losers" to their betrayer. The pitying tone of the actor expresses the pitiless attitude of the director. It is a paltry, poultrylike thing indeed for a man to gain personal liberty at the expense of social honor.

The late Kenji Mizoguchi's *Life of Oharu* closed a few weeks ago at the Toho after an ignominiously unprofitable run, and I have been brooding about that fact ever since. (It is scant consolation that the late James Agee, for all his retrospective prestige, was unable to keep Carl Dreyer's *Day of Wrath* alive in an art house for more than a week.) Most of the reviewers were reasonably, if damningly, respectful of *Oharu*, and I must admit that the film's severest detractors are not entirely in error when they complain about the film's slow pace. Even the infidels who snort "soap opera" are not entirely lacking in plausible arguments.

To synopsize *Oharu* is to condemn it. Every disaster known to woman befalls our eponymous heroine. Her first lover is beheaded for class presumption; Oharu and her family are exiled. She becomes a royal concubine, only to have her child taken from her at birth by the jealous, infertile wife of the ruler. Sold by her parents to a house of ill repute, she is cheated by a counterfeiter. When Oharu is fortunate enough to find a loving husband, he is almost immediately murdered by bandits. Retiring to a monastery, she is hounded by a lecherous creditor; compromised, humiliated, expelled. As an aging prostitute she is pointed up to scorn by a Buddhist priest lecturing his disciples on the ultimate folly of a life of pleasure. Just one misfortune after another. Yet Oharu endures. She sees her son one last time, and then wanders into eternity as a street singer, a pagoda-shaped hat forming her last silhouette. In the last frames of the film Oharu pauses, turns to look at a distant pagoda, her spatial and spiritual correlative, and passes off the screen while the pagoda remains.

From the first frame of *Oharu* to the last, one is aware of sublime directional purpose. To understand the full meaning of a Mizoguchi film is to understand the art of direction as a manner of looking at the world rather than as a means of changing it. There is not much that even the greatest director can do with a face or a tree or a river or a sunset beyond determining his personal angle and distance, rhythm and duration. With Mizoguchi's first tracking of Oharu weaving and bobbing across a licentious world to a religious temple, we are in the presence of an awesome parable of womankind.

No director in the history of the cinema has so completely identified with the point of view of the woman. No, not even Ingmar Bergman. In fact, Bergman is somewhat ambivalent about the female role. It is one thing to worship woman's life force; it is quite another to identify such worship, as Mizoguchi does, as an ingenious rationalization of woman's servitude to man's aesthetic desires. One of the most scathing episodes in *Oharu* concerns a beauty contest set up to select a king's concubine. This is the darker side of the Cinderella legend, the feudal arrogance of the male seeking the lucky foot of his life companion, his soulless mate.

Throughout his long, eminently commercial career Mizoguchi kept returning to the theme of the geisha in both ancient and modern times. It is so bizarre to find a male artist of the first rank persistently agitating for the rights of women that there is a tendency to misread the cinema of Mizoguchi. Those who saw the staggering *Sansho the Bailiff* at last year's New York Film Festival can readily confirm that there is nothing pathological about Mizoguchi's concern with the exploitation of women. For Mizoguchi the rights of women are merely a logical extension of the rights of man. It is difficult to think of any philosopher from Aristotle to Zarathustra capable of such logic.

—Village Voice, May 28, 1964

■ 14. GARBOMANIA

"What, when drunk, one sees in other women," Kenneth Tynan once observed with courtly eloquence, "one sees in Garbo sober." Those seeking spiritual intoxication are advised once more to attend the Garbo Festival at the Coronet. *Ninotchka* and *Camille* were run off last week. Coming up are *Anna Christie, Mata Hari, Anna Karenina, Queen Christina,* and *Susan Lenox—Her Rise and Fall.* I dread to think what these five movies would have been like without Garbo, though even with Garbo, *Anna Karenina, Mata Hari* and *Susan Lenox* would take about seven very dry martinis to pass as milestones of cinematic art. Metro millstones around Garbo's beautiful throat is more like it. Yet the mere fact of Her presence on the screen now constitutes aesthetic redemption. Time has lent an aura of inevitability to a one-studio Hollywood career, bad movies and all. Some have mourned over lost opportunities and defaulted challenges with the repertory of Chekhov, Ibsen, not to mention Shakespeare, Sophocles, and Garbo's insane country-man Strindberg. Such mourning was fashionable on Broadway in the thirties, when mere movie stars were guilty until proven inno-cent and nobody seemed to notice how many crap vehicles were endured for the sake of Lynn and Helen, and above all, "Kit" Cornell too proud to go to Hollywood, where all her moony mis-playing of Chekhov could not deceive the cruel camera.

Let's face it. Hollywood in the thirties or in any other era was hardly a colonial outpost of the Old Vic. For the most part Garbo transcended those vehicles that were unworthy of her, and her ac-complished portrayals of Ninotchka, Camille, and Queen Chris-tina cannot be faulted on either intuitive or technical grounds. On a technical level, it is difficult to compare Garbo's screen magic with the stage mastery of a Judith Anderson or an Edith Evans. If it were possible to ignore Garbo's extraordinary beauty, it might be possible to appreciate more fully the subtleties and ironies of her performances. The difference between Garbo and Anderson-Evans is the difference between surprise and control. One never knows what Garbo will do next, short of sacrificing her emotional sin-cerity for a showy effect. Apart from Chaplin, no player of our time has pirouetted so gracefully between tragedy and comedy, be-tween flickers of expression on an encyclopedic face—and how hopelessly pedantic can one be with the face that launched a mil-lion dreams?

The trouble with analyzing Garbo is that her art dissolves in her myth, and her myth seems to transcend even the cinema that first gave it form. The spine-tingling death scene in *Camille* transforms cinema into sculpture. The masthead close-up of *Queen Christina* flattens out the cameraman's perspective from the transparency of a screen to the opaqueness of a canvas. Without benefit of the perpetually avant-garde mannerism of stop-motion, Garbo stops the flow of images on the screen by enslaving the memory of the spectator. Her demoralizing beauty corrupts the optical habits of the wariest critic. After all, the art of the cinema is concerned with montage and camera movements and spatial relationships and deep focus and the composition of images—but what are all these trappings of mise-en-scène to Garbo or Garbo to mise-en-scène? Let us say simply and finally that Garbo is and always has been her own mise-en-scène.

As myth or mise-en-scène, Garbo's inexhaustible visual force has swept away the petty differences between men and women, outdoor woodsmen and interior decorators, hard-boiled professionals and soft-headed dilettantes. What other goddess of the screen could claim equal devotion from Joseph Alsop and Truman Capote? There are no tears in a Garbo film, or any pathos or self-pity. What Garbo offers her worshippers is a vision of life without compromise, love without disenchantment, sexuality without scabrousness.

It is not surprising that Hemingway's Robert Jordan should link Garbo to the almost mythical Maria in *For Whom the Bell Tolls:*

> Maybe it is like the dreams you have when some one you have seen in the cinema comes to your bed at night and is so kind and lovely. He's slept with them all that way when he was asleep in bed. He could remember Garbo still, and Harlow. Yes, Harlow many times. Maybe it was like those dreams. But he could still remember the time Garbo came to his bed the night before the attack at Pozoblanco and she was wearing a soft silky wool sweater when he put his arm around her and when she leaned forward her hair swept forward and over his face and she said why had he never told her that he loved her when she had loved him all this time? She was not shy, nor cold, nor distant. She was just lovely to hold and kind and lovely and like the old days with Jack Gilbert and it was true as though it happened and he loved her much more than Harlow though Garbo was there only once while Harlow—

—*Village Voice,* June 25, 1964

■ *15. MARNIE*

Alfred Hitchcock's *Marnie* is a failure by any standards except the most esoteric. Unfortunately, Hitchcock has never accepted the martyrdom of being misunderstood. At the very least, he has pre-

ferred, quite sensibly, the loot of the supreme entertainer to the
laurels of the sublime enlightener. Is not the forte of a master of
suspense casualties rather than causalities, corpses rather than consciences?

The critic who thinks there is more than meets the eye in a
Hitchcock film proceeds at his own peril. Hitch will never give
the show away. His peculiarly Chestertonian humor enables him
to play both ends of the brow scale against the middle. Directors
like Huston and Zinnemann function best in the realm of semi-
cinema for the semiliterary. Hitchcock, by contrast, is suspended
by an invisible wire between the mandarins and the masses. Call
it ingrained Catholicism or instinctive ambiguity or inspired formalism, but somehow the cinema of Alfred Hitchcock reverberates
with meaning long after the first shock of recognition.

Why, then, is *Marnie* a failure? The subject seems eminently
Hitchcockian. A beautiful but frigid kleptomaniac is trapped into
marriage with her handsome but masochistic employer. After a
disastrous honeymoon featuring rape and near-suicide, the patient
husband drags his wife back to the scene of her childhood trauma.
After equal doses of Sigmund (*Spellbound*) Freud and Graham
(*Potting Shed*) Greene, Marnie is braced for cure and/or salvation.
Hitchcock has succeeded with similarly abnormal relationships in
the past—*Rebecca, Suspicion, Shadow of a Doubt, Notorious, I
Confess, Rear Window,* and *Vertigo* come to mind with especial
lucidity.

In fact, the key to Hitchcock's characterizations is the twist. If
Hitchcockian suspense alternates between crime in future condi-
tional and guilt in past imperfect, Hitchcockian surprise operates
most ideally in revealing hidden depths beneath polished surfaces.
Who could imagine that Ingrid Bergman and Cary Grant in *Notorious* were so neurotically qualified to torture each other? The
trouble with Tippi Hedren and Sean Connery in *Marnie* is that
their surfaces are not polished enough to lend excitement to their
emerging neuroses. *Marnie* is certainly no less meaningful than
Notorious; it is rather in the ratio of pleasure to meaning that
Hitchcock has fallen short, and this will not do. Eisenstein may be
spinach, pure iron for aesthetic corpuscles, and Dreyer high protein
for the soul, but Hitchcock has always been pure carbohydrate for
the palate.

Even in *Marnie* the conventional plot synopsis is meaningless. Mise-en-scène for Hitchcock is not a wild flourish of style but the story itself. The first shot of *Marnie* focuses on an enormous yellow handbag, receding to a rear view of a leggy brunette on a railway platform. Hitchcock's shot syntax is not "brunette with yellow handbag walks on platform" but "yellow handbag with brunette walking on platform." We know what before we know who. We are cued to money before Marnie. Hitchcock has not lost control of his medium. Not by a long shot. He has simply miscalculated his effects. The manner is present, but the magic is absent. His fake sets, particularly of dockside Baltimore, have never been more distracting, and the process shots of Tippi on horseback are appallingly dated. Again, the inability of the leads to hold the foreground imposes an extra burden on the background. Who cared if Rio were in process in *Notorious* when Bergman and Grant held the foreground?

From the opening fancy-floral lettering of the credits through the flamboyant romanticism of the coupling to the patly Freudian finale, *Marnie* seems to feed on the mystique of the forties. This kind of stylistic nostalgia is a mistake for Hitchcock. A Renoir or a Ford can reminisce, because their relationship to their material has always been direct rather than perverse. Hitchcock has always kept an ironic distance, gambling that he could stay ahead of his audience with purely technical means.

Consequently Renoir, Ford, and, yes, Chaplin can be forgiven more readily for ragged edges than can their more devious colleague. Not only is Master Alfred forced to answer for the clumsy performances of Martin Gabel as Marnie's lecherous victim, Sidney Strutt, and Louise Latham as Marnie's Put-the-Blame-on-Mama. He is also guilty of wasting the interesting faces of Diane Baker and Mariette (*Ride the High Country*) Hartley. Curiously disjointed dialogue with dated slang hardly helps to jolly things along, particularly with the peripheral characters. The binary scenario for costars of equal magnitude is probably to blame for the fact that Sean Connery is introduced much too early in the film, and Tippi Hedren much too late in her larcenous career.

Finally, Hitchcock becomes almost as rhetorical as Martin Ritt about Marnie's modus operandi without giving his audience an adequate frame of reference for his one try at old-fashioned sus-

pense. Marnie is seen long-shot looting her future husband's safe.
The cleaning woman enters an adjacent room encompassed in the
same shot. We see Marnie and cleaning woman at the same time.
Yet the scene fizzles; humorous coda off-key. Reasons? Audience
insufficiently implicated in the action. Lighting wrong. Spatial references vague; i.e., where and how far is safe and out? The master
of suspense has struck out in his own park.

—*Village Voice*, July 9, 1964

■ 16. *MONSIEUR VERDOUX*

I

If this were the most fitting of all possible worlds, Chaplin would
have dedicated the current revival of *Monsieur Verdoux* to the
late James Agee in the generous spirit of Renoir's dedication of the
restored *La Règle du Jeu* to the late André Bazin. Agee's extensive
comments on Chaplin's "comedy of murders" appeared originally
in the *Time* of May 5, 1947, and the *Nation* of May 31, June 14,
and June 21, 1947, and are reprinted in a new paperback entitled
Agee on Film—Reviews and Comments by James Agee. I do not
entirely agree with Agee's position on *Verdoux*, but I admire the
force and lucidity of his arguments. Not only has he prevailed posthumously over the negative critical consensus of his time but he
has kept *Verdoux* alive and legendary through seventeen years of
nonexhibition.

What, then, is left to say about Verdoux after Agee? As Anna
Magnani replies in *The Golden Coach* when asked if she misses
her lovers: "a leetle." Time, no less than seventeen years' worth,
has altered the context of Chaplin's ironic conceits. Back in 1947
Monsieur Verdoux was disconcerting not merely to the rabble of
the right but to the prevailing liberal optimism about the per-
fectibility of man. Agee was most perceptive about this latter aspect of his Zeitgeist: "At a time when many people have regained
their faith in war under certain conditions and in free enterprise
under any conditions whatever, he [Chaplin] has ventured to in-

sist, as bitterly as he knows how, that there are considerable elements of criminality implicit in both."

Note, however, that *Verdoux* follows *The Great Dictator* by seven years, and yet recedes historically to the early thirties of *Modern Times*. The internal evidence of newspapers indicates crucial decisions in 1932. We see newsreels of Hitler and Mussolini like a recurring dream of *The Great Dictator* while the insanely logical world of Monsieur Verdoux collapses around him. When Verdoux taunts his judges about a future war, it is not clear whether he is predicting World War II fatuously or World War III fatalistically.

Why does Chaplin cling to the dead past for his background? To my mind, Agee never satisfactorily answered this question. Normally a retreat into the past indicates an artist's desire to distance his material from a rigorous moral accounting, but Chaplin and Verdoux are so inextricably linked that both creator and creature are implicated in each other's activities. I suspect that Chaplin's solipsism as an artist translates his personal bitterness into political malaise at least as often as his social conscience translates political malaise into personal bitterness. It is only natural that the world seems more wicked as we grow older. What is amazing about Chaplin is the mellowing process between *Verdoux* and *Limelight*. Perhaps it is not so amazing if we consider *Verdoux* as Chaplin's last dialogue with a drifting audience, and *Limelight* as his first soliloquy before a departed audience.

Even today *Monsieur Verdoux* will seem a failure to anyone who has taken half a dozen lessons in film technique. Things were much worse, however, back in 1947 when Chaplin was squeezed between the patrons of Hollywood illusionism on one hand and the partisans of Italian neorealism on the other. *Verdoux* is neither slick enough for the dream merchants nor sincere enough for the humanists, and this is not necessarily all to the good, as Agee seemed to suggest. There are distinct pleasures in both stylistic elaboration of a dream apparatus and the God-given ambiguity and accident of raw realism.

These pleasures are not to be found in *Verdoux* or in the rest of Chaplin. What we get instead is the genius of economy and essentiality, and it follows that the most drab moments in *Verdoux* are also the most functional. Indeed, the opening exposition involving the family of a Verdoux victim is about as bad as anything I have ever seen in the professional cinema. Yet after repeated reviewings, the badness seems not only integral to Chaplin's conception but decidedly Brechtian in the bargain. Chaplin has stacked the deck shamelessly and crudely, but as soon as he makes his first entrance in his rose garden with his meticulous hands and pliers ravishing sweet nature, all is forgiven, particularly the smoking remains of his wife in the incinerator.

II

If 1947 audiences were too reluctant to laugh at the cruelty in Monsieur Verdoux, today's crowds may be too eager. We are becoming so oversatirized that our capacity for pity and terror is rapidly shrinking to bread-and-circuses dimensions. Perhaps all the sick jokes of the past decade have finally come home to roost in the nomination of Barry (Triumph of the Won't) Gauleiter (sic, sic, sic), and we'll all be laughing on the way to the concentration camp. I certainly hope not. However, aside from ultimate consequences, excessive risibility tends to obscure the distinction between jokes and japes. If people can laugh even slightly at the moronic slapstick of Bedtime Story, Chaplin might just as well regress to slipping on banana peels. The paradox here is that Monsieur Verdoux seems much greater as a popular failure than as a popular success. After all, Chaplin ends up thumbing his nose at his audience, a gesture performed with great difficulty when the audience insists on embracing the artist. It may be, as Cocteau once remarked, that it is the fate of iconoclasts to become icons. Then again, Chaplin's reputation may at last be filtering out of his audience all those who are not at least tolerant of his vaguely leftist and agnostic convictions.

There are some bad gags in Verdoux. The fat woman who falls asleep after dinner in the Verdoux cottage is incomprehensibly obvious and overdone. The business with Martha Raye's maid losing her hair is both ugly and uninspired, and the strenuous contrivances by which the poison is misplaced in the same episode are too farfetched for the logic of farce. The functional family of one of Verdoux's victims is a five-pronged ordeal on every occasion it is summoned to advance the plot, particularly when any comically exaggerated reaction is demanded.

Fortunately the great moments are far more numerous and infinitely more memorable. The hilarity I found richest and deepest was inspired not by the famous boat scene with Martha Raye but by that fantastic surprise when Chaplin comes dancing into Isobel Elsom's apartment with satyrlike abandon to embrace Miss Elsom's fat, ugly housekeeper before discovering his mistake. The rest of the scene is drowned out by the convulsed audience as Chaplin commits a second gaffe with Miss Elsom's lady friend and then pauses in perplexity for Miss Elsom herself. Beneath the laughter is the most incisive expression of the pathos and tragedy of Don Juanism I have ever encountered. Until one has seen Chaplin in *Verdoux* one cannot fully realize how little has been done with sex and desire on the screen. We have had gigolos and foolish old women and May-December and December-December romances, but little of the pain and anguish that accompanies the perversion of romantic emotion.

There is a distant parallel, for example, between Chaplin-Elsom and Groucho Marx–Margaret Dumont. Groucho always treated Miss Dumont shamefully, too shamefully, in fact, for realism to intrude on comic fantasy. Deep down we have always known that Groucho is too much of a gentleman and Miss Dumont too much of a lady for anything irrevocably sordid to occur. Groucho's excessive rudeness is actually a form of gallantry, enabling Miss Dumont to withdraw from his bedroom without being deeply humiliated. Groucho takes the burden of outrageousness upon himself because he can afford to let people see through him. He has nothing to hide; his transparency is merely the means by which he deflates the pomposity of others.

Chaplin-Verdoux is more desperate. Despite his courtliness, he is no gentleman. He is a man. Unlike Groucho, he is not a fraud, however hilariously transparent. He accepts his part of the bargain. He seduces his old, ugly victims before he murders them, but he knows the day will come when he will be too old even for the last dregs of wealthy womanhood. It is a measure of Chaplin's incredible instinct for counterpoint that his ugliest victim (Margaret Hoffman) ignites the brightest flame of his poetic imagination. Gazing out the window upon a paper moon against a *papier-mâché* sky, he pauses in the trajectory of his murderous task to choreograph "this Endymion hour" with his eloquent body. His victim summons him to her doom, but the shot of his poetic universe is held. The murder, an act of imaginative schizophrenia, is performed musically offscreen.

Chaplin gets laughs along the way with his businesslike briskness. Whether he is counting his ill-gotten francs with the page-flipping technique of a bank teller or courting a victim by his timepiece or complaining to his adoring wife (Mady Corell) about the stresses and strains of business, Chaplin expertly performs all the scales of social parody. It is possible to deduce that he is attacking capitalism, war, business ethics, family solidarity, bourgeois morality. These are mundane matters for Chaplin's genius. Where he rises with the angels is in the self-revelation of his sexual relationships, particularly with man-eating Martha Raye, the supreme expression of the otherness of life forces in Chaplin's cinema. All the wiles of Verdoux are of course futile against Martha's luck and vitality. (The fiasco on the lake should make it impossible for An American Tragedy to be filmed ever again.) Verdoux is clearly appalled by Martha, a creature of force without style. However, Martha's extreme raucousness may be Chaplin's method, conscious or unconscious, of masking what he really finds objectionable in her, namely her perversity. Perversity doesn't go with pedestals. Chaplin's heroines almost invariably begin by loving outer handsomeness and end by perceiving inner goodness. A casual glance at dating couples on Saturday night should dispel that notion. Even granting that beautiful faces are screen metaphors for beautiful souls, Chaplin underestimates the range of choices involved in feminine free will. Women are too much an extension of his angst-ridden ego, too much an index of his moral sensibility, for him ever to acknowledge their ultimate separateness.

Where Chaplin indulges himself to some extent is in his overly abstract, overly philosophical dialogue. His relationship to Marilyn Nash's tall waif is expressed almost entirely in aphorisms of the I-am-an-optimist-you-are-a-pessimist variety. The beauty of these speeches derives from the effort of Chaplin's expressive face to determine hidden meanings, if any, from the echoes of the sound track. It is interesting that most critics have created the impression that the last line of Verdoux is, in reply to a priest's unctuously routine "May God have mercy on your soul," the metaphysically defiant "Why not? After all, it belongs to Him." The abstraction, it would seem, to end abstractions. However, Chaplin's last line is actually, "Wait, I've never tasted rum." Verdoux drinks the rum. He throws his chest out to the sunlight pouring into the cell as the door opens. The camera follows him through the door and then parks by the hall so that he may turn his back to the audience and show just a hint of the way the Tramp would have walked to the guillotine. The hint is sufficient for sublime recognition. In the end as in the beginning, Chaplin belongs to the things of this world— rum and sunshine—and not to the things beyond—souls and such.

—*Village Voice*, July 16 and 23, 1964

■ 17. THE POOR GIRL:
   A REVIEW OF *HARLOW*,
   BY IRVING SHULMAN

Harlow, by Irving Shulman (Bernard Geis Associates), is the sort of book you can't put down even when common decency demands you throw up. Readability in this instance is directly proportional to reprehensibility, and it is fitting that the dust jacket labels the dirt between the sheets not merely a biography but an "intimate" biography. "Like most people," Irving Shulman confesses at the outset, "I had, at first, been drawn by the sensational aspects of her life, by a desire to know what had really happened in one of the most publicized scandals of modern times. But as the doors were opened and the secrets and sorrows were revealed"—the author adds reassuringly—"I realized that Arthur Landau had told me a truly classic story, the tragedy of a woman and her time."

Mr. Landau, now in his seventies, is described elsewhere as "Jean's discoverer and agent" and "much closer to Jean than any member of her family." From what we are told of Jean's family, Landau's closeness is not that much of a compliment.

Unfortunately, a series of hideously grotesque catastrophes cannot add up to tragedy. Nor can the late Jean Harlow be charged posthumously with hubris. The poor girl seems to have spent most of her life being abused and exploited by a series of leeches and lechers who make the denizens of *Deer Park* look positively saintly by comparison. If the author and his source are to be believed, Jean was finally murdered by the nastiness, pettiness, and meanness that had engulfed her in her short, unhappy life as a nation's sex goddess.

Jean Harlow, born Harlean Carpentier in Kansas City, Kansas, of middle-class parents on March 3, 1911, died of uremic poisoning and Mama Jean's fanatical Christian Science on June 6, 1937. The most prevalent gossip of the time was that Harlow had died of a bungled abortion. Shulman rejects the abortion rumor and many others equally lurid. Injuries to the kidneys inflicted by her first husband, misguided maternal neglect, studied studio indifference all contributed to a medically untimely death. Metro, a studio of jackals masquerading as lions, hushed up the circumstances of death to avoid offending the nation's Christian Scientists. The resulting damage to Miss Harlow's reputation hardly weighed in the balance.

Shulman indicts in his bill of particulars not only an array of villains the late Clifford Odets would have found too odious for *The Big Knife*, but also Southern California, Hollywood, the motion picture industry, the star system, the profit motive, and popular mythology. We have been over this terrain more imaginatively in Nathanael West's *The Day of the Locust*, F. Scott Fitzgerald's Pat Hobby stories and *The Last Tycoon*, John Dos Passos' Margo-Hollywood episodes in *U.S.A.*, and Budd Schulberg's *What Makes Sammy Run?* Shulman's style and sensibility is actually closer to the Harold Robbins level, although the content of *Harlow* is far more sensational than that of *The Carpetbaggers*. Fleshing out the bare bones of scandal with a mixture of two-bit psychology and dime-store sociology, Shulman has achieved the difficult feat of cheapening his fictions with his facts, and his facts with his fictions. The author attains a peak of tastelessness (and readability) with his graphic account of Paul Bern's diminutive member of the wedding and the pathetic pulp-mag-ad device of supplementation. The weird Walpurgisnacht before Bern's suicide evokes the kind of images a more imaginative mind would mask as a nightmare of deformed sexuality. Shulman's sober tone in this satanic context is too ludicrous for words.

Significantly, Shulman provides no filmography, no coherent account of Harlow's career. There is little evidence that the author did any special research on the Harlow movies to determine how they stand up today. His dedication to "Jean Harlow fans who will endure the worst television commercials to see once again their Blonde Bombshell" is also a form of dissociation. Shulman is obviously no Harlow fan himself, and he grossly underrates her talent. Referring to *Bombshell*, Shulman quotes Franchot Tone as complaining about having to read such ridiculous lines as "I'd like to run barefoot through your hair." Tone did read such a line, but the scene was played for laughs as part of a studio-arranged masquerade set up by a glib press agent (Lee Tracy). Also, Harlow's father in the same film is played not by Ralph Morgan, as Shulman mistakenly states, but by Ralph's brother, Frank. These two errors, minor enough in themselves, indicate merely that Shulman has never seen one of the most popular, most characteristic, and most famous of all Harlow performances. He leans heavily on routine reviews of the period, and most of these are unfavorable. He contrasts his own worldliness with the gush printed in fan magazines and tabloids, but ignores the more intelligent pieces written on Harlow in her lifetime.

Elsewhere Shulman betrays an ignorance of movie history generally: "Before 1920 movies still were in the novelty category and studio people and performers held the same status in Hollywood as their predecessors had in 16th and 17th century England: vagrant vagabonds subject to arrest unless they had placed themselves under the protective sponsorship of an influential courtier." The banana oil in the preceding passage is of a sufficient concentration to revitalize the Guatemalan economy. Mary and Doug and Charlie sold zillions of Liberty Bonds in 1918 in mob scenes unsurpassed to this day even by the Beatles. It is Shulman's thesis that the three sex goddesses up to 1937 were Theda Bara, Clara Bow, and Jean Harlow—a thesis most film historians would dismiss as hopelessly superficial.

The author's ignorance is matched by his condescension. Movies, in Shulman's eyes, are fraudulent manipulations of the masses, and Harlow, like Paddy Chayefsky's heroine in *The Goddess*, would have been much happier if she had never become a big movie star. Admittedly, heavenly bodies find their orbits only at the cost of a profound disorientation, but given her parents and her environment, Harlow might have been even more unhappy as a nonentity.

The asylums are full of nonentities, and few movie stars threaten to jump out of tenement windows for the sake of a little attention. Indeed, many of the would-be jumpers are looking for the same attention and recognition accorded to movie stars. Stardom calms as many neuroses as it creates. The price of making the top may be high, but the price of not making it may be even higher.

The exact extent of Jean Harlow's talents is debatable, and Shulman's dislike of Harlow and movies generally hardly disqualifies him as a chronicler. Nonetheless some of his judgments should be taken with a grain of Suetonian salt. For a debunker, Shulman is remarkably naïve about non-Harlow myths. Harlow's posturing at its worst was more interesting than Norma Shearer's cross-eyed sincerity, and at comparable stages in their careers, Harlow was far more adept than Myrna Loy at reading lines for mood and meaning. Harlow's best films—*Dinner at Eight, Bombshell, Reckless,* and *Libeled Lady*—were considerably more entertaining than high-priced limburger like *The Barretts of Wimpole Street* and *The Good Earth,* to which Shulman refers as Irving J. Thalberg's "quality" productions. Thalberg and Shearer are treated like royalty here, and why not? Shulman can't follow this ridiculously affected couple from the boudoir to the bathroom and back as he does Harlow, and so somehow, like the rest of the Hollywood hypocrites, they must be less fleshy than Jean.

Another factor in the author's unfair treatment of Harlow is the ghoulish criterion of exposure. Generally speaking, the dirt is spilled on those upon whom the dirt has been shoveled. Norma Shearer is still alive, and she could sue. Harlow and her family are dead, and so anything goes. This policy of selective scandal causes some bizarre blind spots. Howard Hughes, who has appeared *à clef* in Hollywood novels and films as the King of the Casting Couch, is alive and solvent, and consequently he is treated gingerly by Shulman as the all-business employer of Miss Harlow. William Powell, who gave Miss Harlow a huge engagement ring and paid all her funeral expenses, is too much in this world to be described as anything more than a fraternal adviser. A genuine novelist would strip all characters of their pretenses, or none, and Harlow might emerge as the most honest of the lot.

As it is, Miss Harlow's leading costar is not the late Paul Bern, who serves only for some brutal slapstick, but the late L. B. Mayer, whom Lillian Ross carved up with her stenographic scalpel in *Picture*. Shulman never comes up with anything as precise as the "Kick the old lady down the stairs" sequence reported by Miss Ross, but he does capture some of the colorful crudity of absolute power when Mayer objects to Harlow's second marriage:

"I'm all for religion." Mayer addressed himself to Strickling while he permitted Arthur to stew in the vinegar of penance. "Some of my best friends are Christians. And I know a couple of fine, refined niggers I'd have a cup of coffee with and I wouldn't be offended if they picked up the check. But I don't believe in mixing things up. Jews should get married to Jews. German Jews to German Jews. And Christians should marry Christians."

"Mr. Mayer, please," Arthur raised his head. "I'd like to say—"

"Speak when you're spoken to," Mayer cut him off. "What was I saying?" he asked Strickling. "Oh yes, Christians should marry Christians. Christian people should marry their own kind. That's the way that's best for everybody. And another thing, Howard, in Jewish homes we seldom have divorces. We don't have drunks and run-arounds and we don't have divorces," he stated proudly. "And I don't like to see a nice Jewish boy's heart broken by a divorce."

"Rosson's not Jewish," Arthur said. Mayer gasped, but Arthur continued to nod vigorously. "He was born in England and baptized in an English church." He raised his right hand. "It's true."

Mayer turned to Strickling. "Is he telling the truth?"

"He is," Strickling said.

"So why doesn't someone tell me?" Mayer asked his ceiling.

My favorite scene dramatizes the classic situation of the producer offering the star a mink coat for services to be rendered.

"I don't think I can take it, Mr. Mayer."

He laughed again. "Take it? I'm giving it. It's in there"—he gestured toward the corridor that led to the bath and bedroom—"so get undressed and try it on."

"I can't," Jean shook her head. "You see, I haven't got a present for you. At least nothing I really want to give you."

Mayer trotted from the room and returned quickly with the dark mink coat. He spread it across the sofa, and in the flicker of the flames the skins gleamed with the sheen of burnished copper. Proudly he gestured that the coat was Jean's. "And I'll bet my life and the furrier's too that in your collection there isn't a coat like this. Every skin chosen for the skin and body of a queen. Or a goddess. So what else would you like to give me when I've already made clear exactly what I want?"

"Plenty," Jean said as she crossed to stroke the coat. "I'd like to give you the clap. And if I had it you could have it for nothing. Matter of fact I'd pay you."

Needless to say, Mayer threw her out of his bungalow. But if Jean really said what Shulman has recorded, and if she had never said anything else, there would be through all the eternities of the oppressed a touch of Spartacus in Harlow.

—*Village Voice*, July 30, 1964

■ 18. *NOTHING BUT THE BEST*

Clive Donner's direction of *Nothing But the Best* resembles at first glance the style of a slow-ball pitcher: lots of windup with little follow-through, more manner than matter, effective control gained at the expense of lush entertainment values. Donner's preciseness of effect, so admirably evident in his mise-en-scène for *The Guest,* the film version of Harold Pinter's *The Caretaker,* seems almost too much of a good thing here. Some of the feeling of incongruity can be attributed to the fact that *Nothing But the Best* has been filmed in color. Most of us have been conditioned by decades of formal puritanism to associate color with empty-headed frivolity and scenic delights. Conversely, to be "serious" or "realistic" implies the funereal contrasts of black and white—"superfluous and distracting," complains one anti-color anchorite of nonsensuous persuasion. Old visual habits die hard, but I have finally come around to the point where I think all commercial movies should be in color. Most black-and-white efforts look less serious and realistic than cheap and pretentious. I except, of course, the austere tonal stylization of a Bresson in *The Trial of Joan of Arc* and a Godard in *My Life to Live*, but the colorlessness of *Night of the Iguana* is sheer bargain-basement affectation. Color is a naturalistic resource like sound, and, like sound, it will be denounced as superfluous and distracting long after it has become aesthetically indispensable.

Once we have accepted the incongruity of a dark comedy like *Nothing But the Best* in dazzling color, we are confronted with the apparent superficiality of an anti-cliché scenario adapted by Frederic Raphael from a melodramatic short story by Stanley Ellin. In fact, *Nothing But the Best* has been heralded as a spoof of every creepy climber from *Room at the Top* to *How to Succeed in Business Without Really Trying*. The danger of avoiding clichés too strenuously involves a form of negative predictability that keeps reminding the audience of the original clichés. It may seem clever to have two gunfighters miss each other in their climactic duel at high noon, but this extreme example is sheer stupidity. *Nothing But the Best* manages to be more subtle in its spoofing by exaggerating some clichés and reversing others.

Alan Bates, our ambitious hero, starts out sounding like something left over from *Saturday Night and Sunday Morning* with a precredit reference to "a filthy, stinking world"—as it turns out, the overture to an ironic ritual of conscious self-deception. Donner and his colleagues have perceived the deeper falseness of the room-at-the-bottom, angry-young-man tradition, and that is a lingering sentimentality about the lower classes accompanied by the motivational correlative of the poor being corrupted more by upper-class values than by their own poverty. The dreadfully "sincere" scenes of Joe Lampton with his mum and dad are skillfully parodied by Alan Bates with the vicious grace of a benefactor shipping out his embarrassingly plebeian parents to grotesquely egalitarian Australia. "What have we done to deserve such a son?" says Mum with touching gratitude—an index of the script's occasionally obvious irony.

Obvious, too, is the symbolism of royal substitution in the relationship of Bates (James the Pretender) and Denholm Elliott

(Bonnie Prince Charlie alias Charlie Prince). Bates meets Elliott in a shabby London restaurant with the kind of sweeping camera movement Donner thoughtfully reserves for the expression of identity transference. It is great fun as a down-at-the-heels gentleman gaily instructs a rising plebe in the art of a graybrick education, and there is no moral wrench for Bates when Elliott insists that one never has a kind word for Schweitzer, or an unkind one for Hitler. Bates and the lower classes he represents are sick and rotten to the core even without the intervention of Elliott and his intransigently Blimpish ilk.

Where some critics and audiences part company with *Nothing But the Best* is at the point at which Bates strangles Elliott with the old-school tie, seduces the nympho landlady into silence about the body, and marries Elliott's vergenal (rather than virginal) sister (Millicent Martin), the only girl in London who says no on the first date and yes on the second, and a refreshing switch from the traditionally easy lays of the British aristocracy. The unexpected murder is startling enough in itself, but what is particularly unusual is that the bubbling humor on the surface of the film continues with a dead body in the house. The Bates character, like Billy Liar, expresses his murderous thoughts in interior monologues, but whereas Billy Liar fizzles out, Bates acts with moral logic. Great art never shrinks from the obvious if to do so means to cheat and tease. Early in the first act of Chekhov's *Three Sisters*, Solyoni suggests jestingly that he will put a bullet in Tusenbach's head. The fatal bullet is delivered late in the fourth act. Admittedly on a lower level of creation, Donner makes murder inevitable with three ominous jump-cuts of Elliott brutally divesting Bates of his symbolic trappings.

—*Village Voice*, August 6, 1964

■ 19. THE BEST MAN

The Best Man, Gore Vidal's second play, opened in New York on March 31, 1960, toward the end of the bland Eisenhower era with its aura of invincible smugness. The year 1960 was, of course, a convention and election quadrennial, and for the first time in eight years the ultimate outcome was a betting proposition. In liberal demonology, the McCarthy hard smear had been replaced by the Nixon soft slash. Consequently *The Best Man* functioned best when its allegorical archetypes suggested real-life politicians. A *Time* subscription was not required for the deduction that William Russell, who would rather be pure than President, passed reasonably well for Adlai Stevenson. The fit was even tighter for unscrupulously pragmatic Joseph Cantwell as Dick Nixon. Melvyn Douglas and Frank Lovejoy, two tired character actors, were evenly if uninspiringly matched in Vidal's convention fireworks, but the play, and later the picture, was dominated by Lee Tracy's ripsnorting outbursts as Arthur Hockstader, or Truman transcended.

Now, four years and two Presidents later, *The Best Man* has come to the screen, considerably improved in the process of transition. The original casting imbalance that reduced Douglas and Lovejoy to mere antagonists in the presence of Tracy's protagonist has been righted somewhat by the substitution of Henry Fonda and Cliff Robertson in the Stevenson-Nixon roles. Fonda and Robertson not only act more subtly than Douglas and Lovejoy, they are richer in those iconographical associations that enable movies to excel in the realm of intermediate excellence. Over the years Fonda has become entrenched as Hollywood's populist of the Left, virtually in opposition to James Stewart's populist of the ruggedly individualistic Right. Against Fonda's classic awkwardness, Robertson's compressed grace makes its own comment on the modern politician losing in passion what he gains in poise. In fact, Robertson can serve double duty in 1964 as an approximation of both Dick Nixon and Bobby Kennedy, on record as two of Gore Vidal's lesser enthusiasms. To round out the analogies, Fonda portrayed young Abe Lincoln more than a quarter of a century ago, and Robertson young Jack Kennedy less than a year ago.

Under Franklin Shaffner's intelligently graded direction, *The Best Man* has profited in its adaptation to the screen simply by being exposed to the hot air of Southern California. Even Jo Mielziner's pointedly vulgar stage suites pale in comparison with the camera's casual documentation of a Los Angeles hotel bleached by the sun into a dim replica of a dwelling for humans. More important is the sheer sensuousness of power unveiled for its own sake as spectacle. One shot of a frenzied convention may not be worth a thousand words of Vidal's rhetorical discussion of power and responsibility, but said shot at the very least provides the kind and scope of objective correlative singularly lacking on an austere stage. Finally, the interplay of helicopters, walkie-talkies, and double-entry television screens establishes the cinema's ascendancy over the theater as the medium of modernity.

Casting coups and technical flourishes aside, *The Best Man* remains a writer's picture—that is, one writer's picture—and the critical problem is determining whose ox is being gored. Nixon's? Stevenson's? The electorate's? In an article, "Notes on *The Best Man*" (*Theatre Arts*, July 1960), Mr. Vidal wrote, "I use the theatre as a place to criticize society, to satirize folly, to question presuppositions." Allowing for the inherent pomposity of such statements of intention, the author's tone is a striking blend of condescension and civic-mindedness, a highbrow's acknowledgment of the mass media, an intellectual diving from his ivory tower of self-expression (the novel) into the mainstream of social responsibility (the dramatized pamphlet).

If, as a consequence of Vidal's cultural ambivalence, *The Best Man* is a sample of middlebrow art, it is nevertheless surprisingly good middlebrow art, a domain where talent is more decisive than genius. Curiously, Vidal's scabrous plot intrigues—I-won't-tell-them-you've-been-accused-of-homosexuality-if-you-don't-tell-them-I've-had-a-nervous-breakdown—are even less convincing than similarly lurid contrivances in *Advise and Consent* and *The Manchurian Candidate*. Nor is Vidal too often on target with his political shafts. The idea that a Dick Nixon or Bobby Kennedy could gain national prominence by falsely linking the Mafia to the Communist party is too implausible for even the broadest burlesque of congressional witch-hunting. It is also unlikely that two candidates as far apart on basic issues as Russell and Cantwell would quibble about tactics and personality differences. After all, the difference between Stevenson and Nixon is one of ends as well as means, and the Kennedy-Nixon debate over Quemoy and Matsu was more significant than Vidal indicated in a recent *New York Times* publicity story on *The Best Man*. In the heat of debate both candidates fell back on their reflexes. Kennedy chose to avoid a sign of recklessness, Nixon a sign of weakness. In the light of the subsequent Cuban confrontation, the Quemoy-Matsu exchange was a crucial revelation of character.

For Vidal, however, character is less decisive than image. The author's unsuccessful congressional campaign in New York's heavily Republican Second District has undoubtedly contributed to his cynicism about the effect of issues on the body politic. Consequently the modifications of his stage play for the screen do not alter the basic relationships of his characters. Jokes about birth control have been replaced by jokes about civil rights. References to disarmament and recognition of Red China have been dropped outright, and Lee Tracy's Rabelaisian showstopper—"I personally do not care if Joe Cantwell enjoys deflowering sheep by the light of a full moon"—has been wittily mechanized in tune with the agricultural revolution to "I personally do not care if Joe Cantwell has carnal knowledge of a McCormick reaper."

Where play and screenplay are perfectly consistent is in the focus on command decisions. "My God," Hockstader exclaims to Russell, "what would happen if you had to make a quick decision in the White House when maybe all our lives depended on whether you could act fast . . . and you just sat there, the way you're doing now, having a high old time with your divided conscience?" To Russell's denial of a divided conscience, Hockstader echoes Orwell's essay on Gandhi: "Be a saint on your own time."

The final Russell-Hockstader exchange on power has the eerie ring of Vidal's own internal dialogue as a tormented literary-political creature.

> *Russell:* And so, one by one, these compromises, these small corruptions destroy character.
>
> *Hockstader:* To want power is corruption already. Dear God, you hate yourself for being human.
>
> *Russell:* No. I only want to be human . . . and it is not easy. Once this thing starts, there is no end to it, which is why it should never begin. And if I start . . . Well, Art, how does it end, this sort of thing?
>
> *Hockstader:* In the grave, son, where the dust is neither good nor bad, but just nothing.

Ultimately the "best" man is neither the white knight of liberal idealism nor the white hope of conservative opportunism but a faceless gray compromise candidate. Russell sacrifices himself to stop Cantwell, who displays his first sustained flash of lucidity *vis-à-vis* Russell: "You don't understand me. You don't understand politics. You don't understand this country and the way it is and the way we are. You are a fool."

If *The Best Man* leaves a sour aftertaste, it is because Adlai Stevenson seems to have been savaged unfairly and inaccurately. Stevenson did his best—on the health issue, even his unscrupulous best—to win both elections against Eisenhower. He could probably have defeated Dewey, Taft, Nixon, or Goldwater in turn, but missed all four to confront the one invincible candidate of his time. Bad luck? Of course. But bad luck is not the stuff of drama, and neither is bad timing. What is interesting about the liberal disenchantment with Stevenson is the distinctively American intolerance of failure. De Gaulle can greet Mendès-France with mingled amusement and affection—"Ah, Mendès, you have come to tell me you are torn"—but in America it is two strikes and you're out, Adlai, particularly when otherwise alienated intellectuals are so eager to embrace the cult of experience and to worship men of action.

Nonetheless *The Best Man* is still well above average screen entertainment. If the box office pluralities have not materialized to date in either urban wards or rural precincts, we can blame the last vestiges of the star system up to a certain point. Beyond that is the inescapable conclusion that politics, like baseball, is more fact than fable. The sixty-four-dollar question in '64 is not whether Johnson *should* defeat Goldwater, but whether he *will* or *not*.

—*Village Voice*, August 20, 1964

■ 20. *A HARD DAY'S NIGHT*

A Hard Day's Night is a particularly pleasant surprise in a year so full of unexpectedly unpleasant surprises. I have no idea who is the most responsible—director Richard Lester or screenwriter Alun Owen or the Messrs. John Lennon, Paul McCartney, George Harrison, and Ringo Starr, better known collectively as the Beatles.

Perhaps it was all a happy accident, and the lightning of inspiration will never strike again in the same spot. The fact remains that *A Hard Day's Night* has turned out to be the *Citizen Kane* of jukebox musicals, the brilliant crystallization of such diverse cultural particles as the pop movie, rock 'n' roll, *cinéma vérité*, the *nouvelle vague*, free cinema, the affectedly hand-held camera, frenzied cutting, the cult of the sexless subadolescent, the semidocumentary, and studied spontaneity. So help me, I resisted the Beatles as long as I could. As a cab driver acquaintance observed, "So what's new about the Beatles? Didn't you ever hear of Ish Kabibble?" Alas, I had. I kept looking for openings to put down the Beatles. Some of their sly crows' humor at the expense of a Colonel Blimp character in a train compartment is a bit too deliberate. "I fought the war for people like you," sez he. "Bet you're sorry you won," sez they. Old Osborne ooze, sez I. But just previously, the fruitiest looking of the four predators had looked up enticingly at the bug-eyed Blimp and whimpered "Give us a kiss." Depravity of such honest frankness is worth a hundred pseudoliterary exercises like *Becket*.

Stylistically, *A Hard Day's Night* is everything Tony Richardson's version of *Tom Jones* tried to be and wasn't. Thematically, it is everything Peter Brook's version of *Lord of the Flies* tried to be and wasn't. Fielding's satiric gusto is coupled here with Golding's primordial evil, and the strain hardly shows. I could have done with a bit less of a false saber-toothed, rattling wreck of an old man tagged with sickeningly repetitious irony as a "clean" old man. The pop movie mannerisms of the inane running joke about one of the boys' managers being sensitively shorter than the other might have been dispensed with at no great loss.

The foregoing are trifling reservations, however, about a movie that works on every level for every kind of audience. The open-field helicopter-shot sequence of the Beatles on a spree is one of the most exhilarating expressions of high spirits I have seen on the screen. The razor-slashing wit of the dialogue must be heard to be believed and appreciated. One as horribly addicted to alliteration as this otherwise sensible scribe can hardly resist a line like "Ringo's drums loom large in his legend."

I must say I enjoyed even the music enormously, possibly because I have not yet been traumatized by transistors into open rebellion against the "top 40" and such. (I just heard "Hello, Dolly"

for the first time the other day, and the lyrics had been changed to
"Hello, Lyndon"). Nevertheless I think there is a tendency to
underrate rock 'n' roll because the lyrics look so silly in cold print.
I would make two points here. First, it is unfair to compare R&R
with Gershwin, Rodgers, Porter, Kern, *et al.*, as if all pre-R&R
music from Tin Pan Alley was an uninterrupted flow of melodi-
ousness. This is the familiar fallacy of nostalgia. I remember too
much brassy noise from the big-bands era to be stricken by the
incursions of R&R. I like the songs the Beatles sing despite the
banality of the lyrics, but the words in R&R only mask the pound-
ingly ritualistic meaning of the beat. It is in the beat that the
passion and togetherness is most movingly expressed, and it is the
beat that the kids in the audience pick up with their shrieks as they
drown out the words they have already heard a thousand times.
To watch the Beatles in action with their constituents is to watch
the kind of direct theater that went out with Aristophanes, or perhaps even the Australian bushman. There is an empathy there that
a million Lincoln Center Repertory companies cannot duplicate.
Toward the end of *A Hard Day's Night* I began to understand the
mystique of the Beatles. Lester's crane shot facing the audience
from behind the Beatles established the emotional unity of the
performers and their audience. It is a beautifully Bazinian deep-
focus shot of hysteria to a slow beat punctuated by the kind of
zoom shots I have always deplored in theory but must now admire
in practice. Let's face it. My critical theories and preconceptions are
all shook up, and I am profoundly grateful to the Beatles for such
a pleasurable softening of hardening aesthetic arteries.

As to what the Beatles "mean," I hesitate to speculate. The
trouble with sociological analysis is that it is unconcerned with
aesthetic values. *A Hard Day's Night* could have been a complete
stinker of a movie and still be reasonably "meaningful." I like the
Beatles in this moment in film history not merely because they
mean something but rather because they express effectively a great
many aspects of modernity that have converged inspiredly in their
personalities. When I speak affectionately of their depravity, I am
not commenting on their private lives, about which I know less
than nothing. The wedding ring on Ringo's finger startles a great
many people as a subtle Pirandellian switch from a character like
Dopey of the Seven Dwarfs to a performer who chooses to project

an ambiguous identity. It hardly matters. When we are fourteen, we learn to our dismay that all celebrities are depraved and that the he-man actor we so admired would rather date a mongoose than a girl. Then at fifteen we learn that all humanity is depraved in one way or another and Albert Schweitzer gets his kicks by not squashing flies. Then at sixteen we realize that it doesn't matter how depraved we all are; all that matters is the mask we put on our depravity, the image we choose to project to the world once we have lost our innocence irrevocably. There is too much of a tendency to tear away the masks in order to probe for the truth beneath. But why stop with the masks? Why not tear away the flesh as well and gaze upon the grinning skeletons lurking in all of us?

Consequently, what interests me about the Beatles is not what they are but what they choose to express. Their Ish Kabibble hairdos, for example, serve two functions. They become unique as a group and interchangeable as individuals. Except for Ringo, the favorite of the fans, the other three Beatles tend to get lost in the shuffle. And yet each is a distinctly personable individual behind their collective façade of androgynous selflessness—a façade appropriate, incidentally, to the undifferentiated sexuality of their subadolescent fans. The Beatles are not merely objects, however. A frequent refrain of their middle-aged admirers is that the Beatles don't take themselves too seriously. They take themselves seriously enough, all right; it is their middle-aged admirers and detractors they don't take too seriously. The Beatles are a sly bunch of anti-Establishment anarchists, but they are too slick to tip their hand to the authorities. People who have watched them handle their fans and the press tell me that they make Sinatra and his clan look like a bunch of rubes at a county fair. Of course, they have been shrewdly promoted, and a great deal of the hysteria surrounding them has been rigged with classic fakery and exaggeration. They may not be worth a paragraph in six months, but right now their entertaining message seems to be that everyone is "people," Beatles and squealing subadolescents as much as Negroes and women and so-called senior citizens, and that however much alike "people" may look in a group or a mass or a stereotype, there is in each soul a unique and irreducible individuality.

—*Village Voice*, August 27, 1964

■ 21. *LIMELIGHT*

Frank Tinney I saw when I first came to New York. He was a great favorite at the Winter Garden, and had a gregarious intimacy with his audience. He would lean over the footlights and whisper, "The leading lady's kind of stuck on me," then surreptitiously look offstage to see that no one was listening, then back at the audience and confide, "It's pathetic; as she was coming through the stage door tonight I said, 'Good evening,' but she's so stuck on me she couldn't answer."

At this point the leading lady crosses the stage, and Tinney quickly puts his finger on his lips, warning the audience not to betray him. Cheerily he hails her: "Hi, kiddo." She turns indignantly and in a huff struts off the stage, dropping her comb.

Then he whispers to the audience: "What did I tell you? But in private we are just like that." He crosses his two fingers. Picking up her comb, he calls to the stage manager, "Harry, put this in *our* dressing room, will you, please?"

I saw him again on the stage a few years later and was shocked, for the comic muse had left him. He was so self-conscious that I could not believe it was the same man. It was the change in him that gave me the idea years later for my film *Limelight*. I wanted to know why he had lost his spirit and assurance. In *Limelight* the cause was age; Calvero grew old and introspective and acquired a feeling of dignity, and this divorced him from all intimacy with the audience.

—Charles Chaplin, *My Autobiography*

Limelight seems infinitely more impressive today than it did at the time of its original release back in 1952. That was the year Harry Truman's last Attorney General decided to beat the late Joe McCarthy at his own grime by barring Chaplin's re-entry to the United States through a devious bureaucratic maneuver. The late Elmer Davis remarked at the time that the resourceful Attorney

General would go way down in history as the man who kept Chaplin out of America. Davis was wrong. No one remembers J. P. McGranery—whose name I had to look up in a *World Almanac*.

The year 1952 was also the year that the late Gary Cooper was named best actor for his awkwardly tortured performance in *High Noon* by both critics and Academy. My taste in acting ran at that time more to Trevor Howard and Ralph Richardson in Carol Reed's *Outcast of the Islands*. My standards had been set during the Old Vic's visit to New York back in 1946 when Olivier's Oedipus electrified me, and his Shallow and Puff, buttressed by Richardson's Falstaff and Sneer, completed the conquest. Chaplin? He was just a funny little man with delusions of grandeur, and in *Limelight* he was not very funny even in his set pieces. Buster Keaton was something Billy Wilder had dredged up for his waxworks in *Sunset Boulevard*. However, Claire Bloom was a lovely romantic foil, Chaplin had his moments of tragic insight, and his hesitation waltz gave this spectator the heady thrill of romantic self-indulgence. All in all, *Limelight* was an ambitious failure that lingered strangely in the memory long after more successful works had slipped into oblivion.

Now, twelve years and thousands of films later, and right after a grueling tournament consecrated to cinematic modernity, *Limelight* dwarfs most of its competition. It is as if I had never really seen it before. The opening studio shots of London in the summer of 1914 remind us that Chaplin approaches death, as do most mortals, by receding into the past. The camera, on a Germanic flight of visual exposition rare in a Chaplin movie, floats past the closed doors of a lodging house to the flat of a suicidally inclined ballerina, draped decoratively in baroque white sheets and Victorian long black hair. Back to the street for the entrance of Chaplin alias Calvero. Medium shot out from behind the inevitably atmospheric organ-grinder surrounded by street urchins. The camera moves purposively toward Calvero in transit, and virtually climbs the back of his tweedy jacket. Calvero is drunk, not comically drunk, not tragically drunk, but drunk with a kind of quietly cheerful desperation.

Cut to three street urchins telling him with dramaturgical economy that the landlady is out. A nothing scene, really—but if you look closely today, you can recognize the three street urchins as three of Chaplin's children with Oona O'Neill, namely, Geraldine, Michael, and Josephine. (Michael is later to have a key role in Chaplin's 1957 gibe at McCarthyism, *The King in New York*.) Chaplin surges into the house, smells gas, checks his stogie, then the sole of his shoe, a gesture scatologically reminiscent of his earliest Mack Sennett days. He finally discovers the trouble, rescues the unconscious ballerina despite his tottering equilibrium, placates the landlady, and sets the stage for his soliloquies on life and love and art.

Limelight is full of obvious paradoxes. Chaplin talks about a dead dream world almost fifty years old with all the hindsight he can muster. His "London" is a Hollywood set on which he does not hesitate to quote Gertrude Stein anachronistically and then giggle over his audacity. He condemns Calvero's audience in terms his own audience would understand, and yet Chaplin's art is now limited to the audiences of the art houses. The burden of universality has been lifted from his shoulders, and he is free to edify the few remaining guests with intimations of his mortality.

Back in 1952 I liked the second half of the film better than the first because I felt the mood was more controlled. This time around I prefer the first half because the mood is more ambiguous. Chaplin's two dream numbers, the first before an empty theater and the second with Miss Bloom as his dream soubrette, are cruel and bawdy renditions of the lovable tramp. Until now I always thought Olivier's keen edge in the comic passages of *Hamlet* marked him as the master of the middle register, but I no longer think so. Chaplin can turn the knife of satire upon himself with more subtlety and precision than any actor I have ever seen. There is no test of behavioral range in *Limelight* that Chaplin does not pass superbly. The entire art of a Barrault or a Marceau is summed up in a few seconds of Chaplin's pantomiming a rock, a rose, a Japanese tree, and a pansy, sad or gay. Chaplin in the manager's office is the definitive performance of a man hanging on to his pride with his teeth while his head is being bludgeoned by outrageous fate. Eric Bentley once observed quite aptly that when Chaplin sits down in a chair you feel he has lived in the room all his life. As for Chaplin and Bloom together, this inspired couple pluck May and December out of the calendar for all time.

It is curious, however, that once Calvero renounces Claire Bloom to the young composer, played by Chaplin's son Sydney, there is a loss of enchantment. "In the elegant melancholy of twilight," Calvero rhapsodizes, "he will tell you that he loves you." Claire Bloom and Sydney Chaplin make a handsome enough couple, but the heart of Chaplin *père* is not in the romance. It's that damned solipsism again. Chaplin can never really imagine the world without him, and he cannot really accept the loss of his beloved as his just dessert. Chaplin clings to life and love, and above all to his audience, even when he knows his time is past. Thus in the playing of *Limelight* poetic logic is nullified by poetic license, and Charles Chaplin retains his emotional hold, even in death, upon Claire Bloom, his supreme dream of womanhood. "We are all amateurs," Calvero-Chaplin declares, "because we never have time to be anything more." Chaplin is still perfecting his art in *Limelight*, and the anguish resulting from his fighting the clock as he is telling time is reflected sublimely in the face of an actor capable of playing Lear, Falstaff, and Prospero all at the same time.

— *Village Voice*, October 1, 1964

■ 22. A WOMAN IS A WOMAN

Jean-Luc Godard's A *Woman Is a Woman* has finally obtained a commercial release in New York more than three years after its Paris release. The delay is unfortunate, because few if any of our daily reviewers are ever concerned with restoring a degree of historical perspective to films released way out of sequence. Godard is spoken of invidiously in the present tense for his work on A *Woman Is a Woman* even though he has turned out five features and three episodes since his color and scope adventures with a sort of musical comedy. The point is not that age has withered or custom staled the film's infinite variety, but rather that the sheer newness of A *Woman Is a Woman* at the time of its original release cannot ever be fully appreciated by American audiences.

However, if Godard had nothing but newness going for him, he would be a minor artist indeed. Nothing dates faster than modernity, and already the revolutionary jump-cuts in *Breathless* have become as classical as Murnau's camera movements in *Sunrise*. What impresses me most in *Woman* today is not its inventiveness but its intelligence. Too much stress has been placed on Godard's innovations and not enough on his insights. The most unsophisticated reviewers complain about so-called "inside" jokes, which are actually about as esoteric as Bob Hope asides, but few observers care to believe that subtler meanings may be lurking beneath the surface frivolity. They prefer to attribute profundity to the solemn dirge of the sandpiper in *Woman in the Dunes*, as if the apparent levity of an Oscar Wilde could ever make him less profound than a John Galsworthy.

Part of Godard's trouble with reviewers is that his films are never quite what they seem to be. To take the example at hand, *Woman* bursts upon the wide screen with supercolossal show-biz titles as if a gigantic spoof is imminent, only to have the credit curtain part on a poignant rendering of street scenes in Paris' neglected right-bank neighborhoods. Within the first two minutes of the film Godard has prepared his audience for the analytically fragmented lyricism of the film as a whole. Godard, unlike the presumptuous de Broca, knows that he can never make a decent American musical comedy, and he doesn't even try sustaining rhapsodic effects. The result is that while de Broca is making bad American movies, Godard is making brilliant French films.

The difference between American movies and European films— and I am not speaking here of a generically geographic distinction —is that American movies tend to correspond to reality while European films tend to comment on reality. It might be said, admittedly with a degree of oversimplification, that in the cinema of correspondence the image precedes the idea, while in the cinema of comment the idea precedes the image. American critics who ask plaintively why American film-makers cannot make a *Hiroshima, Mon Amour* or a *L'Avventura* are actually grappling with the first principles of the Hollywood ethos. *Hiroshima* is inconceivable in America because there is not enough plot, *L'Avventura* because the plot makes no sense.

The genius of the American cinema through the years is based on the fact that as the right hand has mastered the technical problems of advancing a plot, the left hand has been left free to improvise stylistic elaborations of almost incredible beauty and complexity. Generally speaking, however, the American cinema tends to be weaker in conception than execution, while the European cinema tends to be weaker in execution than conception. It follows that American directors and players are superior in rendering physical gestures and actions. The genres Hollywood monopolizes—the gangster film, the western, the musical—all depend upon the beauty of the physical graces. When two French gangsters shoot it out, each bullet becomes an existential statement. It is as if the intuitive flow of natural movement were segmented to illustrate the paradox of Zeno's arrow.

Godard is thoroughly European, as are Renoir, Dreyer, Rossellini, Antonioni, Bergman, *et al.* Not only does he realize that Anna Karina, Jean-Paul Belmondo, and Jean-Claude Brialy are lacking in the graceful gestures of their genre; he also realizes that his intellect must intervene between the reality he confronts on the streets of Paris and the illusion he renders on the screen. There can be no direct correspondence. Unlike most of his European contemporaries, however, Godard puts his cards on the screen by taking his audience into his confidence. Look, he says, this is my wife, Anna Karina, and she is going through the motions of playing a stripteaser named Angela Récamier who wants her lover to give her a baby, and incidentally, marry her. She wants the baby so much that she keeps stripping at the shabby Zodiac in St.-Denis and gives up a chance to work in the Lido on the Champs Élysées, where the American tourists are herded in like cattle and the pay is better and the métier fancier. Her lover says no, no, no, but her want prevails over his will. She goes to bed with another man, a man named Lubitsch, who seduces her by playing Charles Aznavour records, then forces her lover to legitimize her desperate indiscretion—for which she stands contritely in a corner—by nullifying her betrayal with a genuine act of love and forgiveness. "Tu es infame," he tells her. "Non, je suis une femme," she retorts, winking once more at the audience, as she did at the beginning of her odyssey to maternity.

Never has a plot had so little to do with what a picture is really about. *Woman* is a documentary not merely of Karina but of the sheer otherness of all women. Not since the most tortured days of Sternberg and Dietrich has the female principle been expressed so triumphantly. Far from representing form over content (whatever that means), *Woman* employs all the resources of the cinema to express the exquisite agony of heterosexual love. This is the enchantment of *Women*, not the "inside" jokes that even the wise women of the *Daily News* can decipher with ease, not the wild suspended-time jokes with quick-change chambers and egg-flips into frying pans, not the references to Lubitsch, Clair, Renoir, Aldrich, Truffaut, Donen, Minnelli, and even Godard himself, and not any precise rendering of Hollywood professionalism. Godard will endure, as Dreyer and Sternberg have endured, not as a flashy innovator but as the conscientious and conscience-stricken chronicler of man's spiritual obsessions. The ultimate paradox of *A Woman Is a Woman* is its genuinely tragic spirit.

—*Village Voice*, November 12, 1964

■ 23. *TO LOVE; BAY OF THE ANGELS*

To Love is at its best as a light comedy of sexual manners, a fantasy of facility that I would like to believe with all my anti-puritanical heart but that in the final analysis my Rock of Ages mind cannot. Not that I particularly care to make a final analysis when the tantalizingly tousled Harriet Andersson—and it's the second *s* that makes all the difference—is on screen evoking the prodigious nostalgia of her Ingmar Bergman period, when the pouting perversity of her Cocteau face was coupled with the sensual complicity of her Rubens body in memorable portrayals of such tasty morsels as the trampish misfit in *Monica*, the tomboyish maiden in *Lesson in Love*, the tigerish mistress in *The Naked Night*, the tempted mannequin in *Dreams*, and the tart maid in *Smiles of a Summer Night*. Fittingly enough, one delectably gratuitous dream sequence restores her pre-Bergman status as a burlesque stripper, and this is one occasion when I prefer to let content transcend context.

To Love is the second film of Jorn Donner, a Finnish-Swedish critic and a (yawn) Bergman biographer. (His first, as yet unreleased in America, also starred Harriet, and where is it, you evil American distributors?) Donner has chosen to treat his subject objectively, and this raises an interesting problem of directorial point of view toward material lacking both dramatic conflict and psychological contrast. Donner begins with an interesting couple in Miss Andersson and Polish actor Zbigniew Cybulski, she a repressed young widow, easily exhausted by meaningless mourning, he a footloose travel agent, casually complacent about his many conquests. They meet at the funeral of her husband, court shortly thereafter, and consummate their courtship immediately after that —and that is pretty much that. There is never another man, and never really another woman, although previous mistresses are dredged up from time to time to make conversation. The girl's mother and little boy are on hand to provide the comedy relief of enlightened attitudes, and a vinegary feminist is squeezed into the plot to dramatize the desirability of sexual emancipation. The bulk of the film is concerned with bedroom intimacy, but Donner ducks the aesthetic problem of duration with the kind of elliptical editing we now recognize at film festivals as "modern." Unfortunately, the objective approach is unable to render the delirious vertiginousness of the subject. You see neither the woman through the man's eyes nor the man through the woman's. You are always looking at both of them together from a studiously objective viewpoint, but there is not enough social and psychological detail to study in this manner, and the option of transforming the bedchamber into a metaphoric universe of subjective emotion is sacrificed for no good reason. For all of the obviously objective charms of the too, too solid flesh of Harriet Andersson, she should be, above all, a sentient being for the discerning director. Ultimately, what she feels in her face is more revealing than what she shows of her body.

Bay of the Angels is Jacques (*Lola*) Demy's second film, and I would hate to think of sitting through its ninety minutes of ultra-philosophical roulette without Jeanne Moreau at the table with one of her most flamboyant performances. I must confess that Miss Moreau, like Bette Davis, with whom she is so often compared, enthralls me more than she enchants me. Her art I find more admirable than affecting, and it is not a matter simply of maturity. It is that she seems so corrupted by experience that she has gone beyond it into a realm where her personality exists for its own sake apart from any dramatic or artistic utility. *Bay of the Angels* is worth seeing solely for the first eloquent smile she bestows on a benefactor. The screen crackles with white-hot irony. But then one gradually realizes that she is acting in splendid solitude, and that *Bay of the Angels* is nothing but a piece of cinematic vaudeville— and that is where a certain type of actress finds her destiny.

—*Village Voice*, November 26, 1964

■ 24. MISFITS AND MISALLIANCES:
REVIEWS OF *THE STORY OF*
"THE MISFITS," BY JAMES GOODE, AND
THE ART OF FILM, BY ERNEST LINDGREN

The Story of "The Misfits,"
by James Goode

The movie-production story, hitherto confined to the entertainment pages of newspapers and magazines, seems on its way to becoming a staple of the book industry, and not entirely in terms of its high yield of gossip and scandal. To take an extreme example— even though more dirt than light was shed in two recent accounts of the shooting, figuratively speaking, of *Cleopatra*—the more dedicated cinephiles could still glean some technical insights into moviemaking before the Nile flowed irretrievably into the Rubicon. However, the movie-production story to end and transcend all movieproduction stories is still Lillian Ross's *Picture,* first published more than ten years ago in *The New Yorker.* If it is unlikely that anyone in the motion picture industry will ever again talk within earshot of Miss Ross, it is equally unlikely that James Goode will be barred from any sets after *The Story of "The Misfits"* goes into circulation. Whereas Miss Ross etches her Hollywood moguls and mandarins with a stenographic stiletto dipped in acid, Mr. Goode prefers to gloss over his array (and disarray) of misfits with the oily prose of the mimeographed press release. Goode's tone is undoubtedly more edifying, but Miss Ross's is infinitely more entertaining, particularly when she draws her material from out of the mouths of boobs.

To carry the comparison further, when Frank Taylor, the relatively highbrow producer of *The Misfits*, is quoted as saying, "This is an attempt at the ultimate picture," the reader is not prompted to laugh or even to smile, because Goode so obviously shares the producer's delusions about the creative credentials of *The Misfits*. By contrast, Miss Ross had no illusions that a sublime production of *The Red Badge of Courage* would emerge from under the leonine aegis of Metro-Goldwyn-Mayer. Consequently *Picture* unfolds less as a tragedy than as a deterministic allegory of a soul-destroying system that demands vulgar compromises at every turn.

Yet, however biased, *Picture* represents a personal point of view, something lacking in *The Story of "The Misfits."* Confusing externality with objectivity, Goode fails to probe even the mythical shells of the late Marilyn Monroe and Clark Gable. The author tends to carp at Marilyn for being late on the set and to gush over Gable's professionalism and virility—though Goode's gush runs a poor second to Arthur Miller's: "By now Clark Gable and Gay Langland are one and the same guy. I don't know where one leaves off and the other begins. Clark is a hero in the mythical sense of the word as well as being real." Where Goode excels is not in character delineation, or in the dramatic expansion of incident into event, both strong points of *Picture*, but in the technical description of how a movie is actually made, day by day, detail by detail. This is the realm of enthusiasm (Goode) rather than cynicism (Ross).

Of course, time had passed and times had changed between the trials of *The Red Badge of Courage* and the tribulations of *The Misfits*. Even Miss Ross had little inkling in 1952 that she was recording the death rattle of the studio system. When Goode ostensibly begins his "diary" on July 18, 1960, he is already chronicling a new era of "packaged projects," which bypass the wicked old studios where L. B. Mayer and Jack Warner used to lurk. The new system will presumably give artists greater freedom, and yet *The Misfits* turns out to be an even bigger mess than *The Red Badge of Courage*. Why? As usual, there are script troubles. Arthur Miller is rewriting well past the last day of shooting, and no wonder. Miller's original story, like all his writing, suffers from the earnestness of being important. Marilyn Monroe is invariably tardy, and for a time is too ill to work at all. The weather goes bad in Nevada, and the wild mustangs are hard to handle. Worst of all, the Monroe-Gable pairing never achieves the desired chemistry. These two screen idols belong to different generations and different worlds. While Miss Monroe is ruminating over Goethe and Stanislavski, Gable is reminiscing about Jean Harlow and Lionel Barrymore. Even the specter of death hovering over both stars cannot dispel the mood of alienation on the screen.

It is probably more causal than coincidental that John Huston happened to be the director on the scene during the recorded misadventures of both *The Red Badge of Courage* and *The Misfits*. No American director has ever projected a more appealing image of the nonconformist battling the crass system, but Huston's career as a director has gone disconcertingly sour. From the testimony supplied by Miss Ross and Mr. Goode, Huston begins to resemble a Hemingway character lost in a Dostoyevsky novel. Whether his failures can be attributed more to a lack of concentration on details than to a loss of confidence in his own judgment is a matter less for analysis than for psychoanalysis. Whatever the diagnosis, Huston emerges as the ignoble yet charming protagonist of both *Picture* and *The Story of "The Misfits."*

The Art of the Film, by Ernest Lindgren

The title of this book is something of a misnomer in terms of its most useful features. "The Technique of the Film" would have defined Ernest Lindgren's contributions to film scholarship more precisely. His chapters on editing and camera work are appropriately concise and lucid, and his appended glossary nothing short of invaluable to the neophyte in the cinema. But the strictures on the "art" of the film, and, for that matter, on "art" in general are something else again, particularly when the reader is forced to cut his way through the tangled underbrush of a passage like this:

> Art does not have its origin at the level of mere sensation and feeling nor, to go to the other extreme, does it have its origin in his intellect, which is concerned with concepts. It originates in his nature as a thinking being, it is true, but at the level at which feeling emerges into consciousness, the level at which we dominate and control feeling by becoming aware of it as idea through the activity of the imagination.

Lindgren has added more recent stills and cited more recent films in an effort to update his text published in its original version in 1948. However, he has managed to avoid more recent controversies about television, wide screen, color, composition in depth, *cinéma vérité*, etc. If the author has not altered his basic Anglo-Russian orientation toward montage as the one indispensable key to cinematic art, it must be remembered that his position in 1948 represents an academic attitude toward the cinema that has not changed essentially since 1928. Mr. Lindgren prefers to argue the vacuous issues of form versus content, entertainment versus enlightenment, social propaganda versus self-expression, documentary versus fiction. At each straw barricade the author gently warns his readers to be wary of extreme positions. Unfortunately, in aesthetics as in politics, the middle position is usually the most muddled.

—Film Culture, No. 34, Winter 1964

■ 25. *MY FAIR LADY*

I

My Fair Lady originally opened on Broadway on the fifteenth day of March way back in 1956 at about the time Adlai Stevenson was locked in mortal combat in the New Hampshire snow with his eventual running mate, the late Estes Kefauver. *My Fair Lady* had still been in rehearsal when the FBI announced the solution of the $3-million Brink's armored-car robbery on January 12. The late Moss Hart was making Julie Andrews letter-perfect as Eliza out of town during the period (February 14-25) of the Soviet Communist party congress in Moscow, where party prexy Nikita S. Khrushchev proclaimed a new party line whereby every comrade worth his salt was exhorted to deStalinize his soul.

Victor Riesel, labor columnist of the late *Daily Mirror*, was blinded by an acid-throwing assailant on April 5. Less than two weeks later Grace Kelly married Prince Rainier III of Monaco in what *Variety* billed as a wedding between an actress and a "nonpro."

Through near-war and peace *My Fair Lady* continued to sell out every performance until long after the Kennedy-Nixon squeaker in 1960. Henry Higginses and Eliza Doolittles came and went, with the males becoming increasingly foppish and the females increasingly sluttish. By radio, television, phonograph, and hi-fi one's ears were assaulted by a million different arrangements of the Lerner-Loewe score. This reviewer can vouch for a medley of songs from *My Fair Lady* accompanying a genteel strip number in London's Casino de Paris in April of 1961.

The point is, as Dooley Wilson observes philosophically to Ingrid Bergman in *Casablanca*, a lot of water's gone under the bridge since Henry Higgins first became accustomed to Eliza Doolittle's face, and I am afraid that much of the bloom is gone from the roses in Cecil Beaton's Covent Garden. Perhaps I should be more impressed than I am by the fact that Jack Warner purchased the screen rights to *My Fair Lady* for $7 million and change, and finally shelled out 17 million clams and change for the completed spectacle now on view at the Criterion at a five-fifty top. As is so often the case, however, the price of a property is incommensurate with the value of the work. *My Fair Lady* may have garnered a hundred times the gross receipts of *Pal Joey*, but its score is still only a tenth as good. Even allowing for the assumed prejudices of self-styled intellectuals against expensive enterprises of any kind, *My Fair Lady* must be described in all candor as an evening of disenchantment. As a longtime admirer of George Cukor's directorial style, I had expected something more in the way of creative adaptation. Unfortunately, *My Fair Lady* is to Cukor's career what *Porgy and Bess* is to Preminger's, a producer's package overstuffed with all the snob stage values so dear to the garment center-garden club tastes of the Warners and the Goldwyns. With justice less poetic than prosaic, Cukor, long slandered as a "woman's director," will probably receive an overdue fistful of awards for one of his weakest jobs of direction. With so much capital invested, *My Fair Lady* has been approached so reverently that transference has degenerated into transcription. This precious property has not been so much adapted as elegantly embalmed, and yet, with few exceptions, the film fails dismally to repeat the click effects of the stage show.

Not that the original show lacked faults of its own. Stanley

Holloway's two vaudeville turns were (and are still) less savagely Shavian than Broadway brass-bound. Holloway himself has always been closer to Noel Coward's conception of the Cockney than to Shaw's, and certainly anyone who remembers the comic bite of Wilfred Lawson's Doolittle in the 1938 Wendy Hiller–Leslie Howard–Anthony Asquith version of *Pygmalion* must feel a lack of mastication in Holloway's sentimentalized characterization.

Even by the standards and aesthetics of the stage, *My Fair Lady* tends to be excessively static. There is no choreography to speak of, and the constriction of the action in Higgins' study for the greater part of two hours would have been fatal to the show if Rex Harrison and Julie Andrews had not brought off the "Rain in Spain" number with such electrifying effect, thus canceling out the tedium and ennui that preceded the inspired celebration of Eliza's victory over her vowels. However, there remained to the very end a gap of sensibility, if also a satisfying contrast, between Harrison's many-layered talk-sing and Miss Andrews' conservatory soprano.

When the time came for casting the movie, the powers that be had three options—go for broke with the Broadway cast, go for the box office with big Hollywood stars, or try mixing a bit of Broadway with a bit of Hollywood. Rex Harrison and Stanley Holloway were retained from the original production, and Audrey Hepburn was brought in to beef up the grosses, particularly abroad. As it turns out, Miss Hepburn is the chief casualty of this compromise. For the next two years audiences will begin to murmur everytime Audrey Hepburn opens her mouth to "sing," "That isn't her voice, is it?" "No dear, it's Marni Nixon's." "Why didn't they use Julie Andrews? She's so nice on records, and did you see *Mary Poppins*, and did you see her on TV with Carol Burnett?"

Poor Audrey will bear the brunt of every imposture since Jeanne Crain didn't sing "It Might as Well Be Spring" in *State Fair* and Rita Hayworth didn't sing "Make Way for Tomorrow" in *Cover Girl* and Natalie Wood didn't sing "Tonight" in *West Side Story* and Deborah Kerr didn't sing the high notes in *The King and I*, not to mention Sophia Loren's *Aïda*! The Broadway-Hollywood feud goes back to all the Gertrude Lawrence–Lynn Fontanne–Katherine Cornell roles played on the screen by Norma Shearer and Joan Crawford, to the chicken-and-the-egg controversies over Bette Davis and Tallulah Bankhead. Certainly Audrey's casting is far less ridiculous than Elizabeth Taylor's in *Who's Afraid of Virginia Woolf?*, even though Uta Hagen is Out of the Question for the screen, with Patricia Neal a reasonable equivalent and almost anyone besides Debbie Reynolds better qualified technically than Miss Taylor. Then, why should poor Audrey be singled out for censure in *My Fair Lady*, particularly when she looks so stunning in her Cecil Beaton costumes? I suggest three reasons. First, she is miscast. Second, she muffs her performance. Third, she undercuts the theme of the play.

It should be noted at the outset that both Miss Hepburn and Miss Andrews suffer badly in comparison with Wendy Hiller's classic Eliza. Her champions to the contrary, Julie Andrews is an inexperienced actress with a degree of camera naturalness and—as Stuart Byron, the associate editor of the *Independent Film Journal*, has so perceptively remarked—just the degree of ugliness necessary to distinguish the star from the starlet. In *Mary Poppins* Miss Andrews comes over too much as Greer Garson's successor with a bad case of Britannia Mews and a granite jaw too formidable for any issue less grave than the Mongolian Invasion of England. There is a bit more meow in her portrayal of the Chayefsky-Huie roundheeled heroine in *The Americanization of Emily* for future star reference.

II

As I was about to say last week before I ran out of space, the substitution of Audrey Hepburn for Julie Andrews in the screen version of *My Fair Lady* would not have aroused so much controversy if there had been corresponding substitutions of, say, Cary Grant for Rex Harrison and James Cagney for Stanley Holloway. Actually, the original idea was to team Audrey with Cary Grant, but since Grant has become incorporated, he is too expensive for anyone as dedicated to breaking even as Jack Warner. Harrison came much cheaper, and fully rehearsed into the bargain. Unfortunately, he was also eight years older, closer to sixty than fifty, and looking every year of it, with the result that the Hepburn-Harrison chemistry is more inorganic than organic.

Audrey herself is somewhat too mature for the role of Eliza Doolittle and hopelessly miscast as the tough Cockney flower girl.

Audrey has always been the gamine, relying more on charm than character, her eyes flirting shamelessly with coy flutters of regal helplessness. Unfortunately, *Pygmalion* is not concerned with a sleeping beauty who is awakened in time for the Royal Ball. Wendy Hiller and, to a lesser extent, Julie Andrews were basically diamonds in the rough given a fine polish by a master educator. The strength and will were always there; only the luster was lacking. By contrast, Audrey Hepburn suggests nothing so much as a *Vogue* model masquerading as a flower girl to create a sense of contrast in the magazine spread that will culminate with her stylish arrival at Ascot. It is distressing to realize that Miss Hepburn has been playing fey, offbeat roles for so long that she lacks the timing and rhythm necessary for classical roles. The comparison to Wendy Hiller is a particularly cruel one in this instance because the two actresses can be judged together, scene by scene, almost syllable by syllable, and Audrey is "off" all the way. Harrison emerges, as he did in *Cleopatra*, with top honors and no context. His is a one-man concert for the benefit of movie audiences who were unable to see his performance on the stage. His songs are as admirably spoken as ever, but his over-all performance suffers in comparison even with Leslie Howard's, and Howard was generally inferior to Harrison. Yet what has always made *My Fair Lady* swing as a show was the inspired idea of putting both Shaw and Harrison to music.

Shaw, like W. S. Gilbert before him, is as arid as the Sahara and as sexy as Louisa May Alcott. With music, Shaw's gruffness and naïve misogyny is transformed into the domestic sweetness of a warm puppy chewing angrily at the bedroom slippers. Audiences recognize the bad manners of Henry Higgins as the reassuring mannerisms of the patriarchs and bachelors of ancient times, when one could hate women without implying a loss of manhood and prefer the company of men without incurring sinister suspicions. For his part, Harrison has always suffered as an actor from a lack of physical extension. On stage or screen he drains the emotional life out of a scene with a voice that is too finely tuned as an intellectual instrument. He would have been dramatically unsatisfactory as a straight Henry Higgins, but Loewe's music enables Harrison to scrape against the lyricism with such force and precision that he succeeds in igniting the Lerner lyrics with a romantic fire Shaw could never have created by himself.

Ultimately, Harrison's virtuosity is futile, because there is no realistic point to the proceedings. *Pygmalion* is not really a Cinderella story but rather, like *The Miracle Worker*, a dramatic projection of the strong bonds between teacher and pupil in the neverending struggle to escape savagery. For all the posh Cecil Beaton effects, audiences have responded all these years to the implied idealism of the plot. What is electrifying about the "Rain in Spain" number is that two attractive people have worked hard to achieve a common purpose, and they have succeeded, and they are happy, and what they have achieved is a degree of civilization that had not existed in the world before, a degree of liberation for a soul that had been previously enslaved by ignorance and poverty. Wendy Hiller conveyed that feeling subtly by stages. Julie Andrews hits it with the first notes of "I Could Have Danced All Night." Audrey opens her mouth and out comes Marni Nixon's jarring American voice, and the audience feels vaguely uncomfortable, because there has been a perceptible loss of idealism in the whole process of pushing Julie Andrews and her years of voice training aside to get Audrey Hepburn into a role for which she was not technically qualified. It is somehow too easy to open your mouth and have some invisible singer ghost for you. It's done all the time, of course, and in all fields of endeavor. The mistresses of Italian producers who pass themselves off as actresses on the screen with the voices of underpaid stage actresses dubbed in on the sound tracks made Audrey's imposture seem relatively harmless, and it would not matter so much normally except that *My Fair Lady* is about training and education being their own rewards, and about people being honest about themselves. If Audrey had used her own voice, people would have said it was inferior to Julie Andrews', but they might have respected her more for trying to make the part on her own steam. Ironically, Julie's voice is even more expressive than Marni Nixon's, which leads one to wonder why Jack Warner didn't come up with Joan Sutherland to give the sound track in *My Fair Lady* the ultimate class.

I may once more be a voice in the wilderness, but I find it appalling that such an uncreative movie can sweep all the awards in 1964. Every change Cukor made in his literal transcription was for the worse, and I was particularly shocked to see him resort to the kind of obvious reaction shots that went out with high button shoes. Some of the director's camera setups are admirable, particularly the one of Ascot, but the picture as a whole lacks any flow and rhythm of its own. The acting, except for Harrison's, is uniformly bad. Wilfrid Hyde White is the biggest surprise, since he seemed to be perfectly cast, but age seems to have taken its toll of his reflexes, as it has of Harrison's and Holloway's. One thing about a movie like *My Fair Lady* is the merciless glare of its spotlight on some of the more abnormal practices of contemporary film-making. The idea of sixty-year-old male stars making love to forty-year-old female stars is shocking not only to Beatles' fans but also to anyone who has any sense of film history. Try to imagine Lillian Gish and Henry Walthall, the stars of *Birth of a Nation,* still doing leads in 1945, or Chaplin marrying Claire Bloom in *Limelight* and living with her happily ever after. Ridiculous? No more so than Harrison and Hepburn in *My Fair Lady,* or Cary Grant and Leslie Caron in the factory-hatched *Father Goose.* And this is not a case of being kind to senior citizens generally, but rather a reflection of the iron grip on the industry held by rapacious talent agencies and idiotic bankers, who lend money only on star names even to the edge of the grave, where the industry coincidentally now finds itself.

—*Village Voice,* December 17 and 24, 1964

iv

1965

■ 1. CONTEMPT

I

I want to say a few words about the job of a script-writer, if
only to give a better understanding of my feelings at that
time. As everyone knows, the script-writer is the one who—
generally in collaboration with another script-writer and with
the director—writes the script or scenario, that is, the canvas
from which the film will later be taken. In this script, and
according to the development of the action, the gestures and
words of the actors and the various movements of the camera
are minutely indicated, one by one. The script is, therefore,
drama, mime, cinematographic technique, mise-en-scène, and
direction, all at the same time. Now, although the script-
writer's part in the film is of the first importance and comes
immediately below that of the director, it remains always, for
reasons inherent in the fashion in which the art of the cinema
has hitherto developed, hopelessly subordinate and obscure.
If, in fact, the arts are to be judged from the point of view of
direct expression—and one does not really see how else they
can be judged—the script-writer is an artist who, although he
gives his best to the film, never has the comfort of knowing
that he has expressed himself. And so, with all his creative
work, he can be nothing more than a provider of suggestions

and inventions, of technical, psychological and literary ideas; it is then the director's task to make use of this material according to his own genius and, in fact, to express himself.

—Alberto Moravia, *Ghost at Noon*

Contempt is not playing anywhere at the moment, and we can only hope that it will not disappear like *Muriel*, another casualty of the currently and locally fashionable anti-intellectualism where movies are concerned. Even in the most enlightened circles, however, the mere notion of Jean-Luc Godard directing a million-dollar international coproduction of Alberto Moravia's *Ghost at Noon* in Rome and Capri for Carlo Ponti and Joe Levine seemed the height of improbability from the very beginning. One might just as soon imagine Norman Mailer standing in for the late Robert Frost on the reviewing stand of JFK's inauguration, or Allen Ginsberg sitting on the speaker's dais at a benefit for the American Jewish Committee, or William Burroughs judging the Miss America Beauty Pageant at Atlantic City—events not exactly impossible, not entirely inconceivable, but somewhat ironically incongruous in the Godard-Levine manner. The casting for *Contempt* of Brigitte Bardot, Jack Palance, Michel Piccoli, Georgia Moll, and Fritz Lang (sic) seemed equally strange, both chemically and culturally. A more plausible production setup for this Moravia property would have starred Sophia Loren and Marcello Mastroianni and have been directed by Federico Fellini on the assumption that Vittorio De Sica had found the script deficient in folk flavor.

Once *Contempt* was completed, Levine was shocked to discover that he had a million-dollar art film on his hands with no publicity pegs on which to hang his carpetbag. Levine ordered Godard to add some nude scenes, then challenged the New York censors like the great civil libertarian he is, and finally released the film with a publicity campaign worthy of *The Orgy at Lil's Place*. The New York reviewers, ever sensitive to the nuances of press agentry, opened fire on Brigitte Bardot's backside. It strikes me that this is attacking *Contempt* at its least vulnerable point, since even if Miss Bardot were to be photographed *au naturel* fore and aft for a hundred minutes of willfully Warholian impassivity, the result would be infinitely more edifying, even for children, than the sickening mediocrity of *Mary Poppins*. Unfortunately, the anal analyses of the reviewers left little space for the story line of either the Moravia original or the Godard adaptation. The striking differences in the two versions reveal the director's intentions in a way few reviewers have even bothered to suggest.

As Moravia has written it, *Ghost at Noon* is a conjugal mystery story told from the point of view of Riccardo Molteni, an ex-film critic, practicing screenwriter, and aspiring playwright. Molteni begins his reflective narrative at the point at which he first felt the beginnings of an estrangement from his wife, Emilia. After two years of marriage, and immediately after beginning to work for a producer named Battista, Molteni is involved in a casually meaningful test of conjugal courage. After dining with Battista, Molteni and his wife accept the producer's invitation to a nightcap at his home. There is room for only two in Battista's red sports car, and Molteni is persuaded, in retrospect too easily, to follow Battista and Emilia in a taxi. Emilia is obviously reluctant to go without her husband, but Molteni insists.

With this tiny miscalculation begins the emotional disintegration of a marriage. For all his context-weaving sensibility, Molteni is unable to fathom the causes of his wife's contempt for him. Emilia is a comparatively primitive being, responding instinctively to ancient codes of strength and honor, and the passionate spirit of Molteni's marriage dies even as its literal obligations are fulfilled. For Moravia, who is more an essayist than a storyteller, sexuality and sensuality are the symbolic currencies of art, history, sociology, politics, and economics. Molteni's membership in the Communist party, for example, can be traced back to a marital incident involving Emilia's longing for an apartment of her own, leading in turn to Molteni's going deeply into debt to obtain the apartment, and causing him to plunge so deeply into self-pity that he identifies his personal plight with cosmic injustice.

Moravia amplifies the theme of marital discord by introducing *The Odyssey* as the subject of script conferences involving Molteni, Battista, and a German director named Rheingold, who according to Moravia, "was not in the same class as the Pabsts and Langs." Battista wants to produce *The Odyssey* as a Levine-like Herculean spectacular. Rheingold prefers an interior Freudian interpretation through which Odysseus is motivated by conjugal repugnance to stay away from Penelope. Rheingold, it seems, had escaped Hitler and followed Freud from Vienna to Hollywood, where psychoanalysis is still taken seriously. Molteni-Moravia prefers the nobility of the Homeric original as filtered through Dante, but Molteni's great discovery is that Emilia would probably understand the interpretations of Battista and Rheingold better than his own. This is Moravia's one novelistic coup: Molteni comes to realize that he is an ignoble being with a noble vision, hence a divided man whom Emilia, with her primitive assumption of appearance as reality, could only misunderstand. The novel ends with two hallucinations, or dreams, in which Molteni imagines that he has effected a reconciliation with Emilia. He learns later that she was killed in an accident even more freakish and more gratuitous than the one Godard depicts on the screen. While sleeping in Battista's car, she snaps her neck in a minor collision, after which Battista drives on without noticing that she is dead.

Molteni's final elegy for Emilia is a striking piece of mise-en-scène: "Driven on by longing for her and for places where I had last seen her, I made my way one day to the beach below the villa, where I had once come upon her lying naked and had had the illusion that I had kissed her. The beach was deserted; and as I came out through the masses of fallen rock with my eyes raised toward the smiling, blue expanse of the sea, the thought of *The Odyssey* came back into my mind, and of Ulysses and Penelope, and I said to myself that Emilia was now, like Ulysses and Penelope, in those great sea spaces, and was fixed for eternity in the shape which she had been clothed in life."

II

The transition from Alberto Moravia's *Ghost at Noon* to Jean-Luc Godard's *Contempt* is largely the transition from a first-person novel to a third-person film. Moravia's Riccardo Molteni is obviously close to Moravia himself, and Molteni's wife, Emilia, merely an extension of Moravia's sensibility, a sort of subjective correlative of what the novelist feels about sex in the life of an artist. However, Riccardo and Emilia are both Italian and, as such, are closer to earthy essentials than Godard's transplanted French couple, Paul and Camille Javal, represented with Gallic perverseness by Michel Piccoli and Brigitte Bardot. Piccoli, grossly hirsute, to the point of parodying the virility many artists like to assume as the mark of their métier, is denied the nobly Homeric vision of Moravia's Molteni, and the audience does not see the problem through his eyes but, curiously enough, through Fritz Lang's. Ultimately Piccoli is crushed between the myth of Brigitte Bardot and the legend of Fritz Lang. Godard pays a high price for destroying Piccoli's character—nothing less, in fact, than the dramatic failure of the film. The fact that Jean-Luc Godard is a director less dramatic than dialectical—that is to say, concerned with the oppositions less of individuals than of ideas—can hardly appease the hunger of audiences for a hunk of the human condition.

Brigitte Bardot presents additional problems as a character, a star, and a myth. She and Piccoli together lack the explosive chemistry necessary for dramatic excitement even under the best conditions. Godard's inventive bits of business with the unfinished apartment only intensify the couple's alienation from their environment, and it is a strange environment indeed that Godard has postulated. Reality without realism seems to be his perennial paradox as he and his photographer, Raoul Coutard, take us on a tour of Rome and Capri, deliberately depopulated for purposes of abstraction. At times Miss Bardot seems to take her nude sun baths in an ancient world blissfully unconscious of the fears of furtive eroticism. Unfortunately, in her waking, walking moments BB is too aware of her feelings to evoke much sympathy in the audience. Godard even supplies her with an anecdote about Martin and the Ass he was forbidden to think about if he wanted his magic carpet to fly—the point being, naturally, that once the unthinkable becomes thinkable, it can never be unthinkable again. This is a good point for Godard to make, but not through Bardot. Her contempt becomes too calculated, her psychology too studied, her indifference too intransigent. Reconciliation is impossible almost by definition, and the audience shifts its sympathy to Piccoli, because he is at least trying to communicate.

Significantly, Godard has passed up the opportunities suggested by Moravia for an illusory reconciliation in the fabulously beautiful red and green grottoes of Capri. That kind of Felliniesque fantasy has never appealed to Godard. The opening stunts of suffocation and levitation in 8½ are clearly labeled: Fantasy—please suspend disbelief. Audiences find it easier to adjust to the conventions of fantasy when they are clearly labeled than when these conventions are compromised by the intrusion of fact into fiction. For example, Fellini would never have the real Fritz Lang speak to a fictional character played by Brigitte Bardot about a real person Lang refers to as our own BB, Bertolt Brecht, invoking not only Brecht's 1943 collaboration on the script of Lang's *Hangmen Also Die* but also the ascendancy of the myth of Bardot over the character of Camille.

This is the domain of the so-called "inside jokes," for which Godard is so frequently criticized. Godard has provided the usual billboards of Howard Hawks's *Hatari*, Alfred Hitchcock's *Psycho*, and Roberto Rossellini's *Voyage en Italie*, to which latter film Godard (and Resnais) owe a great deal of their conceptual montage of moving, turning, pointing, commenting statuary. Piccoli keeps his hat on in homage to Dean Martin in *Some Came Running*, and someone calls out "Vanina Vanini" in reference to Rossellini's film version of the Stendhal novel.

It is generally assumed by Godard's severest critics that he is merely plugging his friends with his references to movies. Some of the inside jokes in *Contempt*, however, are turned against both Godard and his colleagues on *Cahiers du Cinéma*. When Bardot and Piccoli tell Lang how much they admired his *Rancho Notorious* with Marlene Dietrich, he tells them he prefers *M*. This is an anti-*Cahiers* position on Lang's own career, and Lang's description of Cinemascope as a process suitable for photographing snakes and funerals is aesthetically reactionary enough to make André Bazin roll over in his grave. Lang's kind words for Sam Goldwyn are the final confirmation that Godard has allowed Lang to speak for himself rather than as a mouthpiece for Godard. The effect of Lang's autonomy is to complete the degradation of Piccoli as a mere parrot of *nouvelle vague* attitudes, toward which Godard displays mixed emotions. When Piccoli announces that he is going to look at a movie to get some ideas for a script, Bardot asks him with rhetorical scorn why he doesn't think up his own ideas. Piccoli is not even allowed to challenge the vulgar conceptions of Jack Palance's ruthless American producer, Jeremy Prokosch. Lang lines up with Homer, Palance with commerce, and Piccoli becomes a feeble echo of the producer who has set out to humiliate him.

Palance is the one actor who got away from Godard, much as Steve Cochran got away from Antonioni in *Il Grido*. The result is more interestingly ambiguous than either Godard or Antonioni had any idea of permitting. Godard wound up hating Palance as Antonioni wound up hating Cochran—and yet I think these runaway characterizations may suggest that at times the director is well advised, like the jockey on a high-spirited mount, to keep a loose rein on the talent at his disposal and let nature take its course. Palance's conception of Prokosch is closer to Rod Steiger's producer in *The Big Knife* than to Godard's conception of Moravia's Battista, Carlo Ponti, or Joe Levine. The main difference between Prokosch and Battista is that Prokosch sets out to debase Piccoli publicly, while Battista is concerned only with deceiving Molteni in the discreet Italian manner. If in Godard's conception Lang is pure greatness, Palance exudes raw power. Piccoli stands before Lang and Palance as a suppliant before two demigods, and before Bardot as a mistake before a myth.

We are not moved by what happens to the marriage of Bardot and Piccoli. We are not even particularly concerned with what happens to the ridiculous epic Palance wants Fritz Lang to direct (because only a German can understand Homer). The characters keep talking about Homer's classical cosmos of appearance as reality as opposed to our atomic universe under constantly anxious analysis, but the consciously tawdry players in the film-within-a-film indicate that the great Fritz is laboring on a potboiler. Then, what is so moving about *Contempt*? Simply the spectacle of Fritz Lang completing a mediocre film with a noble vision in his mind and at the edge of his fingertips. Godard appears in the film as Lang's assistant, and he repeats Lang's instructions to the camera crew, as if in the bulky figure of this curious man who has always known how far to compromise in order to endure is hidden the real Homeric parable of *Contempt*. Mastroianni-Fellini in 8½ is an artist who just happens to be a movie director, Lang in *Contempt* is a movie director who just happens to be an artist.

—Village Voice, January 28 and February 4, 1965

■ *2. THE RED DESERT*

I have no doubt that Michelangelo Antonioni's *The Red Desert* will become the most controversial conversation piece since *Last Year at Marienbad*. For one thing, even Antonioni's title is moder-

ately mystifying. It is a bit like Humphrey Bogart telling Claude
Rains that he had come to Casablanca originally for the waters,
and Rains responding with Gallic rationality that there were no
waters in Casablanca, situated as it is in the middle of the desert.
"I was misinformed," Bogart states stoically. Conversely, if there
is literally no desert in *The Red Desert*, there is a fascinating canal
conveying oceangoing freighters and tankers past the now petrified
pines that once inspired Dante in Ravenna. Antonioni is at his
best in capturing the ghostly grandeur of these intruders from the
outside world, as fantastic in their subjectively documentary way
as the astrophysical antennae extending their metal tentacles to
hear the stars.

Antonioni's first color film after eight black-and-white features
in fifteen years, *Desert* is more a series of paintings unfurled in
time than the kind of dramatic spectacle we have been calling a
movie for the past half century. Every composition has been
framed with the utmost preciseness, and the signification of every
color has been carefully calculated far in advance. When a young
mining engineer is distracted from the Italian workmen he is re-
cruiting for a Patagonian venture by a streak of blue paint followed
by the camera up the wall, you can be sure that Antonioni has
splashed it up there, possibly as a rub-a-dub reminder of Monica
Vitti's blues, possibly for the stab of sea coldness associated with
far-off places.

Actually, even the plot is a function of the color. When the heroine, the affectedly addled victim of a motor mishap, finally reveals the nature of her neurosis to an uncomprehending Scandinavian sailor in a straight steal from the Gunnel Lindblom–Birger
Malmsten "conversation" in *The Silence*, she includes colors as
well as people and places and machinery as things from which she
is alienated. The pop firehouse-red that keeps stalking the frames
in which she appears takes on a special significance, particularly
when she is flung against pipes and railings painted red so as to
serve as the architecture of her anxiety. The reds and blues exclaim
as much as they explain in the over-all color scheme of relatively
muted greenish grays and reddish browns. Some of the glazed walls
take on the appearance of graphic graffiti, as if Antonioni's canvas
has dispensed with aerial perspective altogether. Effects achieved
by a newspaper fluttering down from a window and the heroine

being masked by a map of the world involve a conscious collage of meanings as well as technical experiments in texture.

Nothing much happens in the old-fashioned sense of things happening. Miss Vitti wanders around fields and factories with her little boy, meets an old school chum of her husband's, winds up committing adultery with him, all to no purpose or satisfaction or even relaxation. There is only the slightest suggestion in the last sequence that she is somewhat more self-assured than she was in the first. As usual with Antonioni, the incidents are more interesting than the events. Three technicians and their women—Miss Vitti, French stripper Rita Renoir, and Xenia Valderi—are sensually deployed in a curious room with red walls in a small shack by the side of a canal. The entire room is taken up by a mattress on which the three couples are sprawled indiscriminately—not three couples actually, Richard Harris being detached from the others while coveting Monica Vitti, who is married to Carlo Chionetti, who is associated with Aldo Grotti, a malignant sensualist married to Miss Valderi while he stalks Miss Renoir. There is an unpleasant intimacy in the abortive conversation about aphrodisiacs, but Antonioni's viciously bourgeois bedbugs are not quite decadent enough to stage a real orgy, though they are too decadent to talk about anything else. This is about as perceptive a view of middle-class morality as I have ever encountered, and its perceptiveness is enhanced by the extraordinary release that follows when Richard Harris pounds his fist through the wall and begins dismantling the red planks for firewood, the most electrifying image ever of a director destroying his decor.

There are layers and layers of meaning to be considered here. These people have a kind of class consciousness. They know that the shack will soon belong to one of the workers who wishes to have a place of assignation with his many girl friends, and as they gleefully destroy his facilities, an act almost of class castration, we see the prefiguration of the corporate state of the future. The vandals are releasing also their own class inhibitions, in which personal propriety is the long-forgotten function of private property.

When our antiheroes and antiheroines see the plague pennant run up on a nearby freighter from which Miss Vitti has heard a muffled cry of anguish, the representative members of cowardly modernity run with cat feet to their cars to escape involvement.

Miss Vitti drops her purse and tries to decide who can go back for it. Standing in the fog, she sees her erstwhile companions dissolve before her eyes, the most stunning conjunction of meaning and mise-en-scène in all the cinematic literature of Michelangelo Antonioni.

Still, I have the feeling that Antonioni would rather curse the discoloration of modern life than distort his contrived decor with one small candle of flickering human hope. I can no longer accept Antonioni's assertion that the modern man fails to communicate, simply because Antonioni refuses to allow his players to allow any garden-variety expressiveness to invade their incommunicado faces. Much of Antonioni's meaningful manner is derived from staring at a rock so long that mere opacity comes to equal profundity.

I must confess that I have had it with Monica Vitti as a stand-in for Everyman or even Everywoman. In fact, Miss Vitti's excessive solemnity engenders in me at times the giddy illusion that I am watching Barbra Streisand adrift in an industrial documentary. As for Richard Harris, he has been subdued to the point of outright suppression of any spark of life. His slicked-down orange hair and bleached eyebrows evoke nothing so much as the brilliantined bravados of Hollywood's gamier past. As for the others, man, women, and child alike seem to have been cuffed about by the director until they have cleansed their faces of any telltale smudges of *joie de vivre*.

Antonioni is so lacking in humor that when Rita Renoir purses her lips lasciviously when someone suggests that aphrodisiacs have been known to extend the suspension principle in sexual engineering for more than an hour, one suspects that Miss Renoir's chucklesome coup somehow slipped by the director's prudish vigilance. Perhaps the key to all the performances is to be found quite literally in the back of a toy robot belonging to Vitti's sleeping son and appearing in an early sequence, walking back and forth, its electric eyes gleaming in the dark. The characters resemble that robot to such an extent that, what with the electronic music on the sound track and the pop modernity of the decor, I began to feel not modernity itself but modernity's modish hatred of itself. Antonioni may be "in," all right, along with the notion that this is the worst of all possible times, but include me out. Why? I suppose I am too sensitive to the fallacy of the Idealized Past even by implication.

The past may have been better, but for whom, Michelangelo, for whom?

—*Village Voice*, February 11, 1965

■ 3. THE TRIAL OF JOAN OF ARC

Robert Bresson's *The Trial of Joan of Arc* opened and closed last week at the enterprising New Yorker Theatre on a double bill with a revival of Roberto Rossellini's *Open City*. Aside from providing a surfeit of religiosity, this pairing of incongruent intentions caused the emotional turbulence of *Open City* to make *Joan* seem unduly dispassionate, and the stylistic austerity of *Joan* to make *Open City* seem unduly facile. Bresson's work had been previously premiered at the 1963 Cannes, Montreal, and New York Film festivals—and that, I am afraid, is where it belonged. Although at sixty-five minutes *Joan* is shorter than any of Bresson's previous films, none is heavier going for the average audience. My pet peeve here is the subject, the Big Subject if you will, already done to death from Shakespeare's witchy strumpet to Shaw's bitchy saint, with stops along the way for Schiller, Twain, Claudel, and Anouilh, among many others. The screen has given us Cecil B. DeMille's version with Geraldine Farrar, Carl Dreyer's with Falconetti, Victor Fleming's and Roberto Rossellini's with Ingrid Bergman, Otto Preminger's with Jean Seberg, and now Bresson's with a one-shot discovery of his, Florence Carrez, a saint more of the Sorbonne than of the soil.

However, in these days when the critical climate is so feeble-mindedly frivolous that *How to Murder Your Wife* gets better reviews than *The Red Desert*, directors like Bresson, Godard, and Antonioni deserve a special asterisk for individuality. Thus, though I don't entirely approve of Bresson's conception, I can't fault the exactness of his execution. From the precredit track of Joan's mother rendered as a black-robed shroud stalking the verdict of Joan's executioners on the altar of history twenty-five years after the event to the penultimate moment in Joan's punishment when her personal possessions are cast in the flames, we are in the grip of a masterly mise-en-scène linked to the deepest meanings imaginable.

Curiously, the Bresson-Carrez Joan may be the first to be viewed entirely within the context of Catholicism. Dreyer's Joan with her enormous close-ups is a basically Protestant conception. One need not stipulate that the close-up is Protestant and the middle shot Catholic to feel that Bresson has reacted against the close-up, either intuitively or intentionally, as a cinematic manifestation of the sin of pride. The face of Florence Carrez never dominates a Bresson frame as the face of Falconetti dominates a Dreyer. Bresson makes us conscious more of Joan's whole body, that temple of sanctity, almost of professional virginity, that Joan longs to present intact to her Bridegroom in heaven. No other version of Joan has dwelled so morbidly on this aspect of the Maid of Orléans.

Richard Roud has described Bresson's art as the chamber music of the cinema, and we wait in vain for the heavy orchestration most other directors would employ to enlist our sympathies for Joan. We must make do with the low-voltage electrifying effect of Joan's bare feet hobbling along the pavestones, the camera clinging to the earth angle as the disembodied feet convey an invisible soul to a stake mounted against the sky. The expressive effect of camera movement, so frugally hoarded for this moment, is released by Bresson with a strategic calculation worthy of the greatest artists.

I might note two other conjunctions of sense and style for the specialists in mise-en-scène. First, Bresson has been criticized on at least one occasion for showing a place a beat or two after the people have departed, thus fading out on geography rather than humanity. Far from being a flaw, this Bressonian mannerism expresses an attitude of man's place in the universe. For Bresson, place precedes and transcends person, since the world was here before we came and will be here long after we are gone. This is hardly the sign of a humanistic temperament, but no one has ever accused Bresson of being a humanist.

My other point is that Bresson's camera setups for the trial itself are skillfully contrived to place Cauchon on trial before Joan rather than Joan before Cauchon. In the repeated cross-cuts the camera angle on Joan is always obliquely off to one side from the point of view of Joan's advocate, while Cauchon's angle is more frontal from Joan's point of view. To intensify this reversal of judicial authority, Bresson isolates all the participants at the trial within their own islandlike frames of identification. Never does Bresson's camera unify the spectacle by moving around the room to show that Joan and Cauchon occupy the same room at the same time. We merely infer this from the editing. The point is that Bresson is not nearly as objectively fair-minded as the muted readings of his players would indicate. Preminger's fluid camera viewpoint of villains and heroines alike is far more genuinely ambiguous than Bresson's somewhat labored air of authenticity. To get down to hard cases, I can understand why some critics consider *The Trial of Joan of Arc* as the first cinematic salvo of General De Gaulle against his favorite targets, the Anglo-Saxons. There is just enough nasty Anglophobia mixed in with this film's more spiritual concerns to suggest that the Cross of Bresson has been subordinated to the Cross of Lorraine.

—Village Voice, February 18, 1965

■ 4. THE COLLECTOR

William Wyler's *The Collector* is the most erotic movie ever to come out past the Production Code, and I urge all my warped friends to rush off and see it. As always, I have strong reservations about Wyler's highly polished but horridly impersonal direction, but the subject is such a splendid one for movies that I'd rather begin by accentuating the positive. First, I like the idea of a two-character movie, particularly when both characters are as attractive as Samantha Eggar and Terence Stamp. A lot of nonsense has been written in supposedly serious film histories about what is cinema and what is not, and a prejudice persists in favor of the great outdoors as against the presumably "stagy" indoors. Yet I can't think of anything more exciting and more cinematic than locking up a boy and a girl in an old house and an intriguing situation. Just as the human voice is the most sublime musical instrument, the human face and body are the most sublime visual subjects, and one shot of Samantha Eggar's elegantly elongated leg turning on a water faucet is worth every shot of every antelope that ever roamed.

Second, *The Collector* should offer conclusive evidence that all movies that can afford it should be photographed in color. There are no black-and-white subjects left anymore. Color should now be taken as matter-of-factly as sound. Without the superb color photography of Robert Krasker and Robert Surtees, *The Collector* would be about 50 per cent of the movie it is now. And if a two-character drama in a predominantly interior setting is enhanced by color, what possible project would not be similarly enhanced—and I am asking rhetorically, of course.

Of the two extraordinary performances I somewhat prefer Samantha Eggar's for its basic directness. Whereas she is perfectly cast as an emotionally vulnerable butterfly, Terence Stamp is somewhat miscast as her nastily repressed collector, and thus while Miss Eggar's performance is all of a piece, Stamp's splits off into two or three different directions. The odd thing is that the girl's skin is photographed in all its blemished splendor while the boy's is unnaturally glossy, almost a variation of the conventional cosmetic formula for beauty and the beast.

The trick in Stamp's performance is that no matter how malignant he looks, his voice and dialect always come out sounding mediocre. Thus while the camera is making him look like something out of the cabinet of Dr. Caligari, the sound track is dragging him back to the whining world of social consciousness. If there is anything truly terrifying about this character, it is that his voice and face don't match. The way Stamp lets his mouth go slack and effeminate is one of the best examples I have ever seen of an actor playing against his looks for the sake of a characterization.

Fortunately, Samantha Eggar is not called upon to play against her looks, and she manages to be stunning through all the dire stress of necessity. It is part of the underlying theme of the movie that her sensuality is never detached from her sensibility, or her body from her soul. This is harder to do than it looks. At one point in the production Wyler fired Samantha Eggar and tried to get Natalie Wood to replace her. He was saved from this disaster by Miss Wood's unavailability, but I still shudder to think of Miss Wood arguing about Salinger and Picasso with Terence Stamp. I'd like to claim a little credit for touting Miss Eggar's performance in *Psyche 59*.

When I was in Mar del Plata earlier this year, some members of the British delegation were embittered by Wyler's takeover of *The Collector*. What had started out as a modest, low-budget, offbeat project was gradually expanded into a $5-million extravaganza for the art houses. Wyler was criticized also for casting Terence Stamp in a part that called for some pimply-faced type. For the most part I'm glad Wyler won out. I'm a little sick of modest, low-budget, offbeat projects, and I don't think it's very wise to inflict unattractive people on audiences for long periods of time. People just stay away from the theater. The point is that I am glad this project went a bit Hollywood.

Nevertheless I have rather strong reservations about some of Wyler's directorial touches. I think he muffs the first chloroforming altogether by jazzing up the action with close-ups and frenetic cutting. For one thing, he tries vainly to agitate the audience to the same degree that the girl is supposed to be agitated, but the audience hardly knows the girl at this point, having seen everything, the girl included, strictly from the collector's point of view.

I think also that Wyler is ill-advised to have the collector celebrate his successful abduction by rolling over and over on the grass and letting the rain splatter his face. This choreography of release is completely inconsistent with a painstakingly acted-out psychology of repression. After all, the only thing that keeps the movie going after the abduction is that the collector is too repressed to rape his captive. The kind of ecstasy in the grass enacted by Stamp may strike even neutral observers of the *nouvelle vague* as suspiciously Truffautish, but it makes the character even more self-contradictory than he should be.

Wyler gags up the first encounter between the girl and the collector by having disembodied feet come through the creaking door à la Count Dracula, and then moving the camera up the collector's body to the tray that reveals that the monster is behaving like a butler. Unfortunately, we already know that the collector is not a conventional sex fiend, because we have seen him decorously lower the hem of his victim's skirt over her knees. That means we know something the girl doesn't know, but, then, the girl obviously sees the tray before the audience does, and so the second part of this suspense gag is just a coy bit of legerdemain for the benefit of the audience.

Wyler might be criticized elsewhere for being needlessly violent, with physical violence, but we don't have to cite chapter and verse on every sequence. The main trouble I find with Wyler's direction is that he doesn't express any personal point of view toward his characters or his material. By the very nature of things, any reasonably sane viewer will feel more sympathy for the girl than for the collector. Aside from the unconscious sexual complicity every male shares with a rapist, it is difficult not to feel sympathetic for a girl who wishes to be free to choose her own destiny. Wyler seems to stand apart from the material, as if he didn't want to intervene emotionally. He gets some very polished effects from the performance, and I can't help wondering how many takes he needed to get that one elegantly decadent shot of the collector tenderly brushing some strands of the girl's red hair from her mouth, one of the most preciously perverted effects that I have ever seen in the cinema.

Some reviewers have suggested that the film is much deeper than it seems, but they don't bother to explore the alleged depths. I think, on the contrary, that the film is an effective but shallow piece of entertainment. Wyler has omitted most of the biographical and motivational background of the novel, but I wouldn't criticize him too severely for that. John Fowles has overloaded his subject with all kinds of social allegory. The girl is quite naturally a ban-the-Bomb, bleeding-heart socialist who loves life and people and animals, and the collector is a nasty Dostoyevskian nihilist who thinks all people are insects. Wyler also omits the collector's charming practice of photographing his bound captive in high heels and black-leather underwear—but I can understand the director's discretion during this primitive phase of film history. More questionable is Wyler's silence on Samantha Eggar's past and point of view, which take up half the novel. It is established in the book that the girl is a virgin, but we never get a yes or no on this crucial question in the movie. All in all, Wyler has limited himself to about as much of the book as he could effectively render in uncluttered narrative. At times he is disconcertingly obvious, as when the girl's face is reflected in the glass case in which some pinned butterflies are mounted. Thus he ducks what I found to be the central message of the novel, that the so-called New People who have risen from the proletariat are the new enemies of the New Left. I think Fowles speaks for a great many of the British and American intelligentsia when he attacks the cold philistinism of the economically but not spiritually redeemed masses. I have been struck by the way organized labor has become a dirty word in the past decade, and the Collector is ultimately every working man who has attained the free time necessary not to give a damn for his fellow man.

A minor footnote to Wyler's anti–*nouvelle vague* interviews: First, Wyler should stop beating a dead unicorn. Second, he might explain why he never used a jump-cut for thirty years until *The Children's Hour*, which happened to follow *Breathless*. Third, he might explain where he got the brilliant idea of shooting a flashback in black and white in a color movie. Resnais' *Night and Fog*, perhaps? It doesn't matter. The cinema is always changing and always renewing. *The Collector* couldn't have been done just a few years ago, and I'm glad that Wyler did it. But he had better watch out for such inside jokes as showing a marquee with *Ben Hur* emblazoned on it. Shades of Jean-Luc Godard!

—*Village* Voice, June 24, 1965

■ 5. THE FASCIST; THE PAWNBROKER

Luciano Salce's *The Fascist* is well worth seeing despite an unappetizing title that seems to keep away the audiences this film deserves. A friend of mine told me about *The Fascist* (*Il Federale*) when he saw it in Florence back in 1961. Signor Salce first attracted this column's attention last year with his oddly sympathetic if technically uneven *Crazy Desire*, a tragicomic trifle about youth versus age featuring Ugo Tognazzi and Catherine Spaak. Tognazzi is on hand again as the Fascist fanatic entrusted with the task of bringing an anti-Fascist professor to Rome in the last days of Fascism. Tognazzi and French actor Georges Wilson achieve a rare rapport in what amounts to a two-character *Odyssey* on the road to Rome. Salce enriches an at times too symmetrically ironic anecdote with a variety of picaresque details. I liked particularly that Beckett-like moment of cosmic comedy when Tognazzi complains that everything is disintegrating into chaos after he sits and collapses on some crumbling masonry. For the most part, intelligent compassion transcends ideological caricature as Tognazzi, the dedicated Fascist, turns out to be something of an idealist, and Wilson, the enlightened liberal, something of an opportunist. The two men commune ultimately over the semireligious ritual of lighting cigarettes wrapped in paper containing Leopardi's verses, the professor's movingly metaphoric gesture denoting the priority of man over art. At its best *The Fascist* is a lyrical evocation of fraternity, and the performances of Tognazzi and Wilson are beautifully large and whole.

Whereas *The Fascist* is a modest anecdote that blossoms beautifully into stature and significance, *The Pawnbroker* is a pretentious parable that manages to shrivel into drivel. In fact, *The Pawnbroker* deserves at least stylistically the subtitle of *Harlem, Mon Amour*. No American film in recent memory reeks so strongly of Resnais, and no wonder. The David Friedkin–Morton Fine screenplay (from the novel by the late Edward Lewis Wallant) was completed sometime in 1961 or 1962 when "Open Mouth" programs were still babbling about Hollywood's hopeless inability to imitate *Hiroshima, Mon Amour*. Director Sidney Lumet came on the scene as a last-minute replacement for Arthur Hiller and glibly executed every last tricky detail of the shooting script. The idea behind the production seemed to be that by combining the Jewish Problem with the Negro Problem the picture would be twice as profound because the audience would be twice as depressed. After about half an hour, however, Harlem seems more remote from Auschwitz than even LeRoi Jones' moral geography would indicate. The main trouble with *The Pawnbroker* is that you can't see the People for the Problems.

Rod Steiger is interesting at first in a mannered, technical performance simply because he underacts and underreacts while everyone around him is declaiming disastrously. Steiger gives it the old Muni-Schildkraut business with the shaved head and the fussily handled eyeglasses, but I would just as soon see a bad actor like Burt Lancaster diverted with these pretenses as a good actor like Steiger fatally distracted. Unfortunately, Steiger's initial inscrutability is soon replaced by message speeches from Western Union delivered in a manner so disagreeable that all you want to do is get out of the pawnshop. Geraldine Fitzgerald's social worker is one of the more nauseating characters in the modern cinema, a sweet-smiling masochist who went out with the late Lloyd C. Douglas of obsessions, magnificent and otherwise. The other performers are wildly gesticulating puppets of contrivance shaped toward a pompous climax in which the pawnbroker atones for his apathy by piercing his palm on a receipt spike. He has been thus moved and redeemed by the impulsive act of self-sacrifice performed by his Puerto Rican assistant. It takes more than Christ's stigmata, however, to return the dead to the living, and it takes more than a death-watch repentance to make a human being. Perhaps one of the penalties of our Judaeo-Christian heritage is that we consider pain more instructive than pleasure—and the pawnbroker's whining certainly gorges itself on that heritage—but I find the ultimate communication of the characters in *The Fascist* much more plausible than I find the redemption of the pawnbroker. First of all, I can't figure out why it is so important for the pawnbroker to be redeemed. There is no law that says every man must love every other man like a brother, and even if there is such a law, it was repealed a long time ago. Certainly the proprietor of a pawnshop may be forgiven for not being friendly with his clients, but it would be almost perverted to love them if he didn't first like and respect them, and if their company did not give him genuine pleasure. This is where *The Fascist* is on so much stronger ground. Salce recognizes, as the perpetrators of *The Pawnbroker* do not, that love is a function of the highest critical faculty.

—*Village Voice*, July 15, 1965

■ 6. *BEFORE THE REVOLUTION;*
   FAMILY DIARY

Bernardo Bertolucci's *Before the Revolution*, an evocation of modern Parmesan passions in the shadow of Stendhal, was one of the more controversial entries in the 1964 New York Film Festival, and it still continued to arouse some controversy at the Pesaro Film Festival I attended last month. In a season when audiences are trooping off giddily to Camp, a work of serious moral sensibility should be welcomed at least as a change of pace.

Some of Bertolucci's more sophisticated detractors have objected to the literalness of his stylistic borrowings from Rossellini and Fellini and Resnais and Truffaut, but this so-called "literalness" I consider a frank quotation rather than a stealthy theft. What cannot be copied from anyone is the richness and energy with which Bertolucci contemplates a life of cowardice and compromise. It is as if he were holding back a torrent of emotion by multiplying his channels of expression. Then in the final movements of his opus all the fragments dissolve into a molten flow of emotional ecstasy as Adriana Asti, she of the luminously liberating eyes, attends her beloved nephew's wedding and tearfully mourns with all the rest of us the glories of life's lost opportunities. *Before the Revolution* is the kind of film a director can make only once in his life, and I rejoice that Bertolucci made it before he became mature enough to learn that he couldn't.

I would like to call attention to one film that has been ineptly distributed in America by Metro-Goldwyn-Mayer, and this is Valerio Zurlini's *Family Diary*, based on an autobiographical memoir by the Florentine novelist Vasco Pratolini. *Family Diary* is both very strange and very moving, and I recommend it to art theaters and film societies as a curiously modern example of the old-fashioned literary cinema, which deep in our hearts we all prefer to so-called "pure" cinema.

Valerio Zurlini was born in Bologna in 1926, and studied dramatic arts at the University of Rome during World War II. He turned out four shorts between 1948 and 1957, and in the latter year collaborated with Alberto Lattuada on the script of *Guendalina*. His first feature-length film, *Le Ragazze di San Fredino*, opened in Italy in 1954, but was never released in America. *Estata Violanta* was released in Italy in 1959, and in New York in 1961 as *Violent Summer*. I caught *The Girl with the Suitcase* (*La Ragazza con Valigia*) at the 1961 Cannes Film Festival. *Family Diary* is thus only his fourth feature in a decade, although I understand he has a new film coming out this year. Up until *Family Diary* I had tagged Zurlini as a lush romantic whose facile emotionalism was initially impressive but ultimately superficial. *Violent Summer*, a kind of Italian *Devil in the Flesh*, struck me as an adolescent fantasy of antisocial *amour* in the midst of a war that meant only the moving mise-en-scène of partings and reunions in railway stations. Eleonora Rossi Drago stays in the mind as a woman whose dignity crumbles under the assault of passion.

The Girl with the Suitcase presented Claudia Cardinale as Aida, every adolescent's dream of a first love, and Jacques Perrin's adoring gaze invested Claudia with an allure she has never exuded since. *Suitcase* was particularly flamboyant in the lyrical sweep of its camera movements, and so when I heard that *Family Diary* was a tearjerker, I was wary. To my surprise, *Family Diary* is notable for the rigorousness and austerity of its direction, proving perhaps that directors don't always run true to form.

There are really only three characters in *Family Diary*, the two brothers played by Marcello Mastroianni and the aforementioned Jacques Perrin, and their grandmother played by the eternal Sylvie. The film opens in a room we are told represents the Rome of 1945. It is some kind of a pressroom, with many telephones, one of which informs Mastroianni that his brother has died in Florence. We then flash back with the narration of Mastroianni-Pratolini to the beginnings of the brotherly relationship in 1918. We are back in Florence in the circumstances of death, illness, and poverty. Mastroianni's mother has died in childbirth, bearing Perrin. Their father is permanently ill in a veterans' hospital, and there is talk that the mother died insane. Mastroianni is five or six years older than Perrin and is brought up in relative poverty by his grandmother, Sylvie, while Perrin grows up in a baron's villa as the adopted son of the butler. From the very beginning this color film establishes a black and orange sibling dichotomy. Mastroianni will always be in black from his hair to his shoes, and Perrin will always complement his brother in orange.

The narration blithely skips around great chunks of time without showing us anything of the world of the thirties and forties. A quick cut disposes of Mastroianni's two years in a sanitarium, and the four years of the war take up a sentence of narration. On one occasion we do see Mastroianni listening dourly to a radio broadcasting Franco's triumph in Spain, and in the same sequence Perrin and his girl friend encounter Mastroianni, but the girl disappears soon after without explanation, and we never see Perrin's wife and daughter. Nor are we ever introduced into Mastroianni's personal life away from his brother. The shots of Florence and Rome are scenically obscure, the underside, as it were, of these two extraordinary beautiful cities.

The streets are always empty in long shot, so that when two figures emerge from around a corner a hundred feet or more away from the camera, you can spot the blob of black as Mastroianni and the blob of orange as Perrin. On one level of expression *Family Diary* is a two-hour drama of chromatic convergence. Zurlini uses camera movement sparingly as he concentrates on compositions of his two protagonists, initially triangulated by the grandmother, but more often isolated from the rest of the world. The scenes are long, and the playing is slow, subtle, and intense.

Despite the austerity of the ambience, the characters do not lack literary complexity and social meaning. For one thing, emotions are enveloped in poverty. Mastroianni has to consign his grandmother to an institution for the elderly, a fate she accepts with the stoicism of the permanently poor. Her last words and thoughts are of her two "orphans," and of what will become of them, the eternal fear of the dying poor. Here we don't see poverty in its usual picturesqueness, since it is a cardinal principle of realist aesthetics that poor pople do not inhabit color films, but rather the drably expressive world of black and white. Poverty, however, is not picturesque, and it is not the presence of ugly things. It is the absence of all sorts of intangibles like freedom, choice, time, and a sense of personal destiny. Above all, poverty is the pettiness of necessity, and it takes its toll in guilt for the love one has no time or means to express. Mastroianni fights the love he feels for his brother with all sorts of rationalizations. Perrin is too formal, beautiful without being charming. He smiles prettily, vulnerably, but somewhat vacuously.

Some of Mastroianni's personal hostility to Perrin is motivated by Pratolini's Marxist beliefs. Whereas Mastroianni is the proletarian intellectual, Perrin is of the servant class, the stronghold of the most intransigent snobbery. It is the trauma of the Italian intellectual that to feel free he must abandon God, family, and country as barbarically bourgeois notions. Of what use are the blood rites and the liturgical vocabularies of the past? Yet, when all is said and done and felt, how far have we come from the cave? Kenneth Tynan once observed very sagely that men of the Right tend to love their fathers, while men of the Left tend to love their mothers.

To love one's brother, however, is to turn in on oneself and to question the justice of one's own existence.

The ultimate triumph of *Family Diary* is due largely to Mastroianni's performance and personality, among the most extraordinarily subtle and sensitive in film history. As Mastroianni gazes at Perrin, this creature who has come through the same womb only to depart into a different darkness, his eyes surrender to the atavistic, unreasoning impulse of love. It is like Goya's splash of red when he paints the infanta of a royal family he despises. Goya's red is his heart's blood pouring out to express a feeling toward innocence his political convictions cannot suppress. *Family Diary*, with its appropriately faded pastel colors, reminds us that social history is but a footnote to family history in the life of mankind.

—*Village Voice*, July 22, 1965

■ *7. HELP!; SYNANON;*
THE SONS OF KATIE ELDER

Help!, the latest bash from the Beatles, was a distinct disappointment to me, not merely because I expected more from a follow-up to *A Hard Day's Night* but also because I had happened to see the brilliant trailer for *Help!* before I saw *Help!* itself. Not that *A Hard Day's Night* can now be written off as a happy accident. Director Richard Lester clearly has the knack as well as *The Knack*, and the Beatles look and sound as if they will endure a while longer. The songs in *Help!* are down a few notches from the extraordinary level of the score for *A Hard Day's Night*, but the title song for *Help!*, despite its drippings of teen-age melancholia, is about the best song the Lennon-McCartney team has conceived. Why, then, am I singing the blues about the Beatles movie? I suppose because I have the feeling that Lester and the Beatles added to each other in their first film together, but that they subtract from each other in their second. Before *A Hard Day's Night* I could never differentiate the three Beatles clustered in front of Ringo's drums. Lester's imaginative cut-and-close-up technique individualized each of the Beatles to the point where I was looking

for their divergent personalities to diverge even further in *Help!*
Instead, the three non-Ringo Beatles are lost in the shuffle of gag
long shots, so that if *Help!* were your first encounter with the
group, you would conclude that the Beatles consisted of Ringo
and his three mopheads.

I understand that Richard Lester and John Schlesinger continue
to work on television commercials in England between their feature film assignments, and this explains a great deal of the doubt
I have had about both their styles. I'm not talking about the Faust-
ian furor such undignified professional behavior would cause in
the more status-seeking States, but rather about a weakness for the
immediate click effect at the expense of an over-all conception.
The difference between Lester and Schlesinger is that Lester usually gets his click, whereas Schlesinger usually gets a busy signal.
It's a matter of taste and timing, and timing, particularly, is about
the hardest talent to describe and evaluate on paper, since it is concerned with the musical dimension of the cinema. There is a scene
in *The Knack* in which a group of grammar-school girls are romp-
ing around the playground in Lolita-like abandon. A sudden fluttering apart of the group unblocks our view of the far fence, where
a group of men are watching. Lester holds the effect just long
enough to get his laugh and no longer. If he had started it sooner,
that is, if he had shown girls and men simultaneously, the audience
could not have made the comic link, since the girls would have
been viewed from the outset in an unsavory context. If he had held
the men a bit longer out of context, the emphasis would shift
away from sparkling social satire to nasty social comment. By contrast, Schlesinger holds every effect in *Darling* a beat or two too
long until the obviousness accumulates into boredom. What saves
Darling from its directorial deficiencies are the click effects of performances within their wobbly guidelines.

Help! does not indicate that Lester has depleted his bag of tricks,
but rather that he is too addicted to fragmentation for its own
sake. It was not a good idea to throw the Beatles into a parody of
old Maria Montez movies and the current vogue for James Bond.
For one thing, the parodies don't work. For another, the Beatles
bear no resemblance to the Marx Brothers, with whom they are
too often compared. A parallel of sorts could be worked out with
Ringo evoking Harpo, the literate Lennon Groucho, the elemental

Harrison Chico, and the cherubic McCartney the procession of straight tenors who followed Gummo and Zeppo. The only problem is that the Beatles are not funny in the classical ha-ha sense. They don't move funny. They don't talk funny. They are basically unfunny performers. If they get chuckles, it is because of the styles of their offbeat alienation from the hysteria that surrounds them. Their reactions to stimuli are out of synch, and they needed Lester's cutting in *A Hard Day's Night* to escape the freak framing of the Ed Sullivan show. The Marx Brothers never really needed direction. An expert comedy director like Leo McCarey helped them polish up their timing to perfection in *Duck Soup*, but most of the time they relied on the laboratory formulas they had perfected before live audiences. If anything, the Marx Brothers were a bit too audience-directed, and their double and triple takes after each laugh look painfully mechanical in television revivals of their movies. But, then, the Marx Brothers were products of a utilitarian tradition of entertainment, whereas the Beatles are somewhat more obscurely motivated. Perhaps the main difference can be summed up in a reworking of Priestley's phrase to the effect that the Marx Brothers tried to be mad in a sane world, whereas the Beatles try to be sane in a mad world.

Synanon sounded so much like an old-fashioned do-good movie that I put off seeing it until it had almost passed out of circulation, and I'm glad I didn't miss it entirely. The acting is very sympathetic, and Richard Quine's direction after an alarmingly jazzy beginning on a merry-go-round settles down to let the performers go through their paces. Alex Cord is a young actor to watch, perhaps as a more hip Steve McQueen. Eartha Kitt was moving in a small part, moving both because of herself and because the movie industry had wasted her so shamefully when her nails were longer and sharper. Edmond O'Brien, Richard Conte, Chuck Connors, Bernie Hamilton all played at the same nice level of no-nonsense camaraderie, with Connors particularly ambiguous in his scenes with Cord and Stella Stevens, scenes rather remarkably free of editorial cant. The big merit of *Synanon* is that the plot is genuinely unexpected in what I would have to call a post–Production Code style. Everyone has been so busy complaining about how salacious Hollywood movies are becoming that they have not realized how much suspense can be engendered in storytelling when you're not sure that the girl who turned a trick for a fix will be automatically run over by a garbage truck in the last reel. My other insight into *Synanon* is how much Stella Stevens has become a prettier Shirley MacLaine, and how, unfortunately, there is never room for two stars of the same offbeat type. Not that I'm wild about the type, but Shirley has done her damnedest, and I'd like to see Stella get a chance to show her stuff.

The Sons of Katie Elder bottles up its violence in the tough manner of action films Manny Farber used to honor for their Homeric virtues back in the late forties and early fifties. The virtues of this kind of western are largely negative, that is, antipop, anti-camp, and antipretentious. John Wayne is old and tough and implacable, but not entirely lacking in moral sensibility and emotional vulnerability. Henry Hathaway has directed Wayne as he has been directing him since *Shepherd of the Hills*, not with the classic force of John Ford and Howard Hawks, but with the serious craftsmanship one professional feels he owes another. Martha Hyer is more natural than I have ever seen her, and Dean Martin and James Gregory are okay as a black sheep and a black villain, respectively. The big switch is George Kennedy's hired gunslinger, the first such character I have ever seen with a slight stammer combined with a fast draw. The spectacle of people in Hollywood trying to do something different in a western at this late date is curiously reassuring.

—*Village Voice*, September 9, 1965

■ 8. *REPULSION; THE IPCRESS FILE;*
THE HOURS OF LOVE

Repulsion is the scariest if not actually the goriest Grand Guignol since *Psycho*. Polish director Roman Polanski had one of the hits of the first New York Film Festival with *Knife in the Water*, a sardonic comedy of manners and morals on a sailboat. Previously the now thirty-two-year-old Polanski had regaled avant-garde audiences with a half dozen imaginatively ironic shorts beginning with the still memorable *Two Men and a Wardrobe*. *Repulsion* is Polanski's first English-language film, and he does fairly well in a language he couldn't speak at all when I met him at the 1963 Montreal Film Festival. In the separatist atmosphere of that time and place the fact that his French was as fluent as his English was nonexistent made him something of a culture hero. The point is that *Repulsion* plays well enough as an unsubtitled talkie, except possibly for Catherine Deneuve's awkward reading of her lines. Fortunately, most of the latter part of the film depends less on articulated speech than on agonizing sights and sounds and, in a manner of non-Huxleyan speaking, even smells gurgling up from the depths of a repressed psyche.

Catherine Deneuve, the sweet bon-bon of *Umbrellas of Cherbourg*, is inspired casting as Polanski's fantasy-befouled virgin. The lack of sensual anticipation in her eyes masks insanity with innocence, while the irreproachable symmetry of her delicate features conveys an illusion of order and discipline in her personality, an illusion belied by the reality of her absentminded alienation from other human beings. Polanski has fashioned the kind of pretty girl we seldom see on the screen, one neither chock-full of character and sincerity nor selfishly narcissistic, but rather a younger version of Bergman's Ingrid Thulin character in *The Silence* without Miss Thulin's compensational literary and lesbian tendencies.

Polanski is actually interested more in the spectacle of repression released than in the psychology of the repressed female, and the direst horror is seldom lacking in dark humor. For example, we are so conditioned to Miss Deneuve's demonic sloppiness by the time she commits her two gruesome murders that the corpses seem to complete the decor. Polanski's direction is equally sloppy on occasion, particularly when he indulges in the subjective surrealism of hands reaching out from the walls with a rhythmic writhing worthy of a Busby Berkeley parody of Luis Buñuel. Nor is he much more effective when he tries tricks of perspective in the midst of his interior desecration. However, his failures of style are related to his triumphs of suspense. By forcing the audience to share the girl's demented point of view, Polanski manages to implicate them in the irrational uncertainty of the plot. We soon accept the fact that the girl is beyond redemption and rehabilitation, even beyond reason, but we still worry about when and how society will invade her subjective world. What Polanski counts on and capitalizes on is the fact that we all fear society's invasion of our subconscious, and that we will somehow identify with the most perverted privacy rather than blow the whistle for the authorities.

All things being equal, Polanski's subjective style is preferable to Wyler's comfortably, almost complacently voyeuristic vantage point in *The Collector*, but Wyler almost makes up the difference with the emotional intensity of Samantha Eggar and Terence Stamp. Almost, but not quite. Polanski's last dazzling track to a telling close-up of a family portrait brings order out of chaos and beauty out of horror. Art, however imperfect, is ultimately preferable to professionalism, however inspired.

The Ipcress File was reasonably entertaining while I was watching it, but after it was over I felt I'd been had. I don't particularly mind pictures that are assembled rather than directed, and Sidney Furie seems somewhat abler as an assembler than Terence Young and Guy Hamilton of the Bond series. Michael Caine is a more attractive performer than Sean Connery; the blur-focusing glasses, the ratty laugh, the sojourns in supermarkets, and the attendant food fetishism all make Caine's character more comically accessible to audiences than Connery's. Caine's success with women is more plausible than that of his predecessor largely because Caine's banter sounds more knowing. Connery's conquests seem to reflect the triumph of wardrobe over wit, and his women almost invariably succumb with all the spontaneity of mechanical dolls in some future interplanetary convention of department-store buyers.

The Ipcress File seems to fall spy-wise halfway between Ian Fleming's glamour and Graham Greene's grubbiness, and Caine's operative similarly splits the difference between Fleming's upper-class sleuth and Greene's lower-caste snoop. Caine starts off with a set of disillusioningly middle-class attitudes. He yearns for more money, job security, the approval of his superiors, the congeniality of his coworkers, and a never-ending concert of sharp girls in his flat. Then suddenly the character acquires some middlebrow modifications with an ostentatious appreciation of Mozart and a sniggering pride in his own virility. Mickey Spillane, where art thou?

Among the tiresome directorial tricks in *The Ipcress File* is the repetitively off-angle anticlimax, with the heavies feeding parking meters, hibernating in libraries, and plotting at band concerts. Nothing happens most of the time, and this is supposed to be funny and ironic. Two CIA agents, one a Negro, are murdered, and we are supposed to react with civilized amusement to the cool aplomb of the British in the situation. International cynicism is one thing, however, and learning that your buddy has been done in on the high road (in a straight steal from a recent Fritz Lang movie) is quite another matter entirely. The hero finally loses his coolness and composure and thus exemplifies, as does Bond, the sentimentality that inevitably overtakes any middlebrow exercise in nihilism. This is one of the less enchanting prospects of popular art in its serial development. When Tarzan, for example, hit the screen in the first Weissmuller version in 1931, Maureen O'Sullivan's Jane went really ape over the Ape Man in a rather frank expression of natural instinct triumphing over social restraints. By the time Metro finished domesticating the series, Tarzan was wearing a Sanforized loincloth and Jane was attending jungle PTA meetings. Bond has steadily declined in arrogant amorality from *Dr. No* to *From Russia With Love* to *Goldfinger,* and before long he will be as fierce as Fearless Fosdick. *The Ipcress File* manages to degenerate between its first hour and its last.

Ironically, what makes the film click even momentarily as drama is a son-father relationship between Caine and his superior, a relationship shattered with classically Oedipal force when the superior turns out to be a double agent. At that climactic moment Freud takes control of the hot firearms away from Marx and Machiavelli and the Cold Warriors. The worst passages in the film are brainwashing sessions involving the projection of pseudo-Pavlovian Op Art, which I doubt could condition a dog to chase a cat. To end on a relatively positive note, I can't remember another movie where the gal takes off the guy's glasses before seducing him. Who says girls don't make passes at men who wear glasses?

The Hours of Love will make the art-house break one of these days, and I recommend it very conditionally only to make the point that as Hollywood films are occasionally very artistic, foreign films can occasionally be fun. In fact, *The Hours of Love* is the kind of good-bad movie that only Hollywood is supposed to have the knack of making. Luciano Salce's direction is more delicately civilized than his rather broad material would seem to deserve, and Ugo Tognazzi and Emmanuelle Riva are pure gold as a couple who find it easier to sleep together than live together. As in *The Fascist* and *Crazy Desire*, Salce is at times the closest thing to an Italian Lubitsch in the graceful discipline that enables his players to shift from near-farce to near-tragedy without losing their lightness. I particularly liked the moment when Riva says that she is not beautiful but that she has beautiful eyes, and then the way she uses her eyes when she cooks Tognazzi his first lunch. The plot is not always profound in illustrating the divergent paths of chemistry and compatibility, but Tognazzi and Riva make this sub-Chayefskian conception worth seeing the way Lombard and Grant used to make a piece of cheese like *In Name Only* worth seeing. There is no law against enjoying bad foreign movies.

—Village Voice, October 7, 1965

■ 9. *BUNNY LAKE IS MISSING*

Bunny Lake Is Missing is a variation of the Paris Exposition story in which a girl's mother mysteriously disappears and the girl is told by all concerned that the mother had never registered in the hotel at which both were staying and that the girl is making up the mother and her disappearance. It turns out that the girl's mother had caught the bubonic plague and the hotel people had been frightened that the Paris Exposition would end in panic and Paris would be the poorer. Alfred Hitchcock's *The Lady Vanishes* was another variation of this plot, and the plot itself with brother switched for mother was made into a charming Jean Simmons–Dirk Bogarde lady-in-distress romance called *So Long at the Fair* some years ago. In both instances the audience knew that the heroine was telling the truth. In *The Lady Vanishes* we see Dame May Whitty before she vanishes from Margaret Lockwood's sight, and in *So Long at the Fair* we see David Tomlinson before he is spirited away to a sanitarium. In both instances romantically inclined males ride to the rescue, Michael Redgrave in *The Lady Vanishes* and Dirk Bogarde in *So Long at the Fair*, but in both instances the heroes are aware of some fact that confirms the heroine's story. The only problem is proof.

However, if you turn the story around, you might just as easily have a paranoiac plot. From the point of view of the authorities and "sane" people generally, people are always imagining cosmic conspiracies. The reason that the plot works in the two contexts I have cited is that there is some overriding social interest at stake to justify the scope of the conspiracy. In *The Lady Vanishes* it is a matter of espionage; in *So Long at the Fair* extensive economic interests. We are not let down at the denouement because we respect the size and plausibility of the motivation.

Bunny Lake Is Missing is something else again. To begin with, we don't see Bunny Lake before she is supposed to be missing. For all we know, Bunny Lake may in fact be nonexistent, and with this aspect of the plot scenarists John and Penelope Mortimer and the author Evelyn Piper are in complete accord. However, it never occurred to me as it did to Frances Herridge of the *Post* that Bunny Lake might be as imaginary as the infant in *Who's Afraid of Virginia Woolf?* I think the purpose of withholding Bunny until the very end is to make the reader or audience see the situation from the point of view of the authorities. If the child were seen from the beginning, the authorities would seem more wickedly obtuse than they are. However, once a doubt is raised about the child's very existence, it is clear that the doubt cannot be sustained for much longer than twenty-four hours, the records and witnesses to human existence being as extensive as they are. Consequently the action has to be confined to one day at the most, and the melodrama works because the mother is too hysterical to wait through a night, and her hysteria adds to the suspicions of the authorities that she is unstable enough to fantasize a child into being. The Paris Exposition plot thus degenerates imperceptibly into mock paranoia.

The screenplay diverges rather drastically from the novel in its climax and final explanation, but the plot collapses in both versions. Why? Curiously, because there is no overriding social interest at stake, but rather an implausibly elaborate caper by a conveniently psychotic character. The biggest mystery of *Bunny Lake*

Is Missing is why Preminger was always so anxious to do the project. As a matter of fact, I once asked him, and he said he was interested in the problem of an unwed mother attempting to establish the identity of her child. I have been aware of Preminger as a producer personality for many years, and he has always answered in a similar way about *The Man with the Golden Arm, Exodus, Advise and Consent, The Cardinal,* and *In Harm's Way.* Always there is some problem, some ticklish situation, some power struggle that intrigues him in the material. I have never once heard him say that he fell in love with one of the characters, and it is perhaps more than a coincidence that what is generally lacking in Preminger's cinema, particularly in recent years, is compelling characterization. Thus I can understand critics and readers reacting violently to even moderate praise of Preminger, but the fact remains that Preminger's mise-en-scène in *Bunny Lake Is Missing* is the most brilliant I have seen all year. The movie is a pleasure to watch from beginning to end, but there are really no characters to consider in Preminger's chilling world of doors and dolls and deceits and degeneracies of decor.

Obviously Preminger hunts about for best sellers and gimmicky projects to avoid paying the piper for box-office costs, but *Bunny Lake Is Missing* is a casting cheat even by Preminger's cut-corner standards. Laurence Olivier is scandalously wasted in a part any second-rate British character actor could have played with ease, and Carol Lynley and Keir Dullea are disconcertingly lightweight in heavyweight roles. This means that the audience soon gets bored with the heart of the drama and begins peering around the edges, and this is just as well, because Preminger has no peer this year around the edges. To watch his camera prowling around a girl's school, an unoccupied house, a pervert's lair, a lackluster pub, from room to room, up- and downstairs, in and out of doors, with the sustained frenzy of a director concerned with integral space is to realize the majesty of mise-en-scène. There is one sequence when Olivier walks up the steps to the school with a fixed focus on the revolving police light in the foreground. Preminger virtually tosses the effect away, and this is only one of many such casual coups that make his movies so hard to evaluate.

—*Village Voice,* October 21, 1965

■ 10. *JULIET OF THE SPIRITS*

I

Federico Fellini's *Juliet of the Spirits* was probably the most eagerly awaited picture of the year. The Venice and New York Film festivals panted for it in vain, and now Fellini has been given the Great Director treatment in New York by a local ad agency hired by the Rizzoli interests. Fellini is certainly nothing if not ambitious. If *La Dolce Vita* was meant to be his *Inferno*, and *8½* his *Purgatorio*, then *Juliet* [or *Giulietta*] *of the Spirits* is clearly his *Paradiso*, or, if not his, at least his wife's.

I may have been too hard on *La Dolce Vita* several years ago when I observed: "Fellini undertook in *La Dolce Vita* to provide a Dantean vision of the modern world as viewed from the top instead of the bottom. Unfortunately, there is more to a great film than a great conception, and Fellini has enlarged his material without expanding his ideas. Consequently, the film is as bloated as the fish that terminates the orgy sequence." In contrast to the increasingly ballooning art of *8½* and *Juliet of the Spirits*, *La Dolce Vita* now seems relatively coherent in its apprehension of some segment of the real world. The scenes with Mastroianni's father and the distant lights of peasant dwellings in the early dawn reminded us that durable facts coexisted with decadent fantasies. The purely subjective oxygen that comprises the artistic atmosphere of *8½* and *Juliet* is not of this world but of some other floating loosely in Fellini's mind.

Nonetheless it is obviously the delayed reaction to *8½* that has made Fellini's reputation. This is the film that is thrown up to me by my lecture audiences as the prime example of modern cinema. There is always some such film in vogue every decade or so. Before *8½* it was *Hiroshima, Mon Amour* and *L'Avventura*, and before these modish movies were *Open City* and *The Bicycle Thief*. The point is that the fashion has now come full circle from raw realism and social consciousness to stylish fantasy and directorial self-indulgence. Even Fellini's confession in *8½* that he had nothing to say seems to have struck a responsive chord in the fantasies of many young film enthusiasts who would probably like to make films that say nothing with great feeling. Also, I suspect that 8½ is the kind of film that seems more impressive after its tedious stretches of intellectual equivocation have been forgotten for the sake of its poignant moments of personal nostalgia. Perhaps, also, Fellini has finally become, like Antonioni, opaque enough to seem profound.

However, it had been a long time since I had seen 8½ and I was beginning to wonder if I had underrated Fellini's achievement. I braced myself at a screening of *Juliet of the Spirits* for what I had predicted would be Fellini's facile assault on my emotional resistance. How could he miss with Giulietta Masina playing his wronged wife with a quivering upper lip and the faintest trace of a gallant smile? As it turned out, Fellini missed by a mile, and I am sorry that I must write this review more in sorrow than anger, but *Juliet* is barely slick enough to pass as middlebrow entertainment on the Rose Franzblau level.

The film opens in the home of Giorgio and Giulietta, a married couple bearing more than a passing resemblance to Fellini and his wife. There are differences, of course. Giorgio is not actually a film director, but does some kind of vague public-relations work. Nor is Giulietta of the Spirits exactly Giulietta Masina. For one thing, the girl in the picture is not an actress, just a simple housewife, though not too simple. She occupies a beautiful home among the lush pine trees of Fregene within walking distance of the sea. She has two maids, many clothes and jewels, and an immense amount of time to worry about her faltering marriage. There are no children, but no one ever discusses the implications of this fact. (Fellini has a long way to fall to reach Arthur Miller's level in *After the Fall*.)

Tonight is Giulietta Masina's anniversary. To the accompaniment of a tinny-melodious Nino Rota score, which gives most Fellini films their distinctively hurdy-gurdy sound, Giulietta busily supervises a surprise anniversary party for Giorgio. Fellini's camera swoops around the house with the wife in true 9½ style as she sets the stage for her husband's entrance. Enter Giorgio. Naturally— one feels typically—he has forgotten the anniversary. He apologizes casually, and then introduces some of his bizarre friends from the office. Giulietta had envisioned a romantically candle-lit dinner for two; the maids must now improvise a feast for eight. Giulietta is

hurt and humiliated as only Giulietta Masina can be hurt and humiliated. After dinner there is a séance for no discernible reason.
Giulietta hears the vague voices of spirits, and thus begins her pilgrimage into the spirit world in search of marital truth.

Fellini has embroidered this simple situation with a vast tapestry
of dreams, myths, illusions, fantasies, memories, and often, most
fantastic of all, grotesque realities. In a Fellini film the world often
looks less strange in dreams than in daily life. For example, Giulietta's next-door neighbor (Sandra Milo) is a courtesan who lives
only for pleasure and stages orgies so desultory as to make those in
La Dolce Vita seem full of high spirits. Surrounded by a court of
gargoyles and eccentrics out of the Arabian Nights via the Marquis
de Sade, she lives in a labyrinth of sensual surprise. Her bedroom
is equipped with a ceiling mirror, and when she is bored, she lures
male motorists to her tree house in the forest.

After Giulietta learns of her husband's infidelity through a battery of audio-visual snoopers acting and talking very much in the
double-edged jargon of cinéma vérité for the benefit of ambiguity-
stalking highbrow critics, she flees to her neighbor's masquerade
ball, where she is offered the revenge of unrestrained eroticism in
the form of a beautiful young Arab lover. But Giulietta runs from
the furies of hellfire inherited from a Catholic girlhood—and truth
to tell, Fellini himself does not seem enchanted by the temptations
of desire. He makes fun of feminine wiles by exaggerating them beyond the point of parody to utter disgust. Giulietta's pretty sister,
Sylva Koscina, is always bouncing her bosom in ridiculous fashion,
or licking her lips, or fluttering her eyes. In the hallucinations Giulietta experiences, the demons of desire are always sticking out
their tongues ceremonially as if to warn the audience about the
wages of sin. Fellini gets some of his most amusing effects from
Oriental mystics and their mumbo jumbo about the rites of love,
but Masina kills most of the humor simply by being the sexless
context of the satire.

What, then, is left to Giulietta after her childhood faith crumbles, her husband betrays her for another woman, and all her potential lovers are rejected out of hand? Simply her freedom to face
reality without myths or ideals, an idea less meaningful in itself
than in the final image of Giulietta Masina embarked once more
on the road of life past the glorious greenness of clustered pines
splashing across the screen as a visual hymn to nature.

II

Giulietta has liberated herself from her Catholic girlhood by unty-
ing herself as a child from the pop-red *papier-mâché* flames she endured as a child in a ghastly religious pageant. Earlier, her vaguely
anarchistic-agnostic grandfather rescues her from the same traumatic flames, but her ultimate liberation, Fellini suggests, is something she must achieve herself. When Fellini is dealing with the
Church and its psychic influence on the Italian spirit, he is both
dramatically compelling and socially relevant. We all know in
some measure the power of religion in imposing taboos on us from
early childhood, and many if not most of us would respond sympathetically to Fellini's call for liberation. But liberation for what?
Here Fellini is not too clear. Like Ibsen in A *Doll's House*, Fellini
is launching his heroine out into the world with confidence that
she will find her way, but what *is* Out There? Like Ibsen, Fellini
doesn't say, but Ibsen at least described and defined what Nora
was leaving and what she was seeking. Fellini sets Giulietta adrift
on a sea of passive acceptance of defeat and rejection, and seems
to confuse what looks like unbearable loneliness by any normal human standard with some vaguely Felliniesque state of liberation.

My strongest reservations about *Juliet of the Spirits* are tied up
with this vague confusion of objective situations with subjective interpretations. Giulietta Masina ceases to exist as a character when
she refrains from any attempt to communicate with her husband.
For all its alleged formalism, *Contempt* does take time for marital
confrontation, and though Bardot's character may be unreasonable,
she is at least comprehensible. Besides, *Contempt* ultimately finds
its consolation in art, whereas *Juliet of the Spirits*, like 8½, implicitly rejects art as an answer. Fellini's only consolation seems to
be a mysterious nostalgia for some unfocused past.

In his first color feature Fellini has drenched the screen with
lurid reds to denote sensuality, pale whites for purity, and dull
blacks for churchly repression. Every last costume counts in Fellini's color scheme, and every last fabric seems to have been invented for the film. If *The Red Desert* is a mobile painting, *Juliet
of the Spirits* is a swirling maze of water colors. Still, I found most
of the film beautiful but boring, because the psychological addition
came out zero. Masina is very much the same in the last scene as

she is in the first, and Mario Pisu as her husband seems more shadowy rather than less after we have learned what little there is to learn about him. All the other characters are creatures of allegory, details of decor, with no dramatic life or psychological meaning. Even Masina herself is not as moving as she has been in the past under her husband's direction in *La Strada* and *Cabiria*. The ingredients for tear-jerking are all there. She is not only a neglected, childless wife. Her sisters and even her mother are infinitely more attractive than she is. Yet she seems to be playing against the ugly-duckling pathos of the situation by emphasizing unpleasantly upper-class aspects of her wifely character, such as spying on her maids, gossiping about her neighbor, and hiring detectives to check up on her husband. By becoming relatively realistic in a poetic fantasy, she only creates a stylistic contradiction, and I wound up not caring about her problem despite her stoic calm in the last scenes of renunciation.

Like so many other films of our time, *Juliet of the Spirits* is a dazzling dead end, and I am thinking of Alain Resnais' *Last Year at Marienbad*, Jean-Luc Godard's *The Married Woman*, Ingmar Bergman's *All These Women*, and Michelangelo Antonioni's *The Red Desert*. These are all films that try to get by almost entirely on directorial personality without any dramatic core, and I don't think this is the way the cinema can go. I preferred Fellini's art in the days of *Vitelloni* and *La Strada*, when he was still telling little stories with great themes, to his present films in which he is exploring great themes with hardly any story at all. And curiously, more of Fellini's personality comes through in *Vitelloni* than in *8½* and *Juliet of the Spirits* put together. Perhaps we may postulate at long last that the cinema is as much the art of indirection as the art of direction.

—*Village Voice*, November 11 and 18, 1965

■ 11. *THE ELEANOR ROOSEVELT STORY*

The *Eleanor Roosevelt Story* is a moving tribute to one of the most famous women of this century. Her early years are reflected in pictures of the ugly duckling growing up shy and lonely in a family where all the other female members were beautiful and most of the male members were drunkards. Both of her parents died before she was eleven, and she lived a loveless life with related elders of the Roosevelt clan. Eleanor was out of place in high society, a disappointment as a debutante, and even her marriage to her tall, handsome cousin Franklin Delano Roosevelt was considered something of a comedown socially. She became a docile wife and dutiful mother in the placid world of privilege that came to an end with the First World War.

The early part of her story is told largely through still photographs; movies, after all, were rather primitive at the turn of the century. There is one striking photograph of Eleanor and her domineering mother-in-law flanking the chair of a polio-stricken FDR like implacable antagonists in an Ibsen play. Eleanor won that now famous battle of Campobello, and the rest is history.

Although Eleanor Roosevelt may have been more a light than a force in that history, she did see many of her objectives realized. She saw Woodrow Wilson's dream die with the dreamer only to be reborn in the UN. She accompanied her husband's casket on the train back from Warm Springs to Washington, and the crowds along the way reminded her of Whitman's verses on Lincoln's last trip from Washington to Springfield. At her own funeral were President John F. Kennedy and Ambassador Adlai Stevenson, now also both dead.

At times the treatment is too loving, and a gracious lady who never took herself too seriously is smothered with affection. Ezra Laderman's musical score is needlessly lugubrious, and Archibald MacLeish's script bites off more history than it can chew. I would have preferred more glimpses of Mrs. Roosevelt herself and less of the meaningless mob footage of the twenties and thirties, periods that were more complex politically than MacLeish suggests. Of the three narrators only Eric Sevareid achieves the proper lightness of tone that is needed to play against the surefire emotions of the subject.

Nonetheless history has vindicated Eleanor Roosevelt's honesty of mind. I wonder how many intellectuals of her time wept for both Spain and Finland, opposed Soviet terror as vehemently as Nazi terror, defended the rights of Japanese-Americans after Pearl

Harbor as staunchly as the liberties of American Communists during the McCarthy madness. She began the war on poverty and racial discrimination long before it was fashionable to do so, and she illuminated the uglier side of America, the middle-class hatred of the needy and the underprivileged, a hatred that lingers today.

In most matters of grave importance, Oscar Wilde has observed, style, not sincerity, is the vital thing. This has been true of Churchill, Roosevelt, De Gaulle, Kennedy, but not of Eleanor Roosevelt. Sincerity was the only style she had. She was awkward, ungainly, and an excruciatingly shrill public speaker. She lacked eloquence, wit, timing, and like any Helen Hokinson clubwoman, she could kill the punch line of any joke. Nor did Shaw's definition of a lady as someone who is treated like a lady always hold true for Mrs. Roosevelt. She was treated by too many with too little of the respect she deserved. Eleanor Roosevelt was a lady simply because she treated every human being as a member of her family. A film worth seeing, though I would have preferred it as a television special so that I could weep in the privacy of my living room.

(The above review was on WNDT, Channel 13, on "The World at Ten," on Thursday, November 11.)

—*Village Voice*, November 25, 1965

■ 12. *THE SPY*
    WHO CAME IN FROM THE COLD

The Spy Who Came In from the Cold is brilliantly cast but badly directed. Before I try to explain what I mean by bad direction, I must warn all my readers who have neither read the book nor seen the movie to read no further in this column, or rather to proceed at their own peril. The reason for this warning is quite simple. I am about to give away every last twist of the plot, to strip the story bare, so to speak, so as to operate on the film. I realize, however, that the most cultivated moviegoers still care about the way things turn out on the screen. Perhaps they don't want to play God by knowing everything in advance, since if certainty is divine, suspense is human. It is difficult for most movie reviewers to be human in

this context. There is always someone in our little world who has
seen the film before we have. There are trade reviews, plugs in the
columns, production gossip, advance peeks at screenplays, and endless conversations about what the distributors think and what they
really think. Thus I usually wind up looking at a movie with all the
wide-eyed innocence of Dorian Gray in his last days of decadence.
The plot? A foregone conclusion. The players and directors? An
IBM (I Bug Movies) computer totes up the odds from past performances, and I just sit back complacently to watch how closely
true to form the execution runs.

Therefore I was not surprised to see Martin Ritt botch up *The
Spy Who Came In from the Cold* despite a relatively literal adaptation by Paul Dehn and Guy Trosper of John Le Carré's runaway
best seller. Not that the book is any great shakes as storytelling. Le
Carré emerges as a poor man's Graham Greene down to Greene's
annoying mannerism of pretending to be bored by his own anti-
Americanism. In a blind genre, however, the one-eyed spy is king,
and Le Carré at his most contrived still towers over the Bond series.
Yet the fact remains that *The Spy Who Came In from the Cold*
is a dull journey to an interesting destination. The plot's the thing
in this instance, and we are treated in the end to a triple twist, and
I can't remember the last time I saw a movie with a single twist.

The plot is built around an elaborate revenge scheme. Alec
Leamas (Richard Burton) heads a British intelligence apparatus in
West Berlin. Both novel and film begin with a gray morning scene
at a checkpoint between the two sectors of the city. Leamas has
been waiting all night for one of his agents to cross from East Berlin. Ritt begins with a rear-view semiclose-up of Burton's vigil
strikingly similar to Jean-Luc Godard's opening in *My Life to Live*.
The agent appears with a bicycle, is passed by the East German
guards, begins riding across the last stretch of East Berlin to the
West. Suddenly sirens, spotlights, Sten guns. This man whom we
have never met is dead, and Leamas is despondent. Leamas returns
to London where Control (Cyril Cusack) makes the stirring
speech (from the book) about spies, starved for approval and affection, becoming useless when they "come in from the cold." Leamas
wants to continue, particularly since it means revenging himself on
the East German intelligence chief who has been murdering British agents in both sectors of Berlin. This murderer's name is

Mundt, and he remains a name through most of the film. Control's plot is never spelled out in great detail, but it seems that it involves framing Mundt as a British agent by arousing the suspicions of Mundt's ambitious subordinate, Fiedler. This maneuver depends also on the facts that Mundt was once a member of the Hitler Youth, Fiedler is a Jew, and both men are still marked by the scars of Hitlerian history. Leamas is called upon to play the most devious role of his career, feigning, in turn, dissipation, disintegration, and finally defection. In the course of his masquerade as a seedy librarian, Leamas makes one fatal error. He falls in love with Nan Perry (Claire Bloom), a fellow librarian, a dedicated Communist party worker, but not a Jewish girl in the film, as she is in the book under the name of Liz Gold.

Leamas slugs a grocer, is imprisoned, then recruited by a succession of Red agents (Michael Hordern, Robert Hardy, Sam Wanamaker) in a daisy chain of petty bureaucratic humiliations of subordinates as the scene quickly shifts from London to Amsterdam to East Germany, where Leamas finally confronts Fiedler (Oskar Werner). The interrogation proceeds with Leamas pretending to begrudge every detail that is intended to frame the still unseen Mundt. One night Mundt appears in the form of Peter Van Eyck. Fiedler turns the tables by having Mundt arrested. A trial is called by the East German Presidium, and Fiedler's case seems very strong at first. Mundt's lawyer (George Voskovec) calls a surprise witness —Nan Perry. Lured from England for a party rally in Leipzig, she unknowingly implicates Leamas in a plot to frame Mundt. Fiedler is completely discredited and destined for a hangman's noose. Leamas suddenly perceives the first twist in the plot. Mundt is indeed a British agent, and Leamas was sent east not to frame him but to clear him. In the process a Jew bothersome to Mundt and the "Free World" would be liquidated. Mundt arranges for Leamas and Nan to escape over the Berlin wall. Then comes the second twist. One of Mundt's men shoots Nan to keep her from telling what she knows outside. The third twist occurs when Leamas decides to stay and die with Nan rather than return to "freedom" on the other side of the wall. Finally and irrevocably, Leamas has come in from the soul-chilling cold of the Cold War.

If Alfred Hitchcock, Joseph Losey, or the Carol Reed of fifteen years ago had directed, *The Spy Who Came In from the Cold* would have been the picture of the year. I remember particularly Claire Bloom watching James Mason die in the receding road from East to West Berlin in Carol Reed's *The Man Between,* and the image still moves me in my memory. Ritt's uninspired mannerisms of "realism" left me completely cold. I could figure out what it all meant, but it was like reading between the images. The heat between Leamas and Nan, Burton and Bloom, is never realized on the screen. There is no sustained tension in the final confrontation of Burton, Werner, and Van Eyck. Ritt has muddled through somehow to give us the facts without the feelings. We know what has happened and why, but there is no emotional resonance in the spectacle as it happens. The spy may come in from the cold, but the audience is left outside.

Despite the wasted opportunities of direction, the acting is superb. Burton is perfectly cast as the uncertain masquerader, impaled finally on his own ironic sensibility like a Hamlet who had spent the whole play mocking the concerns of others until it was too late to respond to his own. Oskar Werner's sensibility is sweeter than Burton's and more likely to be victimized by direct injustice than by devious irony. Claire Bloom is not allowed to develop her role to any meaningful degree, but I can't think of any other contemporary actress, with or without subtitles, who flows from sensuality to idealism without any harsh stops. Similarly, Peter Van Eyck, the vintage Hollywood Aryan of the forties, is wasted by not being brought into focus much sooner as a political correlative of the plot. The name "Mundt" may mean something on the printed page even *in absentia,* but the visual image of the man is the only emotional form the man can take on the screen. Even Godot must be shown. Otherwise there is no point waiting for him, and Tartuffe himself had better not tarry.

I suppose that some critics will defend Ritt's conception as "subtle," "leaving something to the imagination," or even "intellectual." This is a new trend in criticism. Make the plot unclear enough and it seems profound. Of course any imbecile can figure out a plot with enough clues, however dim and dreary. The highest pleasures of moviegoing, however, begin with the enjoyment of plots and not with their deduction. The trouble with Le Carré and Ritt both is that they do not feel their plot all the way down to the denouement, and thus they pad everything out with Bond-like

details about financial and travel arrangements and a sense of fiscal
fealties going back to the bank sagas of James M. Cain. Ultimately,
the characters are less human beings than rhetorical constructs.
Thus though everything we know and feel about contemporary politics asks us to come in from the cold, a lack of meaningful style in
the presentation of the narrative makes us sniff suspiciously at a
sanctimonious odor of self-sacrifice.

—*Village Voice*, December 16, 1965

■ 13. DR. ZHIVAGO

Dr. Zhivago turns out to be three hours and seventeen minutes of
coming attractions for anyone who is thinking of reading the book;
and the book, I suspect, has been honored more on the shelf than
in the subway. As proof of this proposition, you try looking for
pocket editions of Boris Pasternak's celebrated novel. It is not in
stock in most bookstores, and the shelves are usually filled with the
books from which current movies are adapted. I also conducted
my own private poll of my more bookish friends, and fewer people
had managed even to start *Zhivago* than had managed to finish
Herzog. Consequently David Lean and Robert Bolt could have
thrown up any plot on the screen from *Uncle Tom's Cabin* to
War and Peace and few moviegoers would have been in any position to complain about infidelity to Pasternak's text.

Just for the record, however, this column should try to respect
the solemnity of the occasion by filling in some of the background.
Doctor Zhivago earned its author, the late Boris Pasternak, the
Nobel Prize for Literature in 1958. Warned that he would be permanently exiled from Russia if he went to Stockholm to accept,
Pasternak declined the prize. Nevertheless he remained under a
political cloud to the day of his death in 1960. *Doctor Zhivago*, a
poetic projection of Pasternak's own life and feelings, has been
hailed throughout the world for resurrecting the psychological am-
plitude and moral idealism of the great nineteenth-century Russian
novels of Tolstoy, Dostoyevsky, and Turgenev. Americans in 1958,
still recoiling from the imminence of a nuclear nightmare, were

particularly reassured by the evidence of a human heartbeat in the Marxist mechanism of history, the heartbeat, no less, of a dissenting poet who had translated Shakespeare; and everyone loves a dissenting poet in someone else's society.

Enter David Lean with a trophy room full of Academy awards for *Bridge on the River Kwai* and *Lawrence of Arabia*. Off to Spain, Finland, Canada to recreate the Russia of 1905 onward; and now, three years and $12 million later, *Dr. Zhivago* unfurls on the curved Capitol screen as the biggest disappointment of 1965. *Zhivago* is hardly the worst picture of 1965, but it is certainly one of the least interesting. Lean, the impersonal technician, has finally gotten his comeuppance from the very critics who encouraged him in his excesses. (I except, of course, the pathetic Lean idolator on the *Post* who came out with a straight *Cahiers du Cinéma* rationalization of *Zhivago* as a good picture because its director had once made *Brief Encounter*. This apparently is an argument that applies only to Lean, not to Ford or Hitchcock, and a few days later the same critic sneered at French-type critics in a blast at a poverty-row picture by Edgar G. Ulmer. All I can say is that if Ulmer were given three years and $12 million, he'd come out with twenty pictures, quite a few of them more interesting than *Dr. Zhivago*.)

Dr. Zhivago is actually the third time around for what might be called the *Kwai* formula, or the best cinema that time and money can buy. Imperceptibly, David Lean has evolved into the middlebrow's answer to the late Cecil B. DeMille. *Kwai* and *Lawrence* are both spectacularly and exotically produced, *Kwai* in Southeast Asia, *Lawrence* in Arabia. There are no significant female characters in either film and hence no "commercial" heterosexuality. *Kwai* in this regard had a girl in a bathing suit for Holden and some apparently compliant Burmese maidens, but *Kwai* was strictly a man's picture, vague, allegorical, and ironic all at the same time. All the characters meant something, but the ending was unresolved because it was never established how Guinness managed to fall onto the dynamite, that is, intentionally or inadvertently. It didn't really matter, because all the characters were seen from the outside, and the main thing was displaying all the money that was being spent on the bridge.

Lawrence was even more obscure, as the main effect was the marvelous optical illusion created on the desert sands. The all-male plot had more overtones of homosexuality than *Kwai*, but everything was kept vague for Aunt Minny. With *Lawrence*, Lean teamed up with Robert (*A Man for All Seasons*) Bolt and composer Maurice Jarre to create the right, muted, impersonal tone that is needed to impress critics with the seriousness of the undertaking. Now the same team has come together for *Zhivago*, and the result is *Lawrence of Russia*. Peter O'Toole's blue eyes are perhaps to be preferred for this sort of thing over Omar Sharif's cocker-spaniel brown eyes, but the aesthetic fallacy is the same in both instances, though it is more nearly fatal in *Dr. Zhivago*. The fallacy is simply this: the cherished belief of certain aestheticians that words are less "cinematic" than images and every literary idea must be translated into a visual equivalent. This is comparable to composing music that will translate the Constitution or the Rights of Man.

The main appeal of Pasternak's novel is not its plot or even its theme, but rather the extravagant expression of its emotions in poetic language. Most of this poetic language has been stripped from Bolt's simplified and vulgarized screenplay, and the movie is all the poorer for it. Lean seems terrified of being called "talky," perhaps because he spent so much time bringing Noel Coward vehicles to the screen in his earlier days. Yet *In Which We Serve*, *Blithe Spirit*, *Brief Encounter*, and *This Happy Breed*, for all their class condescension, are infinitely more interesting than the dull-as-dishwater dialogue in *Zhivago*. Lean has been quoted to the effect that *Dr. Zhivago* is primarily a personal love story, and yet his lovers never say one interesting thing to each other throughout the film. Whenever possible, Lean will mute his characters behind frosted windows or photograph them from great scenic distances. This is cinema, you see. Well, *Les Enfants du Paradis* runs about as long as *Dr. Zhivago* and is a moving love story, and what do its characters do? They talk and they talk and they talk, poetically, flamboyantly, personally. Is this cinema? Of course it is. Cinema is everything. Image, sound, music, speech, color. It may have been born illiterate, but it has learned to speak, and it is time the aestheticians of illiterate images realized that Carl Dreyer's *Gertrud* is the picture of the year because people sit and talk on a couch, and there is no greater spectacle in the cinema than a man and a woman talking away their share of eternity together.

By contrast, *Zhivago* is full of beautiful shots of ice and snow and moon and sun and fields and flowers and trees and spires, but the shots spill out on the screen like loose beads from a broken necklace. There is nothing holding the effects together, not an idea, or a feeling, or a mood, or even much of a plot, and a relatively capable cast struggles helplessly with Robert Bolt's disconnected, uninspired dialogue as the film bumbles along to boredom. Lean's trouble seems to be the opposite of Stanley Kramer's. Kramer doesn't know enough about his medium; Lean knows too much, and in this instance his artistry has been smothered by his technology.

Even Julie Christie, the most beautiful actress on the screen today, is somewhat hampered by Lean's too deliberate framing. Julie's forte is not embalmed portrait posing, but a whacky, swinging vivacity, with every hair and feature out of place but still swirling together in a wildly stirring harmony. Still, Julie, particularly in her scenes with Rod Steiger, the cynical opportunist Komarovsky, who seduces her and obsesses her, comes closer to life than many of the other performers, who seem to be waiting for tea to be served on the set. Steiger's performance is curiously the most Russian, perhaps because Americans are somewhat closer to the Russian temperament than the relatively restrained British. Tom Courtenay's part is undeveloped, particularly his moving death in the book when he switches from being the celibate Strelnikov to the more human Pasha, but he at least looks the part of the battered fanatic. Normally reliable performers like Ralph Richardson, Alec Guinness, Rita Tushingham, Adrienne Corri, Siobhan McKenna, and Geoffrey Keen play with more intelligence than inspiration.

The highly publicized Geraldine Chaplin emerges with some of her father's charm and warm inner glow in addition to her own considerable good looks, but she has little to do except suffer smilingly as Zhivago's noble wife without even once being allowed to lose her temper. One of the few emotionally effective moments of the film occurs when Omar Sharif runs up the stairs of the old mansion to get one last look from the window at the departing Julie Christie. Lean's camera follows Sharif, the music swells, Sharif reaches the window, but it's locked, and in his impatience to catch one last glimpse of his beloved he breaks the glass. If the movie had given us more of this passion, and much, much more of Pasternak's poetry, that is to say, more literary fat and less visual Lean, it might have had more of a chance to engage American audiences. As it is, when Ralph Richardson expresses shock at the news of the shooting of the Czar and his entire family, it is difficult to stifle a yawn.

If I have not said much about the performance of Omar Sharif in the title role, it is because there is not much to say, and it is not entirely Mr. Sharif's fault. For a title character he is singularly uninteresting. Like most artist-characters on stage or screen, he must be taken largely on faith. Divorced from his muse, Dylan Thomas was just another obnoxious drunk in his recent stage incarnation. Similarly, Zhivago is just a philandering husband who can't adjust to the Revolution, and he seems hardly worth all the fuss and bother dramatically. One would have to look into his mind or allow him to speak it for his full worth to be apparent on the full screen, and this Lean and Bolt have declined to do. Typical of the absurdly realistic conventions of the film is the practice of using Russian characters on signs, letters, and newspapers, with the result that some character or other is always wasting half the scene reading the text in English. A subtle prejudice operates here. The printed and written alphabet is visual and must therefore be authentic; speech is merely an alien accretion to the medium and may therefore be completely unreal. If Lean wanted to be really Russian, he could have had his characters speaking in Russian with English subtitles. Realistic detail is the last refuge of the unimaginative director.

—*Village Voice*, December 30, 1965

1966

■ 1. *THE LEATHER BOYS*

The Leather Boys is one of the strangest (I hesitate to say queerest) pictures around. It starts out as the story of a boy and a girl and it ends up as the story of two boys, one a square fellow and one a quare fellow. Rita Tushingham is ostensibly the star of the film, but she is treated much of the time like a gangly gorgon of femaleness, particularly when she is lurking in the marital bed to lacerate her husband's head with her hair curlers and to enmesh his ruby red lips with her chewing gum. Director Sidney J. Furie seems to have a flair for twisted fantasies of one kind or another. *The Ipcress File* was less a spy thriller than an orgy of father-figuration with a double Oedipal climax in which the hero is given a choice of paters to perforate. Not that Furie creates or even necessarily selects his particular plots, but once a peculiar premise is established, Furie develops it with gay abandon.

The Leather Boys actually precedes *The Ipcress File* by a couple of years; it was released at about the time Rita Tushingham made her first splash in *Taste of Honey*. Furie had previously jazzed up some Cliff Richard musicals, and *The Leather Boys* is still in the mainstream of North Country kitchen-sink and working-class regionalism. Much of the regional slur-slang-slurp requires subtitles, and the various amusements of the poor are treated with the usual condescension. Yet there is no condescension shown toward the mystique of the motorcycle, and the camera seems to caress the black leather jackets within its purview. We are still under the spell here of such pre-mod rockers as Marlon Brando (*The Wild One*) and the late James Dean (*Rebel Without a Cause*), and Furie records the decadence of the genre with soppy slow dissolves and shimmering arcs of light, perhaps as close as a black-and-white film can come to the lisping lyricism of those old blue lights.

The most interesting aspect of the film is the way Tushingham is treated as a sex object. She is most desirable to her young husband when she looks most like a boy and acts most like a pal, preferably on the back of a motorcycle. Normally one would have expected the film to develop this interesting ambiguity in many heterosexual relationships, not only because it is the most normal thing to do but also because Rita Tushingham is supposedly the stellar and emotional center of the plot. Halfway through the movie, however, the emphasis shifts to the emotional relationship of two buddies, and it is this part of the plot that may seem daring to audiences gradually instructed that one of the boys (Dudley Sutton) is indeed abnormal, and the other (Colin Campbell) a bit slow on the uptake.

We are back in that most popular of all cinemas, the cinema that makes the audience feel superior to the situation. The manipulation involved here is worth mentioning. For starters, the most attractive cast credit, male or female, plays the innocent boy torn between Tushingham's termagant and Sutton's Sodom masquerading as paldom. This is, then, the saga of the male beauty tempted by two beasts, one allegedly female and one allegedly male. Campbell's character is even beefed up with sympathetic social consciousness. Whereas he wants to take care of his suddenly widowed granny, everyone else in the family—and particularly Tushingham—would prefer to bundle off the old lady to an institution. Only Campbell's pal understands how sweet an old granny can be. This sort of character-coddling is rather crudely done in this instance, but it establishes a basic bias in favor of the at least latently homosexual relationship.

Still, the old lady from Dubuque might remain in the dark about what was afoot, particularly when these two nice boys keep a proper platonic distance from each other when they sleep in the same bed in Granny's house. They don't even look each other in the eyes for fear of the ayes they (or the audience) may find there. Nor is there ever the vulgar spectacle of a cruisingly appraising in-

spection from head to toe to give the show away. How, then, can
the audience be told the facts of life without the innocent boy
being made too aware on the screen? An outing *à deux* to a seaside
resort is arranged. The square fellow suggests they pick up two
girls; the quare fellow is reluctant and sabotages the pickup with
cutting remarks and antisocial athleticism. The tip-off as far as the
audience is concerned is made clearer by the improbably excessive
physical attractiveness of the two accosted girls. The girls act and
talk stupidly, of course, because this is essentially an antigirl movie,
but the visual signal of a derailment of desire has been flashed.
The quare fellow hates girls, and to make his position symbolically
explicit, he forms an Anger arch on the boardwalk railing with his
outspread legs as he sits, soaking in the deviant rays of the sun.

Now the old lady from Dubuque knows more than the square
fellow, but more is to come. Rita Tushingham walks in on the two
boys innocently rough-housing around their precious motorcycles,
and jabs at their insides with the insight that they are a couple of
queers. The quare fellow responds to this gibe with the kind of
stricken-stag expression Mayor Lindsay might practice on Governor
Rockefeller when money time rolls around. Later the quare fellow
exits his now troubled square friend with a self-wounding remark
about being all out of lipstick, but the square fellow, immune to
innuendo, effects a reconciliation with a boys-will-be-boys pillow
fight.

Life will be life, however, and the square fellow decides to return
to Tushingham. After a voice-breaking, eye-averting farewell scene
with the quare fellow, our heroically heterosexual hero bursts in
on Tushingham, only to find her *flagrante delicto* with another
motorcyclist, and thus his marriage ends on the same sour note on
which it began. This is the key to the irritatingly inconsistent tone
of *The Leather Boys*. The heterosexuality is treated satirically,
while the homosexuality is treated sentimentally. Not quite all the
homosexuality, however. The square fellow finds himself in a queer
bar so infernally insidious it makes Otto Preminger's queer bar in
Advise and Consent look about as sinister as Schrafft's. At long last
the square fellow knows as much as the old lady from Dubuque.
He strides out of the simpering inferno and across a symbolic
bridge while his companion stands in the receding background,
arms akimbo, waiting, no doubt, for the square fellow to look back

in anger. The ending is designed for dramatic pathos, but I found it merely silly and stupid. We are all supposedly more broadminded than we used to be, and homosexuality is certainly human, but more as an aspect of character than as a noble subject in its own right. Roland Curram's fey photographer in *Darling* is more on the right track than Dudley Sutton's solemn sufferer here. Discovery of deviation, for example, should be an initial premise of characterization, not a dramatic climax. Am I saying, then, that homosexual love cannot be treated as sentimentally as heterosexual love? Generally speaking, yes. We may question those of our sexual taboos derived from ancient moralities motivated by the fundamental necessities of survival of the species. We may continue to quarrel with the Chayefskian universe, in which male camaraderie is reckoned a symptom of immaturity, and we may continue to resist some of the games we play nowadays, particularly the one involving the merger of opposites, so that a sweaty locker room invariably gives egress along a path strewn with the pansies of pansexuality to the sybaritic Roman baths. We may continue to be merciful, compassionate, and civilized without bending over backward to deny the very existence of straightness, normality, and order.

Ultimately, I suppose, it is the task of every taste to define the range of its distastes, and homosexuality as a problem subject is among my distastes. Nevertheless back in 1924 Carl Dreyer treated the subject in *Mikhael*, a disguised drama of the sculptor Rodin and his hopeless passion for one of his male models. Dreyer ennobled his obsessed protagonist by emphasizing the feeling rather than the fetish, the passion rather than the perversion. The young male in question, played by a young Walter Slezak, becomes obsessed in turn by a beautiful, possessive woman. Dreyer established the tragic stature of the sculptor and the tawdry stuff of the male model without suggesting or even attempting to suggest that homosexual love was sublime and heterosexual love ridiculous. And it is this latter suggestion that makes *The Leather Boys* a trashy fantasy for fairies and an educational experience for the old lady from Dubuque.

■ 2. OTHELLO

I

Laurence Olivier's *Othello* has been merchandised hereabouts less like a movie than a touring tent show. As a creature of moviegoing habit, I object to the trend toward "special" attractions peddling canned snob appeal with the most archaic film techniques. In this context, Olivier's *Othello* raises certain cultural questions that may not be worth answering in a column ostensibly devoted to cinemah. Certainly the temptation to rewrite one's college term paper is a poor excuse to indulge in the inevitable second-guessing of any possible production of Shakespeare. Besides, how am I to judge if Olivier's is one of the better Othellos? I have seen Paul Robeson's liberal knowingness loftily missing the point and the part—but that was in another generation. On screen I have seen the visually impressive Orson Welles version and fragments of Pierre Brasseur's play-within-a-film performance in *Les Enfants du Paradis* and Ronald Colman's in *A Double Life*. I have only my own sloth and sluggishness to blame for not having seen the interpretation of James Earl Jones in recent years, but I cannot recall offhand any other opportunities to see *Othello* in New York. Nor have I ever been particularly enchanted by the prospect of quasi-professional assaults on Avon by American acting aspirants, who almost invariably read the verse too slowly to make it breathe. Thus to say that Olivier's is the best-acted Othello I have ever seen is almost comparable to saying that Vivien Leigh's Scarlett O'Hara is the best-acted Scarlett O'Hara I have ever seen—and they are.

I do not presume to speak for the London playgoer, with his immeasurably stronger Shakespearean performing tradition, but here in America an educated awareness of Shakespeare is approximately 99 per cent literary and 1 per cent theatrical, and I daresay that the bulk of analytical Bardolatry has been conceived between the sheets of the dramas rather than at performances of the plays. If I were now going for my sheepskin, I would take a Lamb-McLuhan position by arguing that Shakespeare's best media are not theater, motion pictures, and television, but radio and hi-fi recording. The Shakespearean language that projected images on a mental screen in the ages before the advent of visually facile media now submerges this visual facility with a torrent of sound. Perhaps the time has come to admit that Shakespeare and the cinema will never mix satisfactorily. I, for one, can live out the rest of my life without encountering another aesthetically misshapen mongrel like this particular production even though I would not have missed Laurence Olivier's performance for the world, but then I would rush off to see Laurence Olivier in *Charley's Aunt*.

By now it is no secret that Olivier's Othello is so startling in jet-black face makeup that there are moments when the Moor from Venice seems to be auditioning for "Amos 'n' Andy." From *Birth of a Nation* onward (or downward) the American motion picture industry has bequeathed an embarrassing legacy of mocking minstrelsy, caricatures, stereotypes, and downright slanders as incontrovertible evidence of the entrenched injustices of American society. It can be argued, of course, that we Americans should be more sophisticated about Shakespeare and less hypersensitive about color, and I would agree. I suspect, however, that Olivier's makeup would have created less ruckus on the stage than on the screen, not only because the basic shock conception is essentially theatrical rather than cinematic, but also because the theater is a relatively localized and liberalized social arena, whereas the motion picture reaches out across the country and the world. I couldn't help wondering what the good white citizens of Natchez and Montgomery would think about this *Othello*, and it suddenly occurred to me that they would accept Laurence Olivier in the role because he is actually white, whereas they would probably bar James Earl Jones for being black to the core of his Pirandellian being. The southern censors have never objected to plot lines involving interracial romances as long as the players were masquerading about race. Thus the Julie in *Showboat*, the eponymous Pinky, and the entire family of *Lost Boundaries* pass in this double sense on southern screens only because they are bona fide certified Caucasians, but when Gwen Verdon put on some tan makeup in *Mississippi Gambler* to do a voodoo number with authentically Negro bare-chested male dancers, she was neatly snipped out of the version shown in Dixie. Thus, for better or worse, the cinema is both more social and more realistic than the theater, and if Olivier was trying to execute a stylistic parody of Jean Genet's *The Blacks,* he picked the wrong medium. The motion picture camera soon gets bored with the elaborate machinery of imitation and impersonation, and being outlasts pretending. Again, however, I cannot help wondering why Olivier gave us such an unorthodox Othello when most of us have never seen a satisfactorily conventional one. I seem to detect Kenneth Tynan's fine hand in the decision. Indeed, Tynan has gained much of his reputation for critical one-upmanship by questioning Shakespeare's political good faith in such matters as the fulsome praise for the warmonger Fortinbras and a shameless toadying to the Tudors. However, it would be unfair to Olivier, Tynan, and the other interpretative influences on the production to ascribe a purely racial connotation here, and it would be intellectually insulting to all concerned to suggest a conscious effort to reduce *Othello* to the level of *Raisin in the Sun.* As James Baldwin has observed in his admirable essay on Harriet Beecher Stowe, white and black are moral as well as racial tonalities, and Shakespeare himself indulges in the linguistic paradox of a black-skinned husband transferring his blackness metaphorically to the interior being of his alabaster-surfaced wife. The key to Olivier's blackness is, then, not racial outrage but moral absolutism, and his boldface Bodoni makeup operates as a sort of pop Manicheanism.

II

Curiously, there is no sexual passion in this production, no strong sense of conjugal complicity gone sour. Olivier's extreme blackness stylizes Othello out of any possible rapport with the other players, and anyway, Maggie Smith's Desdemona is longer on sensibility than sensuality. In Olivier's arms she seems less like a beloved body than a religious relic, a tangible reminder of the order and decorum he has found to soothe his savage breast. It is perhaps ungallant to suggest that Maggie Smith is no Claire Bloom, and irrelevant as well, though I would question the conventional casting of an unambiguously virtuous type for Desdemona, a character who, after all, did deceive her own father about her passion, as Iago points out to Othello in his one palpable hit.

Unfortunately, this production sets so many arbitrary limits on its scope and effectiveness that it makes little sense to cavil at the casting and conception. The sensuous properties of color, for example, have been largely wasted in a generally drab and ugly spectacle. There is no lulling background music for a show that lingers on the screen for three hours and fifteen minutes, counting the popcorn intermission. Olivier's other Shakespearean productions, *Henry V*, *Hamlet*, and *Richard III*, were lavishly scored, but these were movies, and *Othello* is ostensibly the recording of a stage production—and, as we all know, it is considered bad form to use background music on the stage.

Yet *Othello* is not exactly a filmed document either, because the camera occasionally augments the performances with certain expressive movements, at one point going so far as to rock back and forth as Othello begins to feel the onset of vertiginous jealousy. Generally speaking, Stuart Burge's direction is elementary but logical within the limits prescribed for this hybrid production. The camera occasionally moves in slowly to emphasize the intensification of psychological tension, and moves back to emphasize a lyricism in the larger tableaux, most notably when Desdemona begins singing the Willow Song on the last night of her life. There is one stunning camera angle of Olivier overhearing Iago's conversation with Cassio, an angle that permits Olivier one of his rare opportunities to exploit the electrifying intimacy of his voice. But on most other occasions Olivier seems to be playing to the galleries with the camera down his throat, and one scream of surprise at Iago's mention of Cassio's proximity, undoubtedly electric on the stage, becomes almost grotesque on the screen simply because the camera is too close. Without having seen the stage production, I suspect that Frank Finlay's Iago gains in subtlety on the screen what Olivier's Othello loses in force. (Frank Finlay is, incidentally, the best Iago I have ever seen, but again that is not saying much.) Joyce Redman's Emilia brings back nostalgic memories of her Doll Tearsheet in the 1946 Old Vic production of *Henry IV*, with Richardson playing Falstaff in both parts and Olivier playing Hotspur and Shallow. However, I must express a preference for Fay Compton's Emilia in the Welles version. The other roles, particularly those of Cassio and Roderigo, are indifferently cast, as usual. The great advantage of reading the play is the perfect mental casting of every part, and for my part I would have preferred to see Olivier play every part, including those of Desdemona, Emilia, and Bianca.

Unfortunately, I was somewhat bored by this *Othello* both because Olivier's conception is ultimately too superficial and because his performance once more plays away from his great strength as a comedian to his great weakness as a tragedian. Actually, Olivier's personality has too keen an edge for Othello. He functions best in the middle registers, where the steely precision of his sensibility enables him to shift from one level of awareness to another with humor, beauty, and brilliance. Filtered through Olivier, a line like "Dost thou mock me?" gleams with such iridescent intelligence that it becomes obvious that Finlay's Iago could never in a million years gull Olivier's Othello.

This production is a study also in fitting Shakespeare to the interpretation rather than fitting the interpretation to Shakespeare. There are the inevitable cuts we have come to expect from any Olivier enterprise. First, the clown is cut, and he is no great loss, though the fact that he is listed in the cast credits as being played by Roy Holder suggests that the cut may have been made after the shooting rather than before. A more meaningful cut involves an opening scene showing the Duke of Venice in a political discussion with his advisers concerning the Turks and the Ottomites and Cyprus and Rhodes. Othello has not yet made his appearance in this scene, and who cares about the play's history and geography, which presumably interested Shakespeare's audience? Well, I care, in my puristic perverseness. I cared when Fortinbras was denied egress through Olivier's *Hamlet*, and I cared also when Stanley Baker's Richmond was denied his speech of succession after the fall of Olivier's Richard III.

A still more grievous cut is Emilia's big speech about why wives stray from hearth and home and husband, and here Olivier seems instinctively to protect the centrality of his own role, as he did in *Richard III* when Queen Margaret's scene-stealing and possibly even play-stealing curses were deleted. (I have always longed to see Edith Evans or Judith Anderson do that scene.) Thus we don't even get all of Shakespeare's lines read in this otherwise uninspired document—and so what is the point?

However, I never expect to see a more emotionally effective *Othello* despite all my reservations about Olivier's interpretation. Olivier oversimplifies, it is true. His tendency, particularly in the tragedies, is toward the pathological rather than the heroic, toward the pathetic rather than the tragic. Othello and Macbeth, however, are relatively sub-Aristotelian heroes, whereas Hamlet and Lear are super-Aristotelian. The respective flaws of Othello and Macbeth—jealousy and ambition—are greater than their respective virtues, and they are thereby somewhat deficient in size. The evidence of this deficiency is the virtually coequal importance of the roles of Iago and Lady Macbeth. By contrast, Hamlet and Lear inundate their respective worlds with their feelings. Adapters as diverse as Verdi and Kurosawa have exploited this limitation of the tragic vision in the sub-Aristotelian tragedies, Verdi converting Othello into a creature of passion, and Kurosawa manipulating Macbeth into a henpecked husband—and somewhat fittingly, too, since *Othello* and *Macbeth* are relatively domestic tragedies, whereas *Hamlet* and *Lear* are relatively cosmic.

Yet when the magniloquent Orson Welles confronted the limitations of Macbeth and Othello, he still managed to stand about fifty feet tall in the worlds he created to supplement Shakespeare's vision. Nor is Olivier's primitive twist entirely new in Shakespearean staging. One still shudders at Donald Wolfit's Cro-Magnon Macbeth some years ago. Nonetheless Olivier manages to move me in a role that I approach with dry-eyed preconceptions. Perhaps the pathological and the pathetic are the right keys for this incomplete figure. I must confess an intellectual preference for Welles's conception of Iago as Othello's alter ego—the ironically darker side of the Moor's noble nature—but Welles's monotonous sonorousness as an actor is simply not in the same league with Olivier's sinuous subtlety and devoted detailedness that soar to the highest reaches of acting as an art.

Finally, I must note that times have changed for the cinema since those status-seeking days when aestheticians were concerned about the problem of squeezing the five-foot shelf into the 35-millimeter screen. Quickly, in passing, I wave politely but coldly at Asta Nielsen's female *Hamlet* in the silent era and Richard Burton's post-Freudian Prince, dimly recorded on the screen earlier this year, Cukor's *Romeo and Juliet* with Leslie Howard and Norma Shearer as lethargic lovers, Elizabeth Bergner's revolting Rosalind and Laurence Olivier's callow Orlando in Paul Czinner's *As You Like It*, Castellani's Italianate *Romeo and Juliet*, Joseph

L. Mankiewicz' *Julius Caesar*, in which Edmond O'Brien's Casca outshone Marlon Brando's Mark Antony, Max Reinhardt's disastrous Midsummer Nightmare, in which James Cagney made an intelligent effort to fathom Bottom, Douglas Fairbanks and Mary Pickford struggling with *The Taming of the Shrew* when Lunt and Fontanne were available and now Burton and Taylor are imminent —and aside from moments of high cinema in Welles and high theater in Olivier, I think that Shakespeare on the screen has been almost as much of a loss as the Bible. Fortunately, both Shakespeare and the cinema are such glorious entities in their own rights that their bickering marriage of convenience has not soured their sublimely sweet dispositions. Now back to the cinema.

—*Village Voice*, February 17 and March 3, 1966

■ 3. *LORD LOVE A DUCK*

Lord Love a Duck marks the directorial debut of George Axelrod with a bang rather than a whimper. Not only does Axelrod turn out to be his own best director but his script for *Lord Love a Duck* is by far the best thing he has ever done. Tuesday Weld, Roddy McDowall, Lola Albright, Ruth Gordon, Martin West, Sarah Marshall, Max Showalter, Harvey Korman, Martin Gabel, and a bevy of blank bikini belles make up the funniest comic ensemble since the palmiest days of Preston Sturges. Comparisons have been made with *Dr. Strangelove* and *Lolita* and *What's New, Pussycat?* and *The Loved One*, but *Lord Love a Duck* has them all beat by miles on the laugh meter. In fact, the cavernous guffaws tend to tear apart the flimsy fabric of Axelrod's satiric conception of sun-kissed Southern California, where even God has been converted to a drive-in. The characters and their jokes seem to transcend their contexts. For example, spoofs of psychoanalysis would seem to be automatically mirthless at this late date. Nevertheless Axelrod disproves Seneca's aphorism about there being nothing new under the couch by counterpointing a surly lady psychologist with Roddy McDowall's impishly innocent Rorschach reactor. From then on, Axelrod consistently hits higher notes of hilarity than Kubrick-

Nabokov, Kubrick-Sothern, Donner-Allen, Richardson-Sothern-Waugh, etc.

Part of Axelrod's advantage is with actors. Tuesday Weld is Nabokov's grown-up nymphet come to life in a cavalcade of cashmere sweaters, and closer to Nabokov's original conception than Sue Lyon ever could be. More important than the casting is Axelrod's affectionate attitude toward this creature of inordinate pride and perversity. If the author identifies more with Roddy McDowall's superior intelligence and industriousness, he shares with his protagonist a longing for the natural grace and beauty of American Girlhood flowering amid the absurd vegetation of materialism and gadgetry. Yet Axelrod is, paradoxically, least effective when he attempts to be most serious about his feelings. Ultimately, Roddy McDowall makes too eccentric a spokesman for Axelrod's deeper sensibilities, and it is not always clear what mood the author is attempting to establish, particularly when Luscious Lola Albright is on the screen as Tuesday Weld's Stella Dallas mother updated to a barroom bunny past her prime, yet somehow indomitable, with that glint in her eyes and that catch in her voice and that bunny tail that sums up all the desperate gaiety of our time.

Axelrod is not yet the compleat director. His Resnais flash-memory mannerisms of Last-Tuesday-in-Hollywood are pretentious and wearying, and there is not yet a steady flow or stable rhythm to his over-all direction. The parts are considerably superior to the whole —but what parts! Also, the funny moments are all the funnier because of the admirably serious moments that do not come off successfully. Despite bursts of wild slapstick, Axelrod's direction is wisely calm and contemplative, so that his characters can generate some feeling. He is commendably patient and somewhat original with a sustained oblique two-shot in the touchingly tentative scenes between Roddy McDowall and Tuesday Weld.

Some of the jokes are very broad, but Axelrod's execution of them is never tasteless. (One shudders to think of Billy Wilder running amok in this material.) Thus the humor is often mordant but never malicious; dark but never devious. Special mention should be made of Martin West's all-American ass, a comic reincarnation of Boobus Americanus that would have warmed the heart of H. L. Mencken. West's life force is a perfect complement to that of Weld's all-American girl, and they both seem destined to live pointlessly ever after until Axelrod-McDowall get the bright idea of testing the indestructibility of the male participant in the American Dream. Finally, even the act of murder is morally muddled by the insensate technology of our time.

It has taken me a long time to come to grips with this film. I first considered palming it off with faint praise, but it has stuck in my mind despite all sorts of grave distractions, and I have decided that I am on Axelrod's side in this matter. I like the cast he assembled—not much in the way of marquee value, but admirably appropriate to the task at hand. I believe also that more writers should try directing their own material, particularly in the realm of comedy. Finally, bankers, studios, and producers would be better advised to recruit new directors from the ranks of writers rather than from the functionally illiterate graduates of so-called film academies.

—*Village Voice*, March 17, 1966

■ 4. *LES BONNES FEMMES; JUDEX*

Claude Chabrol's *Les Bonnes Femmes* was originally released in France in 1960, when the *nouvelle vague* was still relatively new. It was not a success, critically or commercially, and it was never imported to America despite some eminently exploitable sequences involving stripteases, seductions, and other step-right-up bits of business. Perhaps the grind-house gurus sensed that Chabrol had driven all the levity out of lechery with his pitiless vision of a silly shopgirl's Paris as hell on earth. In any case, Claude Chabrol became the forgotten man of the *nouvelle vague* as far as Americans were concerned. Now, six years later, *Les Bonnes Femmes* reappears as one of the great films of the sixties and, curiously, as an apparent precursor of all these newfangled theatrical theories involving cruelty, totality, and stylization. I don't want to press these parallels too far, but what was once considered shocking in *Les Bonnes Femmes* now seems standard operating procedure for any self-respecting spectacle. If anything, realism, humanism, literalism are in such disarray that *Les Bonnes Femmes* may even seem too tame to be the same movie that provoked *L'Avventura*-style hissing at the British Film Institute six years ago.

The title of the movie refers ironically to four expressively pretty if not statistically probable shopgirls. Sadly, their names—Bernadette Lafont, Clothilde Joano, Stephane Audran, Lucile Saint-Simon—do not carry any more weight on the marquee in 1966 than they did in 1960, but their relative anonymity preserves a "Group"-like freshness in the playing. The plot is structured in a strikingly asymmetrical pattern of routine and reverie, and Chabrol's style is concerned largely with keeping his audience off balance by turning every situation inside out until every moment of humor is stalked by horror and every beautiful feeling is desecrated by an ugly experience. Consistency is certainly not Chabrol's hobgoblin, and never has there been such an uneasy alliance of realism and romanticism, and yet never has so much beauty flowered out of so much baseness.

The movie starts out with merry malignancy on a frenzied chase, pickup, and bedding down before we have had a chance to "identify" with any of the characters. Chabrol's satiric strokes seem to bold and corrosive for a feature-length movie, but even in the midst of riotous vulgarity, a subtle pathos begins to emerge in the weariness of an aging womanizer hoarding his energies for the crucial volleys, in the way a nice girl looks politely at a provocative stripper, in the marvelously faithful rendering of the poignant spectacle of two girls arguing in pantomime about whether to let themselves be picked up. The evening ends as scabrously as one could wish, with the nice girl escaping and the fun girl tumbled into bed by two men simultaneously. This trollop will later bring us close to tears by noticing her first wrinkle in the mirrored surface that haloes her humanity. A second shopgirl, rejoicing in an advantageous marriage, will encounter silly and needless humiliation in a grotesque encounter with her future in-laws. A third girl will pursue a mediocre career as part-time entertainer. The fourth will open the Pandora's Box of romantic illusions to find a murderous madness. What the late L. B. Mayer would have done with this project! All downbeat and pessimistic and brutal. Nor will this film appeal to those who think *Il Posto* is the acme of screen art. There is nothing discreetly, condescendingly sympathetic in Chabrol's attitude, as there is in Olmi's. Chabrol hates mediocrity, not the people who are engulfed in it. Olmi's satire is gentle enough not to ruffle our sensibilities, but Chabrol's satire is too savage for comfort, and so we react by calling Chabrol brutal, vulgar, and just plain horrid. I have done so myself in the past, but after a third viewing, *Les Bonnes Femmes* suddenly reveals itself as a work of extraordinary compassion, almost a fifth Gospel of four women, essentially and unironically good women, crucified in close-up at the climax of their disillusionment. What Godard has done so obviously and so self-consciously in *My Life to Live*, Chabrol has done in *Les Bonnes Femmes* without once breaking the surface of the illusion to proclaim his own sensibility. Chabrol's Catholicism does not require a schematic analysis of symbols, stigmata, trials, and tribulations. One has only to look into the eyes of a fifth girl, otherwise unidentified, who ends the film on a note of lyrical longing. There is more of the spirit of Christ in the way Chabrol's camera looks into those eyes than in all the high school pageantry of Pasolini's garbage-can Gospel according to superstitious Saint Matthew. This is not to say that Pasolini is insincere or irreverent, merely that his film is fatally afflicted by the negative virtues of neutrality, and that to be inoffensive in religion is to be irrelevant. The cross, the stake, the concentration camp will never rise on hallowed ground, but always on new terrain.

For those who are wary of Batman, Captain Marvel, Superman, and Flash Gordon, but who still are not ready to return to revivals of *Potemkin* and *The Bicycle Thief*, I would like to recommend Georges Franju's *Judex* as a lovely bit of fun without foolishness. Nothing great, mind you, but not to be missed by retarded types (like this reviewer) who have never quite got over the feeling that pretty ladies in tights contain all the secrets of the universe.

—*Village Voice*, May 5, 1966

■ 5. THE GROUP

The Group suggests that what is most wrong with the modern woman is the modern man. Mary McCarthy's tantalizingly, scandalizingly best-selling novel ridiculed a whole generation of college girls who thought they could lead more rewarding lives than their parents. No cause, no ideal, no aspiration escaped Miss McCarthy's satiric stiletto. Marx fared no better than Freud as the Spanish Civil War went the way of psychoanalysis, and the NRA wound up offending one constitution as the progressivism of prophylaxis offended another. As a movie *The Group* has its moments, mainly when it is playing away from the considerable talent of Mary McCarthy as an interior decorator and desecrator. The author has a wicked flair for walking into your apartment and linking the tacky wallpaper to your talky politics. You tend to take her word for the connection, of course, partly because she is so amusing and partly because her tone of critical certitude tolerates no uncertainty—and besides, how many authorities on tacky wallpaper are there, anyway?

Unfortunately, the joke tends to be lost on the screen, where the settings are so given that not even Mary McCarthy can take them away. The wallpaper has to be excruciatingly tacky before the audience can make the link to the character, and even then the more knowledgeable moviegoer will tend to blame the taste of the set designer or that old scapegoat "Hollywood" rather than make too much of a satirical comment on the character who happens to be crawling up the wallpaper at that particular moment. Thus there is no particular paradox involved in the observation that Gene Callahan's sets are admirable without evoking amusement.

If *The Group* succeeds at all as a movie, it is as nostalgia rather than satire. The movie, in fact, represents the revenge of the thirties on the book, and the only tackiness that emerges is in Mary McCarthy's tasteless plots and tedious males. Fortunately, the much-publicized casting coups for the girls in the Group make it seem as if eight bad plots are better than one. Unfortunately, the director, Sidney Lumet, and scenarist, Sidney Buchman, were concerned less with period nostalgia than punctilious fidelity to a Great Work of Art. The script adopts more than it adapts, and the director darts across the period backgrounds without letting the characters get the feel of them. Not that New York lends itself particularly to nostalgia. At that moment in 1933 when the ill-fated Kay and horrible husband get on the Astor Place BMT subway to go to Coney Island for a whimsical one-day honeymoon for career couples, they are standing on about the only street corner in

New York that will look the same thirty years later. Yet the electric effect of the long skirts, the square cars, the references to Roosevelt and Hitler, makes one wish that Vincente Minnelli had been given the assignment, with a free hand to parade pastness for its own sake. As it is, every detail, every line of dialogue moves the plot more than the audience, and there seems to be no time for period atmosphere. In Jean-Luc Godard's latest film, Jean-Paul Belmondo asks the gas-station attendant to put a tiger in his tank—and what could be better calculated to put more zing in the Zeitgeist? By contrast, *The Group* is completely lacking in the enchantment of extraneous detail. We are, then, left with eight girls who create their own nostalgia, not for a particular time and place but for the universal experience of girl graduates starting out life as a bright article in *The New Yorker* and ending up as just another bad movie.

My favorite actress from the Group is Joan Hackett, particularly in those delicious moments early in the movie when she is initiated into sin by Richard Mulligan, the creepy, crawly husband in *One Potato, Two Potato*, and a measure of the monstrousness of the male casting here. Miss Hackett brings a rare blend of humor and dignity to her absurd predicament, and she conveys more than anyone else the sparkle of Mary McCarthy's clear-eyed wise-guy approach to basic biological experience. Joanna Pettet has the most difficult part as Kay, and a whole movie could have been built around her experiences with her punk-playwright husband. Shirley Knight handles the other big part, the old-fashioned star part packaged with a happy ending, and displays a calming capability and emotional restraint with situations in which compassion could easily have degenerated into smugness. The most beautiful girl in the Group is Candice Bergen, Edgar's daughter in real life and a lesbian called Lakey on the screen. Unfortunately, she has a nothing part and a wardrobe designed by Krafft-Ebing to match. Jessica Walter's performance as a tiresome teaser out of Booth Tarkington is generally underrated, because no one likes a tiresome teaser out of Booth Tarkington. Elizabeth Hartman wastes her talent on a character it would depress me too much to describe, while Mary-Robin Redd and Kathleen Widdoes sort of get lost in the shuffle. If the *Harvard Lampoon* is still in business next year after selling out to Natalie Wood's press agent this year, it should award a

special prize to Hal Holbrook to prove once and for all that acting
is more than the application of makeup, and that on this occasion
straight acting has exposed the fraudulence of "character" acting,
and seldom the Twain shall meet.

Perhaps the movie camera is not the subtlest of artistic instruments, but it is one of the most honest, and the camera eye on
the Group exposes the emotionally hollow core of Miss Mc-
Carthy's art. For all her cleverness, Mary, Mary quite contrary,
turns out to be the Rona Jaffe of the *Partisan Review* set.

—*Village Voice*, May 12, 1966

■ 6. SEVEN WOMEN

John Ford's *Seven Women* has caused a slight stir in the trade by
opening on the bottom half of a double bill with Burt Kennedy's
The Money Trap, by all odds the daily double of the decade. My
critical colleagues were more pitying than scornful as they confronted this latest opus of a director who has been in the business
for more than fifty years. Some of them knew how I loved and admired John Ford and tried to break the news to me gently. Ford,
after all, was now past seventy, and perhaps it was time to put the
old war horse out to pasture. Ford's premature burial crew had the
advantage of me, because Metro had neglected to invite me to its
screenings several months before, and I had had to wait for the
not-so-grand opening on good old Forty-second Street. Even so, I
had braced myself for the worst. *Cheyenne Autumn* had been a
failure—a noble failure, but a failure. Ford was never able to get
inside his stone-faced Indians, and his best scene, the Wyatt Earp
episode, had been truncated by the studio. Besides, what was one
failure more or less in a career that has soared to so many new
peaks? Ford has passed the point where he has to pay any install-
ments on his place in the Pantheon. His standing would not be
jeopardized if he chose to direct the Three Stooges in a nudist
movie, much less seven actresses in a Chinese adventure.

I could have saved my defensive rationalizations. *Seven Women*
is a genuinely great film from the opening credit sequence of a
Mongolian cavalry massing and surging in slashing diagonals across

the screen to Anne Bancroft's implacable farewell to Mike Mazurki's Mongolian chieftain: "So long, you bastard." No lingeringly bitter tea of General Yen for Ford.

Not that I blame Metro for releasing *Seven Women* as unobtrusively as it did. The movie is at once too profound for the art-film circuit and too personal for the big, brassy Broadway houses. Ford's films are passing into history and legend, and the veteran director may have heard his last hurrah. No matter. The beauties of *Seven Women* are for the ages, or at least for a later time when the personal poetry of film directors is better understood between the lines of genre conventions. Ford's gravest crime is taking his material seriously at a time when the seriousness of an entire medium is threatened by the tyranny of trivia. *Seven Women* is not being defended here because it is an old-fashioned kind of fun movie, outstanding solely for its outrageousness. Far from it. Ford represents pure classicism of expression in which an economy of means yields a profusion of effects. No one will ever catch John Ford at the Paris Cinémathèque studying *nouvelle vague* techniques. There is not a single jump-cut or freeze-frame in *Seven Women*. Nor are there any coy asides to the audience. Nor any concessions to "modernity." But, then, it would never occur to Ford, as it has to De Sica, to masquerade as a great director in search of the mass audience. Ford does not need to masquerade when any of his compositions selected at random will reveal an attention to nuanced detail and over-all design such as make a directorial monstrosity like *The Spy Who Came In from the Cold* look cinematically illiterate. Where Ritt ruins a trial scene with excessive cutting and unimaginative camera placement, Ford sustains psychological tensions with almost no interior literary support. Ford gets more drama out of a darkened hallway than Ritt can get out of a whole restaurant. There is one sequence in which Bancroft simultaneously surrenders her body and asserts her authority simply by striding toward the camera and forcing three people to react to her movement within the same frame. This movement triggers a series of abrupt actions with explosive force. When Ford finally does cut back and forth between Bancroft and Mazurki, the Eisensteinian collision is supplemented by a more supple sensibility capable of transmitting a touch of tenderness between two deadly antagonists.

Some critics have ridiculed the casting of Mazurki as a Mongolian chieftain. Mazurki, like Ford's Negro giant regular, Woody Strode, is cast less as a realistic Mongolian than as a fantasy male. Here we have seven women stranded in a Protestant mission in China in 1935. They have virtually excluded men from their sanctuary, and yet when the men swarm down on them, they are the worst kind of males the female psyche can envisage. These rampaging males wander around the countryside raping, killing, plundering, and worst of all, smashing all the windows, furniture, and bric-a-brac. They affront every canon of order imposed upon the male by the female since the beginning of time, and yet the seven women must somehow come to terms with this monstrous maleness to survive, and a sacrifice must be made—a sordid sacrifice, it would seem, in the mere telling of the story, but a sublime sacrifice in Ford's filming.

The actresses—Anne Bancroft, Margaret Leighton, Betty Field, Sue Lyon, Flora Robson, Anna Lee, and Mildred Dunnock—constitute a configuration of Ford's vision of order. It is interesting to speculate what Patricia Neal would have been like in the part Bancroft took over for the stricken Neal, but Bancroft is admirably forceful and direct, perhaps closer to the Manchus than the Method, and perhaps all for the better. Ford's vision is open to criticism. He obviously finds women incomplete without men, but he nevertheless admires their gallantry and generosity and courage. In the end, women, like men, must submit to some order. The merits of the order are irrelevant, and here Ford leans more to the right, in opposition to a Brecht, who distinguishes between good and bad orders.

If Ford is not as fashionable as Brecht, however, it is simply because not as much has been written in the right places about "distancing" in cinema as there has been about distancing in theater. The same fur-coated audiences at Lincoln Center that sit patiently before the extravagant adventures of *The Caucasian Chalk Circle* would hoot at *Seven Women* with its infinitely subtler distancing. The fake Metro set and sky, and the arbitrariness of the plot, are the materials of one of the cinema's greatest poets, though he would be the last to say so himself.

—*Village Voice*, May 26, 1966

■ 7. *GERTRUD; THE THIRD LOVER*

Gertrud heads the third of four double bills at the New Yorker Theatre, which Dan Talbot has turned into a Mecca of the modern cinema. Carl Dreyer, Claude Chabrol, Francesco Rosi, Andrzej Wajda, Satyajit Ray, Henri Colpi, and Chris Marker are directors any serious moviegoer or genuinely scholarly critic studies as a matter of course. I much prefer Dreyer and Chabrol to the others, but there are truths and beauties to be discerned in them all. In Wajda's *Lotna*, for example, the symbolism of the beautiful white horse is obvious enough and the expressionistic carnage is artificial enough, and yet the entire experience evokes that almost forgotten newsreel image of the Stukas diving down on a Polish column as horse-drawn artillery frantically scurries off the road and off the precipice of history, the old order of ornate snobbery perishing before the icy terror of iron men. The obtrusiveness of Wajda's art is out of style at the moment, but there is something to be said about solidity and solemnity in an era of prankish pillow fights, an era in which even a dour monument like Dwight Macdonald seems to be teetering from giddiness.

Gertrud is a sternly beautiful work of art with none of the fashionable flabbiness of second-chance sentimentality exemplified most vividly in Monica Vitti's compassionate caress of Gabriele Ferzetti in the final, ultimate blank-wall composition of *L'Avventura*. Dreyer has lived long enough to know that you live only once and that all decisions are paid in full to eternity. Some critics have attacked Gertrud herself as a Hedda Gabler character, consumed by her destructive demands for perfection in others. The difference between the two, however, is the difference between a genuine idealism, however intolerant, and foolish fantasizing. Dreyer did not create the character of Gertrud; he has "merely" adapted a play to the screen. Yet no mere adaptation could capture the lyrical intensity and lucid interiority of this film. Dreyer has poured his soul into the luminous light into which the actors float on an ever so subtly and ever so slowly moving camera. "But this isn't cinema!" snort the registered academicians with their kindergarten notions of kinetics. How can you have cinema when two people sit and talk on a couch as their life drifts imperceptibly out of their grasp? The academicians are right of course. Dreyer simply isn't cinema. Cinema is Dreyer.

That wildly beating heart struggling against its mortal coils, that fierce resignation one encounters in characters who realize too late that love is the only meaningful issue of life, the only consolation of memory. Admittedly there is something cold and merciless and implacable in Dreyer's vision of life, and the *Mensch*-munch audience may be put off by the film's intolerant attitude toward inadequacy. The whining of Herzog is more in the mode than the settled solitude of Gertrud, but Dreyer should not be tagged as an elitist. He grasps and treasures what he has held despite his tortured awareness of what he has lost. The tenacity of his art is summed up in the ceremonial style Gertrud maintains to the last flickering light of her life, to the last conversation on a couch, to the last warm, human encounter before the meaningless mists of eternity enshroud her. *Gertrud* is the kind of masterpiece that deepens with time because it has already aged in the heart of a great artist.

Claude Chabrol's *The Third Lover* opened here technically in 1963, and about thirty-eight people saw it, while everyone else thronged to see *Tom Jones*. There is no particular moral to be deduced from the fact that the Chabrol is infinitely superior to the Richardson. Merit and popularity intersect only infrequently and then usually for the wrong reasons. (Taste can be measured as the difference between the number of people who started reading *Lolita* and the number who finished reading *Pale Fire*.) The American release title is misleadingly salacious in terms of the original French title, *L'Oeil du Malin*, which suggests the eye or point of view of a cunning rogue. *The Third Lover* is mainly an exercise in telling a story from the point of view of a jealous, mediocre, destructive journalist who cannot bear to be in contact with people of greater moral resources. Chabrol thus violates the tradition of the innocent, impersonal, objective narrator without making the roguery sympathetic. The Dennis Price character in *Kind Hearts and Coronets* is at least intellectually superior to his victims, but Chabrol's poltergeist remains decisively inferior. The point of view is thus morally diseased from beginning to end, and whatever amusement we derive from the pranks directed against a vulnerably big-hearted man and wife is an index of our own repressed aggressions against those we envy and admire. With Dreyer and Chabrol on the same program, the New Yorker is hardly a citadel of liberal complacency during these days and nights of our discontent.

—*Village Voice*, June 2, 1966

■ 8. SUNDAY IN SAN SEBASTIAN

San Sebastian, Spain, June 23—People who complain that film festivals tend to be arty and highbrow should try San Sebastian next year as a change of pace. The scenery is beautiful, almost too beautiful, and the artistic atmosphere is about on the level of the Photoplay Awards. A genial Spanish actor interviews actors and directors on a level of sophistication Art Linkletter would find too fatuous, and the audience applauds politely as everyone looks around to see what everyone else is wearing. The Festival Theatre is one of those ornate affairs ringed with boxes for royalty and society and peanut galleries for the peasants. The kids outside are so hungry for autographs they even pester the journalists, and even when you tell them (albeit halfheartedly) that you are nobody—an offbeat journalist for a Greenwich Village paper, an editor of the English-language edition of a French film magazine, a member of the selection committee of the New York Film Festival, or a panelist on radio and television—even then they seem to want the autograph of an American. Nonetheless San Sebastian was an alienating experience, and David Wilson, the astute correspondent for *Sight and Sound*, confirmed my feelings of angst. There was no place and no occasion to meet other critics, and no sense of seriousness in the proceedings. The films were so-so, and most of the better ones were swept in on the backwash from Cannes. The American pictures were *The Glass Bottom Boat*, *Cast a Giant Shadow*, and *Nevada Smith*—real fun pictures all, and a symptom of Hollywood's exploitation of San Sebastian for valuable government visas enabling films to open commercially in Spain.

Anyway, Sunday rolled around in San Sebastian, and it even stopped raining. What to do? There were no bikinis on the beach because the law forbade them and the starchiness of the Spanish cuisine discouraged them. A press conference was scheduled for noon for Sarah Miles and Desmond Davis, the star and director of *I Was Happy Here,* a film that had been shown the night before, and I hoped to use the press conference as a means of focusing my day on a journalistic gesture, and perhaps even meet some of my colleagues. I walked over to the Maria Cristina Hotel, which is about a ten-minute walk from the Continental Hotel, where I was staying, only to find that the press conference was scheduled for 12:45, and so, like everything else in San Sebastian, Sunday was turning out to be another shaggy dog story. There was nothing for me to do at the Maria Cristina, and so I decided to walk back to my hotel, simply for the exercise. One of the nicest things about San Sebastian is that you can walk along the river (the Rio Urumea) right out to the Atlantic Ocean, where the waves occasionally surge over the parapets right into the streets and the natives try to time them and then leap out of the way—a sort of poor man's surf-boarding. The same path that leads from the river to the ocean then curls around a small mountain and leads into the bay and the beaches.

I had taken this route before, and I had noticed a small building, almost a baroque barracks, guarded by a single soldier with a carbine slung over his shoulder. It was the military governor's house, apparently. (I never figured out where Franco and his entourage stayed when they made San Sebastian their summer capital.) Sunday, however, was slightly different. I heard the noises as I approached, not noises exactly, but chants, and then as I got closer, I saw about fifty young people, students, mostly boys, with no more than a dozen girls among them. They were taunting some of the soldiers and the local constabulary, who were looking into the crowd as if to memorize the faces there. Suddenly, for no reason, I remembered Tom Dewey giving this steely-eyed look to my late brother for heckling Eisenhower when Ike was campaigning in 1952 from the steps of Queens Borough Hall. Every so often the kids would stop staring back and begin chanting "Libertad! Libertad!" The police did nothing but stare and shuffle around with an amused just-you-wait attitude common to the constabulary everywhere.

After about fifteen minutes of chanting the students turned and began walking along the boardwalk overlooking the bay and the beach. The chanting increased in frequency and frenzy as the students tried to sweep the Sunday throngs along with them. People just stopped and looked, and most of the expressions seemed unsympathetic, and off in the distance, in one long panning shot, as it were, were the antlike masses dotting the beaches, the masses of the indifferent middle class, the people who vote for Balaguer over Bosch and who prefer Franco to the risks of chaos. Suddenly the students, like all idealists and intellectuals, seemed terribly alone, defenseless, and vulnerable. Here they were in Basque country that had defied Franco in 1936 and defeated him for a time, and they were alone. *La Guerre Est Finie*, the title of the new Resnais film, seemed to sum up the feelings of the weekend revelers: Don't bother us. We work hard all week, and we want to relax with our families on Sunday. Pay is still too low, and the Falange is still too corrupt, but we have food on the table, and there is no blood on the streets. The students didn't seem to care. They were young, and their blood had not yet run cold from caution and compromise and "maturity," that most dreadful affliction of the human spirit. They turned off the boardwalk and into the center of the town, where I assumed, mistakenly as it turned out, that they had dispersed. I went back to my hotel, and then remembered that I had completely forgotten about the press conference. I got back to the Maria Cristina at about 1:10 and learned that Sarah Miles and Desmond Davis had said their piece. David Wilson told me that the level of the questioning never rose much above the indiscreet inquiry about the marital intentions of Sarah Miles and Robert Bolt, which was the first I knew that the chap in the British box at the screening had been none other than England's answer to Arthur Miller.

Coming back from the Maria Cristina I saw police wagons jammed with some of the young students, now with very frightened expressions. Some Americans told me afterward that the police had begun swinging their clubs, and that a priest, several young girls, and even innocent passersby had been injured. But I saw none

of this myself. Nor could I confirm the report that two young
Czechs had joined the group. I don't even know what the occasion
was for the demonstration. One very unconfirmed rumor was that
the students were protesting a twenty-year sentence meted out to
one of their fellow students for illegal political activity. All I know
is that on the twelfth day of June in the year of our Lord 1966 at
about noon a group of Spanish students chanted "Libertad!" in
front of armed authority in San Sebastian. I don't know if anyone
else has reported the incident, or where it fits into the total picture.
All I know is that I felt I owed something to the frightened-look-
ing faces in the paddy wagon.

—*Village Voice*, June 30, 1966

■ 9. McLUHANISM AND *MADAME X*

Berlin, June 29—This reviewer recently experienced his first in-
flight movie on a TWA flight from New York to Madrid. Aha! A
new medium with a new message, he thought. And what is the
movie, he asked the hostess with the neatly creased smile. *Madame
X*, she said proudly. *Madame X!* There was the paradox of McLuhanism in a nutshell. Here we were flying *x* hundred miles an
hour at an altitude of *y* thousand feet into a brave new world and
our cultural bill of fare was a plot that had already sprouted whiskers when Ruth Chatterton parlayed it into an Oscar nomination
back in 1929. Fortunately I had not yet seen this universally
panned clinker from the Ross Hunter claim, and there was nothing
better to do on the plane than sleep (which is difficult when one
is constantly composing one's last words), and so I plunked down
my $2.50 for the earphone apparatus that provides the sound for
the movie and six channels of canned music besides.

But first a word about the immediate "audience." On my left
was a well-mannered young man from the University of Colorado
en route to Paris, where he wanted to study philosophy at the Sorbonne and palaver with his generation at sidewalk cafés. He was
always addressing me as "sir" and writing entries in his journal
with words like "real" and "communication" and "feeling" and

"honest" and "sincere." On my right was a Spanish-American lady from Columbus, Ohio, a dead ringer for Carmen Miranda with a sensibility to match. So much for the international intrigues of plane travel, I thought, as I sat squeezed between Holden Caulfield and Carmen Miranda to await the arrival of *Madame X.*

It didn't take more than a reel to establish the fact that David Lowell Rich was no Douglas Sirk, and that there was no chance of transcending a bad plot when the director was obviously ashamed of it. After a few minutes Holden Caulfield took off his earphones and drifted off into a deep, quiet sleep to dream his beautiful dreams. Carmen Miranda was deeply absorbed in the spectacle to the very end, when Lana Turner dies nobly.

For myself, I kept noting fringe facts that would interest only the most devoted followers of films. Like the late Constance Bennett looking more like Lana Turner's sister than her mother-in-law, and Ricardo Montalban's slightly beat-up maturity making him look more like a real-life womanizer than was usual on the screen. Burgess Meredith and Keir Dullea were worth a look, and John Forsythe really wasn't, despite the chuckles he would evoke from time to time as he stood with a telephone receiver in his hand and lamented lamely, "The Secretary of State wants me to go to Africa." Most of the movie unwinds like one of Russell Metty's animated abstractions with firehouse-red gowns for passion, blue for cooling off, and dull pastels for degradation. But nothing works, and once more the emptiness of expertness without feeling becomes evident as *Madame X* ends up in deadly dullness.

The fact remains that I watched it to the bitter end. Why not? Aside from my professional inclinations I had nothing better to do, and certainly nothing better to see. There was no walking out of the spectacle, only a turning off, and turning off is entirely different from walking out. This is one of the messages of McLuhan. Media *do* encroach on meanings. Watching a movie in a drive-in is quite different from watching a movie in a theater or on TV. The differences may be difficult to measure, but they exist, and at least part of one's critical sensibility should be devoted to evaluating these differences. Values are fine until they begin replacing facts, and the trouble with most critics of McLuhan is that they blame him for Ross Hunter and *Madame X* when he is actually talking about the implications of in-flight movies. Not that the technology and aesthetic of in-flight movies can convert a *Madame X* into a *Madame Bovary*. Far from it. McLuhan is only marginally relevant to the revaluation of works of art. As a movie specialist I find McLuhan completely irrelevant. It is in the realm of sociology that he is most useful, or rather, that sociology that is concerned with the world more as it is than as it should be. And *Madame X* is most interesting as a piece of in-flight sociology. When I turned around to stretch after the lights went on, I noticed many a tear being furtively dabbed away, and when I remarked to the stewardess that I hoped that the in-flight movie on the way back was more interesting, she seemed genuinely surprised by my reaction. Most of the passengers, she reported, had volunteered favorable comments.

Of course, public opinion has little to do with aesthetic judgment, particularly in the realm of executing conventional conceptions. That is to say that *Madame X* could have been a great deal better and the Holden Caulfields would still drift off into dreamland, and *Madame X* could be a great deal worse and the Carmen Mirandas would still be absorbed. Part of my role as a critic consists of defining exactly how well *Madame X* was executed, and that concern automatically alienates me from both the Holden Caulfields and the Carmen Mirandas of this world.

However, once having diagnosed the artistic worthlessness of the entire experience, I am still left with the probability that most of the passengers liked the movie. Is it simply a matter of bad taste? Not entirely. It suddenly struck me that one of the most ridiculous aspects of the *Madame X* plot had become somewhat commonplace in my own lifetime—the travels and tribulations that beset our heroine after she is forced to leave home and hearth because of scandal and a vindictive mother-in-law. Off she goes to Switzerland, across Europe, and finally to the depths of Mexico City, but she can never forget the husband and child she left behind. Not even when a concert pianist proposes to her. Her past is too strong, her memories too painful. She can never escape from herself. Soap opera? True confessions? Women's fantasies? Of course. But there is social truth as well. We are traveling more than we ever have in the past, but look around at all the faces of the travelers and you can see the dreadful banality of remembered experience, of family ties and emotional dislocations. This is the point Antonioni makes. We are flying by jet, but our emotions are still in the horse-

and-buggy era, and we find that we cannot escape from ourselves, dreadfully banal as that sounds. We have grown wings and we fly faster than any bird, but our hearts are still chained to those groundlings we left behind, and it is our misfortune that the promise of the future never obliterates the poignancy of the past. Despite all our technological advancement we are still yesterday's children, and it is not in our nature to mature into tomorrow. This, then, is the ultimate paradox of McLuhanism: *Madame X* in the jet age.

—*Village Voice*, July 7, 1966

■ 10. WHO'S AFRAID OF VIRGINIA WOOLF?

Who's Afraid of Virginia Woolf? has been hailed by some critics as a daring adventure for Jack Warner, a dazzling vindication of Elizabeth Taylor, and still another directorial coup for Mike Nichols. The movie isn't all that good, but it's reasonably entertaining and effective within certain limitations, some evitable and some inevitable. Why Jack Warner should be applauded for bringing a Broadway hit to the screen is a bit beyond me. I certainly won't hold my breath until *The Zoo Story* and *The American Dream* materialize on the screen as further manifestations of Jack Warner's addiction to the Theater of the Absurd. From a Hollywood standpoint *Virginia Woolf* is no more daring a venture than *My Fair Lady*, especially with Elizabeth Taylor and Richard Burton providing box-office insurance. Indeed, Mike Nichols was probably hampered somewhat by the studio's reluctance to tamper with a pretested property, not to mention Broadway's traditional scorn for any liberties taken with the sacred text of a play. Ernest Lehman's screenplay is so timidly faithful to the original that the additions require microscopic analysis. We have come a long way since the 1929 credits for the Pickford-Fairbanks *The Taming of the Shrew*: Play by William Shakespeare, Additional Dialogue by Sam Taylor. The pendulum has swung so far in the other direction that there was never any serious question of a major infidelity to Edward Albee's original text. Consequently many of the flaws in the film have been transcribed intact from the stage.

As it happens, *Who's Afraid of Virginia Woolf?* is a brilliant

play about Living and a bad play about Life. Albee is at his best in
dramatizing the existential problem of survival through a night of
drinking and divulging, and it is no accident that the best moment
in the movie is Richard Burton's quiet pronouncement, "The
party's over." Even Haskell Wexler's overheated camera rises to
the occasion with a reflectively lofty angle of weary compassion.
Where Albee goes bad is in projecting his fantasies as marital realities. The notion of the imaginary child is too elaborate a conceit
for people whose total existence is rendered by a scream in the
night. There is no yesterday or tomorrow in Albee's theater, only a
neurotic now of masks and metaphors and masquerades and tinkling symbols.

By contrast, Eugene O'Neill's *Long Day's Journey into Night*
is as weak with the rhythm of Living as it is strong with the resolution of Life. We endure the numbness of O'Neill's Now for the
sake of the grandeur of his Then and After, and it is the last line
of the last act that redeems all that has gone before. With Albee,
the third act of *Virginia Woolf* degenerates into hysterical cha-
rades that can be vulgarized by middlebrow audiences into the conventional pieties. "You couldn't have children of your own?"
George Segal asks solicitously. "Aha!" the audience responds.
"That's what all this yelling is about. They really love each other
very much, but they can't have children. No—it's not just that.
Their yelling is really a form of communication. To show they're
alive. That's what it all means."

It's too bad, really, because *Virginia Woolf* is at its best when
it doesn't Mean anything, but simply Is. Albee touched a sociological nerve with his first two acts. The shrill horror of the cataclys-
mic cocktail party on the campus has become a document of American attitudes, and Taylor and Burton complete the portrait as real-
life archetypes of artists of abuse. When they were first announced
for the parts it struck me that Burton was miscast and Taylor too
well cast, but it turned out that Burton was inspired miscasting.
You can't believe that he'd put up with Taylor for twenty years, or
even twenty minutes, and you can't believe that Taylor had been
exposed to a college campus much past her prime, and you can't
imagine Burton and Taylor together anywhere except in a suite
full of stooges in the St. Regis—but it doesn't matter, because
Burton has given a performance of electrifying charm. (In regret-

ful retrospect, the ideal casting for *Virginia Woolf* would have been Burton and Patricia Neal.)

If Taylor does not match Burton, it is not for want of trying. Nichols has worked hard with her on her big scenes, and she is never less than competent. What she lacks is Burton's heroic calm, particularly in the all-too-rare quiet moments when she is supposed to be listening and reacting, moments that are the supreme tests of acting. It is at those moments that a sullen coarseness invades her dulled features, and Burton simply soars by contrast, with inscrutable ironies flickering across his beautifully ravaged face. Without Burton the film would have been an intolerably cold experience. Not alone does Taylor's performance lack genuine warmth. George Segal and Sandy Dennis are degraded even more than the script demands by overemphasized reactions and unnecessary mannerisms. Nichols should have restrained Miss Dennis from acting so much with her teeth, and Segal should have been quieter, but the performances are merely symptomatic of a more serious defect in the direction.

Nichols has actually committed all the classic errors of the sophisticated stage director let loose on the unsophisticated movies. For starters, he has underestimated the power of the spoken word in his search for visual pyrotechnics. Albee's script is pretty strong stuff. There is no need to jump up and down with the camera every time a character suggests humping the hostess or getting the guests or humiliating the host. Nor is there any need to take the action outside, where the hypnotic spell of an alcoholic mood can be dispelled by the fake emptiness of exteriors. Nichols gained nothing in the way of genuine cinema with his screeching station wagon. He would have been better advised to develop his main interior into a visual vortex where his characters could sink into their stupor. Compare Losey's apartment in *The Servant* or Cocteau's in *Les Parents Terribles* with the fragmented setting of *Virginia Woolf*; but, then, Losey and Cocteau knew that a sense of hell can never be achieved with facile shock tactics. Hell is, instead, a room or a house with no exit, a spatial enclosure in which human beings are rendered helpless by their unwillingness to confront the Outside. Such an expression requires a visual style emphasizing the spatial contiguity of the characters. Nichols goes so far in the other direction that at the climax of the film Elizabeth Taylor's face in

the background actually goes out of focus so as to concentrate attention entirely on Burton's reading of his line. This kind of arty
effect is ludicrous in the context of a scene in which the marital relationship is hanging in the balance. Mr. Nichols has always been
more of a tactician than a strategist, but by trying to win every
battle, he has lost the war, and in the process he has come up with
a film that looks pretentious and old-fashioned at the same time.
All that remains is an evening of Richard Burton reading the jokes
of Edward Albee, and that is more than enough entertainment for
most occasions.

—*Village Voice*, July 28, 1966

■ 11. BELMONDO

There are times when Jean-Paul Belmondo seems almost too good
to be true. His public personality has not altered appreciably since
1959, when he electrified Parisian audiences as a hard-boiled Humphrey Bogart worshipper in that tribute to American gangster movies, Jean-Luc Godard's *Breathless*. Now, seven years and more than
thirty movies later, enough of his easygoing, unpretentious, Rabelaisian personality has seeped across the Atlantic to appeal to those
of his campus admirers who are tired of Daddy's heroic declama-
tions on the Great Depression and the Great War. At the advanced age of thirty-three Belmondo is still one of the New People.
In a Times Square shop window that serves as a fever chart of adolescent addictions a gigantic poster of Belmondo shares space with
such other luminaries as David McCallum, Robert Vaughn and
the Beatles. Yet, unlike these unlikely companions, Belmondo has
not benefited from the promotions of the mass media in the States.
His English, minuscule as it is, is execrable, and few of his movies
have had wide international distribution. Despite his press clippings, Belmondo doesn't even have a press agent. In short, his
career seems to have more Zen than zing.

In *Breathless* Belmondo was cast as a cop killer, washroom mug-
ger, purse pilferer and taxi jumper, just to mention some of his non-
sexual outrages. "Belmondoism" was consequently regarded as a

new style of affluent amorality, and Belmondo himself was identified invidiously with everything from foppery to fascism. Yet four years after *Breathless* Belmondo starred in a real-life drama with the Paris police. While arguing the right of an injured motorcyclist to speedier service from the policemen on an ambulance crew, the actor was clobbered from behind by a cop and rendered *hors de combat*. Belmondo sued, and the police brought countercharges. Though Belmondo was fined for "insulting language," the impulsive gendarme was given one month's suspended sentence for "unnecessary violence." The latter penalty was virtually a milestone of human rights in a city where the law men make Okefenokee sheriffs look like charter members of the American Civil Liberties Union.

At the time I read of the incident I was reminded of an infantry officer in basic training instructing us in the submachine gun with the comment that its kick "would knock a runt like Humphrey Bogart flat on his ass." Undoubtedly there is something in Belmondo, as in Bogart, that deeply disturbs a certain type of authoritarian personality. This something may be largely a myth, but not entirely. In two very different generations a genuinely independent spirit flows out of an actor's apparently casual on-screen gestures. The surface arrogance of both Bogey and Belmondo conceals a tough-guy gallantry underneath.

It is no accident that the rediscovery of the forties Bogart has enhanced the reputation of the sixties Belmondo, and vice versa. Nevertheless there is much, much more to Belmondo than the Bogey bit. Much more and much else. If at times Belmondo seems like the last of the real movie stars, it is because his extraordinary range encompasses so many different functions and traditions. Who among contemporary actors can simultaneously evoke Douglas Fairbanks and James Dean, Marlon Brando and Marcello Mastroianni, Errol Flynn and John Garfield? Only Belmondo, the first actor in film history to combine the intelligence and athleticism of America with the intellectuality and aestheticism of Europe.

Part of Belmondo's image in France as a modern Fairbanks is based on his doing his own stunt work in films. Nowadays no Hollywood studio would permit its star to dangle from a skyscraper in Brasilia or from a helicopter over the Amazon. It would certainly never allow him to hurtle over a cliff on a motorcycle going eighty miles an hour. Belmondo's stunting is the ultimate demonstration of the nonsissiness of his métier. But in his homage to the American action movie, Belmondo has become more royalist than the king, since few, if any, of the Hollywood heroes Belmondo admires so much have ever done their own stunt work. Which only goes to prove that Americans, being more attuned to action and violence, are also more practical about it. With the French intellectual, action and violence have become articles of faith. Belmondo, sensitive to the tastes of the French public, seems to have decided, perhaps instinctively, that there is no substitute for the real thing in a country starved for authentic heroes.

Belmondo is also addicted to speeding in sports cars, much like his ill-fated predecessor the late James Dean. Unlike Dean, however, Belmondo does not seem afflicted by a death wish arising out of a lonely morbidity. Belmondo still shudders at the memory of a reckless drive that nearly cost the life of Jeanne Moreau's young son, who was riding in the "death seat." The speed generated by his many sports cars is merely an expression of Belmondo's essentially extroverted zest for physical sensations. Driving is also an expression of the actor's oft-quoted attitude of taking life as it comes.

Even in the limited context of the French cinema, however, Belmondo is hardly the first actor to project virility on an international scale. Jean Gabin was the proletarian prototype of the thirties, full of grand illusions and earthy nobility. The late Gérard Philipe embodied the Existential Pilgrim of the late forties and fifties, the anguished age of Camus and Sartre. Philipe was beautiful, austere, puritanical and cerebral. His was a sensibility of memory and regret in a world that had witnessed the obliteration of the values Gabin incarnated. (Gabin, incidentally, has called Belmondo his logical successor.)

Jean-Paul Belmondo was born in Neuilly-sur-Seine on April 9, 1933, the year after Jean Gabin made his screen debut. Belmondo was only six when Paris fell, and only eleven when Paris was liberated, an event he is helping commemorate this season in the Paramount superproduction *Is Paris Burning?* There is no reason to believe that Belmondo was particularly scarred by memories of World War II, and consequently his personality is reasonably free of the tics and angsts of the thirties and forties. His father, a noted academic sculptor, provided an atmosphere of taste and elegance against which the young Belmondo rebelled in the recognizable style of the ruling classes. He was expelled from some of the best schools of France, and took up a boxing career so seriously (twenty-three amateur bouts as a lightweight) that his parents were relieved when he went into acting. His boxing bequeathed him part of the squash in his nose, that noble emblem of his Experience, and more important, the kinetic frenzy of movement and gesture, such as we have not seen since Cagney jabbed his way across the early talkies. Belmondo is six feet tall and weighs only 143 pounds, a compact combination of sinewy muscles that makes him a heavyweight in his chosen medium. Since highbrow culture seldom exploits the expressive potentialities of the human body, Belmondo would never have made it as a big star without an accompanying revolution in the cinema.

Belmondo made three films in 1959, but only *Breathless* managed to give birth to Belmondoism. Jean-Luc Godard had worked with him previously in a short film entitled *Charlotte et son Jules*, a directorial conceit consisting of a Belmondo monologue to his departing mistress, who limits herself to a wide range of gestures and grimaces pantomiming female perversity. Godard's flair for improvising bits of business for his players found its fullest expression in *Breathless*, where a universe of meanings could be contained in the way a character lit a cigarette or opened the door to a car. Godard and Belmondo thus anticipated many of Marshall McLuhan's media probes; the characters in *Breathless* became the instruments of the gadgets they manipulated. Furthermore, the key objects in Belmondo's world are luxuries, whereas the key objects in Gabin's world were necessities, and in Philipe's world there were no objects, only moral situations. By contrast, Belmondo functions and even flourishes in a world of machines and gadgets, to the neurotic point of experiencing more and enjoying less.

Belmondo fits into a time when the need for a personal style is predicated on a loss of faith in the larger configurations of religion and history. The importance of the Now, the temporal constituent of style, is related to the decline of the hereafters of heaven and utopia. Not that Belmondo has rationalized his own role to this extent. Far from it. He has merely followed his instincts to a more vigorous response toward the world around him than custom dictates. From his first days at the Conservatory of Dramatic Art, Belmondo felt compelled to pump life, however vulgar and bawdy, into the most revered classics. (Anna Karina, Jean-Luc Godard's Galatea and ex-wife, was later to sum up Belmondo's appeal in the wisecrack, "He's not handsome, but at least he's vulgar.")

There was no Actors Studio in Paris to channel these impulses; Belmondo had to swim alone against the current of convention. Gradually he acquired a coterie of lesser-known admirers, Jean-Pierre Marielle, Jean Rochefort, Michel Beaune, Pierre Vernier and Guy Bedos. Belmondo has retained these friendships long after the big payoff of *Breathless*; and friendship, more than coincidentally, is one of the recurring themes in his movies.

One of the forgotten films of 1959 is Claude Sautet's *Classe Tous les Risques*, a gangster saga of the devotion of a young man (Belmondo) to an aging mobster (Lino Ventura). The French cult of Howard Hawks movies is derived largely from this kind of idealization of male *amitié*. Ironically, Leslie Fiedler finds this theme in American literature a symptom of the suppressed and not-so-suppressed homosexuality in American culture. Belmondo has re-enacted this Hawksian relationship in two striking films of Jean-Pierre Melville, *Magnet of Doom* and *Duolos—the Finger Man*. Only Belmondo's unquestioned virility makes the treatment of this theme feasible even in France, where homosexuality is not nearly as scandalous as it is in the more susceptible States. For his part, Belmondo prefers the relative stoicism of American *amitié* movies, in which the characters never talk about their fraternal feelings, to the gushing lyricism of François Truffaut's *Jules and Jim*, in which Jules and Jim are always reassuring each other about how much they like each other.

Nevertheless Belmondo does not deserve special credit for his virility. Such matters are not subject to choice. Nor is it particularly significant that virile actors are always in short supply and great demand. The trouble with acting, generally and universally, is the predominance of delicate, sensitive, effeminate types far beyond the correct casting percentages. The necessary narcissism is lacking in too many of the stronger personalities who would make more interesting actors. Consequently a diamond in the rough like the late John Garfield will always be a rarity and an irreplaceable treasure.

Yet Belmondo, in real life as well as in reel life, seems to have

developed few of the complexes of the big movie star. Not only has
he remained loyal to his old friends and reserved toward the most
prominent of his new ones, he has kept the same wife (Élodie, a
former dancer), whom he married on the way up, through three
children and a score of curvaceous costars without seeming sanctimonious about home and hearth. His name has been linked romantically to many of his leading ladies, most recently to the frequently
undressed Ursula Andress, his tantalizing trial in United Artists'
Up to His Ears. Such gossip, however, is standard publicity procedure for actors far less virile than Belmondo, though admittedly
some of the choicer Belmondo-Andress gossip items seem to be
getting out of hand, almost like a B-picture remake of the Burton-
Taylor tryst on the Tiber.

There is no strong evidence, fortunately, that Belmondo has lost
the sense of proportion that goes with a sense of humor. The prevailing pattern of Belmondo's personality is still a gusty irreverence
for all the cobwebs of culture and convention, but he is hardly
lacking in the finer feelings. Qualities like loyalty and fidelity are
rare enough these days, but there is also in Belmondo a restless
search for new standards of taste. He takes on a great many assignments a canny careerist like Alain Delon would scorn as beneath
contempt. Yet for all of Delon's calculations, he is merely another
pretty boy in a sea of smooth-faced anonymity, another stereotyped
French lover in the Hollywood tradition that has wasted such formidable talents as Charles Boyer and Louis Jourdan. Belmondo,
by contrast, has gone international by staying national, become universal by being French. He has become that biggest kind of star,
the kind whose sparkle is enhanced even by his bad movies.

Belmondo's instincts are probably sounder than some of his
carping critics imagine. The job of a movie star is to keep making
movies. It's all very well to say that one must pick only the best
projects, but even the best projects have been known to go bad.
What Belmondo's critics really object to is the actor's tendency to
go for "movie-movies" rather than serious cinema. Belmondo apparently passed up opportunities to work with Truffaut and Visconti in order to romp around Brazil and Hong Kong in simpleminded adventure spoofs. On the other hand, Belmondo has never
priced himself out of the way-out projects of Jean-Luc Godard, and
has undoubtedly brought many movies the financing they needed

to see the light of day. Many of the movies were bad, granted, but they were all worthy trying, and Belmondo's reputation did not suffer in the process of trial and error. Who knows which of his thirty-odd movies will next catch fire in some lonely moviegoer's soul? As it is, Belmondo has more than held his own with such international luminaries as Gabin (*Monkey in Winter*), Moreau (*Banana Peel* and *Moderato Cantabile*), Loren (*Two Women*), and Jean Seberg (*Breathless* and *Backfire*), of whom he has said, "She is what every American girl should be." His roles have ranged from a priest (*Léon Morin, Prêtre*) to a peasant (*La Viaccia*) and from a vulgar intellectual (*A Woman Is a Woman*) to a vulgar idealist (*Leda*). *Leda*, in fact, was his third film in 1959, the film in which he most closely resembled Brando, particularly at the dinner table, but with none of Brando's anguished *Streetcar Named Desire* sensitivity.

The point is that Belmondo is ultimately an original. Despite his fracas with the police, Belmondo is not a cop hater like Sinatra, or a hardheaded nonconformist like Mitchum, or an amateur agitator like Brando. Belmondo is a performer, hoping to perform as well as he can, and, up to now at least, as often as he can.

—*Gentleman's Quarterly*, Fall-Winter 1966

■ 12. *THE TORN CURTAIN*

The Torn Curtain is the fiftieth film of Alfred Hitchcock's delightfully deceptive directorial career. This ultracommercial package of Paul Newman, Julie Andrews, Hitchcock himself, and a spy subject is doing boffo business around the country even though the reviews have ranged from mixed to mildly unfavorable; and there is a general feeling that Newman and Andrews have been somewhat wasted in routine roles. It is possible also that so-called cult criticism of Hitchcock's mystical mise-en-scène has made audiences and reviewers concentrate so much on the implications of each image that they miss the plot flowing by. Like Edgar Allan Poe's "Purloined Letter," Hitchcock's meanings are in full view on the surface of the screen. Hitchcock's direction, such as it is, is not mere decoration but the very shape and substance of his story. We further stipulate that *The Torn Curtain* is basically a Hitchcockian plot even though Brian Moore receives sole credit for the script.

The opening credits of *The Torn Curtain* show a succession of faces writhing in anguish against a background of fire. The faces seem to swirl in a red sea of suffering; the pain is palpable. A strangely serious visual overture to be composed in an age of painless pop and batty camp. Dissolve to a cruise ship sailing up a Norwegian fjord against an icy blue sky. Immediate temperature contrast with opening credits. A series of establishing shots determine that the ship's heating is being repaired, and further, that the grotesquely bundled-up passengers in the dining room are members of an international scientific conference. In the midst of this comic discomfort a character later identified as Professor Karl Manfred (Gunter Strack) glances with concern at an empty table for two. Hitchcock achieves this mood of malaise with one of his patented crisp reverse cuts. We already sense that this table for two should be occupied by Paul Newman and Julie Andrews. Who else could cause such concern? Our suspicions are immediately justified by a quick cut to a stateroom where, as one suspiciously ingenuous young reader of *The New York Times* remarked, Harper is in bed with Mary Poppins under a pile of bedclothes and overcoats. Cut to badges on coats hanging on the chairs. Newman's badge identifies him as Professor Michael Armstrong, presumably the all-American male. Julie Andrews is simply Sarah Sherman, an innocent young girl enjoying an assignation before breakfast and a honeymoon before marriage.

We are already many degrees Fahrenheit away from the world of James Bond, where no one ever sweats or shivers. Hitchcock has taken us from fire to ice, and in the process he has denoted a fundamental disorder in the world he has created. As far as we can ascertain, Newman and Andrews are the only Americans on the cruise ship, and They Are Not Where They Are Supposed To Be. In some subtle way they have broken the rules of the community around them by circumventing its suffering. Indicative of how Hitchcock's form comes full circle is the fact that the very last shot of the film shows Newman and Andrews escaping once more to the sanctuary of a blanket, the couple's cocoon, the warp and woof and womb from whence the Ugly, Quiet, and Innocent Americans emerge periodically to bring chaos and confusion abroad. And make no mistake about it. *The Torn Curtain* is at least partly a parable of American meddling in the world.

When there is a knock on the door the audience is immediately apprehensive that the worried-looking scientist has come to check up on the indecorous behavior of his colleagues. Fortunately it is only a bellboy with a radiogram. There is almost a sigh of comic relief as Newman reads the apparently meaningless message, but then our hero inexplicably denies that he is the intended recipient. Suddenly we sense that Newman is hiding something from Andrews, and in that moment she becomes both the temporary protagonist and the audience's point of view.

We are subsequently launched into a succession of commonplace incidents infected with the intrigue of Hitchcock's reverse cuts. A cryptic radiogram is dispatched by Newman, a book is picked up in a shop specializing in religious tracts, a luncheon date is canceled, a fake flight to Stockholm is announced. Newman is up to something—but what? Julie Andrews feels rejected, rebuffed, and humiliated, but she perseveres to the point of following her man to East Berlin, where, as it turns out, he is apparently defecting to the East Germans.

If we could forget the espionage trappings for a moment, it would seem almost as if Newman was clumsily arranging an assignation with another woman, and Andrews was checking up on him. There is never really any meaningful communication between Newman and Andrews, and there is a classic one-take sequence in a hotel room that would inspire rapturous essays for its meaningful use of color if only it had popped up in an Antonioni film.

Nonetheless Julie Andrews is emotionally released by elaborate camera movements all the more expressive because Hitchcock is too adept at montage to require camera movement for merely mechanical assignments. Hitchcock's economy of expression makes him infinitely superior stylistically to such non-montage directors as Kubrick and Fellini, whose camera movements often degenerate from gratuitousness to monotony from sheer overwork. In fact, Hitchcock is about the only director alive today who could tell a story replete with emotional relationships without using a line of dialogue.

Of course, the audience inevitably disbelieves in Newman's defection. Yet the discomfort persists. The East Germans are too sympathetically civilized to seem stock villains. Hansjoerg Felmy, the canny catalyst of *Station Six—Sahara*, plays the security chief with warm charm and cool competence. Wolfgang Kieling's Communist watchdog, Gromek, is a gem of a cameo characterization as the gum-chewing fan of Warner's gangster movies and a former inhabitant of Eighty-sixth Street. These people have not initiated the intrigue. They are merely reacting to it with justifiable suspicion. All the other characters in the film, Communist, non-Communist, and anti-Communist alike, belong to a world of fixed, even orderly ideologies and duties. Newman and Andrews have disrupted this world; they have torn the curtain, and human blood, not theirs, has been spilled—but for what purpose? We soon find out. Newman tells an Allied agent that the bogus defection is designed to obtain a secret from the enemy. Newman's funds had been cut off in Washington because he was unable to calculate the ultimate formula of the antimissile missile. An East German scientist (Ludwig Donath) has the secret, and Newman intends to pick the scientist's brain by cajoling his curiosity. Newman is obviously no patriot. Otherwise there would be an obligatory scene of his superiors imploring him to pose as a defector for national security, and there is no such scene even implied. Newman goes it virtually alone, endangering friendly agents and innocent bystanders in the process. He is simply a conniving petty bureaucrat out to steal a trade secret from the enemy, in this case the East Germans, but it could just as easily be a rival company. Paul Newman is the organization man par excellence, using unscrupulous means to achieve dubious ends, and Julie Andrews is the perfect company wife, smug, superior, completely confident that enough money can compensate for anything. That Newman, particularly, is antitype-cast makes Hitchcock's statement on Americans of the sixties come over more forcefully.

The most admired scene in the film, and rightfully so, is the one in which Newman and a woman accomplice kill Gromek, slowly, torturously, painfully, with a knife, a shovel, and finally by sticking Gromek's head in a gas oven, a sequence culminating morally with Newman's palm stained with Gromek's blood. This is the only murder in the movie, and it constitutes Hitchcock's comment on the Bond casualness about killing, and perhaps also on the perversion of a genre that Hitchcock and Fritz Lang so often transcended with their noble art.

—*Village Voice*, September 1, 1966

■ 13. *THE WILD ANGELS*

The Wild Angels has caused somewhat of a stir on the international scene by being chosen to open the recently concluded Venice Film Festival. We don't have Clare Boothe Luce on hand to instruct Italians in the American image, as she did more than a decade ago when *The Blackboard Jungle* threatened to besmirch the glories of our big-city secondary schools. *The Wild Angels* is undoubtedly stronger stuff than *The Blackboard Jungle*, but the principle is the same. Let's not hang out our dirty linen in public, at least not where the European Left can see it and draw its own diabolical conclusions. There is some virtue if not much validity to this argument. The European Left is now so completely bankrupt intellectually that American self-criticism serves no constructive purpose. In fact, Europeans seem to have picked up every American vice except self-hatred.

Still, it is no secret that the Venice Film Festival would have preferred *Who's Afraid of Virginia Woolf?*—and how does that rate, image-wise? No, the only solution is to delegate the festival film-supplying job to Walt Disney, capitalism's answer to Bertolt Brecht.

In all fairness to Roger Corman and his colleagues on *The Wild Angels*, a Festival appearance was probably the farthest thing from his mind. Most Corman movies fall into the demimonde of conventional horror and violence, a realm that regular reviewers seldom take seriously enough to appraise its incidental and intermittent beauties. It is hard enough to get the literary Establishment to appreciate the artistry in such relatively respectable genres as the western and the thriller. When you descend to ghouls, vampires, and tunic-and-toga specials, only the most esoteric cultists accompany you with any kind of coherent commentary. Corman is consequently a cult figure with critics who regard *Cahiers du Cinéma* as a sellout to the Establishment. Also, Corman's movies are stronger visually than dramatically; the acting is always atrocious, and the scripts spectacularly uneven. In this context *The Wild Angels* runs true to form. Peter Fonda and Nancy Sinatra may reverberate on the marquee with hereditary hubris, but their performances on screen demean the names they bear. Therefore, the inevitable echoes of *Rebel Without a Cause* and *The Wild One* only remind us of the now classical art of Marlon Brando and the late James Dean. Peter Fonda, in particular, virtually destroys the mythos of the motorcyclist with his bad artiness.

Unfortunately, there are no secondary characterizations to take up the slack, and this is one of the limitations of the script and of most C-picture scripts as well: a lack of density and detail. To make matters worse, the print now circulating in the States is allegedly a butchered version of the one that opened in Venice and was previewed here in New York for the critics. An orgy sequence in a church was deemed particularly offensive to certain groups, and most cuts have been made with reference to a gang rape of a motorcyclist's young widow, which seems to be the main point of the orgy. Some viewers will be consciously outraged by the spectacle of a swastika being flaunted as part of a Black Mass and others will be subconsciously startled to witness the attempted rape of a Negro nurse by a white hoodlum, an unintentional reminder, perhaps, that white power long antedated black power. Many critics will complain that this sort of thing is irresponsible and even untrue. The newsreels of swastika-bearing youths in Cicero are all too real, however, and nothing is to be gained from burying our movies in the sands of decorum. A frightful tension haunts our society. However, much as a movie like *The Wild Angels* exploits this tension, it also exorcises the evil involved by simply acting it out. Not that *The Wild Angels* is concerned exclusively with the direst deviltry. There are moments of soppy, sweet-colored lyricism on the road when one begins to understand that most social evil is a perversion of noble impulses by mediocre sensibilities. And the noblest and yet most perverted impulse of all is that lyrical leap toward liberty, the subject and substance of politics and cinema. Artistically *The Wild Angels* may be a *Scorpio Rising* for Scopitones, but there is more genuine audacity here than there is in a whole season of Iron Curtain cartoons attacking conformity, always, of course, in the most abstract terms.

—*Village Voice*, September 15, 1966

■ 14. *THE CHELSEA GIRLS*

The Chelsea Girls has made the move uptown from the Film-Makers' Cinematheque to the Cinema Rendezvous, where, ironically enough, many family-type flicks have premiered or returned for the kiddies over the years. Needless to say, *The Chelsea Girls* is not for the kiddies, or for adults of kiddy-car coyness. Functional voyeurs will be bored to distraction. Warhol doesn't exploit depravity as much as he certifies it. Most pornography is antierotic because of the crudity of its certification, but *The Chelsea Girls* isn't even pornographic. The flashes of male Caucasian nudity depress the viewer with intimations of a pitiful passivity. Warhol has refined the old Hollywood tease into a kind of tepid torture in which organisms talk away their orgasms.

I am not sure the version of *The Chelsea Girls* now on view at the Cinema Rendezvous is the same film that played at the Cinematheque. The running time was originally reported at four hours; it is now three and a half. The "ending" seems to have been changed somewhere between the Cinematheque and the Rendezvous. All the reviews I have read pro and con seem to be vague about details. Part of the problem is the studied unprofessionalism of the presentation. Neither Andy Warhol nor the Cinematheque provided press sheets, credits, synopses, and so forth. The reviewer is left to his own recollections. Many of his predecessors have proclaimed that they have been put upon, or worse still, "put on." Is *The Chelsea Girls* a "put-on"? I would say it's probably no more a "put-on" than *Lawrence of Arabia*. *Lawrence* may have an advantage around the edges, but *The Chelsea Girls* has more conviction at its core.

Andy Warhol presents his material on two screens simultaneously and uses the double screen to develop the most obvious contrasts. One screen is usually synchronized with a sound track while the other is silent. One screen may be in color while the other is in black and white. One screen may show "girls" while the other shows "boys." The quotes around "boys" and "girls" are applied advisedly. The only polarities Warhol projects are homosexual and sadomasochistic. No one in Warhol's world is "straight" or "true," and the percentage of deviation is a flagrant exaggeration even for the fetid locale. Fortunately *The Chelsea Girls* is not concerned with deviation as a clinical subject, or with homosexuality as a state of fallen grace. Some of the more sophisticated Establishment reviewers write as if everything that happens south of Fourteenth Street comes out of Dante's *Inferno*. Warhol is not bosh, but neither is he Bosch. The Chelsea Hotel is not hell. It is an earthly, earthy place like any other, where even fags, dykes, and junkies have to go on living twenty-four hours a day. This is where Warhol has been heading through the somnambulism of *Sleep* and the egregiousness of *Empire*—toward an existential realism beyond the dimensions of the cinema. Warhol disdains the conventional view of film as a thing of bits and pieces. Perhaps "disdains" is too strong a term for an attitude that is at best instinctive, at worst indifferent. As his scene segments unreel, the footage is finally punctuated by telltale leaders and then kaplunk blankness on the screen. This indicates that each scene runs out of film before it runs out of talk. If there were more film, there would be more talk. If there were less film, there would be less talk. How much more gratuitous and imprecise can cinema be? Goodbye Sergei Eisenstein. Hello Eastman Kodak. Besides, what with the problems of projection and the personalities of projectionists, each showing of *The Chelsea Girls* may qualify as a distinctly unique happening.

Andy Warhol displays some disturbing flourishes of technique. His zooms are perhaps the first antizooms in film history. Unlike Stanley Kramer's zooms (in *Judgment at Nuremberg*), which go boi-ing to the heart of the theatrics, Andy Warhol's zooms swoop on unessential details with unerring inaccuracy. With a double screen, the gratuitous zoom is a particularly menacing distraction to the darting eye. (Is that a girl's bare thigh? No, it's a close-up of the kitchen sink.)

A less conspicuous addition to Warhol's abacadabra arsenal is the traveling typewriter shot, which consists of a slow horizontal camera movement from left to right culminating in a rapid return shot from right to left. What does it mean? Nothing that I can figure out. Warhol has been experimenting with jazzy effects ever since one of his camp parties on film. The most glaring weakness of *The Chelsea Girls* is its attempts at art through cinematic technique. The color LSD frames don't work as hallucinations; the close-ups and camera movements don't work as comments. Nonetheless a meaningful form and sensibility emerge through all the apparent arrogance and obfuscation.

Richard Goldstein's excellent critique in the Sunday *World Journal Tribune* gives the impression that Warhol's vision is as glossy and popeyed as Richard Lester's. I don't find Warhol *au courant* in this way at all. *The Chelsea Girls* is actually closer to *Nanook of the North* than to *The Knack*. It is as documentary that *The Chelsea Girls* achieves its greatest distinction. What Warhol is documenting is a subspecies of the New York sensibility, a sensibility that Paddy Chayefsky only mimicked in the party scene in *The Bachelor Party*, a sensibility that Clifford Odets only hinted at in *Sweet Smell of Success*—and let's not even mention such contorted Village vileness as *Two for the Seesaw*, *A Fine Madness*, and *Penelope*.

When the "Pope" of Greenwich Village talks about sin and idolatry, when a creature in drag "does" Ethel Merman in two of the funniest song numbers ever, when a balding fag simpers about the Johnson admenstruation, when a bull dyke complains about her mate getting hepatitis, it's time to send the children home and scrap Lillian Hellman's *The Children's Hour*. Warhol's people are more real than real, because the camera encourages their exhibitionism. They are all "performing," because their lives are one long performance, and their party is never over. The steady gaze of Warhol's camera reveals considerable talent and beauty. The Pope character is the closest thing to the late Lenny Bruce to come along in some time, and his Figaro repartee with a girl called Ingrid is an extraordinarily sustained slice of improvisation. The film begins with the beautiful blonde Nico on the right screen, the Pope and Ingrid on the left. The film ends with Nico on the left, the Pope on the right, and I felt moved by the juxtaposition of wit and beauty. Warhol's people are not all this effective—Marie Menken, particularly, is a big bore—but they are There, and though I wouldn't want to live with them, they are certainly worth a visit if you're interested in life on this planet.

—Village Voice, December 15, 1966

■ 15. A MAN FOR ALL SEASONS

A *Man for All Seasons* is the most edifying experience to hit the screen since *The Life of Émile Zola*. It seems that almost every year at this time some film or other inspires me to play Horatio at the Bridge. It was *Lawrence of Arabia* in 1962, *Tom Jones* in 1963, *My Fair Lady* and *Dr. Strangelove* in 1964, and *Who's Afraid of Virginia Woolf?* for most of 1966. Does pure perverseness play a part in this reviewer's reactions? Not as much as most nonreviewers suppose. Even the most captious critics have a hankering to come in from the cold, and it is generally much easier and more "human" not to resist the rape of the click film, the hit play, the runaway best seller, the bandwagon bonanza, the "of course" complacency of the success story. Even in moments of maximum hysteria, however, there is a place for the long view, and in this corner at least, there is grave doubt that A *Man for All Seasons* is a film for all time.

Actually the film version of A *Man for All Seasons* will probably follow the same cultural path as the play. The daily reviewers, surfeited with sensationalism, spoofery, and just plain silliness, are primed to endorse the slightest semblance of seriousness. Then along comes Robert Bolt, England's answer to Arthur Miller, both men monstrous mouthers of rhetorical redundancies. And what is Bolt's message? Simply that every individual must preserve his integrity. Fortunately, Sir Thomas More's martyrdom is remote enough and hence abstract enough to serve as allegory for covert nonconformists from Madison Avenue to MacDougal Street. Barry Goldwater will be edified. So will Norman Thomas. After all, Sir Thomas More doesn't go around burning draft cards or babbling about Black Power. Such contemporary confrontations of authority might offend much of the audience that now applauds More's steadfastness in a world of King-Pope intrigues to which the modern religions of nationalism are relatively indifferent. In fact, the film, even more than the play, tends to subordinate historical facts and ideological issues to abstract arguments about personal conscience. The Spanish ambassador disappears as a character, and with him the information that Spanish troops are terrorizing the Pope in Rome. More's theological arguments in the film actually smack of a rigid medievalism, against which Henry VIII's capricious sensuality seems almost sympathetic. What validates More's position is his sufferable moral superiority. Like Jesus Christ and Joan of Arc, he is simply better than anyone else around at the time, but this situation is more the stuff of dogma than drama.

Not that Bolt isn't entitled to write a play about Sir Thomas More, but there is something wrong when the noble hero gets all the best lines, with a veritable stuffing of staircase wit. The bad guys in good westerns get a better break than do the bad guys in *A Man for All Seasons*. To make matters worse, Leo McKern is cast as the arch villain. McKern is effective when he plays hysterical bullies in Losey's films because Losey has a flair for lyrical love-hate scenes in which characters flail at each other with their uncontrolled feelings. Under Fred Zinnemann's tight direction, with Bolt's tight script, opposite Paul Scofield's tight-lipped ironies, McKern is reduced to stock villainy. The one high note of the film is struck by that wondrous wailing banshee, Wendy Hiller, in the defiance scene in More's dungeon. This is the only scene in the film in which a character is able to shut up Thomas More, and it takes his wife to put her hand over his mouth to do it: "S-s-sh . . . As for understanding, I understand you're the best man that I ever met or am likely to; and if you go, well, God knows why, I suppose —though, as God's my witness, God's kept deadly quiet about it!" Wendy Hiller has only one more sentence to go in her one big scene, but anyone who has ever seen her in *The Heiress* or *Moon for the Misbegotten* knows that it takes her only an instant to bring the heavens crashing down on the stage. Lifting her arms, and looking upward in a slow, clumsy, aged, earth-laden movement, this gruff tradesman's daughter and cleric's wife discards the prudence of a lifetime to defy all the universal power arrayed against her poor husband: "And if anyone wants my opinion of the King and his Council they've only to ask for it." The line really isn't that good, but in Hiller's hands it becomes the stuff of sublime theater. "Why, it's a lion I married! A lion! A lion!" Scofield quips fatuously, and as he puts his stage arms around his wife, the mood is muffled by a return to rhetorical display. From frenzy we descend back to forensics, and Scofield takes us the rest of the way to the chopping block with one or two good one-liners, most notably: "For Wales? Why, Richard, it profits a man nothing to give his soul for the whole world . . . but for Wales!" The foregoing line is so good that Zinnemann resists nudging the audience with a reaction shot of period extras chortling at More's wit in the courtroom. Would that Zinnemann had altogether resisted this vulgar method of telling audiences in Topeka that grammatical English prose can get laughs, but then A Man for All Seasons would not be the successful middlebrow enterprise that it is.

In all fairness to Zinnemann, his direction is about as effectively expert here as it was ineffectively expert in Behold a Pale Horse. Every frame is etched and chiseled in terms of the most precise placement of characters, colors, costumes, and period decor. As an academic exercise, A Man for All Seasons will probably be snapped up by the 16-millimeter catalogues unless there are purists who still object to filmed stage plays. The film will probably look better in 16-millimeter. Zinnemann avoids close-ups and sweeping camera movements like the plague, and some of his imagery with stone lions evokes Eisenstein's October. On the whole, Zinnemann's visual style is recessive in that everyone is always seen at a safe distance. I don't like this style particularly. It's safe, tactful, and tentative for a director who doesn't want to get too involved with his characters. Yet it is probably wise for this project. Scofield and Bolt don't really take close-ups. They lack feeling and empathy. Scofield is a virtuoso on the stage, where the dry inflections of his voice can ripple across the footlights with layers and layers of expressive irony and biting cynicism. When you look at his face on the screen, however, you get a guilty desire to look somewhere else. Actually, it's hard to remember what Scofield looks like from one performance to the next. I can't think of another actor of comparable skill with so little physical presence.

A Man for All Seasons is blessed with an extraordinary supporting cast—Wendy Hiller, Susannah York, Orson Welles, Robert Shaw, and Vanessa Redgrave in an unbilled appearance as Anne Boleyn. All I can say is wow! There was Orson Welles down in Spain shooting Chimes at Midnight which will have trouble finding a theater while A Man for All Seasons rolls on and on. Despite such coups as getting Gielgud and Richardson and Moreau, Welles had to make do with such eminently dubbed Shakespearean actresses as Marina Vlady, whose perfect English diction led one wag to dub the film *Singin' in the Reign*. *Chimes at Midnight* has all kinds of technical deficiencies, and Welles makes many more mistakes than Zinnemann ever could, and yet I wouldn't trade one shot from the Welles for the entire oeuvre of Zinnemann. With all the faults of the Welles, and all the virtues of the Zinnemann, I firmly believe that the massive passions of *Chimes at Midnight* will long outlive the miniature pageantry of *A Man for All Seasons*.

—*Village Voice*, December 22, 1966

■ 16. *BLOW-UP*

Michelangelo Antonioni's *Blow-Up* is the movie of the year, and I use the term "movie" advisedly for an evening's entertainment that left me feeling no pain (or Antoniennui) whatsoever. It is possible that this year's contributions from Ford, Dreyer, Hitchcock, Chabrol, and Godard may cut deeper and live longer than Antonioni's mod masterpiece, but no other movie this year has done as much to preserve my faith in the future of the medium. If you have not yet seen *Blow-Up*, see it immediately before you hear or read anything more about it. I speak from personal experience when I say it is better to let the movie catch you completely unawares. One of its greatest virtues is surprise, and the last thing you want to know is the plot and theme in advance. Unfortunately, most of the reviewers have given the show completely away. Judith Crist coyly conceals the plot gambit in *Gambit*, but she spills the beans on *Blow-Up* with no qualms whatsoever. Why? I suppose she considers *Blow-Up* too esoteric for audiences to enjoy in the course of mindless moviegoing. It's a pity, since, purely on a plot level, *Blow-Up* provides more thrills, chills, and fancy frissons than any other movie this year.

The excitement begins with the opening credits, which are stenciled across a field of green grass opening into a pop blue rhythm-and-blues background of dancing models perceived only partially through the lettering that, among other things, implicates Antonioni in the script and heralds Vanessa Redgrave, David Hemmings, Sarah Miles, and a supporting cast of unknowns. The billing is misleading. Miss Redgrave and Miss Miles make only guest appearances in what amounts to a vehicle for David Hemmings and Antonioni's camera. *Blow-Up* is never dramatically effective in terms of any meaningful confrontations of character. The dialogue is self-consciously spare and elliptical in a sub-Pinteresque style. Fortunately, the twenty-four-hour duration of the plot makes it possible for Antonioni to disguise most of the film as a day in the life of a mod photographer in swinging London town. What conflict there is in *Blow-Up* is captured in the opening clash between vernal greens on one plane and venal blues, reds, yellows, pinks, and purples on another. The natural world is arrayed against the artificial scene; conscience is deployed against convention.

The film itself begins with more obvious contrasts: A truck loaded with screaming revelers made up in garishly painted mime faces. Cut to derelicts trudging silently out of flophouse with bundles and belongings. One would suspect Antonioni of facile Marxist montage in his cross-cutting between mimes and derelicts, between noisy merriment and quiet morning aftermath, but one would be wrong. The mimes are merely an Italianate mannerism in London, and the derelicts are simply the grubbier side of a photographer's visual concerns. Nevertheless the cross-cutting functions by itself without any explicatory dialogue or commentary. Even the protagonist is identified for us only by degrees. Antonioni can afford a leisurely exposition for two reasons. First, we are going to be looking at Hemmings all through the movie, and a slightly mysterious materialization will not hurt him at the outset. Second, the emphasis throughout is not so much on the protagonist himself as on what he and his camera see and on how well he blends with the background. Gradually we are filled in not so much with a plot as with a routine—a day in the life of a candid cameraman.

Blow-Up abounds with what Truffaut calls "privileged moments," intervals of beautiful imagery while nothing seems to be happening to develop the drama or advance the narrative. Very early in the film the camera confronts the photographer's long black convertible head-on at a crossroads. Suddenly the entire screen is blotted out by a blue bus streaking across from right to left, followed quickly by a yellow truck. That sudden splash of blue and yellow defines Antonioni's mood and milieu better than any set of speeches ever could. Wherever Antonioni's camera goes, doors, fences, poles, even entire buildings seem to have been freshly painted for the sake of chromatic contrast or consistency. Part of Antonioni's ambivalence toward his subject in *Blow-Up* is reflected in the conflicting temptations of documentary and decoration. After painting the trees in *The Red Desert* a petrified gray, Antonioni feels no compunctions about painting the grass greener in *Blow-Up*. If reality is not expressive enough, a paint brush will take up the slack. The theory of controlled color is carried about as far as it can go in *Blow-Up* before its artistic limitations become too apparent. Antonioni is heading in a dangerous direction, but the Pirandellian resolution of the plot saves him on this occasion from the stylistically bloated decadence of *The Red Desert*.

The ultimate beauty of *Blow-Up* is derived from the artistic self-revelation of the director. *Blow-Up* is to Antonioni what *Lola Montès* was to the late Max Ophuls, what *Ugetsu* was to the late Kenji Mizoguchi, what *Contempt* was to Godard, what *French Can-Can* was to Renoir, what *Limelight* was to Chaplin, what *Rear Window* was to Hitchcock, what *8½* was to Fellini—a statement of the artist, not on life but on art itself as the consuming passion of an artist's life. As David Hemmings moves gracefully through off-beat sites in London, his body writhing to meet the challenge of every new subject, we feel that Antonioni himself is intoxicated by the sensuous surfaces of a world he wishes to satirize. Curiously, he is more satisfying when he succumbs to the sensuousness than when he stands outside it. The unsuccessful sequences—the rock 'n' roll session, the marijuana party, the alienation conversations Hemmings has with Vanessa Redgrave in one scene and Sarah Miles in another—all suffer from the remoteness of cold chronicles recorded by an outsider. Antonioni is more successful when he forgets his ennui long enough to photograph a magnificent mod fashion spectacle that transcends the grotesquely artificial creatures lending themselves to the illusion. Even more spectacular is the teenybopper sandwich orgy that digresses from the main plot. An entire generation of mini-teasers and inhibited exhibitionists are divested of their defenses in a frenzied choreography of bold beauty and heartrending contemporaneity. The stripping away of pink and blue leotards may explain why the Metro lion has decided to skulk away from the opening credits like a timid pussy cat scared of the Production Code.

The fact that Antonioni can be entertaining even when he is not enlightening makes the eruption of his plot all the more stunning. It starts simmering in the midst of apparent aimlessness. The photographer-protagonist wanders out of an antique shop, drifts by chance into a park, where he ignores a grotesquely sexless park attendant jabbing trash with her pike, passes by a tennis court, where two children are playing a clumsy brand of tennis, photographs pigeons afoot and in flight, then stalks a pair of lovers up a hill. At a distance it looks as if a tall girl is pulling at an older man in what later will be recalled in retrospect as a spectacle of carnal Calvary. Here Hemmings becomes a weak-kneed voyeur as he scurries behind fences and trees with his telescopic lens. This is raw, spontaneous life in an ominously leafy setting. Vanessa Redgrave, she of the incredibly distracting long legs and elongated spinal column, which is here extended vertically through an ugly blue-plaid mini-suit, making her look at a distance like a seven-foot girl guide—in short, Vanessa Redgrave via Antonioni rather than Karel (*Morgan!*) Reisz—runs up to Hemmings to plead for the pictures. Everything in the movie has been so fragmented up to this time that we accept her trivial invasion-of-privacy argument at face value. Hemmings refuses to return the negatives, and later tricks her into accepting bogus negatives while he develops and "blows up" the real ones. What seemed like a tryst in a park is magnified into a murder. Death, which has hovered over Antonioni's films from the very beginning of his career, makes its grand entrance in a photographer's studio through the eyes of a camera that sees truth where the eyes of the photographer see only reality. This, then, is the paradox of Antonioni's vision of art: The further we draw away from reality, the closer we get to the truth. Vanessa Redgrave, an irritating, affected personality in her "live" scenes, comes to life with a vengeance in the "blow-up" of her photos.

From the moment of his artistic triumph, the protagonist becomes morally impotent. He has discovered truth, but is unable to pass judgment or secure justice. He returns to the scene of the crime that night and finds the corpse of the murdered man. He visits a neighboring artist and mistress only to find them furiously *flagrante delicto*. He returns to his studio and discovers the theft

of his blow-ups. He is physically frightened when he hears footsteps
and begins to cower in a corner of his decor. It is only the artist's
mistress (Sarah Miles), treading as beautifully as ever on her cat
feet and in her transparent dress. He tells her about the murder,
but she is too preoccupied with her own problems to give much
help. The rest of the film threatens to degenerate into one of Antonioni's shaggy dog Odysseys to futility when the photographer
returns to the scene of the blown-up crime. The wind is blowing.
The body is gone. The leaves flutter with chilling indifference.
Then suddenly the mime revelers from the opening sequence reappear in their loaded truck and disembark at the tennis court. Two
mimes play an imaginary game with somewhat clumsy gestures
while the others watch with silent, swivel-headed concentration.
Antonioni's camera begins following the action of the imaginary
ball back and forth across the net until it is "hit" over the fence
near where the photographer is standing. He walks back to the spot
where the "ball" has landed and throws it back. He then begins
swiveling his head back and forth and even hears the ball bouncing. He smiles at his own susceptibility, but suddenly an expression
of pain flashes across his face. The camera cuts to an overhead shot
of the photographer, a self-judgment of both contempt and compassion. Antonioni, the ex-tennis player who once sold his trophies
to live, has come out in the open with a definitive description of
his divided sensibility, half Mod, half Marxist. Unlike Fellini, however, Antonioni has converted his confession into a genuine movie
that objectifies his obsessions without whining or self-pity. As befits
the classical tradition of movie-making, *Blow-Up* can be enjoyed by
moviegoers who have never heard of Antonioni.

—*Village Voice*, December 29, 1966

vi
1967

■ 1. *LA GUERRE EST FINIE*

Alain Resnais' *La Guerre Est Finie* embellished the 1966 New York Film Festival with its extraordinary excellence. It's a long way from the Abraham Lincoln Brigade to Lincoln Center, but memory and nostalgia have a way of preserving lost causes as the conscience of history. Thus simply for its subject *La Guerre Est Finie* should regain for Resnais most of the admirers he lost somewhere on the track between Hiroshima and Marienbad. The almost irresistible temptation to insult the Idiot Left must be resisted at all costs. Who is to say that people should not admire the right films for the wrong reasons? It is for the critic to register the right reasons. The creator prefers profitable misunderstandings and confusions, so that he can find the funds to continue his career.

If *La Guerre Est Finie* is in some ways the most satisfying movie Resnais has made, credit is due largely to the lucidity and integrity of Yves Montand's characterization of Diego, a revolutionary engulfed by fears, fantasies, and futilities. However fragmented the director's feelings may be, Montand remains a rock of commitment, and with Montand's solidity as an actor serving as an anchor of style, a sea of images can be unified into a mental characterization. Whereas the awesome majesty of the late Nikolai Cherkassov obliterated montage in the late Sergei Eisenstein's *Ivan the Terrible,* the humanity of Montand domesticates montage in *La Guerre Est Finie.* We are no longer concerned with the pretentious counterpoint of love and the Bomb, past and present, illusion and reality,

285

society and the individual, and so on. We are obsessed instead with the doubts and the fantasies of Diego. Through his mind passes what we know and feel about the heritage of the Old Left, that last, desperate camaraderie commemorated in kitchens and cemeteries as old comrades grapple with the old rhetoric they are doomed never to forget and the new reality they are doomed never to understand.

For Resnais it is enough to celebrate remembrance and mourn forgetfulness as fragments of personality and politics disintegrate in the void of time. Civilization is the process of trying to remember, and Resnais once did a documentary on the Bibliothèque Nationale as the supreme ornament of civilization. Cinema, however, is more than remembering and forgetting. It is also acting, doing, resolving, indeed being. Cinema, like life, is a process of creating memories for the future. Resnais has always drawn on the past without paying for the future. His cinema has been hauntingly beautiful if dramatically improvident in its ghostliness. His characters have been paralyzed by the sheer pastness of their sensibilities. Montand's Diego is no exception, but a marvelous thing has happened. Montand's dignity and bearing have broken through the formal shell of Resnais' art to dramatize the doubts and hesitations of the director. Diego has become a hero of prudence and inaction. He has shown what it is to be a man without the obvious flourishes of virility so fashionable today. (Even the stately explicitness of the lovemaking is a measure of the hero's stature.) To be a man it is above all necessary to be patient as one's life dribbles away on the back streets, blind alleys, and dead ends of political impotence. The at times agonizing slowness of *La Guerre Est Finie* achieves the pathos of patience by expressing a devotion to detail common to both Diego and Resnais. It has always seemed that Resnais was more suited to documentary than fiction because of a preoccupation with facts rather than truths. The parts in Resnais always seem superior to the whole, and if *La Guerre Est Finie* is an exception, it is because the integral behaviorism of a performer has buttressed the analytical style of a director. It is as if Resnais were dropping things all over the screen, and Montand were walking around picking them up. That *La Guerre Est Finie* finally makes us weep is a tribute to Montand's tenacity.

As for what the film actually "says," Jorge Semprun's script is explicit enough for the least sophisticated audiences. The meaning is in the title. The war is over, and Resnais, unlike Zinnemann in the grotesquely unfeeling *Behold a Pale Horse*, makes no attempt to reconstruct the agonies of antiquity with old newsreels. The ultimate tragedy of the Spanish Civil War is that all its participants are either dead or thirty years older. Spain still exists as a geographical entity, but it has been repopulated with an indifferent generation. Tourists swarm through Madrid and Barcelona while old Bolsheviks haul pamphlets into Seville. The New Left sneers at the Old Left. But it doesn't matter as long as one man can keep faith in the midst of uncertainty.

—Village Voice, February 2, 1967

■ 2. BOUDU SAVED FROM DROWNING

Jean Renoir's *Boudu Saved from Drowning* is a film of unexpected freshness despite the fact that it has taken thirty-five years to cross the Atlantic. Looking at Michel Simon's aggravatingly accomplished tramp ("un clochard réussi") bedevil a bookselling benefactor and his household, I was struck by the prefiguration of today's peevish black power–white liberal confrontations. Michel Simon is an irritating actor even on his best behavior, but when his brash Boudu wipes off shoe polish from his hand with milady's bedspread he is well-nigh intolerable. Boudu belongs to that incorrigible tribe of troublemakers Shaw described in *Pygmalion* as the "undeserving poor." They are always with us, these lowly wretches who lack humility, who make too much noise in the streets, who defile our cultural monuments and scrawl obscenities in our temples, who show disrespect to upper- and middle-class humanitarians.

Boudu himself goes so far as to spit into a book by Balzac. When a customer asks for a first edition of *Les Fleurs du Mal*, Boudu answers that the shop sells books, not flowers. Later when he is scolded for spitting on Balzac, Boudu can't remember any bloke by that name. Hopeless. Simon-Boudu reveals no redeeming qualities. None whatsoever. Yet after he has drawn a winning lottery ticket and married the maid and rowed down the river to respectability with a silk topper, he reaches out of the rowboat to pick a water lily and overturns his entire middle-class existence in one motion. He floats in the womb of the river downstream until he reaches a point on the shore whence he can find his road. He passes a scarecrow and pulls it over the fence for its old clothes, and in the process props it across his back like a cross, but only for an awkward instant. Renoir never milks his effects. His exquisite evocations float across the screen like forgotten features of the landscape. A full appreciation of *Boudu* depends to some extent on an appreciation of Renoir's total career as a river of personal expression. It helps also to remember the thirties, when bands used to play in outdoor casinos and young girls in long dresses would lean on the bandstand in the shimmering sunlight. The sky was not yet the menacing realm of air raiders, and people went to the country and believed naïvely in nature, and no one really expected a lasting depression.

This was the world of my parents, and I can still remember them going out in their Pierce Arrow touring car to go dancing, and I can even remember the rotogravure section in the Sunday papers, and the long, slim silhouettes of the international fashions. Renoir evokes these childhood memories with just one or two shots of a destination Boudu will never reach, for Boudu is less a character than a bundle of impulses forbidden to the bourgeoisie. Freedom, earthiness, irresponsibility, even impulsiveness itself are denied to people and classes that yearn for or settle for mere respectability. But ultimately there is no dramatic conflict between Boudu and his benefactors. They are all part of Renoir, part of his joyful sadness, part of the feeling he expresses so lyrically about the irreconcilability of life's choices. *Boudu* documents the Paris left bank of 1932, that is literally the left bank of a wet river in which people may drown and from which they may be saved from drowning much like Cabiria in Fellini's chronicle of loneliness and despair. The time and place are entirely different. Chilling Roman indifference in the fifties can be contrasted with warming Parisian camaraderie in the thirties. Renoir's Paris is the Paris of class distinctions and bookish habits and corrupt gendarmes and fraternal feelings and rabid individualisms.

Renoir records these paradoxes of coexistence in a matter-of-fact manner. There is little in his shot-sequencing of what aestheticians like to call "dynamic progression." *Boudu* meanders along like its eponymous protagonist, indeed like the shaggy dog and soul mate Boudu loses at the beginning of the movie and never finds. There is no sense of urgency in Renoir's style, no tricks of tension, only an insistent inevitability that engulfs all the gags and irritations and beauties. Even back in 1932 Renoir was beyond mere technique. His camera simply breathes with life. His compositions flow across abstract space into behavioral reality. When Michel Simon sprawls across a table, the entire screen seems to stretch to accommodate the physical release. Many scenes seem to go on too long. A minute here, a minute there, Renoir waiting all the while for his creatures to finish their business. Then at the end, a feeling of poignancy, a stab of pain, a realization of loss. And all with a tinkling tune and a gallant smile. Not to mention the Pipes of Pan, the presumptions of Priapus, the early variation of Vittorio De Sica's maxim that the only drama of the middle class is adultery. Renoir demonstrates that the only farce of the bourgeoisie is hypocrisy, which applies equally to adultery and charity.

By most standards *Boudu* is a minor work in Renoir's career, but even the minor works of great artists contain great truths. The reiterated truth of *Boudu* is that Renoir will always sacrifice form for truth, and that though his films may be disconcerting experiences to others, they are never dishonest expressions of his own vision of life.

—*Village Voice*, February 23, 1967

■ 3. *PERSONA*

Ingmar Bergman's *Persona* seems to bewitch audiences even when it bewilders them. The perennial puzzle of What It All Means is quite properly subordinated to the beauty and intensity with which faces, beings, personae confront each other on the screen. The feeling spectator can supply his own psychic fantasies to fill Bergman's blank spaces. Identity, communication, alienation, even schizophrenia: those are not so much the director's subjects as they are his spectacles. Two characters, a nurse and an actress; two actresses,

Bibi Andersson and Liv Ullmann. Tensions, conflicts, ambiguities, confessions, intimations, and, as always, impending violence. Take it as it comes, and don't worry about the puzzle. When pieces to a puzzle are lost forever, the puzzle ceases to be a mystery and becomes instead a permanent incompleteness.

Certified Bergman-watchers may be awed by the Pirandellian pyrotechnics fashioned with arc lights, loops, and leaders, but students of Stan Brakhage are more likely to yawn. Brakhage has spent (wasted?) his whole life taking the medium apart. By contrast, Bergman has turned out twenty-seven feature films without even beginning to suggest an instinctive affinity to the medium. His stylistic flourishes have always been strained, derivative, archly symbolic, or obtusely obscure. Some reviewers have indicated that more than one viewing is necessary to understand *Persona* fully. I doubt it. A hundred viewings will not bring what is off the screen onto the screen. A thousand will not unlock Bergman's mind. What Bergman chooses not to tell must remain unsaid.

The Bergmaniac can canvas the artist's career for such cross-references as the animated cartoon unrealistically projected (*Illicit Interlude*), the surfside sonority of dialogue on a beach (*The Seventh Seal*), the magic-lantern mystique of childhood (*The Magician*), the emphasis on the role of costumes (*The Naked Night*). But why bother? If Bergman is not yet beyond interpretation, he is certainly against it. As compared to *Brink of Life* and *Wild Strawberries*, *Persona* is devious in its intransigence, perverse in its denial of pleasure. Bergman has taken his place with the modern deities of the cinema—Antonioni, Fellini, Godard, Resnais. Paradoxically, his greatest talent is as a classicist, a writer of dramas and a director of actors. Pier Paolo Pasolini and Jean-Luc Godard have both understood this paradox about Bergman, but they have failed to perceive its consequences. Godard dismissed Bergman's avant-garde mannerisms a long time ago, and Pasolini has never even acknowledged them. Nonetheless Bergman himself remains obsessed by technique for its own sake. I wonder if there is a director of his rank who worries so much about the cinematic form he will devise to express himself. Bergman is so uptight technically that his characters often have difficulty breathing in his rigid frames. And no director of a comparable sensibility is so clumsy. Which brings us back to Brakhage, who is not one-hundredth the artist Bergman is. The trouble with Brakhage is that he cannot surrender to any of the illusions his mind conceives. He must intervene in every shot with an outside insight into his basically didactic personality. Bergman can leave two beautiful actresses at a table, withdraw behind his camera, and let them ultimately illuminate the screen with the crackling urgency of their dramatic personalities.

I remember Jonas Mekas once criticized Bergman's *Brink of Life* for focusing on the anguished faces of Ingrid Thulin and Eva Dahlbeck rather than on the miscarriages that were causing the anguish. I remember also that Brakhage has recorded on film the actual delivery of his wife's child. I remember also that the late Maya Deren once started an anti-Bergman fan club back in the late fifties. The strength of underground cinema is basically documentary. The strength of classical cinema (including Bergman's) is basically dramatic. The moderns—Godard, Resnais, Antonioni, Fellini—are suspended between these two polarities. It is Bergman's problem that he wishes to join the moderns without possessing a strong visual style of his own. Thus when Bergman tries to go obscure and superaesthetic, he is passing from his strengths to his weaknesses. Unfortunately, audience tastes have swung so wildly away from classicism toward kookiness that Bergman can hardly be blamed for pumping some pretentiousness into *Persona*.

All in all, Bergman's stature is incontestable. His vogue began at a time when audiences were rejecting facile equations of art and politics. The collapse of liberal optimism and Marxist aesthetics opened the door to the dourest Swede since Strindberg. Bergman has no politics to speak of—or film of—simply because Sweden itself lacked significant political tensions. The angst of alienation came more naturally in a country that was not suffering from overpopulation. Aldous Huxley once observed that the Lake Poets would not have taken such a benign view of nature if they had grown up in equatorial Africa. Similarly, Bergman's metaphysical concerns might not have been as asocial if race riots exploded now and then in Stockholm. Bergman's American admirers on the arthouse circuit were nonetheless ripe for Bergman not only because his concerns were more relevant to the angst of sheer affluence but also because he seemed immune to the corruptions of mass taste. His small crew in Sweden was an eloquent rebuke to the massive apparatus of Hollywood films.

Bergman is still apolitical, if not apathetic. His random references—Chinese A-Bomb in *Winter Light* and self-immolation of Saigon Buddhist in *Persona*—are more gratuitous than Godard's. Ingmar Bergman remains essentially an artist in an ivory tower in an isolated country. Still, he manages to invest the faces of his players with an expressive excitement and their characters with a demonic energy none of his technically more accomplished colleagues in Sweden can approach. The Bibi Andersson of *Persona* towers over the Bibi Andersson of *My Sister, My Love,* and therein lies the mystery and magic of Bergman's art.

—*Village Voice*, March 23, 1967

■ 4. *FALSTAFF* AND
     A *COUNTESS FROM HONG KONG*

Orson Welles's *Falstaff* and Charles Chaplin's A *Countess from Hong Kong* deserve the support of every serious moviegoer. Bosley Crowther has panned both films in no uncertain terms, but Mr. Crowther panned *Citizen Kane* and *Monsieur Verdoux* in their time. I don't wish to single out Mr. Crowther as a critic, only as an awesome power on the New York film scene. He is certainly not alone in panning A *Countess from Hong Kong*. To my knowledge, only William Wolf of *Cue* has rallied to Chaplin's defense. Happily, *Falstaff* has found powerful defenders in Joseph Morgenstern of *Newsweek*, Judith Crist of the *World-Journal Tribune*, and Archer Winsten of the *Post*. Even so, Mr. Crowther is entitled to his opinion, and he is scarcely the least enlightened of American film critics. Henry Hart of *Films in Review* has earned that dubious distinction with ease. The problem with Crowther is power. Not only can he still make or break most "art" films in New York; he can dictate to distributors what films they may or may not import. Lately he has been credited even with determining what will or will not be produced. In a letter to the *Times* the producer of *Dutchman* whined that Crowther had seemed to encourage the project at a preproduction dinner. The producer in question is not the first person in the industry to learn that Crowther cannot be had for a free meal. I'll say that much for Bos. He is not corruptible in the vulgar way most of his detractors suspect. He is affable, urbane, polite, genial, and easy to misunderstand in personal relationships. The industry is full of glad-handers and promoters who claim to have Crowther's ear but who only get the back of his hand when the early editions of *The Times* hit the stands. This kind of unpredictability is all to Crowther's credit. United Artists planned a Bond-like promotion of Sergio Leone's *A Fistful of Dollars* and the sequels largely because Crowther seemed to have been impressed by the Italian western cycle on his European jaunt for *The Times* last year. When it turned out there was too much pasta in them thar oats, Crowther backtracked and UA had to dump the project.

Power must always be fought, however, because power itself tends to corrupt. The moviegoer should think for himself to the point that he would find it unthinkable to miss a Welles or Chaplin work simply because a critic, any critic, said it was not worth seeing. What I object to in Crowther's review of *Falstaff* is the implication that he is going to punish the distributors for bringing Falstaff to *America* against his express wishes announced in a dispatch from Cannes last year. We in America can thank Mr. Crowther for having waited almost a year to see *Falstaff*. The distributors even changed the film's title from *Chimes at Midnight* to *Falstaff* in a naïve attempt to confuse the readers of *The Times*. The distributors should have known better. While I was reading Crowther's review of *Falstaff*, I suddenly understood what the real issue had become. The cyclical pattern of regular reviewers made more sense than even Truffaut had realized when he discovered it many years ago. The reason a Crowther will pan a Welles or Chaplin, the reason a Crist will complain about "cultists," the reason the daily reviewers loathe the New York Film Festival, is simply power. Crowther and Crist and all the critics combined cannot keep a so-called "cultist" from seeing *Falstaff* or *A Countess from Hong Kong*. Consciously or unconsciously, the power-oriented critic tries to keep these cults under control by giving every director a certain quota of pans so that he doesn't get too uppity. With Welles or Chaplin there are additional incentives. The critic can call them old-fashioned and dated and used up, as if critics stayed young forever and only directors became senile. I would expect old critics, particularly, to understand what *Falstaff* and *A Countess from Hong Kong* are all about. But no, the older the critic, the more up to date he must pretend to be, even though anything genuinely modern from *Citizen Kane* to *Masculine Feminine* has always filled him with revulsion.

The great sin of Welles and Chaplin is their failure to abandon their own personal visions of the world to current fashions. Welles is still Humpty-Dumpty from Wisconsin, and all the king's lenses and all the king's screens can't put Humpty together again. *Citizen Kane* was made by an old man of twenty-five. Welles seems to have been rehearsing for Falstaff and Lear all his life. Welles the actor now sounds like a muffled echo of everything he once wanted to be. Welles the mountainous man is a monument to compulsive self-destructiveness. The important thing is that Welles feels Falstaff from the inside out, and that he is enough of an artist to look at himself with ironic detachment. He is enough of an intellectual to give Shakespeare a distinctive shape and size. The production is Gothic and pastoral at the same time, towers above and mud below. Prince Hal, the Shakespearean hero who most resembles Dick Nixon, resembles in Keith Baxter's interpretation Welles himself. Welles, like Hal, is cursed with the ability of seeing even the present as some future past. For Hal, Falstaff is life as it endures. Hal's real father, John Gielgud's death's-head Henry IV, is life as preparation for death. Welles's *Falstaff* dramatizes the conflict of two fathers, or two aspects of fatherhood. Falstaff is gross, warm, animal affection, but also genuine love. Henry is pride and authority. Falstaff's world is horizontal, Henry's vertical. The final renunciation scene is thus inevitably shaped by the geometry of the setting.

Welles displays here a sensibility from the thirties and forties when choices, however anguished, still seemed morally meaningful. Despite his ironic humor, Welles is not in tune with current mannerisms of cruelty and absurdity. His Falstaff is graced with dramatic grandeur of an intelligent sobriety we have almost forgotten in our search for new sensations. Welles's battle scenes are especially noteworthy for not blinking at the brutal spectacle of war, and yet not winking at the audience for its satiric indulgence. Consequently the spectacle of the fat knight in glorious retreat becomes a beautiful piece of mise-en-scène.

Chaplin's *A Countess from Hong Kong* had me hooked from the precredit sequence when a sailor in Hong Kong struts into a dance hall where all the girls are "countesses." Chaplin's sentimental music closes in on a succession of medium shots of not particularly attractive, not particularly unattractive girls, and Charlie loves them all, and everyone begins dancing awkwardly in silent-movie style, and we are back in a world Chaplin both inhabited and invented a long time ago. Few reviewers have bothered to observe that Chaplin's role is being played by Sophia Loren, the tramp with oversized men's pajamas and a heart of gold. Chaplin had problems with both Loren and Brando simply because neither is Chaplin, but the movie still generates a surprising amount of charm and wit. Chaplin's writing still strains for many of its ironic effects, and the plot is almost too sentimental to synopsize safely, but the lines are underplayed almost to a whisper, and one particularly sticky scene is brilliantly redeemed by the slapstick of seasickness.

Attacks on Chaplin for his sentimentality and/or vulgarity date back almost to the beginning of his career. John Grierson wrote learnedly on why Chaplin should not have wound up with the girl in The Gold Rush. People who attack A Countess from Hong Kong in the name of the Chaplin they once allegedly loved have probably forgotten what Chaplin was like in the past. If you ever liked Chaplin, you will probably like A Countess from Hong Kong. It is the quintessence of everything Chaplin has ever felt. One reviewer complained about the doubling up of sets, but Chaplin has never worried that much about sets. His is too much of a one-man sensibility for nuanced detail. Nor has Chaplin ever achieved his effects through camera movement, montage, or Rembrandt lighting. His basic axiom has been that comedy is long-shot and tragedy is close-up, and most of Countess is long-shot. Chaplin's genius resides in that secret passageway from the physical to the emotional through which bodies and faces are transformed by grace and expressiveness into universal metaphors.

A Countess from Hong Kong is far from Chaplin's past peaks, but one scene with a momentarily irrepressible butler (Patrick Cargill) in Sophia's bedroom is as comically exhilarating as anything Chaplin has ever done. Chaplin might have been more modern, of course. He might have read selections from Lady Chatterley's Lover at five dollars a throw. Better still, he might have displayed the footage featuring Chaplin directing Loren and Brando in A Countess from Hong Kong and called the whole shebang 80½.

Unfortunately, Chaplin will die as he has lived, an unregenerate classicist who believes in making movies he can feel in his frayed lace-valentine heart.

■ 5. *THE DIRTY DOZEN;*
   DON'T MAKE WAVES; CAPRICE

The antiauthoritarianism in Robert Aldrich's *The Dirty Dozen* amounts to a glorification of the dropout. The fictional premise of the film is well suited to slum fantasizing. Twelve of the most depraved criminals in the American Army are recruited for a top-secret mission, namely to kill as many German officers as possible at a lavish rest and recreation center. First, however, the dirty dozen must convince the American top brass that they are worthy of the assignment. Most of the movie is devoted to their earning the privilege of dying, and the last celebration at a banquet before almost total annihilation finds the dozen apostles of violence and hoodlumism deployed around Lee Marvin's crew-cut Christ-figure in an updated version of the Last Supper. The drama of *The Dirty Dozen* is then concerned primarily with redemption, not through death but through the military mystique of twelve isolated individuals becoming a single unit.

Jean Renoir has observed that people are moved more by magic than by logic. To sit in the balcony of the Capitol while Clint Walker and Jim Brown are demolishing two finky noncoms is to confirm this observation. All the well-intentioned Operation Bootstrap cinema in the world cannot provide underdog audiences with the emotional release achieved almost effortlessly with one shot to the solar plexus. It's sad, but true. Blood is thicker than progressive porridge.

Two Aldrich themes run through *The Dirty Dozen*, one antimilitaristic from *Attack* in the mid-fifties, when World War II was being demystified, and the other democratic-didactic from *Flight of the Phoenix* in the mid-sixties. Putting the two themes together, Aldrich re-enacts the German description of British soldiers in

World War I as "lions led by donkeys." *The Dirty Dozen* is anti-authority down to Charles Bronson's last line about getting into the habit of killing officers. Unfortunately, Aldrich lays on the anti-Establishment humor a bit too thick. His jokes are played too broadly in an obvious bid to the balcony. Worse still, his casting is uneven. Robert Ryan is particularly misplaced as a stuffy West Point chicken colonel. Ryan has had a wide-ranging career, but dull conformity is hardly his forte. There is a subtly neurotic curiosity in his eyes operating against the stability of a scene. His is a personality perpetually on edge, and it is as wrong to enlist him in the Establishment as it was for Tony Richardson to recruit Michael Redgrave for an insidious authority role in *Loneliness of the Long Distance Runner*. On a lower level of miscalculation, Ernest Borgnine is nothing less than catastrophic as a cynical general. Of the dirty dozen themselves, fewer than half emerge with any clarity, and of these Telly Savalas is spectacularly implausible as a Bible-thumping misogynous psychopath. He makes no sense as a character on any level, including the most lurid.

Perhaps twelve characters are simply too many to chisel out of the hard rock of an action scenario. Even so, Aldrich managed a modicum of physical differentiation even without a corresponding psychological distinction. The final flurry of action suggests that even in World War II, and indeed in all wars, you can't really tell the hoodlums from the soldiers without a scorecard. Through all the absurd carnage, Lee Marvin's solidity and tenacity hold the picture together.

Don't Make Waves is one of the more underrated comedies of the season. Alexander Mackendrick's direction is longer on quiet chuckles than noisy belly laughs, and Tony Curtis gives his most perceptive performance since *Sweet Smell of Success*, also directed by Mackendrick. Most critics didn't "get" the movie because it has moods for all genres, and the ending is too sentimental for the cynicism that has preceded it. The biggest liability, however, is Claudia Cardinale, who should never act in English until she can read lines as skillfully as Sophia Loren, the only pizza queen who ever held her own in repartee with Cary Grant. Claudia's troubles are compounded by the fact that she is out-vavavoomed by Sharon Tate in the biggest Hollywood cheesecake robbery since Betty Grable displaced Alice Faye in *Tin Pan Alley*. All in all, *Don't*

Make Waves is the latest of what promises to be a long line of frightening documentaries on the state of California.

Caprice receives better direction from Frank Tashlin than it deserves. I hesitate to recommend the film even to specialists in marginalia because of the optical obscurities that now enshroud any Doris Day project. Even the subject—cosmetics espionage—conspires to remind us that we have been on a long Day's journey into naught.

—*Village Voice*, June 29, 1967

■ 6. *GUNN*

Gunn brings Blake Edwards full circle as a creative force in Hollywood film-making. Adapted from his own long-running television series, *Gunn* is the private-eye movie of the decade. (So much for *Harper*, which was more a big slip than a *Big Sleep*.) Some critics have complained that devotees of the video version would find nothing new in Peter Gunn's screen reincarnation. This devotee of the video version found everything from the decor to the denouement brand new on the screen. The only element regrettably lacking was Lola Albright's low-key libido as a nightclub canary. Laura Devon still has a long way to go to capture the wan smile that expresses the disparity between what Lola wants and what Lola gets.

The plot cannot be discussed in any detail without calling too much attention to it. Edwards has not escaped the anticlimactic and anti-Aristotelian conventions of serial writing through which the notion of beginning, middle, and end is scrapped for that of a self-contained circularity, neither tragedy nor comedy, but unruffled melodrama. The compensation Edwards provides is all incidental to the main thrust of the action, said compensation consisting of the vicious glossiness of the modern look, the casual pervasiveness of evil seeping even into the pores of the detective-hero, the harsh paradoxes of permissive heterosexuality, and the very, very contemporary view of individual lives as being composed less of experiences than of auditions. Hence the incessant, almost compul-

sive wit of the dialogue, and the somewhat detached distancing of
the performers.

Gunn is a movie of the sixties as Kiss Me Deadly was a movie
of the fifties and The Big Sleep a movie of the forties and The
Maltese Falcon a hangover from the thirties. Craig Stevens' patented coolness looks a bit worn by now, but the feeling of fleshy
corruption is more subtly expressed in Gunn than in the more
socially concerned Spades and Hammers of yesteryear. Edward
Asner and Albert Paulsen are two actors to keep in mind when
anyone asks you what happened to all the good character actors
from the good old days of movie-movies. All in all, Gunn makes
the Bond series look like child's play.

—Village Voice, July 13, 1967

■ 7. EL DORADO;
   THE BIG MOUTH; MY HUSTLER

> Gaily bedight,
> A gallant knight,
> in sunshine and in shadow,
> Had journeyed long,
> Singing a song,
> in search of Eldorado.
>
> But he grew old—
> This knight so bold—
> And o'er his heart a shadow
> Fell as he found
> No spot of ground
> That looked like Eldorado.
>
> And, as his strength
> Failed him at length,
> He met a pilgrim shadow—
> "Shadow," said he,
> "Where can it be—
> This land of Eldorado?"

*"Over the Mountains
Of the Moon,
Down the Valley of the Shadow,
Ride, boldly ride,"
The shade replied—
"If you seek for Eldorado!"*
—Edgar Allan Poe, "Eldorado"

That the new Howard Hawks–John Wayne–Robert Mitchum western called *El Dorado* has been given short shrift hereabouts is not
surprising. The heroic and professional virtues Hawks celebrates are
not the stuff of scintillating think pieces. Indeed, careless juxtaposition of the names Wayne and Hawks may remind the urban dove
of Wayne's forthcoming war-hawk project dealing with the Green
Berets.

Cosmopolitan audiences and taste-makers are not particularly
fond of westerns anyway, and the Hawksian brand lacks even scenic
compensations. There is really nothing to look at in *El Dorado*
except people, or more precisely, heroes. Those aesthetes who believe the cinema should look at everything except people will always find Hawks boring and commercial. Man is the measure of
all things Hawksian in a cinema defined by the boundaries of faces
rather than spaces, a cinema more Protagorean than Pythagorean.
For Hawks, as for Poe, El Dorado is less a place than a state of
mind. Perhaps even a state of grace. And Hawks, like Poe, has been
appreciated more by the French than by his own countrymen. Unlike Poe, however, Hawks has found the opportunity to discharge
his debt to the French. There are veiled allusions in the dialogue
to François Truffaut's *Shoot the Piano Player* and to Jacques Rivette's critical insight into Hawksian comedy as an index of human
folly. "No other critter," a character in a coonskin cap observes,
"would make such a fool of hisself."

Above all, Hawks has dared to repeat himself shamelessly from
Rio Bravo, and revel in the repetition and the self-awareness. Ironically, most of the local reviewers didn't even remember *Rio Bravo*,
which came out eight long years ago, and the director's self-pla-
giarism went by unnoticed. No matter. The beauties of *El Dorado*,
like the beauties of *Rio Bravo*, are as obvious to one critical faction
as they are obscure to another, and never the twain shall meet.

However, there was as much of Hawks in *Red Line 7000* as there is in *El Dorado*, and yet *El Dorado* never comes close to succumbing to the self-parody that made *Red Line 7000* such an uncomfortable experience for this Hawks enthusiast. Part of the difference may be the mythic force exerted by John Wayne and Robert Mitchum. Wayne, particularly, is in the Poe spirit "gaily bedight, a gallant knight." He has looked old for such a long time that his oldness has become spiritually resurgent. His infirmities ennoble rather than enfeeble him, and every wrinkle on his skin has come to terms with his endless quest. Years from now art-of-the-film critics will study Wayne's features in *El Dorado* for clues to the psychic energy that enabled him to keep the notion of action cinema alive in a culture that was beginning to worship lethargy.

El Dorado is funnier and more charming than the anti-Hawksian critics give it credit for. Hawks has never been more resourceful with props as running gags about character. James Caan, who recites the Poe poem to Wayne, is especially endearing with his stovepipe hat, blundering blunderbuss gunmanship, and his fumbling quest for a father-figure. The comic camaraderie shared by Wayne, Caan, Mitchum, and Arthur Hunnicutt looks too easy and casual to be appreciated for the accomplished artistry it demands. Also striking is Christopher George's extraordinarily sympathetic professional killer, "professional" being the operative word. One reviewer complained that all the Bad Guys are killed, and none of the Good Guys, even though the Good Guys consist of cripples, kooks, and certified incompetents. The criticism is irrelevant to a poetic fantasy in which there is as much of Hawks in Christopher George's Bad Guy as in Wayne's Good Guy. What Hawks seems to be saying is that life is hard on heroes, but they must go on in good humor even if they have to walk on crutches to gunfights. For all its apparent levity, *El Dorado* is tinged with melancholy. The women in the film render their lines in a dirgelike tone that befits the debatably marginal role of women in the world of Howard Hawks. So much is coming to an end in *El Dorado*. Wayne, Hawks, Hollywood, the heroic western, the classical cinema. Or, as Shaw has said of Shakespeare, "The lot of the man who sees life truly and thinks about it romantically is despair." Fortunately, *El Dorado* is a western that sticks to its guns by affirming the spirit of adventure instead of trampling it in the dust of a fashionable misanthropy. Humor and affirmation on the brink of despair are the poetic ingredients of the Hawksian western. And now memory. Especially memory. Only those who see some point in remembering movies will find *El Dorado* truly unforgettable.

The Big Mouth still leaves this juror out on Jerry Lewis. The Forty-second Street audiences roar at his antics, the French rank him with Chaplin and Keaton, and even the local intelligentsia look at him more closely in the fear that he might be "in" one of these days. Lewis is nothing if not ambitious, and he is the only American comedian working full time on slapstick comedy. Bits and pieces are effective. His Kabuki routine here, his karate routine in *Three on a Couch*, his nightclub routine in *The Patsy*, and so on. The films he directs himself become increasingly ambiguous and self-conscious, but he still hasn't put together one comically coherent work of art. The films of Chaplin and Keaton may not be the works of great intellectuals, but they are the works of naturals. Lewis is not a natural. His jokes involve a certain strain either on his physiognomy or our credulity. He is funny, but almost never witty. As an artist he is particularly weak on transitions, on little things, and these are the things at which Chaplin and especially Keaton excelled. I hate to say this to my French friends, but Lewis should be seen, not heard.

Andy Warhol's *My Hustler* is better heard than seen. It is reported that Chuck Wein wrote the viciously matter-of-fact conversations that accompany the epicene camera glimpses of a blond male beauty sunning himself on Fire Island's sand. The talk is outrageously funny and worthy of Restoration comedy, though lacking a moral or a *raisonneur* or dramatic action. This is the first movie in which I've heard the term "fag-hag" used. Of course, the subject is laid on the line, and I doubt that even homosexuals are charmed by such brutal frankness. This is an ugly, joyless movie. It is also anti-erotic despite its scabrous insertions. The underground has moved to the sexploitation circuit, and the victims of sexploitation pay exorbitant prices to be punished for their erotic expectations. One kind of hustle is very much like another.

—Village Voice, July 27, 1967

■ 8. *THE WHISPERERS;*
THE FAMILY WAY;
DIVORCE AMERICAN STYLE

The Whisperers strives to express through Dame Edith Evans what
it is to be very old and very poor in a well-meaning welfare state.
That Dame Edith looks every weary day of the seventy-two-year-
old character she plays only contributes to the drab documentary
look of this latest Bryan Forbes film. The title refers to the creatures the addled old lady imagines in her paranoid fantasies. They
lurk behind every drip, drip, drip of a leaky faucet. They listen all
coiled up in a silent radio. No matter. The old lady is onto all their
tricks, and she tells them so repeatedly. She reports them regularly
to the police, who scoff at her behind her back. The whisperers,
however, are only part of her fantasy life. She imagines also that
she is a daughter of the aristocracy, an heiress waiting for her
money to arrive so that she can pay back the nice gentleman at the
Welfare Board. The routine of her day consists of a visit to the
free warmth of the public library, the free soup of a revival meeting, the free pillage of trash cans, and then back to her flat and the
reassuring torment of her enemies, the whisperers. When a political
candidate takes over the wireless to shed crocodile tears over the
plight of lonely old people, the lady murmurs sympathetically and
without a trace of bitter irony, "Poor souls."

The routine is shattered irrevocably by the return of the old
lady's thieving son and vagrant husband, a brief fling with stolen
money ending dismally in the gutter, where the poor prey on the
poor. Pneumonia, mental breakdown, welfare-state paternalism,
gangland melodrama, and life generally all conspire to drive away
the whisperers and all the other comforting features of the old
lady's fantasy landscape. Society, with its obsessive concern for
sanity and order, has stripped a lowly creature of all its protective
plumage of the mind. The cost of the cure has been a broken spirit.

The Whisperers is an apt title for a Bryan Forbes project. Indeed, the world of Bryan Forbes is one of wisps and whispers.
Whistle Down the Wind was muted allegory, *The L-Shaped Room*
muted soap opera, *Seance on a Wet Afternoon* muted melodrama,

King Rat muted adventure, and *The Wrong Box* muted slapstick.
Always nibbling at nuances, always straining for subtlety, never
quite breaking an egg to make an omelet, never quite exploding a
theme into dramatic excitement. Unfortunately, *The Whisperers*
starts out as submerged material, and the director's fear of obviousness only drives the material deeper into the ground. Dame
Edith Evans is never moving either as a character or as an actress
largely because Forbes keeps the dramatic electricity turned off. He
never seems quite sure whether the old lady is a subject or an
object. For the longest stretches she is helpless or unconscious or
inert or uncommunicative, and the action of the film simply washes
over her. Edith Evans is denied Sylvie's heroic irony in *The Shameless Old Lady*, or Ida Kaminska's ignoble pathos in *The Shop on
Main Street*, or Beulah Bondi's tactful stoicism in *Make Way for
Tomorrow*. Forbes has avoided any suggestion of corniness and
sentimentality like the plague. In the process, he has made a monotonous movie lacking both contrast and coherence.

The Family Way has been blurb-excerpted thus from our most
eminent reviewer: "The problem of the bridegroom who finds he
cannot consummate his marriage and the bride who does not com-
prehend his nervous tension is the device for conducting the cinematic transition of Hayley Mills from maidenhood to marriage
couch." The advertising has concentrated on this aspect of Bill
(*Alfie*) Naughton's script, and that is what I thought the film was
about until I saw it. Bill Naughton seems to be a very clever reactionary on sexual subjects. The antiabortion sequence in *Alfie*
was blatant enough, but a completely gratuitous sequence in *The
Family Way* that ridicules birth-control advertising in a nasty way
is even more revealing. What Naughton seems to be driving at is
that the common people in their ageless wisdom know what they
are about when they glorify the family at the expense of the individual. All of *Alfie* could be summed up in that one aching moment when Michael Caine's Alfie looks longingly at his own son
being swallowed up in another man's family. The theme of *The
Family Way* is that the institution of family eventually resolves
personal hang-ups, and, as in *Alfie*, Naughton seems to rest his case
on a condescending class attitude toward the little people who are
the salt of the earth. Fortunately or unfortunately, British acting is
so good that the author's condescension is effectively concealed.

Where Naughton is particularly dishonest in *The Family Way* is in his raising serious issues about his reluctant bridegroom and then dropping these issues to pursue another plot. Hywel Bennett's badgered hero seems to have legitimate grievances. He reads books and listens to Beethoven while his dear dad swills his ale and makes jokes about people who read books. Naughton is not mocking his hero's cultural pretensions; he endorses them by having Hayley Mills's adoring bride approve them. Also, the boy here is even more attractive than the girl, and the philistines put up with his airs because of the genuine sensitivity reflected in his delicate good looks.

Nor is there anything unreasonable in his pathetic desire to find a place of his own with an indoor toilet and walls thick enough so that he doesn't have to hear his lumbering pa pissing into the family chamber pot every night. All in all, Hywel Bennett reincarnates the incredibly refined Dickensian heroes of the slums. The fact that he can't cut the mustard with his bride is only one symptom of a general cultural dislocation, and if he is to be accepted as an authentic character, whether of sociology or autobiography, it is hard to see why he ever married the Hayley Mills character in the first place. She is lower-class conformist all the way despite a warm, womanly generosity. After the bedroom, what on earth would they talk about?

Naughton ducks this problem with a devious bit of dramaturgy. Here we are waiting to come to grips with the frustrations of the newlyweds when suddenly the focus shifts to the bridegroom's parents. They are discussing the problem with the bride's parents when suddenly they begin reminiscing about their own peculiar honeymoon two decades before. Marjorie Rhodes and John Mills lurch into stage center with an unforgettable memory looming out of the past. The memory is named Billy. We have heard his name mentioned before on the wedding night. Billy has been well "planted" in the script. He was the best friend of the smugly manly father played by John Mills. He was such a close friend, in fact, that he even came along on the honeymoon to Blackpool. Then one day he disappeared without a word and never returned. Only the wife knows why exactly, and she has never told her spouse. She has waited many long years for her endearingly blind husband to recognize Bill's walk in the "son."

Marjorie Rhodes is marvelously, almost manically sensitive to the theatrical possibilities of this turn in the plot. She and Mills contrive to move us to tears with nostalgic hysteria in much the same way that Caine does in *Alfie*. This is not the stuff of great art. I'm not even sure that it's truthful, but it is damned clever just the same. If I have not talked a great deal about Hayley Mills, it is because her character is sidetracked by the hereditary locomotion of the family, waywardly portrayed by Hywel Bennett, Marjorie Rhodes, and John Mills. The Paul McCartney score is lyrically appropriate.

Divorce American Style is concerned more with the institution of divorce than with divorced people as hooman beins, which is just as well when Debbie Reynolds and Dick Van Dyke turn out to be the protagonists. Miss Reynolds has never outgrown her long career as the all-American teaser and emasculator, and Van Dyke is too much the rubber-faced comic to just be whatever he is supposed to be. Between them they make a stronger case for divorce than for marriage despite the conventionally happy ending. Director Bud Yorkin displays more style than one would have expected after *Come Blow Your Horn* and *Never Too Late*, and somewhere in the Norman Lear screen play from the Robert Kaufman story are to be found directions where all the bodies are buried. *Divorce American Style* is viciously comic, not so much about divorce itself but rather about the avarice and instability hovering around the edges. One sequence dealing with the disposal of multiparented children is alone worth the inflated price of admission. Jean Simmons and Lee Grant lend some charm to the proceedings with their presence, and Jason Robards is almost refreshingly clumsy with his outsized Irish face next to the muggings of Van Dyke, but the big merit of the film is its ice-cold images of life and debt in America.

—*Village Voice*, August 10, 1967

■ 9. *IN THE HEAT OF THE NIGHT*

In the Heat of the Night is not a very good movie. Not awful, just not very good. The mystery plot makes so little sense that the audience is forced to concentrate exclusively on the vaudeville routines performed by Rod Steiger and Sidney Poitier. In this year of Clay and Carmichael, Black Power and blackened Powell, Hollywood will probably follow the lead of the rest of the country in bending over backward to be unfair to the Negro by giving the Oscar to Steiger rather than to Poitier. Not that Poitier deserves a second Oscar before Steiger has received his first. Not at all. Steiger is long overdue for recognition of previous performances in *On the Waterfront, The Big Knife* and *Across the Bridge.*

Nonetheless Poitier merits consideration for making Caucasian actors look good. Richard Widmark stole the show from Poitier way back in 1949 in *No Way Out,* one of the first screen manifestations of Black Power fantasies fabricated by white liberals. This was the first American movie in which Negroes fought back against white bigots with sticks and stones, but Poitier's character was too antiseptic for street brawls even when Widmark's bigot spat in his face. Poitier played a doctor who ends up treating his tormentor. Widmark was still outacting Poitier in the sixties in *Bedford Incident,* Widmark as a juicy fascist, Poitier as a dubiously debonair implausibly far-flung correspondent for *Life* magazine.

Poor Poitier is damned if he does and damned if he doesn't. If his role confines him to the Negro community, his picture acquires the box-office-poison labels of "Problem" and "Ethnic." If his role pushes him into the white world, he is subtly ridiculed for his presumption or subtly patronized for his purity. He can never escape the servitude of his negritude. His very first entrance is made conspicuous solely by his color. As with all Negro actors, Poitier's essence precedes his existence. His blackness enshrouds all the subterfuges of the scenario. He is not a Negro before being a man. He is a Negro instead of being a man. The white audience does not wait suspensefully for his character to emerge from out of the total tapestry of the plot. A Negro character is not entrusted with a dramatic life of his own. Nor with a morsel of moral ambiguity.

Nowadays, particularly, Negroes are never condemned in the movies. Their faults, if any, are tolerated as the bitter fruits of injustice, and thus their virtues are regarded less as the consequences of free choice than as the puppetry of liberal propaganda. The white audience tolerates the Negro character on the screen only as a walking civil-rights commercial. All that is expected of the Negro, as of any commercial, is that he be inoffensive, and Poitier has finally perfected his craft to the point of being heroically inoffensive.

Poitier's finest moment in the Mississippi of *In the Heat of the Night* comes almost at the beginning of the picture when he is tensely still in a train station as a minion of the local law frisks him. Poitier communicates to the audience the instinctive awareness of racial murder as the kind of hobby that launches white Mississippians into political careers (*vide* the thousands of votes cast for Byron de la Beckwith as a rebuke to the zealots who sought the murderer of Medgar Evers). Besides, anywhere an adult Negro can still be addressed as "boy" one moment, he can probably be murdered with impunity the next.

Steiger's advantage over Poitier as a performer is a repetition of Widmark's. Steiger can call Poitier "boy" and "nigger" on the screen without jeopardizing his standing in the liberal community off the screen. Steiger represents neither his race nor himself, but only an actor playing a character against type. Steiger can act out the drama of redemption because he can release all his furies of damnation. Poitier has nowhere to go dramatically because he must repress too many impulses for the sake of a race image. To put down the red-neck constabulary of Sparta, Mississippi, Poitier's character must trot out the sleuthing finesse of a Sherlock Holmes and the insightful sensibility of a Jean-Paul Sartre.

But if Poitier ultimately wins a modicum of respect from Steiger, it is a respect more for aptitude than for negritude. To read anything more into this fantasy of racial reconciliation is to return to the fatuousness of special exemptions for George Washington Carver, Booker T. Washington, Jesse Owens, Joe Louis, Ralph Bunche, and the rest of the rhythm and sports entertainers.

Norman Jewison has been blessed with perfect timing this year, as he was last year with *The Russians Are Coming*. Liberal optimism and nonviolence have been badly wounded in many ghettoes across the country. *In the Heat of the Night* has managed to restore some faith in "responsible" behavior. It is not Poitier's fault that he is used to disinfect the recent riots of any lingering racism. It is his destiny to be forbidden the individuality to say "I" instead of "we."

Jewison gets extra points from some critics for muffling his violence. Every time some unpleasantness is about to occur, the camera watches from the next county. Poitier's noble northern detective is nearly killed on two occasions, and repeatedly threatened as well while investigating a murder. Yet the tone of the film is light and airy, with more laughs than were in *The Russians Are Coming*. As is often the case these days, the reality of the setting conflicts with the contrivances of the plot.

Jewison errs further by overdirecting characters—notably a bereaved widow and a hunted fugitive—before the audience has had a chance to identify with them. Lee Grant, whom Bud Yorkin handled gracefully in *Divorce American Style*, is so cluttered here with pretentious mannerisms that she might be mistaken for a different actress. The final directorial absurdity consists of concealing the face of a murderer whose identity is stupefyingly insignificant to the issues of the film.

But what bothered me most about *In the Heat of the Night* was the bland assumption that any Negro, however noble and privileged, could find rapport with a white man who was capable of addressing (and undressing) him as "boy." Some words in our social vocabulary are irrevocable, and "boy," I should think, is one of them. A little word indeed for so many centuries of slavery and emasculation.

—*Village Voice*, August 17, 1967

■ 10. DON'T LOOK BACK

William Zanzinger killed poor Hattie Carroll
With a cane that he twirled 'round his
Diamond ring finger
At a Baltimore hotel society gathering
And the cops were called in
And his weapon took from him
As they rode him in custody down to the station
And booked William Zanzinger for first degree murder

William Zanzinger, who had just 24 years
Owns a tobacco farm of 600 acres

With rich wealthy parents
Who protect and provide him
And high office relations in the politics of Maryland
Reacted to his deed with a shrug of the shoulders
And swear words and sneering
In his tongue it was snarling
And in a matter of minutes on bail was out walking

Hattie Carroll was a maid of the kitchen
She was 51 years old
And gave birth to ten children
Who cleaned up the table and hauled out the garbage
And didn't even speak to the people at the table
And never sat once at the head of the table.
Who just cleaned up all the food from the table
And emptied the ashtrays on a whole other level
Got killed by a blow, lay slain by a cane
That sailed through the air
And came down through the room
Doomed and determined to destroy all the gentle
And she never done nothing to William Zanzinger

And you who philosophize disgrace
And criticize all fears
Take the rag away from your face
Now ain't the time for your tears.

I heard Bob Dylan sing the above lyrics in a movie called *Don't Look Back*. I remember being moved by the last stanza without understanding what it really meant. Somewhere in the song I had lost all the connections. All that moved me was the strange intensity of Bob Dylan's climbing up the meter of his song-poem as if he were on all fours, wailing at a world he never made but understood too well. When I got home I consulted a transcript thoughtfully provided by D. A. Pennebaker to assist reviews of his movie, but not for publication. I was startled to discover that I remembered the case from a few years back. It had really happened, and I had been outraged, as any self-respecting liberal should be outraged, and then I had completely forgotten the incident. Bob Dylan's song is the only memorial Hattie Carroll is ever likely to have. Her misadventure is too morally one-sided to interest our more stylish moralists. Art Buchwald would find her caning too lacking in parody potential. Murray Kempton would be frustrated by the absence of irony and paradox. The civilized intellect finds it difficult to render a simple cry of pain. Or to respond to the more obvious outrages. Dylan is made of sterner stuff. He made me remember something I never should have forgotten. I am grateful to him. I dig Dylan. I don't even mind the accusatory tone of the refrain. And I am far past thirty.

Why didn't I understand the song fully when I heard it? It wasn't the fault of the audience. Though the house was packed with Dylan devotees, they were very quiet and attentive during the songs. They obviously were listening to the words. But they probably knew most of the words from listening to Dylan's records. They were educated in Dylan, as I was not. Dylan is not the easiest singer to understand at first hearing, but there is something electric in his performance that justifies a second and third effort. However, some anti-Dylan critics assume that Dylan's fans listen to him in mindless incomprehension simply because the critics themselves are unsophisticated in pop-rock-folk-jazz recordings. It is as if the cultivated playgoer went to a performance of Hamlet without any prior acquaintance with the play. (Did he say "What a ruddy peasant slave am I," or what? The actor doesn't enunciate properly.) Of course, there is less cultural pressure and pretense with Shakespeare than with Dylan, but ignorance of either is not the best qualification to evaluate either. Dylan's fans are probably more qualified to discuss Dylan than are his detractors, but since the former are usually younger than the latter, it is easy to put down scholarship and expertise as the whims of youth.

Some of Dylan's critics seem to think that the singer is taking impressionable young people away from the poems of John Donne. Bob Dylan should be compared to Bobby Darin rather than to John Donne. Indeed, young people who dig Dylan will probably be more responsive to Donne and all poets as a consequence of their devotion. When I think of Dylan and the Beatles and compare them to Perry Como and the Andrews Sisters and Bing Crosby and Al Jolson and the pop singers of the past, I hold my head in collective shame for all of us over thirty. Kids today have so much better taste in pop singers than their elders did that the human race may still be saved.

Many reviewers of *Don't Look Back* indicated a preference for the personality of Joan Baez. (She smiles more than Dylan does.) I disagree. Joan Baez is a relatively conventional folk singer. She takes the sting out of everything she sings with her very professional charm to the point that she could make "La Marseillaise" sound like "My Love Is Like a Cherry." Dylan projects a unified personality as a performer. He is what he sings—warts, obscurities, and all. He is certainly not a great musician, and it can be argued that he is not a great performer. The value of his lyrics as literature is still debatable, as are the facile shock effects of electronic noise for its own sake. What makes Dylan electrifying is that his art is connected to the wholeness of his personality. What makes Dylan modern or even ahead of his time is the lack of coquettishness in his despair. What makes him truly admirable is the absence of self-ridicule in his arrogance.

Don't Look Back does Dylan's fans a service by giving them a closer look at their hero. What of Dylan's enemies? It is unlikely they will be converted in the numbers credited to the Beatles after *A Hard Day's Night*. Richard Lester gave the Beatles a showcase for their talents, and although they played themselves, we never imagined for a moment that we were getting the inside story. *A Hard Day's Night* was a self-enclosed movie. *Don't Look Back* seems to be a contrived documentary, but most of the time the audience is not let in on the joke. Even with the transcript, I can't figure out what some of the scenes signify. The Leacock-Pennebaker school of documentary holds that a film-maker should not impose his point of view on his material *a priori*. As the material emerges, its truth emerges with it. This entails a passive, voyeuristic role for the camera. The truth exists; the camera must capture it. Robert Rossellini attacked Jean Rouch at a film festival for abdicating his (Rouch's) moral responsibility toward the material recorded by the camera.

Florence Fletcher of *Cue* claims that Pennebaker wants *Don't Look Back* treated virtually as a fictional movie, starring Bob Dylan as Bob Dylan. Joe Morgenstern of *Newsweek* and most of his colleagues have treated *Don't Look Back* as an authentic record of Dylan's tour through England in 1965. Nothing in the film led me to suspect that it was being staged for my benefit. I am certainly not going to call up Pennebaker to find out what is truth and what is jest in *Don't Look Back*. The work of art should speak for itself. I didn't have to call up Richard Lester to review *A Hard Day's Night*.

Besides, I don't trust the Leacock-Pennebaker school of documentary. Ugliness and awkwardness are subtly transformed from technical necessities to truth-seeming mannerisms. When Leacock came up to Montreal in 1963 with *Jane* and *The Chair*, the National Film Board people were skeptical about the crudities in the films. It wasn't the usual underground problem of money, but something more insidious, an attempt to con an audience into thinking that something is more real when it is awkward, or rather that awkwardness is truth. The fact that you can't hear conversations clearly in *Don't Look Back* makes you strain to listen to something that presumably you are not supposed to listen to and that makes you "in" if you listen to it. Even when you can make out the words, you can't figure out the context. What is Joan Baez laughing at? You don't know, man? Well, you're just not where it's at, man. Just sit in your seat and listen and don't make any noise and don't expect any exposition or heavenly-Father narration. All right, I abase myself for the sake of Bob Dylan's very real talent, and then I am told all this ear strain and eyestrain is contrived to make me suffer for a spurious realism. Am I angry? Hell, no. It doesn't really matter.

What comes through *Don't Look Back* is beyond dissembling. Jean-Luc Godard put it well when he said that Leacock was interesting when he dealt with Kennedy in *Primary* and boring when he dealt with Crump in *The Chair*. In this kind of cinema the subject is everything and the style nothing. *Don't Look Back* makes me want to fill in on Dylan's recordings, but not Pennebaker's movies.

The camera can capture only that truth that chooses to exhibit itself. If there were nothing of the exhibitionist in Dylan, the camera would register a blank. Many truths are hidden from the camera, and this is a fact that too many makers of documentary refuse to face. The great ideal of the documentary movement was to tell the truth about everything, but the truth was often lost in a collection of external details. The highest art of the cinema consists of relating what is shown to what is not shown, and of defining essences in terms of surfaces. Pennebaker's mock passivity before his plastic material does not alter the fact that Dylan is performing in front of a camera. What Pennebaker records is not Bob Dylan as he really is—whatever that means—but rather how Bob Dylan responds to the role imposed upon him by the camera. Compared to most of the public figures of his time, Dylan responds very well indeed.

—*Village Voice*, September 21, 1967

■ 11. THE NEW YORK FILM FESTIVAL

The trouble with think pieces is that you spend all the time in the forest without looking at the trees. And since no two trees are exactly alike in the forest of the cinema, a few ungeneralized observations are in order.

The Rise of Louis XIV: Roberto Rossellini has given us an austere spectacle of power. Many in the New York Film Festival audience were disappointed by the lack of lushness. Logic and rigor are not the most appealing graces, but there are beautiful passages of unbearable precision in the playing. I particularly like Jean-Marie Patte's Louis XIV for his relentless imperturbability, particularly in the scene when he throws himself with mock repentance into his mother's arms and then quickly and impassively withdraws from the embrace and escapes from the possible emotional trap. It is a moment of gleaming intelligence. For the rest, Rossellini is content to remain relatively impersonal. Unfortunately, an impersonal film requires more objective scope in its spectacle. I would have preferred more Rossellini or more Versailles. I get too little of either. Too little only by the highest standards. Rossellini's was the one film at the Festival with a clear claim to greatness.

Bariera and *Le Départ*: I prefer *Bariera* to *Le Départ*, if only because *Bariera* is Polish and *Le Départ* is ersatz Parisian. Also, Jan Nowicki and Joanna Szczerbic are more engaging a couple than Jean-Pierre Léaud and Catherine Duport, two rather shopworn items from *Masculine Feminine*. I have come to loathe Léaud's raw insolence as an expression of anarchic youth. *Le Départ* is the four-hundred-and-first blow and the last straw. *Bariera* is handicapped by a weighty allegory, but Jerzy Skolimowski's lightness of touch is more appropriate for something serious like *Bariera* than for something already giddy like *Le Départ*. Skolimowski is undeniably talented, but he seems to be caught in the aimless cosmopolitanism that seems to afflict every Polish director sooner or later. *Le Départ*, particularly, suffers from the superficiality of a man without a society.

Funnyman: I don't understand the hostility to *Funnyman*. What are we really looking for in American cinema? I think John Korty has grave weaknesses as an artist. His asthmatic lyricism is less bothersome here than it was in *The Crazy Quilt*, but it still weakens the second half of the film. Still, the set pieces do click despite the awkwardness of their framing. We've been complaining that American independent movies can't handle dialogue with a smidgen of behavioral charm, and here comes a movie that can make an audience full of people laugh without indulging in facile satire, and all the reviewers hate it. Indeed it is a puzzlement. Peter Bonerz' performance alone should have tipped the scales in favor of the film. His is the first American screen characterization that succeeds in adapting itself to the new documentary spirit of fictional films. I am proud that the New York Film Festival recognized merit in a product of the American language, the nuances of which the international film crowd will never begin to appreciate.

The Feverish Years: Are the Yugoslavs coming on strong like the Czechs? Will Dragoslav Lazic be remembered in later years without a scorecard? Tune in to next year's Film Festival. I frankly don't know. There is something depressing in the film renaissance of an austerely socialist society. The artist is suspended between the rhetoric of idealism and the reality of opportunism. He is just discovering the problem of materialistic decadence when here in the West we are already bored by it. An example is the all-night orgy in wicked Belgrade. At first glance it looks like a session with pot and LSD, but it turns out to be merely a matter of whiskey and cigarettes. A big deal for Belgrade perhaps, but for New York a big bore. Or should we take an ethnographic interest in Yugoslavia for the sake of Yugoslavia? Even for a director with the good taste to admire *The Birds*, which he screens in his own film.

Yesterday Girl: Alexander Kluge is trying to say something about Germany today, but he gets lost in a scenario hopelessly alienated from itself. His sister, Alexandra Kluge, stays in the mind as a kind of modern girl who keeps asking embarrassing questions out of the black pools of her questing eyes and never finding satisfactory answers. One dog-training sequence makes a devastating comment on the *Achtung* aberration of the Germans. The rest of the time I was bored.

An Affair of the Heart: This is a big year for Mayakovski (here and in *Les Carabiniers*). Dusan Makavejev has it all figured out. Modern man is not cast in the mold of the socialist hero of song and dogma. Men are pathetically human and vulnerable, and they are swallowed up by their own weaknesses to the swelling chorus of the party songs. Marx is eclipsed by Freud, *Das Kapital* by *Cahiers du Cinéma*. It all works out intellectually, but there is an emotional lag. The characters are created solely in terms of their ultimate destruction. They never get around to breathing life into their author's conception.

Puss and Kram: Jonas Cornell's screenplay reminds me of nothing so much as a Swedish translation of *Luv*. Another example of the cinema of the absurd going nowhere with a flourish of humorless put-ons.

Young Toerless: Barbara Steele lives up to her cult reputation in a cameo gem for this parable of totalitarianism in early twentieth-century Germany. The square virtues of good ensemble playing and orderly storytelling are particularly refreshing in this time of calculated chaos.

The Other One: Rene Allio has come a cropper, to coin a phase. The mixture of Chekhov and Pirandello never jells, and Malka Ribovska is no more a Garbo than Marie Laforet before her. Allio's problem is that he has too civilized a sensibility for the outrageous demands of drama. He could use some of the corn that makes

Chekhov and Pirandello so exciting despite their exquisite sensibilities. Too much modern art is merely the brain severed from the heart and other vital organs. *The Other One* is smothered by Allio's unyielding good taste.

Portrait of Jason: I enjoyed listening to Jason until Shirley Clarke made the mistake of trying to find the "real" Jason. I much prefer Jason's con to his conscience. In this instance the man's style does not so much conceal as constitute his substance. Why pick at Jason's tattered soul when it is only his surface charm that keeps him from screaming out of his skull? There should have been more songs and fewer tears. Don't cry, Jason. Just try to entertain us.

Elvira Madigan: Bo Widerberg reminds us that romanticism is not dead even in Sweden, only dormant since the early, relatively carefree days of Ingmar Bergman. Widerberg is no Bergman. Widerberg's romanticism is too consciously lyrical to be genuinely romantic. His chromatic intoxication is closer to the Agnes Varda of *Le Bonheur* than to the Jean Renoir of *Picnic on the Grass*. But the film works in spite of its limitations by remaining within them. Pia Degermark and Thommy Berggren evoke the fragility of love with appropriate delicacy, and it is good to see acting of conviction in costume in an age when the omnipresent Now threatens to swallow up the cinema.

Far from Vietnam: Zero as art. Some polite applause for Jean-Luc Godard, Alain Resnais, Joris Ivens. They at least tried to make a personal statement. But where was Chris Marker's "unifying" editing? I haven't seen such a patchwork quilt since *Mondo Cane*. The English-language commentary sounds like a parody of the thirties' Stalinist sermon. Why? As for the footage on the big parades in New York earlier this year, the point being made is unclear. The "peace" marchers are presented as grotesquely as the "loyalty" marchers, as if all Americans of every political persuasion had gone mad over Vietnam. By contrast, the Vietnamese peasants are neat, alert, and dedicated. It struck me that the film was intended neither for Paris nor New York but for Hanoi. I don't believe French intellectuals really expect American intellectuals to divert Johnson from his course. French intellectuals remember too well their own impotence over Algeria.

It struck me also that Ivens was back to sentimentalizing peasants and the soil as he did in *The Spanish Earth* back in the thirties. How curious this cult of the peasant abroad, when it is usually the peasant who is the most reactionary member of any society. The urban left in America will sob over peasants in Spain, Vietnam, and even Marcel Pagnol's studio in Nice, but they are mortal enemies of the American farmer, whose political influence in Congress is devoted to strangling the cities. Curiously, the one failure of all Communist countries without exception is agriculture. Both Russia and China were grain-surplus areas before communism and grain-deficit areas after, but no one can argue that the Communist leaders were not correct in sacrificing agriculture to industry. No modern nation can achieve economic power until the peasants are driven off the land and into the cities. There is thus nothing sacred about the role of the peasantry anywhere.

Joris Ivens might have devoted some footage to industrial workers in Hanoi, but the image of machinery would have compromised the image of a poor, primitive society battling jets with pitchforks. All in all, *Far from Vietnam* qualifies as hard-core propaganda. It is a time, as Jean Renoir observed in *The Rules of the Game*, when everyone is lying. Do the lies from Saigon and Washington justify the lies from Hanoi and Paris? This is a question only the individual conscience can answer, and the individual artists in *Far from Vietnam* obviously surrendered their consciences for the sake of a collective statement. Resnais, Godard, and Ivens even surrendered the supposedly sacred right of cutting their own footage. It may be argued that the cause was worth the sacrifice. The film certainly wasn't.

In retrospect I prefer D. W. Griffith and John Ford to Abel Gance and Mark Donskoi. Gance was often spectacular with his big effects, but very weak with his transitions. At his best, the sublime coexists with the ridiculous. *La Roue* and *Napoleon* are staggering achievements, and we have to take them as they are, and there is nothing else quite like them, but there have been better things. King Vidor's *Show People* and Rouben Mamoulian's *Applause* made a nice double bill of which Hollywood can revive hundreds more with comparable quality.

—*Village Voice*, October 12, 1967

■ 12. *UP THE DOWN STAIRCASE;*
    POINT BLANK; GAMES

Up the Down Staircase can be considered a failure for asking questions it is afraid to answer. Why should ghetto children receive an
education modeled after middle-class values outside the ghetto?
How do educators break the vicious circle of hopeless home environments causing hopeless classroom situations that will perpetuate hopelessness into the next generation? With updated
lesson plans on *Silas Marner* and *A Tale of Two Cities?* With tea
and sympathy, or faith, hope, and charity? Or by pretending that
problems do not exist except in the minds of bigots, and that all
children are created equal and treated fairly?

Curiously, *Up the Down Staircase* is more depressing than *The
Blackboard Jungle.* Even back in 1955 *Jungle* was discounted for its
pulp sensationalism. Things were not really that bad in the dis-
advantaged districts, we smugly assured ourselves. A dozen years
later things seem much worse. The ridiculous villainies of *Jungle* at
least exuded some of the thirties' vitality of the Dead End Kids.
Staircase is infinitely more discouraging than *Jungle,* particularly in
those moments when insensate noisemaking reflects an inarticulate
despair shared by the adult victims and castoffs of tomorrow. Good
and evil become irrelevant issues to those without pride in their
personal identity, and thus *Staircase* never really comes to grips
with the myth of mass education in a society that is becoming increasingly class-structured. Part of the credibility gap in the movie
can be attributed to the simpering, sniffling schoolteacher incar-
cerated in the mannerisms of Sandy Dennis, the adenoidal Greer
Garson of the sixties. Indeed, all the adult characters are contrived
caricatures of authority, strangling themselves and their charges
with an inexhaustible supply of red tape. The scenario begins
satirically for audience guffaws (in Calvin Coolidge High School,
no less) and ends sentimentally for audience gulps on the order of
"Goodbye, Mrs. Chips."

The criticism of *Up the Down Staircase* as a conceptual whole
fails to do justice to Robert Mulligan's perceptive direction of his

younger players, particularly Ellen O'Mara as the heartbreaking incarnation of every ugly, awkward, vulnerable adolescent that ever
wallflowered a high school gymnasium while the handsome instruc-
tor she adored tried to make time with a wise and pretty instruc-
tress from that mysterious planet of adulthood. There is a five- or
six-minute sequence in *Up the Down Staircase* that is better than
anything I have seen on the screen this year. The sequence begins
with an act of compassion at a high-school dance and ends with an
adolescent's suicide the next day. The lyrical link between the two
time sequences is composed of a gliding camera movement that
follows the young girl as she shuffles away from and back to the
teacher's letter box in which she has deposited a note of heartfelt
gratitude for the night before. The teacher summons her for a cruel
lesson in "composition." As he corrects her grammatical (and emotional) errors, Mulligan's camera glances at the girl's poignantly
inexpressive face and then cuts to her hand clutching the sleeve of
her coat. Between them, Robert Mulligan and Ellen O'Mara have
resurrected the behavioral beauty of those old Hollywood movies
that amaze us with their privileged moments in the midst of punk
scenarios. Despite the over-all failures of form in *Baby the Rain
Must Fall*, *Inside Daisy Clover*, and *Up the Down Staircase*, the
emotional delicacy and intensity of Mulligan's style marks him as
the successor to Leo McCarey. He even manages to hold down
Sandy Dennis from time to time, but he has had ample practice
with Natalie Wood.

Point Blank begins more pretentiously than any picture I've
seen this year, but I wound up liking it just the same. British director John Boorman attracted some attention in 1965 with *Having a Wild Weekend*, a kind of mobile "in" exercise that tried
to do for the Dave Clark Five what *A Hard Day's Night* had done
for the Beatles—and whatever happened to the Dave Clark Five,
anyway? In any case, Boorman seems to have completely digested
the films of Alain Resnais. He establishes a conventional dishonor-
among-thieves plot as if he were directing an Alain Robbe-Grillet
script entitled "Last Year at Alcatraz." Even with all the stylistic
pyrotechnics that enable modern directors to tell stories backwards
and sideways, the plot of *Point Blank* never makes too much sense.
But the forward momentum of Lee Marvin's mysterious vendetta

against the skyscraper underworld manages to overcome Boorman's laborious exposition. *Point Blank* has a meaningfully modern look to it as Marvin demonstrates the adaptability of the actor to his architecture with much the same striking effect that Mastroianni achieves in demonstrating the alienation of the actor from his architecture in Antonioni's *La Notte*. It is also nice to see Angie Dickinson getting a chance at long last to project some genuine sexuality into an American movie. The violence is imaginatively handled, and for those critics who wish to continue carping on this subject, a certain television commercial for razor blades features a gangster chieftain shooting his subordinates with a silencer for stealing a shipment of the wrong razor blades. This commercial was used during the telecast of the World Series, the same World Series during which Sandy Koufax was blipped off the sound track for asking Jim Lonborg about bean balls. The television networks seem to have inherited the fastidious hypocrisy of the old movie companies.

Curtis Harrington's *Games* is about the shrewdest movie title of the year, and the movie itself is not as disappointing as its plot, which is riddled with implausibilities. The difference is the decor in all its dazzling popeyed presence as the main protagonist of this horror film. If there are chills in the film, they emerge from our expectations that the walls are going to start climbing up the characters, rather than vice versa. The best way to enjoy *Games* is to case the joint and forget the tenants.

—*Village Voice*, October 19, 1967

■ 13. *REFLECTIONS IN A GOLDEN EYE*

Reflections in a Golden Eye may mark a new era of high fidelity adaptions of "adult" novels to the screen. Henceforth movies will not merely shed their fig leaves of decorum and discretion; they will even add a few fetishes and perversions of their own. Thus what the late Carson McCullers was content to leave implicit on the printed page, John Huston, Chapman Mortimer and Gladys

Hill have chosen to make explicit on the screen. The covertly homosexual officer created by Mrs. McCullers has not only been upgraded from captain to major; his covertness has been boldly and brilliantly transformed by Marlon Brando into a course in cruising along Third Avenue. To watch Brando smiling smugly at his own irresistible reflection is to witness a privileged moment of acting reflecting being. Unfortunately for the film as a whole, Brando is woefully miscast as a dedicated but devious officer on an Army post in the South. Seeming more crackers than cracker, he never suggests military discipline as part of his sublimated past. For Carson McCullers, Captain Weldon Penderton repressed his true sexual feelings until it was too late to act rationally on them. Her gossamer Gothic plot exorcised the ghosts of repression in the name of emotional veracity. ("There is a fort in the South where a few years ago a murder was committed. The participants of this tragedy were: two officers, a soldier, two women, a Filipino, and a horse.")

Mrs. McCullers enmeshes her characters in a network of defective affinities. The covertly homosexual officer is ignominiously impotent to the point that his cuckoldry takes the form of an infatuation with his wife's lover. The harebrained heterosexual officer fancies that his own wife knows nothing of his adultery even after she has cut off her nipples with garden shears as a form of retribution. For her part, the adulterous wife is sensually complacent but conspicuously stupid. The two couples form a crisscross of sensitivity and stupidity, a pattern preserved in the screen casting of Marlon Brando and Elizabeth Taylor as the sensitive-stupid Pendertons, complemented by Brian Keith and Julie Harris as the stupid-sensitive Langdons. The Langdon ménage is further embellished by a Filipino fairy houseboy christened Anácleto. Abnormal as these two interlocking households may seem, there is no psychic force capable of jolting them out of their dull routine. Enter the sixth character as catalyst in the person of Private Elgee Williams, a creature who intersects the lives of the Pendertons and the Langdons at the strategic coordinates of sexuality and violence. It is Private Williams who steals into Mrs. Penderton's bedroom every night to stare in mute wonder at the sleeping woman. It is Private Williams who arouses a homosexual passion in the woman's impotent husband, and it is Private Williams who indirectly causes the death of Mrs. Langdon. Finally, it is Private Williams who is murdered in a woman's bedroom by the woman's husband in a fit of perverted jealousy.

Carson McCullers wrote her story in a matter-of-fact manner, as if it could be recorded on a morning report. Significantly, her most truthful characters—the sparrowish Mrs. Langdon and her devoted Anacleto—are also the strangest on the surface. There is a message in all this madness. Homosexuality, heterosexuality, and asexuality all merge into one muddy stream of consciousness. The main thing is to know thyself so that nothing human will ever be alien to thee. Certainly nothing human was alien to Mrs. McCullers. The trouble is that restraint of latent impulses is as "human" as their release, and that so-called Gothic fiction falsifies surface fact in the name of subterranean truth. It may be that many if not most heterosexuals suppress their latent homosexuality in order to play the roles for which they have been cast by society, but it does not follow that role-playing is necessarily ridiculous or dishonest. Homosexual fiction is too often guilty of taking a lofty attitude toward the games people play by pretending to be impartial between the quares and the squares, but underneath the veneer of objectivity is the muck of vicious gossip. Still, a writer as skillful as Mrs. McCullers had no trouble implicating her readers in her horror stories because she sensed intuitively the abiding abnormality of American sexuality. Indeed, if there was not a widespread uneasiness over heterosexual hedonism à la *Playboy* magazine, *Reflections in a Golden Eye* would be more vulnerable to the charge of treating heterosexual instincts as the stuff of farce and homosexual instincts as the stuff of fantasy.

John Huston has devised all sorts of visual equivalences to match the literary style of Carson McCullers. He has drained out all the color from the color film until the fatal climax, as if to fulfill Sergei Eisenstein's dictum on chromatic expressiveness found in the Russian director's overrated treatise, *The Film Sense*. (Eisenstein had criticized Alexander Korda for not varying the tonality of the film *Rembrandt* to correspond to the aging of the painter's palette.) Huston plays the horses for all they are worth, both symbolically and rhetorically, a bad habit he picked up from Arthur Miller in *The Misfits*. He succeeds in keeping a consistent distance from all his leading characters, and the ensemble playing of Brando, Taylor, Keith, and Harris cannot be faulted. Where Huston falters is in the atmosphere he provides for the action. Like Robert Wise with *The Haunting*, Huston overdirects *Reflections* for the sake of a mass audience in which he has little confidence. His film lacks the special stillness of the novel. There is too much expressionistic foliage on the screen and too much declamatory thunder on the sound track.

The star structure of the casting may be to blame for the failures of Zorro David as Anacleto (too broad) and Robert Forster as Private Williams (too dim). The private is particularly weak in the movie because he was so private to begin with in the novel. He is the one character that cannot be articulated by dialogue, and he is not crucial enough to justify a novelistic narration on the sound track. Huston does his best to characterize the private through the camera, but the character remains a boring mystery and the actor a hollow shell sharing only empty space in a shot frame with such mythic personalities as Brando and Taylor.

Huston attempts a Hitchcock effect to dramatize the intensity of Brando's obsession. Brando's mad major is following, virtually stalking Private Williams, when there is a screech of brakes and a crash of two cars behind Brando. Up ahead, Private Williams and his buddies turn around to see what has happened. Brando, never turning for an instant, keeps his gaze fixed on the private, now facing him. Huston's cutting and camera placement succeed only in confirming the motivation of the Brando character. There is no visual impact in the incident. By contrast, Alfred Hitchcock presented a similar situation more strikingly in *Strangers on a Train* in which Robert Walker watches a tennis match with his eyes fixed on one of the players (Farley Granger) while the rest of the spectators are swiveling their heads back and forth to follow the play. Hitchcock's image of an obsession is disguised as a gag, and the Robert Walker and Farley Granger characters are mere puppets in a contrived murder intrigue. The homosexual implications of the Walker-Granger relationship are beneath the surface, whereas those of the Brando-Forster relationship are above the surface. Thus the difference between Hitchcock and Huston, here and elsewhere, is that Hitchcock is visually direct and psychologically oblique, Huston psychologically direct and visually oblique. This is not only the difference between two directors but between two kinds of cinema.

Huston pulls out all the stylistic stops when Brando finally shoots Forster in Taylor's bedroom. The screen splashes into color. The camera jerks about madly in erratic lateral bursts between the dead soldier, the screaming wife, the slumping officer, and finally, almost eerily, the grayish figure of the officer next door, a figure caught in the blur of the camera movements like some ghostly retribution. Except for this latter figure of style, Huston's mise-en-scène is clearly inferior to Mrs. McCullers': "The reports from the pistol aroused Leonora and she sat up in bed. As yet she was still only half-awake, and she stared about her as though witnessing some scene in a play, some tragedy that was gruesome but not necessary to believe. Almost immediately Major Langdon knocked on the back door and then hurried up the stairs wearing slippers and a dressing gown. The Captain had slumped against the wall. In his queer, coarse wrapper he resembled a broken and dissipated monk. Even in death the body of the soldier still had the look of warm, animal comfort. His grave face was unchanged, and his sun-browned hands lay palms upward on the carpet as though in sleep."

—*Village Voice*, November 30, 1967

■ 14. THE GRADUATE; IN COLD BLOOD

The Graduate has been adapted by Mike Nichols, Buck Henry, and Calder Willingham from a novel of the same title by Charles Webb. I like the movie much better than the book, but I had no idea how literally faithful the screenplay was to its source. Charles Webb seems to be the forgotten man in all the publicity, even though 80 per cent or more of the dialogue comes right out of the book. I recently listened to some knowledgeable people parceling out writing credit to Nichols, Henry, and Willingham as if Webb had never existed, as if the quality of the film were predetermined by the quality of its script, and as if the mystique of the director counted for nought. These knowledgeable people should read the Webb novel, which reads more like a screenplay than any novel since John Steinbeck's *Of Mice and Men*.

Webb's book is almost all dialogue, with the intermittent straight prose passages functioning as visual tips for the director. That is not to say that Nichols, Henry, and Willingham are not entitled to their credits, but merely that their contributions pertain more to nuance than substance, more to the how than the what.

The Graduate, more than Who's Afraid of Virginia Woolf? is Mike Nichols' diploma as a director. Whereas Nichols merely transferred Albee, he actually transcends Webb. The Graduate is a director's picture not because Nichols wrote all the dialogue and acted out all the parts and sang and composed all the songs under the double pseudonym of Simon and Garfunkel and directed the cinematography under the alias of Robert Surtees, et cetera, ad infinitum, ad credit sheetum. The Graduate is a director's picture because even its mistakes are the proofs of a personal style.

Style is more an attitude toward things than the things themselves. It can be a raised eyebrow or a nervous smile or a pair of shrugged shoulders. It can even be an averted glance. By playing down some of the more offensive qualities of the book, Nichols expresses his own attitude toward the material. The main trouble with the book is its reduction of the world to the ridiculous scale of an overgrown and outdated Holden Caulfield. The catcher in the rye has been perverted by time and affectation into a pitcher of the wry. Charles Webb's Benjamin Braddock expresses himself with a monosyllabic smugness that becomes maddeningly self-indulgent as the book unravels into slapstick passion. Ben even goes "on the road" for a brief period to demonstrate his beatification at the expense of the beatniks. He is superior to his pathetic parents and adults generally. He is kind to the wife of his father's law partner even though she seduces him with cold-bloodedly calculating carnality. Ben then falls in love with Elaine, his mistress' daughter, and makes her marry him through the sheer persistence of his pursuit.

The screenplay has been improved by a series of little changes and omissions constituting a pattern of discretion and abstraction. The hero is made less bumptious, the predatory wife less calculating, the sensitive daughter less passive. The "on the road" passage is omitted from the movie, and the recurring parental admonitions are reduced in number and intensity. The very end of the movie is apparently the result of an anticliché improvisation. In the book Ben interrupts Elaine's wedding (to another) before the troths have been plighted or the plights have been trothed or what have you. In the movie the bride kisses the groom before Ben can disrupt the proceeding, but the bride runs off just the same. And this little change makes all the difference in dramatizing the triumph of people over proceedings. An entire genre of Hollywood movies had been constructed upon the suspenseful chase-to-the-altar proposition that what God hath joined together no studio scriptwriter could put asunder. The minister could turn out to be an impostor, the bridegroom a bigamist, but once the vows were taken, that was the old ball game. *The Graduate* not only shatters this monogamous mythology; it does so in the name of a truer love.

The emotional elevation of the film is due in no small measure to the extraordinarily engaging performances of Anne Bancroft as the wife-mother-mistress, Dustin Hoffman as the lumbering Lancelot, and Katharine Ross as his fair Elaine. Nichols is at his best in getting new readings out of old lines and thus lightening potentially heavy scenes. The director is at his worst when the eclecticism of his visual style gets out of hand. The opening sequence of bobbing, tracking, lurching heads in nightmarishly mobile close-ups looks like an "hommage" to Fellini's 8½. A rain-drenched Anne Bancroft splattered against a starkly white wall evokes images in *La Notte*. The languorous lyricism of Ben at Berkeley seems derivative of Varda's *Le Bonheur* and even some of John Korty's landscape work in the same region. Unfortunately, the cultural climate is such that the intelligent prose cinema of Mike Nichols tries to become the intellectual-poetic cinema of Michelangelo Nichols. Still, I was with *The Graduate* all the way because I responded fully to its romantic feelings, and my afterthoughts are even kinder to a movie that, unlike *Morgan*, didn't cop out in the name of "sanity." Some people have complained that the Bancroft-Hoffman relationship is more compelling than the subsequent Ross-Hoffman relationship. I don't agree. As Stravinsky once observed, it is easier to be interesting with dissonance than consonance. Similarly, it is easier to be interesting with an unconventional sexual relationship than with a conventional love pairing. *The Graduate* is moving precisely because its hero passes from a premature maturity to an innocence regained, an idealism reconfirmed. That he is so much out of his time and place makes him more of an individual and less of a type. Even the overdone caricatures that surround the three principals cannot diminish the cruel beauty of this love story.

In Cold Blood is not Greek tragedy, either in the original book
by Truman Capote or in the movie version written and directed by
Richard Brooks. What Truman Capote wrote was an extended
New Yorker profile on all the circumstances surrounding the slaying of the Clutter family of Holcomb, Kansas, by two young drifters
named Richard Hickock and Perry Smith. At 150,000 words, Capote's book is obviously too long for an average-length movie. (*The
Graduate* runs only about 60,000 words.) Besides, Capote's strength
is in the sheer accumulation of detail, particularly irrelevant detail.
If his book is not one of the mountains of world literature, it is certainly one of the most mountainous molehills. Its main limitation
is its author's detached journalistic stance, particularly in that mysterious moment when the murders were willed, that moment
known only to God and artists, but never to "objective" journalists.
The main strength of the book lies in its configuration of two
Americas heading accidentally and insanely on a collision course.
The America of the Clutters is comfortable, wholesome, puritanical, generous, complacent, and singularly uncurious. The America of the killers is insecure, hallucinatory, irrational, impermanent,
and infinitely treacherous and oppressive. The Clutters represented
the American dream of Republican editorials, Smith and Hickock
the American nightmare of writers from Melville to Burroughs,
embracing Kerouac's *On the Road* and Leslie Fiedler's "Come up
to de raft, Huck honey." The Clutters were rich—at least mod-
erately—and the killers were poor—desperately and criminally. Capote shuns the Marxist determinism of Dreiser's *American Tragedy*, but he propounds no theory of his own. He merely quotes
witnesses and "authorities" to his heart's content and lets the devil
take the hindmost.

Richard Brooks has transformed Capote's journalistic caper into
a tract against capital punishment. A journalist (played by Paul
Stewart) is superimposed on the film as the writer-director's liberal,
humane mouthpiece. Capote himself seemed singularly uncom-
mitted on the issue. However, Brooks seems to have sacrificed too
much of the book in order to make the murderers more sympathetic.

It is not a question of dropping some of Capote's details; Brooks
has dropped entire dimensions of the book. The Clutters, for example, take up much of Capote's book, as do the neighbors around
them. Nancy Clutter goes steady with a boy of whom her father

disapproves because of the boy's Catholicism. The boy is treated as a suspect after the murder. Nancy's mother has been sick for years, and one day she bursts into tears in a neighbor's arms because she feels that in these years when the children are growing up she is so ill that the children will remember her in years after only as a ghost in the house. The detective's wife dreams of Mrs. Clutter months after the murder. In the dream Mrs. Clutter stands in the doorway and cries. The neighbors of the Clutters gossip about all the possible suspects in their own midst, and are almost disappointed when it turns out that outsiders were responsible.

None of these "details" turn up in the movie. The first half of the film looks promising; the second half becomes boring. The trouble is that Brooks has focused almost entirely on the killers and their sick minds and childhood dreams. Consequently the movie is motivated by the kind of facile Freudianism that is supposed to have gone out in the forties. Brooks goes so far as to suggest that Perry murdered Mr. Clutter in a straight case of father-identification. Even the hangman is momentarily represented as Perry's father on the screen. The whiplash documentary style of much of the photography clashes with the tired German expressionism of dreams and hallucinations, and the mixture is a bit dishonest besides, in that it places an aura of subjectivity around the killers and around no one else. In the book the dead and even the detectives were allowed the dignity of their own dreams and reveries.

Other minor discrepancies are symptomatic of Brooks's biased treatment: Language—Brooks introduces such profanity into the dialogue as "bullshit" and "friggin." Hickock and Smith are denied such language in Capote's book, probably because Capote decided that these words should be used casually and continuously or not at all. Brooks uses the words purely for shock effect and as part of the subjective isolation of the two killers from humanity.

On the other hand, the characters in the book repeatedly use the word "nigger," which Brooks deletes from their dialogue in the movie.

Finally, Brooks deletes from the odyssey of Hickock and Smith an incident that would have turned every audience in the world against them. In the book Hickock blithely swerves his car to the side of the road to kill an old dog walking out its last moments.

Even the inspired castings and performances of Robert Blake and Scott Wilson in the central roles would not have sufficed to save them from the wrath of audiences. Mass murder is one thing, but stomping a pooch is quite another.

—*Village Voice*, December 28, 1967

vii
1968

■ 1. *THE STRANGER*

The Stranger is more an inevitable failure than an interesting fail-ure. As a producer's package, the combination of Albert Camus, Luchino Visconti, and Marcello Mastroianni seems like a logical ploy for the culture vultures. Ever since the project was announced, the cocktail-party line of the literati was that Mastroianni was mis-cast as the emotionally detached hero. I disagree. It is not Mastro-ianni who is miscast, but Camus. *The Stranger* should never have been made into a movie. Nor *War and Peace* and *The Brothers Karamazov*. It is not that Visconti and Mastroianni have botched up Camus. Quite the contrary. Visconti has prostrated his own directorial personality before the cultural monumentality of Camus. The quiet browns and blues of sand and sea and sky pertain less to a director's images than to a writer's. Even the stunningly gray living-death masks of aged mourners are coups less of a personal visual style than of an impersonal illustration of novelistic ideas. Nothing spills over in *The Stranger* from Visconti to Camus. No previous Visconti film has been so schematically subservient to its literary source, and all in vain. For all his fidelity to Camus, Vis-conti succeeds only in vulgarizing him.

The vulgarization of Camus reaches its crescendo in the court-room sequences of blustering bigotry triumphant. Mastroianni's Meursault, tried for the senseless slaying of an Arab in the blind-ingly hot sun on an Algerian beach, is convicted and sentenced to death largely for his indifference at his mother's funeral. Meursault

further offends his peers by his disbelief in all divinities. The beauty
of the Camus prose arises from the author's stripping away the
sentimental rhetoric of life and death the better to bare the sensuous essence of existence. Camus pours his own sweet sensibility
into the empty vessel of a character he calls Meursault. Mastroianni in turn incarnates the beautiful interior of Camus with the
beautiful exterior of Mastroianni, and this is as it should be in a
medium in which the internal can be expressed only through the
external, and in which the beauty of a face is both the mask and
the metaphor of the beauty of a soul.

Unfortunately, Camus constructed *The Stranger* philosophically
rather than dramatically. The Algerian crowds representing conformity and hypocrisy were never meant to materialize on a movie
set for the titillation of urban art-house God-is-dead-and-living-in-
Argentina sophisticates. The brief, spasmodic action of the novel
was inserted merely to allow the heroic nonhero the opportunity
for detached self-contemplation, the province more of literature
than cinema. Hence the direst of dilemmas. Mastroianni is too attaching and affecting to audiences to convey the dry-as-dust detachment Camus intended, but an actor substantially less affecting than
Mastroianni would make the movie unsittable-through. It is not
Mastroianni's fault that he seems most endearing to Karina when
he tells her he doesn't love her. Camus died before the romanticism
of alienation engulfed the screen through the lushly sensual lethargy of Mastroianni, and *The Stranger* is now as dated cinematically as Gérard Philipe's cerebral *Caligula* would be dated the-
atrically. Modern existentialism was inspired by the desperate
either-or choices posed by totalitarian politics through the thirties
and forties, and it is impossible to appreciate the audacity of
Camus' conception without an awareness of those two desperate
decades, an awareness as much in the audience as in the players
posing uncomfortably in period bathing suits. As it is, Mastroianni–
Camus–Meursault seems to exist apart from any time or place, an
apartness emphasized by the distracting dubbing of Mastroianni
into French.

The best moments in the film are manifested in Mastroianni's
appreciative reaction to the feelings erupting around him in the
very mortal spectacles of his mother's aged admirer fainting at her
grave, a scabrous widower lamenting the loss of his equally scabrous

dog, and an Arab mother waving encouragement to her imprisoned son. Apart from the out-of-key forensics in the courtroom and the prison cell, the gravest defect of Visconti's direction is the unconvincing staging of the murder. Not that Visconti is entirely to blame. Camus thought the murder through as a philosopher without feeling it out as an artist.

The debut of Anna Karina's bare bosom deserves at least the immortality of a footnote in any review of *The Stranger*. What Godard gallantly withheld in the name of love for so long has finally been exposed in the name of culture. It seems in retrospect that Godard astutely perceived that the reality could never equal the illusion.

—*Village Voice*, January 4, 1968

■ 2. *JULES AND JIM* MEETS *PSYCHO*:
A REVIEW OF
HITCHCOCK, BY FRANÇOIS TRUFFAUT

The most extraordinary fact about *Hitchcock*, by François Truffaut, is that such a book was written at all. There is not another instance of one practicing director paying homage to another in the entire history of books on cinema. Even if the spirit had been willing, the scholarship would have been weak. Film directors until very recently were not noted for their literary gifts and critical insights, and they were especially reluctant to reveal the tricks of their trade to outsiders. The Hollywood director concealed his technique for the sake of his audience's illusions. His style, such as it was, served the scenario logically and faithfully, or at least seemed to serve even when it was full of personal flourishes. The idea that a Hollywood director would ever be discussed as a creative force seemed particularly remote in the studio-dominated thirties and forties, when "serious" film histories wrote off American movies as the products of vulgar capitalists.

François Truffaut represents a new breed of critic-director, who is conscious of what he owes to his predecessors in the cinema. As a critic for *Cahiers du Cinéma* in Paris, Truffaut helped force a reconsideration of the American cinema by looking through the total output of Hollywood directors for elements of a personal style. But as a film-maker Truffaut revealed himself as an overtly personal artist modeled more after the impudent individualism of Jean Renoir and Jean Vigo than the commercial masks of Alfred Hitchcock and Howard Hawks. Ironically, the American art-house crowd that admires Truffaut for *The Four Hundred Blows, Shoot the Piano Player,* and especially *Jules* and *Jim,* tends to despise the films of Alfred Hitchcock. Truffaut is fully aware of this discrepancy in tastes: "I know that many Americans are surprised that European cinéphiles—and the French in particular—regard Alfred Hitchcock as a 'film author,' in the sense that the term is applied to Ingmar Bergman, Federico Fellini, Luis Buñuel, or Jean-Luc Godard."

Truffaut does not argue that Hollywood movies and directors have been underrated as a whole, but rather that Hitchcock alone should be singled out for revaluation. "If Hitchcock, to my way of thinking, outranks the rest, it is because he is the most complete film-maker of all. He is not merely an expert at some specific aspect of cinema, but an all-round specialist, who excels at every image, each shot, and every scene."

Truffaut can document his admiration with citations of shots from any of Hitchcock's 50 films turned out over the past 40 years. The book itself consists largely of approximately 500 questions and answers dealing with "(a) the circumstances attending the inception of each picture; (b) the preparation and structure of the screenplay; (c) the specific directorial problems connected with each film; (d) Hitchcock's own assessment of the commercial and artistic results in relation to his initial expectations for each picture." Truffaut had little English, and Hitchcock less French. The indispensable intermediary was Truffaut's friend Helen Scott, of the French Film Office in New York. Still, the language barrier would seem grotesque were it not for Truffaut's conception of Hitchcock as a director capable of expressing the subtlest emotions with purely visual means.

Language is not the only barrier between Hitchcock and Truffaut. They are of different ages and different worlds. Hitchcock sounds more professional and less intellectual than his persistent questioner. Truffaut seems almost embarrassingly deferential in the early stages of interrogation, and at times he seems to overreact to Hitchcock's jokes, more on faith than amusement. But Truffaut's analytical intensity never falters. Film by film, detail by detail, a web of meanings is spun from the raw silk of Hitchcock's memories. Hitchcock keeps talking about effects, and Truffaut keeps countering with ideas. Hitchcock instinctively resists being intellectualized. He has survived too long in the film industry to let himself be captured by the fickle highbrows, and he has been plagiarized too much to enjoy supplying a detailed blueprint of his methods to his competitors. But Truffaut is relentless. He will not be put off by Hitchcock's coarseness and perverseness. He has cased Hitchcock's career too thoroughly to be distracted by the familiar defense mechanisms of an artist who wishes to remain a mystery to the critic.

Then suddenly comes the collision. Truffaut presumes to criticize the subjective style of *The Wrong Man*. Hitchcock bristles at this break in the uninterrupted litany of praise. The two men argue back and forth to an impasse, but Truffaut has broken Hitchcock's shell of unconcern when it seemed least vulnerable. This is the drama of the book: the psychological penetration of a devious artist by a devoted admirer.

Much of the book's success can be credited to the 300 illustrations of Hitchcock's art in action. Truffaut, unlike too many French critics, does not shirk menial details. There are efficient plot synopses of all the Hitchcock films, and no tidbit of production gossip is considered too trivial for mention. Indeed, the Truffaut-Hitchcock conversation often resembles a scene from a cat-and-mouse Hitchcock thriller in which the most banal anecdotes contain dangerous clues and hidden traps. Significantly, Truffaut draws a complete blank when he tries to get Hitchcock to talk about his dreams. He is more successful in establishing a link between Hitchcock's themes of guilt and a very formal Catholic upbringing in childhood.

Truffaut's *Hitchcock* may leave the unfortunate impression that there is no sympathetic criticism of Hitchcock in the English language. Robin Wood, Peter Bogdanovich and Ian Cameron have covered much of Truffaut's terrain—Robin Wood with particular profundity—but no mere critic is likely to match the influence of the director of *Jules and Jim*. Truffaut may not convert all Hitch-

knockians into Hitchcockians. Still, a second look at *Rear Window,*
Notorious, Vertigo, and *Psycho* may confirm Truffaut's thesis that
a major artist lurks beneath the façade of a master entertainer.

—*Book World,* January 14, 1968

■ 3. CHINA IS NEAR

Marco Bellocchio's *China Is Near* may not be running much
longer, and more's the pity for an art-house scene that is usually
starved for genuinely artistic attractions. Bellocchio's direction is
brilliant to the point of brilliantine. Not a hair or shot is out of
place, or a cut or camera movement. Everything counts and everything matters in this Stendhalian comedy of mores, but Bellocchio
seems to have offended some of the reviewers by violating the
sacred rules of exposition. The first shot of the film is a rigidly
framed, discreetly distanced glance at two lovers dormant on an
improvised bed in an unidentified room in the cold, gray light of
dawn. Bellocchio cuts briefly to the stirring couple simply to identify their faces and then retreats quickly to the discreet distance
that will keep the sensations of the plot from ever seeming sordid.
We shall never completely escape the chilling grayness of this opening sequence. Indeed, *China Is Near* explores all those frayed feelings of conformity that awaken in the five o'clock of the morning
of the soul when the ancient alarm goes off like the dreaded church
bells of Italian Catholicism.

We are barely accustoming our eyes to the dimly lit and drably
furnished scene before this first stage of exposition is supplanted by
the next and then the next and then the next, until three separate
plots and five major characters merge into one comic canvas of
Italian Leftism in complete disarray. Bellocchio's young lovers,
Carlo (Paolo Graziosi) and Giovanna (Daniela Surina), are first
introduced as the beleaguered victims of a class society, specifically
the servants of a family of spoiled, self-indulgent aristocrats who
dabble in the politics of the Old and New Left. Vittorio (Glauco
Mauri) is a plump, pink plutocrat with acute guilt feelings about
his enormous wealth. After a fling with the Communist party he

settles down with the staid Socialists when they present him with a place on the ticket as councilman. The candidate's younger brother, Camillo (Pierluigi Apra), leads a three-man Maoist cell in the municipality and refuses to countenance the brother's disgraceful desertion. The candidate's sister, Elena (Elda Tattoli), confounds her brothers with her political conservatism and sexual radicalism. Even when the world is going to pieces, Vittorio reminds her, an Italian expects his sister to retain her honor.

However, Bellocchio is no mere satirist like Pietro Germi, and his characters never degenerate into Germi caricatures at whom we can laugh so complacently. Bellocchio's five characters struggle vainly and grotesquely to escape their common destiny, but they are ultimately helpless against the fundamental lethargy of Italian history. Bellocchio very cleverly keeps the audience off-balance by never allowing any moral situation to linger on the screen long enough for facile audience identification. The fact that the impoverished Carlo is passed over for the Socialist nomination so that the wealthy Vittorio can attract bourgeois votes is soon forgotten when Carlo takes Vittorio's sister as his mistress. Discarded by Carlo, Giovanna retaliates by allowing Vittorio to take her at long last from his typewriter to his bed.

The plot takes an ugly turn when Elena becomes pregnant and decides to escape her trap by obtaining an abortion. Carlo sets all the machinery of family, Church, and state into motion against her, and the only truly admirable character in the film is broken by all the bigotry arrayed against her. And yet she, too, is part of the system that entraps her. She is not as cowardly as her two brothers, or as calculating as the two proles who inveigle their way into her household, but in the moment of truth she is not quite courageous enough to sacrifice her reputation for her principles. The film ends with Elena and Giovanna practicing their maternal exercises together in the splendor of a room seen for the first time in its awesomely ornate verticality. Elena will marry Carlo. Giovanna will marry Vittorio. Unbeknownst to Vittorio, both women have been impregnated by Carlo. It doesn't matter. The accommodations have been made. Life must go on. China must wait a bit longer, like any hope too long deferred.

On my first viewing of the film I somehow missed the posters advertising Sean Connery in a James Bond film and Michael Caine in *Alfie*. Also the reference to Bernardo Bertolucci's *Before the Revolution* at a performance of Verdi's *Macbeth*, through a lens dimly. On a second viewing everything in the film fell into place too neatly and concisely for comfort. Bellocchio's economy of expression is more impressive on first viewing than second, and yet it takes two viewings to appreciate the initial brushstrokes of characterization. Truffaut maintains in his introduction to his Hitchcock interview that clarity is the supreme virtue of a director. Bellocchio's opening is anything but clear. Not only does he confuse the audience with unexplained shifts of locale for the unheralded entrances and exits of unidentified characters on unmotivated mission; he also makes jokes about the characters before they have been properly introduced to us, and hence throws away his punch lines. For example, Glauco Mauri as Vittorio makes the most spectacularly farcical entrance of a character since Alberto Sordi, bedecked in Arab garb, sang on a swing in Fellini's *The White Sheik*. Our first glimpse of Mauri's Vittorio is a medium (i.e., waist-high) shot of a man in the throes of masturbation or constipation begging God's forgiveness. Bellocchio then cuts discreetly but still devastingly to a long shot of Vittorio virtually lurching out of the water closet to confront the guilt of a new day.

It all happens so fast that even the most discerning spectator lacks the buildup to give this gag the laugh its sheer audacity deserves. Indeed, there is barely time for a quiet chuckle, but it all turns out for the best, because Glauco Mauri's performance is one of the most beautiful characterizations in the history of the cinema. Mauri is the main reason I missed decorative trivia like the Connery-Caine posters. I couldn't take my eyes off his face, the face of a gloriously helpless bungler and bumbler, a frustrated lover and humanitarian, an inept traitor to his class who cannot persuade even his maiden aunts to vote for him, a born dupe and cuckold, in short, a poor little fat rich boy who never outgrew his childhood dreams of romance and adventure and who, in a useless sort of way, is infinitely more precious than all the realists who make sport of his illusions.

The most beautiful moments in the film are derived at least in part from the richness of Mauri's characterization. The much-admired off-key children's serenade to an ailing priest forms both background and counterpoint to Mauri's earnest plea for forgiveness from his unyieldingly fanatical younger brother. Later when the two brothers are confronted with the imminence of their sister's abortion rather than world revolution, a crisis more practical than theoretical, they are embarrassed to encounter each other in a movie theater, that modern refuge from reality. The older brother flees in panic, the younger averts his eyes with a shame-driven snap of his neck. Still later, Vittorio's sister drags him from bed for an impromptu night inventory of the library. Vittorio bounces a ball; Elena takes it away from him. He calls out the titles of first editions, then pauses over a bound comic book containing his childhood memories. He smilingly yawns, and Elena follows with a yawn of resignation to her own private five o'clock in the morning of the soul. Elda Tattoli as Elena (and coscenarist with Bellocchio) gives a quite lovely performance, as do the other principals and supernumeraries, but Glauco Mauri is something special in making you smile when you really want to cry.

Bellocchio's direction may be too controlled for some tastes; his vision of the world too naïvely neurotic for others. I found myself liking and admiring *China Is Near* almost in spite of myself. There has always been a grotesque credibility gap between ethics and politics, between personal opportunism and social idealism, between the muddy trenches of man's sexuality and the marble pillars of his intellect. Perhaps never more so than in this very fateful moment in world history. The fact remains that a politician's truth can become an artist's truism. Fortunately, Bellocchio avoids the trap of schematization by implicating all his characters in his fluid frames, even in those most dreadful moments when an honest civil servant is forced into corruption and a priest rolls his eyes skyward as he breaks in on an abortion. *China Is Near* is perhaps a prophetic film in its total despair.

—*Village Voice*, February 1, 1968

■ 4. *CHARLIE BUBBLES; TELL ME LIES*

Charlie Bubbles is the most pleasant surprise of a year that has thus far been less surprising than disconcerting. First of all, the idea of

Albert Finney doubling as star and director did not seem too promising, and not because there is any taboo against working both sides of the camera. Chaplin, Keaton, Welles, and Renoir come to mind immediately as impressive precedents for aspiring actor-directors. Even on a lower level of personal style, directing seems to bring out the better qualities of an actor. Gene Kelly was less of a ham in his own (and Donen's) musicals (*Singin' in the Rain*, *It's Always Fair Weather*) than in Minnelli's (*The Pirate*) or Sidney's (*Anchors Aweigh*); and Brando was less of a hog in the self-directed *One-Eyed Jacks* than in the Lumet-directed *The Fugitive Kind* and the Englund-directed *The Ugly American*. The real problem nowadays is that everyone, including the leggy chorus girl in the *New Yorker* cartoon, wants to be a director, with the result that aspiration too often exceeds inspiration.

The biggest surprise in *Charlie Bubbles* is that Finney's direction succeeds on its own terms as a tasteful stew of acting vignettes. Indeed, I'd have to go back to the Mercury Theatre casts of Orson Welles in *Citizen Kane* and *The Magnificent Ambersons* to find a comparable level of ensemble playing, down to the smallest bits and pieces. Finney is certainly no Welles in the realm of intellectual and emotional expressiveness. As a work of art *Charlie Bubbles* finally bursts into cop-out fantasy, because its wholeness is unable to reconcile the perfection of its parts with any coherent attitude toward its subject. The film's ending leaves the audience up in the air literally and figuratively—literally because Finney's beleaguered Bubbles ascends in a balloon *ex machina*, figuratively because the ascent forestalls an obligatory scene Shelagh Delaney neglected to write for Charlie and his estranged wife, Lottie (Billie Whitelaw).

Shelagh Delaney happens to be the girl who wrote *A Taste of Honey*, reportedly after becoming disgusted with the contrivances of a Terence Rattigan play performed in a theater for which she worked as an usherette. It is natural for artists reacting against contrivance to let some air into characterizations. Unfortunately, it is equally natural for these artists to inflate individual characterizations at the expense of an over-all conception.

Albert Finney and Shelagh Delaney confront a familiar phenomenon of recent years in our popular culture—the movement of raw talent and energy from the north of England to the south. (In America and Italy the analogous movement is from south to north.) Albert Finney's Charlie Bubbles is ostensibly a successful writer from the north who has settled in the sybaritic luxury of London, but the instant recognition of the "writer" in the film is more appropriate for an actor very much like Finney. The film begins a good deal like the standard satire of success. The setting is the murmuringly posh atmosphere of a London restaurant where Charlie meets with an agent and accountant to talk of roast beef and residuals. Charlie spots a less successful colleague named Smokey Pickle (Colin Blakely) dining indecorously with a wart-encrusted solicitor. Charlie and Smokey have barely said hello before they are spattering each other with the specialties of the house. Finney's *Tom Jones* fans chortle appreciatively at the anal level of the slapstick satirically intercut with the discreetly disturbed expressions of the still murmuring diners. The strange thing about the scene is Finney's extraordinary self-effacement. At first it seems only the modesty of an actor, and there is no end of that, but eventually the modesty of the actor is translated into the meaning of the character. Charlie Bubbles is not bored; he is tired. He is afflicted less with ennui than with downright exhaustion.

And so we have a double vision of Charlie's world, the satirical and the hallucinatory. The satire is cued by the kooky nomenclature—Charlie Bubbles and Smokey Pickle as the authors, Mr. and Mrs. Noseworthy as Charlie's devoted servants, Mr. and Mrs. Fettuchini as a slightly sinister movie couple, and Eliza Heyho as Liza Minnelli's sensitive rendering of the ugly Americaness in Charlie's cluttered life. But though the names suggest caricature, the characterizations do not. By forcing himself into the background of every scene, Finney functions like a solid double-brass player with a jazz trio. Every performer resonates through Finney's personable bulk and generous passivity. Finney's tact extends to his directing technique. He indulges in an occasional visual stunt like the closed-circuit television screens through which we see the childish disorder of Charlie's town house existence and a Felliniesque procession through the muddy bleakness of the industrial north. But even in these profoundly scenic sequences Finney's players are enhanced.

Nowhere is Finney gentler than in his scenes with Liza Minnelli, an ill-featured, ungainly girl, who emerges triumphantly from the apparent humiliation of a sex scene during which her Eliza does not so much seduce the played-out Charlie as service him in the nether regions of his libido. By the time Finney is achieving new ecstasies of rapport with Billie Whitelaw as his casually earthy ex-wife and Timothy Garland as his emotionally crafty son Jack, Charlie's tiredness transcends any possible social or psychological interpretation. Satirical reality seems to sink into the swamplike realism of a dream. It is as if Charlie Bubbles dreamed the whole film in those few moments of semiwakefulness during which he was suspended between north and south, failure and success, innocence and guilt, hope and regret.

The beauty of the film is that it shifts imperceptibly from the Pickwickian to the Earwickian as attitudes flow into feelings. *Charlie Bubbles* falls short of greatness both because its feelings never coalesce into ideas and because its eponymous protagonist never wakes up long enough to resolve his relationships. Nonetheless a score of memorable performances must count for something on any ultimate scale of values. Albert Finney, Billie Whitelaw, and Alan Lake as a disconcertingly direct celebrity hound in an airman's uniform deserve special commendations.

Tell Me Lies has concluded a short run to make way for more conventional entertainment. Far from ending the hostilities in Vietnam, Peter Brook's film has started a feud between Nat Hentoff and Renata Adler. At the risk of taking a cowardly middle position between the two extremes, I must say that the film struck me as intellectually provocative and artistically unsuccessful. But, then, Peter Brook has always been intellectually provocative and artistically unsuccessful. *The Beggar's Opera, Moderato Cantabile, Lord of the Flies,* and *Marat/Sade* all looked better on the drawing board than on the screen despite impressive castings and performances by Olivier, Belmondo, Moreau, McGee, (Ian) Richardson, and the boy who played Piggy. Brook seemed to have used up all his artistic options from the extreme determinism of *Moderato Cantabile* to the extreme improvisation of *Lord of the Flies,* but *Tell Me Lies* provides an entirely new set of cinematic conceptions, which miscarry in the messiest ways imaginable.

Tell Me Lies is reportedly based "loosely" on the recent Peter Brook–Royal Shakespeare Company production *US.* I don't know what "loosely" means exactly in this context, but what undeniable traces of the original stage show I could discern seemed more strident than searching. By the time I had figured out what the performers were trying to do, I was wishing they wouldn't do it. I was never offended by the film. At its core was the same healthy skepticism I respected in the Resnais and Godard episodes from the otherwise deplorable hodgepodge called fittingly (for Brook's film as well) *Far from Vietnam*.

Tell Me Lies must be judged ultimately as a protest film that questions its own effectiveness at every turn. It is drenched in doubt. After all, how *can* British intellectuals affect events in Vietnam? How can demonstrations and poetry readings end the horrors of bombing and napalming? One speaker asks if British intellectuals really want the war to end. It is such a safe, comfortable, and distant cause. (I might add parenthetically that Vietnam is a much safer issue in Britain currently than that of the immigration of "colored" British subjects to a homeland that is only 2 per cent "colored" but apparently more than 50 per cent racist. Brook can hardly be criticized for avoiding an issue that did not explode until very recently, but I wonder why Brook, unlike Fruchter and Machover in *The Troublemakers*, never bothered inquiring into the failure of the New Left in both Britain and America to rouse the masses of labor and the poor.)

The major problems of *Tell Me Lies* are time and space—time, because the events in Vietnam change too quickly for the normal gestation period of a film; space, because television can bring Vietnam into our living rooms instantaneously. It can be argued that television coverage restructures Vietnam into a manageable shoot-em-up series for the general viewer, but the shock mannerisms of *Tell Me Lies* are hardly likely to rouse viewers from the torpor of their TV dinners.

Actually, *Tell Me Lies* may irritate a great many Americans who are against the war more because the war is genuinely un-American than because it is quintessentially American. The British actors and intellectuals treat a political phenomenon like Morrison's self-immolation on the steps of the Pentagon as a heroic manifestation of individual conscience, but when the film's conversations take on an overtly revolutionary tone, Americans are lumped together in genocidal generalities. Suddenly the actors stop straining to imitate American accents, and reassert their social and cultural superiority as snobs lecturing slobs.

Brook undercuts the arguments within his own film through the peculiar stylization of his spectacles. The players act out incidents from America and Vietnam in England. An American GI wanders into Saigon in the guise of a British actor in Soho. The screen being the vivid medium that it is, the most casual viewer cannot escape the impression that Peter Brook and his associates are establishing some meaningful link between Saigon and Soho beyond mere impersonation. It is all right on the stage to say that these bare boards equal Agincourt and this hobbyhorse the French cavalry, but every screen setting, however stylized or allegorical, must answer for its own plastic reality. Also, the screen audience can never be assumed to possess the cultural cohesion of the stage audience.

If I find it difficult to come to grips with Brook's film, it is because too much of it is fragmented and undigested. Brook goes off in too many different directions without reaching any destinations. Stokeley Carmichael livens up the proceedings for a while simply by being Stokeley Carmichael. I couldn't take my eyes off his button-down shirt and striped tie as he recited his revolutionary rhetoric. He is playing a role like the rest of us, but he has staked his life on that role. The stars of Vietnam are LBJ and Ho, Westmoreland and Giap, and they are all playing the parts history has assigned them. Senator Eugene McCarthy is waiting in the wings for a piece of scenery to fall on the actor he is understudying, and Senator Robert F. Kennedy is sulking in his dressing room. And after looking at this multibillion-dollar Hollywood superproduction of *Tell Me Lies* week after week and month after month, it is difficult to see how a threadbare, cut-rate British company that can't even afford the proper scenery and sound effects is going to change the course of history.

—*Village Voice*, February 29, 1968

■ *5. BENJAMIN*

Michel Deville's *Benjamin* may not restore civilized heterosexuality to twentieth-century New York from eighteenth-century France, but it tries. We should be grateful for the grace and lightness of the effort at a time when latent homosexuality and permissive pansexuality seem to rule the roost and a columnist can report that Elizabeth Taylor is pleading with Richard Burton not to play a homosexual role in *The Staircase* and the great chase is degenerating into a drag race. At the very least, *Benjamin* reminds us of the distinctions and differentiations between men and women, and *Vive la différence* and all that. Catherine Deneuve, Francine Berge, Catherine Rouvel, Anna Gael, and even the poignantly aging Michèle Morgan and Odile Versois and an array of less prominently featured females provide all the delectable distractions a nostalgic libertine could desire. However, the body (*le corps*) is merely the scenic gateway to that holiest of holies, the heart (*le coeur*).

The eponymous hero of *Benjamin* (Pierre Clementi) is a male virgin initiated into the rites of love by a society that lives for little else. Elaborate rules have evolved in this realm of overflowing bodices and courtly cruelties. The sentimental and sensual education of a young man prepares him for a life through which he will pursue women till he finds the dark at the end of the tunnel. His life's pleasures will be measured by the women he has wooed and won. It is a chase to death, but *Benjamin* stops short of death to let its weary males catch their breath and regain their dignity. Swelling bosoms and sparkling eyes taunt the hero at every turn. Happiness lurks in the next rendezvous, on the next bed, but intrigue intervenes with maddening perversity until wisdom has finally been acquired at the expense of innocence. Two virgins participate in mutual defloration without love and the diary ends in disenchantment.

Michel Deville orchestrates desire with movement. Benjamin and his aunt's lover (Michel Piccoli) ride off furiously in all directions in pursuit of elusive pleasures. Benjamin runs hither and yon against an inexorable clock toward his inexhaustible yearnings. But Benjamin's and the film's finest moment comes at a rendezvous less with beauty than with truth in front of a mirror at which Michèle Morgan's jilted countess surveys her own faded charms. (Miss Morgan's beautifully stark cheekbones in *Symphonie Pastorale* have finally dissolved into mushy makeup; her eyes have lost their austere luster to make the Pirandellian pathos of her performance complete.) Benjamin looks into that same mirror and tells the countess that she is the most beautiful woman of the region, and at that moment he finds his soul by perceiving the pain and vulnerability of another human being.

Nina Companeez' dialogues may be modeled after Marivaux, but the editing of anguished expressions and reactions is worthy of Turgenev's *First Love*. Indeed, the eye-play quadrille of Morgan, Deneuve, Clementi, and Piccoli confirms Deville's early promise (*Ce Soir ou Jamais* and *La Menteuse*) as the French Lubitsch. And if Deville should happen to be underrated by Americans, well, so was Lubitsch. Directors who make difficult things look easy are seldom appreciated adequately.

—*Village Voice*, March 28, 1968

■ 6. CARL DREYER 1889–1968

Carl Theodor Dreyer, a man always out of season, now belongs to the agelessness of art. He died a few days ago in Denmark at the age of seventy-nine. All in all, fourteen features and five documentaries constitute the legacy of half a century of Dreyer's desperately personal film-making. No fewer than nine of his features were silent movies commissioned and delivered in the decade between 1918 and 1928, and culminating in his most celebrated achievement, *The Passion of Joan of Arc*, with Marie Falconetti. Thirty years later Godard paid tribute to Dreyer by cross-cutting Karina's tears with Falconetti's within his own Passion of a prostitute, *My Life to Live*.

Unfortunately, Dreyer's Passion did not end with *Joan of Arc*. It was only beginning. The intervals of inactivity in the next forty years speak for themselves. *Vampyr* (1932), *Day of Wrath* (1943), *Two People* (1945), *Ordet* (1955), and *Gertrud* (1965). Along the way Dreyer acquired admirers, but not backers. His talking films were stronger in the long haul than in the short run. *Day of Wrath* ran for only one week at the Little Carnegie despite raves from Archer Winsten and the late James Agee. *Vampyr* never achieved the vogue of such inferior horror films as James Whale's *Frankenstein* and Tod Browning's *Dracula*. *Gertrud* concluded Dreyer's career on a note of critical scandal and commercial disaster. His difficulties with financiers made such intransigent individualists as Buñuel and Stroheim seem like Dale Carnegies by comparison.

Buñuel and Stroheim could at least promise the titillation of shock and sacrilege; Dreyer, like Bresson, could offer nothing but austerity and eternity.

Dreyer was never so much ahead of his time as out of his time. No critic ever described him as "modern." *The Passion of Joan of Arc* seemed backward in its period, not only because it was a silent movie released in the midst of talkies with all the self-consciousness of an "art" film but also because Dreyer's enormous close-ups lacked the structural dynamism of Eisenstein's dialectical montage in *Potemkin* and *October*. *Day of Wrath* struck most critics of its time as too slowly paced for the demands of film art. The sin of *Gertrud* was that it dared to be deliberately slow and stately in an era in which film critics worshipped the cinematic virtuosity of elongated television commercials. For Dreyer, unfortunately, there were no short cuts or even jump-cuts to eternity.

Dreyer was never as interested in jazzy film techniques as in the subtlest feelings that could be expressed through the human face by a staring camera. He was therefore less a dramatist than a portraitist, but a portraitist gifted with a metaphysical urgency and implacability. His gallery of witches, bigots, persecutors, sensualists, and perverts never became a rogues' gallery, simply because Dreyer saw the torments of his characters in terms of a world still governed by God. For Carl Theodor Dreyer, man, not the medium, was the message.

—*New York Times*, March 31, 1968

II

The death of Carl Theodor Dreyer (1889–1968) last week finally ended his quest for funds to film the life of Jesus in Israel. Dream films have a way of never being made, and perhaps that is all to the good. A director's loveliest and most lucid works are often those he turns out in the wakeful interludes between his dreams. *The Parson's Widow, Mikael, Master of the House,* and *The Bride of Glomdale* constitute the peak of Dreyer's classical, commissioned period. They round out the Dreyer we might have known only from *The Passion of Joan of Arc, Vampyr, Day of Wrath,* and *Ordet,* and for this rounding out of the director we are deeply indebted to the Museum of Modern Art Dreyer retrospective organized in 1964 by Miss Eileen Bowser. Indeed, Miss Bowser's *The Films of Carl Dreyer* is one of the few sustained pieces of scholarly writing I have ever encountered on the Danish master.

I met Dreyer very briefly in 1965 when he came to New York for the showing of his last film, *Gertrud,* to a generally disastrous critical reception. I felt a curious spiritual resemblance between Dreyer and Robert Frost, and even now the lines from *The Road Not Taken* come to mind: "Two roads diverged in a wood, and I—/ I took the one less traveled by,/ And that has made all the difference." *Gertrud* was Dreyer's *The Road Not Taken,* a visual sigh on the screen for the emotional aridity of art as a vocation, a vocal curse on the inability to compromise. Both Dreyer and Frost have been carelessly categorized out of modish urban indifference to their personalities, Dreyer as a mindless mystic, Frost as a rousing rustic. Both, I think, were brilliant monsters with the ability to express the chill in their hearts. The past was for Dreyer what the country was for Frost—a refuge from the living in the midst of life.

It is too soon and too late to write more definitively of Dreyer, but the gallery of Dreyer faces will never fade, particularly the old actress playing the dying *Parson's Widow* as her own life is ebbing away, and then invisibly passing on her wifely-hooded silhouette to the young woman replacing her in the last shot of a film in which Dreyer dances comically on the edge of eternity. *Mikael* is the perverse side of *Gertrud.* Here Dreyer's characters follow their sensual impulses to the point of self-destruction as Dreyer establishes once and for all his view of sensuality as treacherous and illusory. The homosexual theme (supposedly based on the life of Rodin, according to Miss Bowser) is subordinated to a moral accounting in a world still (and in Dreyer's world always) governed by God. *Master of the House* and *The Bride of Glomdale* were Dreyer's sunniest films, his only excursions into the emotional alternatives of normal family life and romantic courtship. With the *Passion of Joan of Arc* Dreyer embarked irrevocably on the road of abnormal obsessiveness, and that made all the difference.

—*Village Voice,* March 28, 1968

■ 7. *LA CHINOISE; MADIGAN*

Jean-Luc Godard's *La Chinoise* is as successful with its fragmented forms as *Made in USA* and *Two or Three Things I Know About Her* were unsuccessful. Almost everything works as it should in *La Chinoise*, and the result is the kind of charm and enchantment we had almost stopped associating with the increasingly joyless Jean-Luc. What bothered me most about *Made in USA* and *Two or Three Things* was Godard's confusing his fleeting impressions of reality with reality itself. The visual flair was still evident, but the ideas were banal. The poet was pontificating like a pundit, and his films were becoming bloated with redundant rhetoric. More and more, Godard was saying what he meant instead of showing what he felt. After the suicidal climax and confessional of *Pierrot le Fou* it seemed that he was following the safe path of cerebral deviousness by exploiting the most provincial prejudices of the Idiot Left. Anna Karina in *USA* and Marina Vlady in *Two or Three Things* were less characters than puppets, less directed than manipulated by their master's voice.

Godard's apparent decline could not have come at a worse time for his American admirers. It was hard enough getting any of his films distributed without publicizing his clinkers. Godard's inane interviews did not help matters very much. His description of Hollywood movies as "the gangrene of world cinema" could be chalked off to the political passion inherent in a project called *Far from Vietnam*, but his cranky comments about other people's movies and motives sounded as if the thousand flowers of the *nouvelle vague* were withering away into the jealous, poisonous weeds of anti-Hollywood conformity. Long, long ago I had loved Godard's criticism for its open-mindedness. The movies were everything, Godard had insisted, from Hitchcock to Rossellini, from Eisenstein to Flaherty. Now suddenly the movies were only what Godard and his cronies permitted them to be. This moviegoer still prefers the original description of the cinema as everything from Jean-Luc Godard's *La Chinoise* to Donald Siegel's *Madigan*.

Critical orientation aside, *La Chinoise* is the most perceptive film about modern youth since *Masculine Feminine*, which is another way of saying that Godard is the only contemporary director with the ability to express through graceful cinema what young people are feeling at this time in world history. Not all young people, of course, only the heroic hotheads. Anne Wiazemsky, out of Bresson's *Balthazar*, has replaced Anna Karina as Godard's Galatea. At first it seems that Godard has sought to transform a severe ascetic into a Sorbonne soubrette, perhaps even Anne into a facsimile of Anna—eyes wide and lips slightly parted—but the impression fades. Anne Wiazemsky is all mandarin, as Anna Karina was all marshmallow, and Godard has learned to keep his distance. Jean-Pierre Léaud is the actor of the troupe, and he, too, transcends himself by being himself as he walks the tightrope between Mao and Artaud, between the politics of terror and the theater of cruelty.

La Chinoise is filmed as if it were in the process of being filmed. We see the clapper boards banging together at the beginning of scenes that do not always come to a conclusion. Godard's voice can be heard in the background of *cinéma vérité* scenes, but softly now, always softly, as if he were conversing with beings possessed of otherness rather than mere reflections and echoes. Perhaps Godard does not yet understand Anne Wiazemsky well enough to know her every move and calculate her every mood. Perhaps he was simply fascinated by the facility with which she expressed the inexorable intolerance of youth.

La Chinoise is beautifully photographed. Never have I seen posters and photographs so well integrated with characterization. This is what I missed in *The Edge*. Robert Kramer is too intellectual to let us see even the graffiti we encounter accidentally. No two people ever talk about a subject that could possibly be of interest to a third person. Kramer's directorial tact dooms him to inexpressiveness and boredom. I respect the dignity and intelligence of *The Edge*, and I might even be willing to grant that Robert Kramer is a better human being than Jean-Luc Godard, but *La Chinoise* remains a mountain of scenic splendor, whereas *The Edge* remains an arid plain of unrelieved flatness except for the mechanism and symbolism of Kramer's Golden Bowl.

Such articulate defenders of *The Edge* as James Stoller, Roger Greenspun, and Stuart Byron have focused attention on the cups of coffee involved in the deliberations of the protagonists. By a strange coincidence Godard has one of his characters dunk rolls into a bowl of *café au lait* while he is explaining his defection from a young Maoist cell in the New Left of Paris. Godard's character would rather eat than talk; Kramer's would all rather talk than eat. They handle their utensils as if they were sacramental objects. They are never dominated by their decor or by the food they eat, but by thus being somewhat more than human, they are much less than human. Godard's character succeeds in emphasizing what is most poignantly ephemeral about the proceedings because Godard's vision enables the director to see a meal and a message on the same level of history. Kramer's direction suffers from a visual paranoia that causes him to blame objects for human misery. Perhaps it is unfair to compare Godard and Kramer, but, unfortunately, *La Chinoise* makes *The Edge* and Clive Donner's *Here We Go Round the Mulberry Bush* seem somewhat superfluous as statements of the Zeitgeist. It might be argued that *The Edge* is what happens to the people in *La Chinoise* ten years later, except that Godard will probably be on hand ten years from now with a superior version of *The Edge*.

Ultimately, Godard is superior to the New American humanists because he is cursed with a fantastic memory of the medium. There are bits of Lubitsch and Ophuls in the back-and-forth tracks within scenes, across the obstacles of walls, and the apertures of open shutters. These tracks, so effective here, were often irritating in *A Woman Is a Woman* and *Contempt*. (Godard even repeats a song from *A Woman Is a Woman* to link Anne to Anna.) However, the most extraordinary movements in the film come out of Murnau —a sliding gate reminiscent of the ship's sail entering the frame in Murnau's *Tabu*, and an extraordinary trip viewed through a train window situated between two speakers, to remind us forcibly of the Janet Gaynor-George O'Brien trolley ride in Murnau's *Sunrise*. The fact that the two speakers—Anne Wiazemsky and Francis Jeanson—are debating the uses of terror in a smug society as the country to be terrorized passes serenely outside their window only enhances Godard's stylistic coup with thematic relevance. The world is so big, Godard implies, and time is so short (for youth as well as for revolution), and the bravest men of the past seem like cowards in the present. Jeanson himself was exiled for his stand on the Algerian war, but he can offer no encouragement to the Parisian Maoists. For his part, Godard now perceives fully the chasm between thought and action. He stays with the students for their summer and takes them on their own terms, but in the very heat of summer he can anticipate the winter of their discontent. *La Chinoise* is more than Godard's valentine to youth; it is also his valedictory.

Madigan is a reminder of the often forgotten virtues of classical editing. Don Siegel's most successful films express the doomed peculiarity of the antisocial outcast—Neville Brand (*Riot in Cell Block 11*), Steve Cochran (*Private Hell 36*) Mickey Rooney (*Baby Face Nelson*), Eli Wallach (*The Line-Up*), Elvis Presley (*Flaming Star*), Steve McQueen (*Hell Is for Heroes*), and now Richard Widmark in *Madigan*. In addition, *Invasion of the Body Snatchers* is one of the few authentic science-fiction classics by virtue of its matter-of-fact visualization of paranoia.

Madigan sports a lovely New York look from Graeme Ferguson's title shots of the Big City to Russell Metty's expert match-ups of location and studio footage. The screenplay by Henri Simoun and Abraham Polonsky is characterized by that note of urban romanticism we associate with *Body and Soul* and *Force of Evil*, and it is good to see Polonsky back from exile on a credit sheet.

The strength of *Madigan* is the seriousness of its genre and the morally grayish tint of its characterizations. Henry Fonda's police commissioner walks around as if he has something else on his mind, and he usually has. Richard Widmark's detective on the spot lives on the edge of his nerves. Between them Fonda and Widmark express the two aspects of life in New York—Fonda the clouded view from the top, Widmark the desperate urgency around the next corner. New York is a city where the future is always colliding with the past, and the moral arithmetic never quite adds up.

The characterizations are finally wrapped up when the string runs out on a manhunt for a cop killer, and, to Siegel's credit, the ending explodes with emotional force without a wasted move or extra shot. The characterizations would not have been sufficient in themselves, or the action sufficient in itself, but welded together by Siegel's familiar style of editing, *Madigan* turns out to be the best American movie I have seen so far in 1968. It was particularly heartening to find adulterous situations stopping on the brink of the abyss because of the character's feelings rather than the censor's wrath. After all, it is as naïve for Hollywood to assume that every sexual fantasy is fulfilled in "real" life as that none are, or that the libidinous realm of Jeanne Moreau is any less fantastic than Doris Day's filtered vale of virginity.

—*Village* Voice, April 4, 1968

■ 8. *BELLE DE JOUR*

Luis Buñuel's *Belle de Jour* has evoked in many critiques that all-purpose adjective "beautiful." Catherine Deneuve is undeniably beautiful, never more so than in this context of Buñuelian perversity, and almost any meaningfully designed color film seems beautiful, if only because the vast subconscious sea of the cinema is safely gelatinized within the frames of an academic painting. Describing a film as beautiful is unfortunately too often a device to end discussion, particularly nowadays when irrationality and hysteria have become institutionalized as life styles. *Elvira Madigan* is beautiful in the way flowery poems are poetical, not through functional expressiveness but through lyrical excessiveness. *Bonnie and Clyde* is beautiful when its concluding slow-motion ballet of death and transfiguration takes the audience off the hook by distancing the characters back into legend and fantasy. The fact that the close-ups contradict the distancing is immaterial to the film's admirers. *Bonnie and Clyde* is beautiful, and consistency is the hobgoblin of little minds.

I would argue that *Belle de Jour* is indeed a beautiful film, but not because of any anesthetizing aesthetic of benevolently mindless lyricism. Nor is the film beautiful because its director's visual style transcends its sordid subject. The beauty of *Belle de Jour* is the beauty of artistic rigor and adaptable intelligence. Given what Buñuel is at sixty-seven, and what he has done in forty years and twenty-seven projects of film-making, and what and whom he had to work with and for, *Belle de Jour* reverberates with the cruel logic of formal necessity. From the opening shot of an open carriage approaching the camera at an oblique ground-level angle to the closing shot of an open carriage passing the camera at an oblique overhead angle, the film progresses inexorably upward, an ascent of assent, from the reverie of suppressed desires to the revelation of fulfilled fantasies. But whose desires and whose fantasies? Buñuel's? His heroine's? Actually, a bit of both. The exact proportion of subjective contemplation to objective correlative can best be calculated by comparing Joseph Kessel's basic anecdotal material with what appears on the screen.

In his preface to *Belle de Jour* Kessel writes: "The subject of *Belle de Jour* is not Severine's sensual aberration; it is her love for Pierre independent of that aberration, and it is the tragedy of that love." Kessel concludes his preface with a reprovingly rhetorical question for those critics who dismissed *Belle de Jour* as a piece of pathological observation: "Shall I be the only one to pity Severine, and to love her?"

The "sensual aberration" of which Kessel writes undoubtedly seemed more shocking in 1929, when the first French edition was published, than it would seem in the current period of erotic escalation. Severine Serizy, happily married to a handsome young surgeon, goes to work in a house of ill repute, actually less a house than an intimate apartment. The money involved is less the motivation than the pretext for her action. Pierre, her husband, provides for her material needs handsomely, but his respectfully temporizing caresses fail to satisfy her psychic need for brutal degradation, a need first awakened by a malodorous molester when she was a child of eight. To preserve a façade of marital respectability, Severine works at her obsessive profession only afternoons from two to five, the mystery of her matinee schedule causing her to be christened Belle de Jour. Kessel's novel, like his heroine, is fatally divided between clinical observations on sexual psychology and novelistic contrivances to overcome the innate lethargy of a woman of leisure. Husson, a weary sensualist in her husband's circle of friends, is a particularly intricate contrivance in that he triggers much of the novel's intrigue. It is Husson who first alerts Severine to her own frustrations by his unwelcome advances. It is he who inadvertently supplies her with the address of her sensual destiny, and who, discovering her double life, poses such a threat to her non–Belle de Jour existence that he precipitates, almost innocently, the final catastrophe.

Marcel, a gold-toothed gangster infatuated with Belle de Jour, provides a violently melodramatic climax to the novel by agreeing to murder Husson to preserve Severine's secret and Belle de Jour's respect. Irony is piled upon irony as Marcel's assault on Husson is deflected by Pierre, who is so grievously wounded that he is confined for life to helpless paralysis in a wheelchair. Marcel and Husson remain silent about Belle de Jour, thus enabling Severine to escape a public scandal and even prosecution. But perverse to the end, she confesses everything to Pierre, and is rewarded not with his forgiveness but with his stern silence.

Buñuel and his coscenarist, Jean-Claude Carrière, have retained most of the characters of the novel. Severine goes to work for Madame Anaïs in both novel and film, and Belle de Jour's colleagues are Charlotte and Mathilde in both versions. The most striking variation between novel and film is in the elaborately structured dream apparatus of the film. Kessel's Severine never dreams the concrete images of Buñuel's surreal reveries of feminine masochism. There are no floggings in the book, as there are in the film, no binding of hands with ropes, no sealing of mouths, no splattering with mud. Kessel's Severine never really dreams at all; she merely recollects the past and anticipates the future. If the novel had been filmed in the thirties or forties by a French director trained in the Tradition of Quality, a Marcel Carné or Claude Autant-Lara perhaps, Severine would probably have been played with many shimmering close-ups to dramatize the desperate conflict between her feelings and her senses. The background music would have been exquisitely sentimental. Except for the bells that signal the movement of the horse-drawn carriage, Buñuel uses no music whatsoever. No Simon and Garfunkel, no Beatles, no Donovan, not even the realistically based music of radios and record players. There is no radio or television in the modern world of Belle de Jour, but there is a Geisha Club credit card. Buñuel has stripped modernity of its specificity. Thus we are not bothered so much by the suspicion that horse-drawn carriages are not as likely to figure in the reveries of Severine's (or Catherine Deneuve's) generation as in the memories of Buñuel's. The fact that Buñuel does not employ music in *Belle de Jour* is not significant as a matter of general aesthetic policy. Buñuel himself has derived ironic counterpoint from the musical backgrounds of such recent films as *Viridiana* and *Simon of the Desert*. He must have felt that he didn't need music to underscore the fundamental irony implicit in a woman with the face of an angel and the lusts of a devil. Still, *Belle de Jour* overcomes an awesome handicap of affect by disdaining the facile frissons of music.

Many of the script changes were dictated by the differences in the media. Pierre emerges through Jean Sorel as a much duller character than in the book, but it is difficult to see what any director could do with the character of the Noble Husband in such a grotesque context. The changes in Husson's character are more meaningful. Kessel's Husson was more mannered in his ennui, but he takes advantage of Severine's degraded status as Belle de Jour to possess her body. Buñuel's Husson (Michel Piccoli) is more fastidious; he loses interest in Severine at precisely the instant she becomes available to him as Belle de Jour. But it is Buñuel's Husson who tells Pierre of Belle De Jour after the accident; Kessel's Husson never seriously contemplated such a course of action before or after.

Kessel wants us to love Severine by identifying with her; Buñuel wants us to understand Severine by contemplating the nature of her obsession. Instead of indulging in Kessel's sentimental psychology by staring into Catherine Deneuve's eyes, Buñuel fragments Deneuve's body into its erotic constituents. His shots of feet, hands, legs, shoes, stockings, undergarments are the shots not only of a fetishist but of a cubist, a director concerned simultaneously with the parts and their effect on the whole. Buñuel's graceful camera movements convey Deneuve to her sensual destiny through her black patent-leather shoes, and to her final reverie through her ringed fingers feeling their way along the furniture with the tactile tenderness of a mystical sensuality—Severine's, Deneuve's or Buñuel's, it makes little difference.

The beauty of the filmed version of *Belle de Jour* arises from its implication of Buñuel in its vision of the world. It is Buñuel himself who is the most devoted patron of Chez Madame Anaïs and the most pathetic admirer of Catherine Deneuve's Severine–Belle de Jour. Never before has Buñuel's view of the spectacle seemed so obliquely Ophulsian in its shy gaze from behind curtains, windows, and even peepholes. Buñuel's love of Severine is greater than Kessel's, simply because Buñuel sees Belle de Jour as Severine's liberator. The sensuality of *Belle de Jour* is not metaphorical, like Genet's in *The Balcony* or Albee's in *Everything in the Garden*. Most writers, even the most radical, treat prostitution as a symptom of a social malaise and not as a concrete manifestation of a universal impulse. Buñuel reminds us once again in *Belle de Jour* that he is one of the few men of the Left not afflicted by puritanism and bourgeois notions of chastity and fidelity.

The difference between Buñuel and, say, Genet is not entirely a difference of ideology. It is more a difference between a man of images and a man of words. What distinguishes *Belle de Jour* from most movies is the impression it gives of having been seen in its director's mind long before it was shot. There is a preconceived exactness to its images that will inevitably disconcert middlebrow film critics, especially those who are highbrows in other cultural sectors. It is only the specialist in film who can fully appreciate the directness of Buñuel's images above and beyond the novelistic nuances he sacrifices on the altars of shock and laughter.

II

The ending of *Belle de Jour* is tantalizingly open as narrative. Husson has told Pierre about Belle de Jour, or at least we presume so. Buñuel does not show the scene, and we are not obliged to believe anything we do not see, but there is no particular reason to believe that Husson has not carried out his stated intention. Buñuel does not cast his audience adrift in a sea of ambiguity at every opportunity; he is simply not that interested in dramatic suspense. Severine enters Pierre's room, and for the first time in the film Buñuel's technique obscures the flow of action. Buñuel breaks up the spatial unity of the scene with alternative sights and sounds to indicate a range of possibilities. Cut to Jean Sorel's tear-stained face. Pierre Knows All and Feels Betrayed. Cut to his crumpled upturned hand. Pierre Is Dead from the Shock of His Grief. Cut on the sound track to the bells of a carriage, and to Sorel's voice asking of Deneuve's pensive face what Severine is thinking. Everything Turns Back to Fantasy.

Or does it? Some critics have suggested that Severine has been cured of her masochistic obsession by becoming Belle de Jour.

Hence the empty carriage at the end of the film. She will no longer take *that* trip. One French critic has argued that the entire film is a dream, but the big problem with such an argument is Buñuel's visually explicit brand of surrealism. Earlier in the film Husson calls on Severine at her home and is rudely rebuffed. Buñuel cuts immediately to a shockingly "cute" boy-girl profile two-shot of Severine and Husson at the ski lodge. As the camera pulls back we see Jean Sorel and Macha Meril at the same table. It must be a dream, we assure ourselves, while Severine and Husson slip out of sight under the table to perform some unspeakable act of sacrilege against bourgeois society. The table begins to bump up and down, but the deserted partners, Sorel and Meril, are only mildly concerned. Buñuel has transported *Belle de Jour* back to *L'Age d'Or*, but the effect of the scene is unsettling if we accept it as occurring in Severine's mind. Here I think Buñuel slipped into a sadistic attitude of his own toward Pierre, since this is the only scene in the film in which Pierre is made to look completely ridiculous. The key to the scene, however, is not Severine's characterization but Buñuel's satiric attitude toward Hollywood sentimentality. The profile shot more than the table-bumping gives the show away, but audiences would never "get" the joke without the table-bumping, and Buñuel does not disdain vulgarity as one of the strategies of surrealism.

Actually, we are such puritans that we talk of surrealism almost exclusively in the solemn terms of social defiance. Humor is only a means to an end, but not an end in itself. No, never? Well, hardly ever. And in Buñuel's case laughter serves to disinfect libertinism of its satanic aura. If we can laugh at the prissiness of perversion and the fastidiousness of fetishism not with smug superiority but with carnal complicity, we become too implicated to remain indifferent. Buñuel's masochist, unlike Genet's in *The Balcony*, satisfies his devious lechery by stroking the thighs of his professionally cruel mistress. Buñuel's brothel is a brothel and not one of Genet's microcosms, and Buñuel's sensuality turns in upon itself as an enclosed experience devoid of allegorical signification.

Similarly, the entire film turns in upon itself by ending with the same question with which it began: "Severine, what are you thinking of?" And Severine tells the truth, in her fashion. She thinks of places and conveyances and trips and herds of Spanish bulls named Remorse, except one named Expiation. At the end she is still dreaming, and who is to say that the dream is any less real or vivid than the reality it accompanies? Certainly not Buñuel's probing but compassionate camera. There are several possible interpretations of Buñuel's ending, but the formal symmetry of the film makes the debate academic. Buñuel is ultimately ambiguous so as not to moralize about his subject. He wishes neither to punish Severine nor to reward her. He prefers to contemplate the grace with which she accepts her fate, and Buñuel is nothing if not fatalistic. Even the hapless husband is granted a mystical premonition when he sees an empty wheelchair in the street. It is destined for him, and the concreteness of Buñuel's visual imagery is so intense that we feel that the wheelchair is as destined for Pierre as Pierre is destined for the wheelchair.

Buñuel's fatalism actually undercuts the suspense of the narrative to the extent that there is no intellectual pressure for a resolved ending. Between the fatalism and the formal symmetry, *Belle de Jour* seems completely articulated as a Buñuelian statement. We do not have to know what we are not meant to know, and Buñuel establishes a precedent within his film for the ambiguity of his ending. This precedent involves Madame Anaïs, after Severine the most absorbing character in the film. Alone of all the characters, Madame Anaïs is the truth-seeker, and she is inevitably far from the mark. She misunderstands the motivations of Belle de Jour from the outset, and she misinterprets Belle de Jour's departure. Still, she is always staring at Belle de Jour as if it were possible to peel away layers of lacquered flesh to the raw impulses underneath. The scenes in which Genevieve Page's Madame Anaïs gazes with loving curiosity at Catherine Deneuve's Belle de Jour gleam with a psychological insight not customary with Buñuel, or as rigorously empirical aestheticians would have it, the scenes gleam with the appearance of a psychological insight, the very beautiful appearance derived from two extraordinary screen incarnations.

The great irony of *Belle de Jour* is that a sixty-seven-year-old Spanish surrealist has set out to liberate humanity of its bourgeois sentimentality only to collide with the most sentimental generation of flowery feelings in human history.

—*Village Voice*, May 2 and 9, 1968

■ 9. DIRECTORS,
HOW PERSONAL CAN YOU GET?

Back in the days when producers were Hollywood deities a reporter began a remark to Sam Goldwyn by saying, "When William Wyler made *Wuthering Heights*—" The reporter never finished his sentence. "I made *Wuthering Heights*," Goldwyn snapped. "Wyler only directed it."

Goldwyn was merely applying the gold standard to the question of authorship when he chose to slight his employe's contribution as a form of creation. Nowadays there are complaints that the pendulum has swung too far toward the director. The new breed of film historian devotes chapters to the Wylers of this world and only footnotes to the Goldwyns. Since producers and other studio satraps always took the lion's share of the loot, few tears have been shed for their downfall.

But what of the other artists and craftsmen? Should Wyler now be honored for *Wuthering Heights* to the exclusion of original author Emily Brontë, scenarists Ben Hecht and Charles MacArthur, composer Alfred Newman, cameraman Gregg Toland, editor Daniel Mandel and players Laurence Olivier, Merle Oberon, Flora Robson, Geraldine Fitzgerald, Donald Crisp and David Niven?

Who, then, *is* the author of a film if not the director? The answer to this question is actually less important than the fact that the question is asked at all. Until very recently it was considered bad business to build up personality cults behind the camera. The Hollywood dream factories had a vested interest in convincing the public of the spontaneity of illusions on the screen, and most reviewers played it the company way by treating movies as corporate products rather than personal statements, however marginal. After a season's run, a movie would disappear from circulation as if it had never existed, and there would be no chance to compare the progress of a director from year to year.

Besides, some movie reviewers suffered from attacks of amnesia so acute that the studios could use the identical plot twice within four years with no one being the wiser. (Warners was so notorious in this regard that its script department was called the "echo chamber.") If movie reviewers were thus incapable of remembering plots from one year to the next, it was inconceivable that they could recall nuances of visual style with any consistency.

To make matters more hopeless, most scholarly works on the cinema were written from a predominantly sociological viewpoint, whence no director with a bank account escaped the stigmas of compromise, commercialism and corruption. The occasional exception to directorial decadence was usually long ago and far away, and a *Caligari-*to-*Potemkin* repertory was devised for those aesthetes who chose to see only a dozen films a decade. Another type of intellectual preferred to treat movies as raw material for his refined sensibility. Indeed, the currently fashionable poses of pop, camp and trivia have replaced kitsch as rationalizations for the guilt intellectuals feel when they see movies they shouldn't instead of reading books they should.

The fact that most directors do not write their own scripts is enough to discredit the role of the director in the eyes of the literary establishment. Such discredit is often unjustified even on literary grounds simply because many directors decline to take credit for collaborating on the writing of their films. John Ford, Alfred Hitchcock and Howard Hawks may never win the Nobel Prize for literature, but each of these directors has created a world of his own on film, a world no less unique for having been filtered through the varying verbalizations of scores of scriptwriters.

Furthermore, screenwriting involves more than mere dialogue and plot. The choice between a cut and a camera movement or a close-up and a long shot, for example, may quite often transcend the plot. If the story of Little Red Riding Hood is told with the Wolf in close-up and Little Red Riding Hood in long shot, the director is concerned primarily with the emotional problems of a wolf with a compulsion to eat little girls. If Little Red Riding Hood is in close-up and the Wolf in long shot, the emphasis is shifted to the emotional problems of vestigial virginity in a wicked world. (To cut back and forth between the two characters is to emphasize their conflict; to enclose them within a circular camera movement is to emphasize their complicity.)

Thus two different stories are being told with the same basic anecdotal material. What is at stake in the two versions of Little

Red Riding Hood is two contrasting directorial attitudes toward life. The first director identifies more with the Wolf, the male, the compulsive, the corrupted, even evil itself (Hitchcock, Lang, Buñuel, Chaplin, Welles). The second director identifies with the little girl, the innocence, the illusion, the ideal and hope of the race (Ophuls, Mizoguchi, Griffith, Fellini, Cukor).

Most movies are composed of approximately 600 separate shots. (One of my students counted over 1,800 separate shots in Sergei Eisenstein's *Ten Days That Shook the World*, but Eisenstein is, almost by definition, an extreme case.) When all this fragmentation is multiplied by all the possible choices of focal length and camera angle, the visual vocabulary of cinema is comparable in its expressive variety to verbal vocabulary.

The disparity between good direction and bad direction is thus as marked as the disparity between good writing and bad writing, but how many movie reviewers are capable of making the distinction even today? Visual atrocities like *The Tiger Makes Out* and *Barefoot in the Park* are reviewed respectfully in some quarters because of the theatrical prestige of Murray Schisgal and Neil Simon, respectively, while visually graceful but verbally awkward works like Orson Welles's *Falstaff* and Roman Polanski's *The Vampire Killers* are denounced out of hand as complete disasters. This is only the most recent proof that most reviewers do not really look at movies, but merely listen to scripts being read aloud on the screen. Similarly, the visual wit and beauty of *Gunn* (Blake Edwards) and *Point Blank* (John Boorman) cannot be appreciated by movie reviewers afflicted with genre prejudices and an inability to adjust to the age of the color film.

If directors have been enthroned as the authors of films, it is only because they are expected to be if film is to be considered an art. Directors, like kings, may reign and not rule. There is no doubt that the author and prime mover of *The Americanization of Emily* is writer Paddy Chayefsky rather than director Arthur Hiller, but the weakness of the film is precisely its lack of a consistent point of view that only direction can provide. Not that even the most influential screenwriters are necessarily as original as they seem. Dudley Nichols' script has received almost as much credit for *Stagecoach* as John Ford's direction, but the literary ghost hovering over the entire project is de Maupassant.

Authorship is thus a subtler issue than mere origination, and the innumerable exceptions to directorial dominance do not alter the strategic position of the director. Only the director is capable of preserving formal order in all the chaos of filmic creation. Only the director can provide a unity of style out of all the diverse ingredients at his disposal. The writer will find his words chopped up into shots. The actor who performs continuously on the stage is recorded intermittently on the set, where his part is slowly eroded out of sequence into little bits and pieces. Under these conditions, a stage Hamlet is reduced on the screen to the impotence of Rosencrantz and Guildenstern.

For more than half a century, Hollywood directors have devised the most economical methods of expression. To understand anything genuinely new in the cinema, we must come to understand the classical tradition these directors represent, but an understanding of any director requires a comprehensive view of his work. Only in the total context of a directorial career is it possible to perceive the chilling professionalism of Howard Hawks in *Scarface,* the Pirandellian precision of Ernst Lubitsch in *Angel,* the political resurgence of Jean Renoir in *Diary of a Chambermaid,* the numbing nostalgia of Orson Welles in *The Magnificent Ambersons,* the tragic sensibility of Max Ophuls in *Letter From an Unknown Woman,* the evocation of lost family in John Ford's *The Searchers,* the delirious tremors of Alfred Hitchcock's *Vertigo,* and the vertiginous descent into childhood and infantilism of Otto Preminger's *Bunny Lake Is Missing.* Against these intimations of personal expression, the relatively impersonal direction of Fred Zinnemann for *A Man for All Seasons,* David Lean for *The Bridge on the River Kwai,* and William Wyler for *The Best Years of Our Lives* seems relatively boring.

Zinnemann, Lean and Wyler are undeniably talented men, and their best films are impressively mounted, but in a certain school of criticism these directors are derogated for their lack of an emotionally expressive style. François Truffaut became the spokesman of this school back in 1954 in the pages of *Cahiers du Cinéma,* where he quoted the aphorism of Giraudoux: "There are no works; there are only authors." The Saganesque seducer asks *"Aimez-vous Brahms?"* without specifying the symphony, and we speak of "Tolstoy" and "Shakespeare" and "Nabokov" for a body of work rather than a single specimen. Truffaut argued that the same principle should be applied to certain film directors, and to emphasize his point he declared that the worst film of Jean Renoir was more interesting than the best film of Jean Delannoy, a director remembered mainly for *Symphonie Pastorale* and represented most recently by *This Special Friendship*.

Why was Renoir so transcendentally superior to Delannoy? Because, according to Truffaut, Renoir transcended his scripts and script writer with a personal style that reflected his vision of the world rather than any literary formula. Being for Renoir and against Delannoy constituted one of the canons of Truffaut's *Politiques des Auteurs*, later shortened in America to the "auteur theory" to explain a critical approach by which every critique assumes the historical burden of artistic biography. To review John Ford's *Seven Women* in 1966, it becomes relevant to the *auteur* critic to cite a frame in Ford's *Straight Shooting* of 1917.

A by-product of the *auteur* theory is a preference for small subjects over large, adaptations of pulp novels over adaptations of literary classics, westerns over working-class allegories. By this standard, Mike Nichols earned his diploma as an *auteur* more for *The Graduate*, with its humble literary origins, than for *Who's Afraid of Virginia Woolf?* with its awesome dramatic laurels. Whereas Nichols merely *transferred Virginia Woolf*, he *transcended The Graduate* with his very personal way of directing actors in action.

Ultimately, the search for meaningful authorship on the screen does not denigrate the roles of writer, actor, composer, cameraman and editor. Ideally the director should write his own films and, failing that, should at least be in emotional and intellectual sympathy with his scripts. If novelists and dramatists wish to take over the cinema, and they may have to some day, they must accept the problems of direction. Frederic Raphael has observed that writers tend to change the world while directors have to face the world as it is in all its intransigence. The writer can create a glorious heroine, but the director must cope with a ham actress. The writer is a creature of aspirations, the director a creature of limitations. In any event, the search for the author of a film is beneficial if only because it keeps the searchers concerned with questions of personal artistic responsibility at a time when all art is threatened by the impersonality of an environmental happening. The search is dedicated also to the proposition that art and even effective entertainment cannot be entirely accidental.

—*The New York Times*, May 12, 1968

■ 10. *THE YOUNG GIRLS OF ROCHEFORT*

Jacques Demy's *The Young Girls of Rochefort* tries to float like a butterfly and sting like a bee, but too often it gets tangled up in its fancy footwork. The imitation Jerome Robbins slouch-shouldered choreography is ludicrous enough in a Gallic context, but the casting of Gene Kelly (too late) and George Chakiris (too smilingly slight) is fatal to the spell of this latest Demy-monde. *The Young Girls* is less graceful than *Lola* and less lyrical than *The Umbrellas of Cherbourg*, but it is curiously charming just the same. Demy has not really revitalized the musical form. He has merely taken from the musical those liberties and contrivances that serve his own poetic sensibility. In his Odyssey from Nantes (*Lola*), to Cherbourg (*Umbrellas*), to Rochefort (*Girls*), Demy comes ever closer to the glossy sophistication of Paris.

There is an increasing urgency and desperation from film to film, as if Demy were trying to remember something he would never have time to realize on the screen. Even within the film itself, the sister act of Catherine Deneuve and Françoise Dorléac is shadowed by the offscreen death of Miss Dorléac in an auto accident last year. Demy keeps referring to characters from his earlier films, but he can only cite names of characters. The faces are all mixed up. Long before Lelouch's *A Man and a Woman* Demy wanted Jean-Louis Trintignant to appear with Anouk Aimée in *Lola*. The director settled for Marc Michel instead, and used Michel again for *Umbrellas*. Demy wanted Danielle Darrieux for the mother role in *Umbrellas*, but had to make do with Anne Vernon. He took over the town of Rochefort and repainted it to his aesthetic specifications, but he didn't have enough money to repopulate it with singing-dancing sprites of all ages, genders, and callings. In a sense, he had too much money but not enough.

Demy did not really "use" Rochefort the way he used Nantes. Rochefort remains more a set than a place, partly because Demy's sense of color is too functionally expressive and partly because dancers tend to transform real space into abstract space. Once a dancer begins gliding down a street in pursuit of the camera, the street loses its spatial coordinates. To make matters worse, the choreography in *Young Girls* seldom advances or even enhances the plot. George Chakiris and Grover Dale romp about (with faceless female partners) with all the narrative relevance of station breaks.

Fortunately, the "straight" people are more effective. Michel Piccoli is particularly affecting as Simon Dame, the failed composer and music-store proprietor, the man with a name so ridiculous for a prospective wife (Madame Dame) that he is jilted by Danielle Darrieux as the mother of twins (Deneuve and Dorléac), who grow up to find their romantic destiny in an abstract painter (Jacques Perrin) and an American composer (Gene Kelly, alas) respectively. In Rochefort, as in Nantes and Cherbourg, there is the feeling of irrevocable destiny. There are the people who venture forth and the people who are left behind, and sometimes the people who have ventured forth come back to the people who have been left behind. Making it, in the world of Jacques Demy, is a sad, futile business. Wherever you go and whatever you do, you inevitably end up in a bistro somewhere telling stories about some lost love or cherished ideal. Legrand's music has been criticized by some critics for its excessive sentimentality, but I thought it was just right for the feeling of yearning it sought to express. If the dramatic people—Piccoli, Darrieux, Perrin—are infinitely superior to the musical people—Kelly, Chakiris, Dale—the Rochefort girls themselves fall somewhere between. For some reason Demy has directed Deneuve and Dorléac with more brass and pizazz than they seem capable of absorbing. When they do their big slinky, sleazy red-dress number, there is something of the put-on in the production. There is none of that marvelously knowing female rapport Bardot and Moreau projected in Louis Malle's *Viva Maria*. Somehow Bardot and Moreau managed to be more themselves by sharing their private joke on all males.

With all that is wrong with *The Young Girls of Rochefort*, it is amazing how much pleasure it provides. I have enormous respect for Demy's effort, simply because it is so much easier to make a cosmic statement full of open-ended ambiguities than to turn out a reasonably entertaining musical. Jean-Luc Godard's *La Chinoise* may be more successful in what it sets out to do, but it is not one-tenth as ambitious as *The Young Girls of Rochefort*. Intellectuals have always been baffled by the mystique of the musical. The more serious film histories barely mention the subject, but the fact remains that while the aesthetes were moaning about the loss of pantomime and visual metaphor back in 1929, the musicals burst upon the scene with an unappreciated poetic force. People who talk about cinema as a visual art form seldom acknowledge the enormous debt the "purest" cinema owes to music. Fellini is taken seriously largely because he knows how to exploit Nino Rota's imitation Chaplin melodies without implicating himself in their sentimentality. Everything is passed over as lower-class pathos, middle-class nostalgia, or upper-class satire. The so-called Brechtian musical of our time prides itself on its conscious ironies because it is catering to an audience that feels superior to musicals. Demy deserves credit for making a musical at all in this poisonously self-conscious atmosphere, and even more for discovering the source of poetic enchantment in all musicals.

—*Village Voice*, May 16, 1968

■ 11. *PETULIA*

If a project called *Petulia* had been tossed into the Hollywood hopper back in the thirties (that somewhat tarnished but still tawdry decade), the first change would have been in the title. Too close to Petunia, an executive of that era can almost be heard saying, and who'd ever go out with a girl called Petunia, forgodsakes! Of course that's the whole point of Petulia as a piece of contemporary nomenclature. Petulia is a consciously ugly, spikey, I-don't-care-what-you-call-me-as-long-as-you-see-me-as-I-am kind of name, and it fully fits the arch kook Julie Christie cooks up in Richard Lester's *Petulia*. Julie clearly belongs more to the miniskirts and memory-and-anticipation cuts of the sixties than to the long skirts and watch-and-listen reaction shots of the thirties.

But once the plot of *Petulia* is unscrambled from Lester's mini-montage, the story line takes on the sentimental motivations of an era three decades ago, when kooks were called screwballs. Let's imagine that Carole Lombard, the loveliest screwball comedienne of her time, played the wistfully wiser but sadder wife of spoiled little rich boy Robert Montgomery in his anyone-for-tennis period. Lombard and Montgomery drive down to Mexico, where a cute little Mexican boy hitches a ride and refuses to get off. Lombard worries about what to do with the boy, but Montgomery treats the whole thing as a lark, and so the cherub comes north to San Francisco to live in rich daddy Lionel Barrymore's palatial home. After a Vorkapitch montage of marital stress, Montgomery shows a touch of *Night Must Fall* neuroticism by regarding the Mexican boy as a reproof to the vagueness of his own virility, and so *adios* to the boy, who runs distractedly into the street and is run over by a truck. Enter Spencer Tracy as the skillful surgeon operating on the boy while Lombard looks with grateful adoration through the observation window. She and Tracy then meet at a charity ball. He has just been divorced from Margaret Sullavan and is at loose ends. Lombard comes on like a high-society floozie, because out of some screwball shyness she doesn't want Tracy to suspect what she really feels about him. They go to a hotel, but she changes her mind, and thus they're hooked for life in a relationship that bypasses the flesh to go straight to the heart. Tracy sees Sullavan again, but it's no go. Even their two little boys can't bring them together again. Lombard comes to Tracy's bachelor apartment and spends the night there (platonically in the thirties and dialectically in the sixties). Tracy comes home from the hospital the next day to find Lombard brutally beaten by Robert Montgomery in a jealous rage right out of *Rage in Heaven*. Tracy rushes her to the hospital and saves her life.

Lionel Barrymore comes to the hospital and pleads with Lombard not to press charges against his son. She agrees and returns to Montgomery, and the whole family goes off on a cruise. Tracy does not see her again until she is back in the hospital to bear her husband's baby. At this point the Hays Office would have rigorously upheld the sacrament of marriage against any possibility of dramatic suspense. Tracy and Lombard would have been compelled to renounce each other, he to return to Sullavan and their

children, she to Montgomery and her child to be. Even if Montgomery were killed off violently as a jealous psychopath with suicidal inclinations, there would still be Sullavan. Whatever happened would have to be for the best in terms of the moral health of
the audience.

The ending of Lester's *Petulia* observes the letter but not the
spirit of the Hays code. George C. Scott's doctor stands over the
perilously pregnant Petulia and tells her there is still time for him
to call a private ambulance and take her away to where he would
never have to leave her again and she says yes yes, and he goes to
the phone but he cannot dial it because he lacks the courage of
his romantic sensibility, and the moment passes with the anguish
of a light joke and a tortured smile but she calls out his name
before she goes under the ether because deep down the girls of the
sixties are no different from the girls of the thirties.

Nonetheless Richard Lester's syncopated style disguises the material more than it develops it. Lester himself describes *Petulia* as
a "sentimental love story," and it is clear that his mini-montage
strives for the fragmented poetics of a "Petulia, Mon Amour." Unfortunately, Lester is no closer to Resnais than Jack Clayton was
to Antonioni in the poetically pregnant pauses of *The Pumpkin
Eater*. Not that Resnais and Antonioni are entirely free of sentimentality. Far from it. *L'Avventura* and *Muriel* achieve pathos
through a facile contrast between feeble feelings and the fearsome
expanses of time and space. But whereas the styles of Antonioni
and Resnais are related to the way these two directors see reality,
the styles of Clayton and Lester are related more to the manipulation of dramatic conventions to beguile the audience with the surface if not the substance of modernity.

Still, *Petulia* emerges as Lester's most effective film since *A Hard
Day's Night*, not so much because the style fits the subject but
because Lester deftly maneuvers a dangerously eccentric cast—
Christie, Scott, Richard Chamberlain, Shirley Knight, Joseph Cotten, Arthur Hill—into an expressive ensemble. Scott and Chamberlain are the biggest surprises, Scott for his first intimations of
behavioral charm on the screen, Chamberlain for his first flashes
of a demonic pretty-boy talent. By making us take his cast in bits
and pieces, Lester manages to make us overlook the fact that
modern performers are not geared for the steady voltages of the

ancient stars. Julie Christie, for example, is good at giving off
sparks, but she can't burn for any length of time with the low
flame of a Lombard.

Lester's con game in *Petulia* consists of making the audience
suspect that there is more to the characters than meets the darting
eye. What hidden perversions, for example, lurk behind the Chris-
tie-Chamberlain marriage? None whatsoever. The Chamberlain
character is merely weak in the most old-fashioned way, and Christie, for all her boisterous bravado in bedrooms, turns out to be less
a compulsive slut than a compassionate saint. The whole thing is a
bit of a tease, sort of like a tasteful Chinese dinner that leaves you
feeling hungry an hour later, reinforcing the impression that Lester
is a minor artist but potentially a masterful entertainer. If I haven't
mentioned the hippie elements on the fringes of the film, it is
because they have nothing to do with its action. The first scene of
the film gives us a glimpse of Janis Joplin with Big Brother and the
Holding Company, but Lester treats these interesting performers
as part of the meaningless noise and chaos of our time. Curiously, it
was not too long ago, sometime before *A Hard Day's Night* in fact,
that middle-aged skeptics had the same impression of the Beatles.
Lester, like most artists, is least affecting when he seeks to satirize
things he neither loves nor understands. But after *Petulia* it will be
difficult to argue that Lester lacks charm, wit, and a very personal
insight into people.

—*Village* Voice, July 4, 1968

■ 12. GENERATION GAP

The Over-Thirty Backlash has taken many curious forms in this
summer of doddering discontent. John Osborne is quoted in the
Observer as describing Paris student revolutionaries as "instant
rabble." Stephen Spender (in the *New York Review of Books*)
and Paul Goodman (in the *New York Sunday Times Magazine*)
express their doubts about youthful anarchism—and Osborne,
Spender, and Goodman represent only the thunder from the Left.
What is the Right supposed to be doing while Marcuse's minions
are wrecking things? Even to ask this question nowadays is to be
dumped into the generation gap.

Students don't seem to be frightened by the specter of another Hitler arising out of the ashes of anarchy. And why should they be frightened of someone they don't really remember? A few years ago petulant American parents would complain that their spoiled children had no idea what the Depression had been like. Nowadays adolescent amnesia is beginning to enshroud Buchenwald and Dachau, Hiroshima and Hungary. What is frightening about today's youth is not so much its skepticism about its elders as its complete lack of historical curiosity. Even Marcuse was badly received in Germany for dwelling morbidly on the past. An Oxford graduate in his twenties was struck by the widening gap between his own sense of history and the England Year One sensibilities of current students. History is always the weakest subject on a British college TV quiz program, particularly recent history.

Hence the recurring complaint about young people lacking a sense of humor. Humor is a function of memory and history with just a dash of frustration. Humor never arises from a situation in which the young bang their plates all day to attract attention. The biggest danger, however, is not from the young people themselves. (I can't buy the overhysteria of *Wild in the Streets*.) The biggest danger is actually the excuse young rebels give old reactionaries to set repressive forces into motion. The silliest thing I've ever heard is the student strategy of "using" the police to force a new alignment of social forces. That's like dumping man-eating sharks into a crowded pool to demonstrate human solidarity against a common peril. As it turns out, the police are not above "using" the students for their own ends. Any institution that trains its members (sic) to entrap citizens in public urinals is capable of the direst deviousness.

Film, like most arts, does not lend itself to the clamoring of the Now generation. This is what I think Osborne and Spender and Goodman are really getting at when they question the antics of young anarchists. Anyone who has ever tried to write even the most mechanical column, the most perfunctory article, knows that at some point he must lock himself away from the madding crowd to labor in maddening solitude. I'm not talking about ivory towers, just plain hard work that is especially pertinent in a time when many student revolutionaries are strongly suspected of rationalizing their own laziness. I doubt that even one good movie will emerge from all the student cadres that presumed to prescribe the future course of the cinema at Cannes and Pesaro. That is not to say that the current system of film production is above criticism and beyond reproach, or even that the banning of dinner jackets from festival rites is necessarily a social tragedy. Unfortunately, the festival disrupters have shown themselves more adept at stopping screenings than curtailing cocktail parties. The Berlin film students would not allow their own films to be screened for the press, and they did not seem overly enthusiastic about the special film program of young Canadian film-makers. They were more interested in issuing revolutionary leaflets on the inadequacy of their film education.

The students at Berkeley have gotten their heads bashed in a gesture of solidarity with the French students, but the Berkeley martyrs had better not count on any gratitude or recognition from abroad. There is little genuine internationalism in the student uprisings, despite the handy catchphrases of Vietnam. Rudy the Red was so rudely received by British student leaders that he publicly recanted the cult of his own personality. French directors scuttled Cannes one month and scintillated Berlin the next. History had been rewritten in Paris and Berlin to indicate that the uprisings in Berkeley and Columbia were imitations of European initiatives. Few dissident students in the Western democracies showed much concern for the bruised sensibilities of Canadian separatists, Czech liberals, or, for that matter, the millions of starving Biafrans. Hitler, it should be remembered, came to power as a National Socialist atop the corpse of the Weimar Republic, dissected and dismembered by both the Left and the Right.

Dr. Erwin Leiser, head of the Berlin Film Academy and producer of *Mein Kampf*, has come up with another compilation of Nazi film footage, this time of feature films. The American title will probably be *To Die for Hitler*. As I sat watching the film in a small Berlin projection room, I wondered what the student anarchists would make of it. Would they roar with laughter at the outrageousness of the manipulation (and the corniness of the costumes) or would they experience the slightest frisson of horror and recognition? I am never entirely happy with compilation films. I prefer to see everything in its full context, and I have special reservations about Leiser's ideologically schematic organization of his material. This section deals with Nazi attitudes toward war, this with Jews, this with German minorities, this with Communists, and so on. Nonetheless *To Die for Hitler* cannot help but be fascinating for anyone concerned with memory and history. There is something for every taste. Shots of Stuka pilots singing in their cockpits as they go off merrily to war are uncomfortably reminiscent of similar sequences in Hollywood war films. As a popular (in Germany) Swedish chantoosie sings about needing the world still, row upon row of Wehrmacht officers sing along while swaying in alternate directions as if in an inspired "Springtime for Hitler" production number from Mel Brooks's *The Producers*.

Hardly surprising but strangely disconcerting is the tendency of Nazi characters to act as though they were the Good Guys. In one excerpt a German girl is stoned to death by Polish brutes after they discover a swastika hanging around her neck. In another a little Nazi storm trooper is chased through the streets by evil Communists. The poor lad is found face down in the mud by his brownshirted buddies. As they lift up his head his glazed death-eyes gaze skyward to the clouds where young storm troopers are marching to the strains of still very stirring martial music and to the banners of the most evil regime the world has ever known, but now merely the campiest. Leiser and his generation of Germans try to tell the students that history could easily repeat itself. But to believe that history repeats itself is often merely the means of remembering what one has experienced, and even worse, of foreclosing the future. Thus in a political context, memory and history may be the alibis of a useless sentimentality, but memory and history are also the very stuff of cinema, itself hardly the last refuge of callow youth.

—*Village Voice*, July 18, 1968

▪ 13. ROSEMARY'S BABY

Rosemary's Baby has been blessed with such extraordinary popularity from the printed page to the silver screen that it seems superfluous, if not presumptuous, for a critic to recommend the movie as good hot-weather-goose-pimply entertainment. Everybody read the book and now everybody's going to the movie; book and movie are discussed interchangeably as media permutations of the same basic formula. Good luck and perfect timing have played a part in these proceedings. Certainly only luck can explain the fortuitous conjunction of a strong commercial property like Ira Levin's novel with a strong directorial personality like Roman Polanski without the novel being distorted or the director diluted. Indeed, Levin and Polanski actually reinforce each other, Levin being more a storyteller than a stylist and Polanski more a stylist than a storyteller. Even in *Rosemary's Baby* there are moments of excessive embellishment in the beginning when good old Elisha Cooke, Jr., is showing Mia Farrow and John Cassavetes through the Dakota Apartments. Polanski's camera seems a bit too jittery and his cutting a bit too jazzy and the over-all effect a bit too ostentatiously ominous. But then Levin's potent plot takes over, and Polanski seems to relax into a contemplative calm, with only occasional touches and asides to remind us of his impish irreverence.

By now the plot of *Rosemary's Baby* is familiar enough to analyze without spoiling anyone's fun. In an age of themes, Ira Levin has come up with a plot so effectively original that it is deserving more of a patent than a copyright. The qualities of a good plot are simplicity, directness, and an oblique treatment of essentials. *Rosemary's Baby* can be synopsized in one sentence as the adventures of an actor's wife, delivered to the devil and his worshippers by her ambitious husband so that she might bear the devil's baby, which she does. The beauty of the plot is that it virtually conceals its real subject. On the surface *Rosemary's Baby* seems merely a diabolical reversal of Mary's baby, a reversal made even more flagrantly sacrilegious by Polanski's God-Is-Dead gaiety. A Catholic group has bitten on the bait by condemning the film, though probably more for the director's deftness with nudity than for his disrespect for the sacraments. Many critics have missed the point of the story because of their prejudice against melodrama as a meaningful dramatic form, a prejudice traditionally diagnosed as the anti-Hitchcock syndrome.

Rosemary's Baby is more than just a good yarn, however. Its power to terrify readers and viewers, particularly women, derives not from any disrespect toward the Deity nor from any literal fear of embodied evil. Ghosts, holy or unholy, have ceased to haunt our dreams in their metaphysical majesty. The devil in *Rosemary's Baby* is reduced to an unimaginative rapist performing a ridiculous ritual. It could not be otherwise in an age that proclaims God Is Dead. Without God the devil is pure camp, and his followers fugitives from a Charles Addams cartoon.

What is frightening about Rosemary's condition is her suspicion that she is being used by other people for ulterior purposes. She has no family of her own to turn to, but must rely on a husband who seems insensitive to her pain, neighbors who seem suspiciously solicitous, a doctor whose manner seems more reassuring than his medicine, and a world that seems curiously indifferent to her plight. When she tells her story to a disinterested doctor, he dismisses it as pure paranoia, as most doctors would if a pregnant woman walked into the office and told them the plot of *Rosemary's Baby*. The disinterested doctor calls the witch doctor, and Rosemary is delivered to her satanic destiny. And then comes the final twist. After spitting in her husband's face, Rosemary approaches the rocker where her yellow-eyed baby is crying, and by slowly rocking the infant to sleep acknowledges her maternal responsibility toward a being that is after all a baby and ultimately *her* baby.

Thus two universal fears run through *Rosemary's Baby*, the fear of pregnancy, particularly as it consumes personality, and the fear of a deformed offspring, with all the attendant moral and emotional complications.

Almost any film that dealt directly with these two fears would be unbearable to watch because of the matter-of-fact clinical horror involved. By dealing obliquely with these fears the book and the movie penetrate deeper into the subconscious of the audience. It is when we least expect to identify with fictional characters that we identify most deeply. If Levin had been fully aware of the implications of what he had been writing, he would have been too self-conscious to write it. Conversely, Polanski, who is too aware of implications and overtones, could never have invented the plot of *Rosemary's Baby*. Hence the fruitful collaboration of instinct and intellect on this occasion.

Levin's lady-in-distress mannerisms are misleading in that they are designed merely as plot devices to tighten tension during the period of pregnancy, a period during which even witches and warlocks lack the ability to accelerate events. At times the suspense of the story is more rhetorical than real, since we are always more curious about what Rosemary is trying to escape from (witchcraft) than what she is trying to escape to (the normal, neurotic everyday world). Consequently Rosemary is infused with a feeling of helplessness and Zen passivity that creates in the reader and viewer a mood of voluptuous self-pity. Where the story does succeed as melodrama is on the level of persecution trying to prove that it is not paranoia, and of course the best way for an artist to project his own paranoia is to describe real persecution. The great stories are acts of faith in the reality of feelings. The wondrousness of a story or a movie is a plea to the audience to be less skeptical about the possibilities of human experience.

No movie succeeds without a reasonable number of casting coups, and *Rosemary's Baby* is more fortunate than most in this regard. The biggest surprise is Mia Farrow as a Rosemary more ideal than anyone would have suspected after *A Dandy in Aspic*. Even her curiously pallid and awkward artificiality works to her advantage in a role for which it is desirable not to seem too credible to the outside world. Polanski is especially good in directing her physical movements of escape and evasion in a way that makes her plausibly but affectingly ineffective. And when she apologizes for her husband's rudeness by observing that even Laurence Olivier must be self-centered, her gaucherie is heartwarming to the point of heartbreak.

The supporting people are uniformly excellent, Ralph Bellamy being the outstanding revelation as the bearded witch doctor and yet typical of a cast that plays against the strangeness of the situation with a tenaciously tweedsy folksiness mixed with an air of perpetual preoccupation. Ruth Gordon, Sidney Blackmer, and Maurice Evans match Bellamy with an energetic seriousness that is amusing without ever being ridiculous. John Cassavetes is somewhat miscast as the actor-husband, a part that would have been more appropriate for the narcissism Richard Chamberlain displayed so precisely in *Petulia*. Cassavetes is too intelligent and offbeat an actor to project self-absorption. Above all, he lacks the beautiful self-sacrifice mask of an actor capable of selling his wife to the devil for a good part. Cassavetes is simply more than his character calls for, but he, too, has his moments in an almost flawless entertainment.

—*Village Voice*, July 25, 1968

■ 14. THE STRANGE AFFAIR

The Strange Affair is one of the most disturbing movies I have seen in years. David (Sebastian) Greene directed the Stanley Mann screenplay adapted from a novel by Bernard Toms. Not having read (or even heard of) the novel, I am unable to apportion responsibility for the various touches and ambiguities that make The Strange Affair so troublesome to digest morally. However, I do detect in David Greene's taut direction a contempt for the mod(ern) world consistent with the stylish misogyny of Sebastian. But whereas Sebastian functioned almost entirely on a fantasy level of sexual hostilities, The Strange Affair opens out onto the real world with a frightening literalness befitting a film that derives its banal title from the name of its apparent protagonist, Peter Strange (Michael York), a British bobby who turns out to be something of a booby in the curiously conspiratorial atmosphere of Scotland Yard.

Most of the review synopses have been sidetracked by the admittedly distracting spectacle of Strange's bawdy bath with a hippie harlot named Fred (Susan George) under the prying pornographers' cameras of Fred's dear old Aunt Mary and Uncle Bertrand. Not that Michael York and Susan George act with unnatural lewdness in their ribald roles. Far from it. All they do and show is graced with a youthful innocence hopelessly out of key with a society drenched in evil and hypocrisy.

Although the film begins and ends from the fateful viewpoint of Michael York's Peter Strange, the most compelling characterization is that of Jeremy Kemp's Detective Sergeant Pierce, a fanatically honest plainclothesman on the narcotics squad. Pierce spends most of the movie trying to get the goods on a dope-smuggling ex-detective named Quince (Jack Watson) and Quince's two sniggering sons (David Glaiser and Richard Vanstone), the latter visually a veritable Rosencrantz and Guildenstern of filial felony. Ultimately, the Quinces, father and sons, get away with murder and assorted crimes. A corrupt Scotland Yard inspector stymies Pierce at every turn, and a combination of bureaucratic police pro-

cedures and judicial restraints does the rest. The movie ends with
the relatively good guys in jail, and the absolutely bad guys at liberty. But the audience is not amused by the hilarious immorality of
it all. Indeed, the denouement is so unsatisfying that some of the
reviewers have tried to pass it off as an idle jest lacking any foundation in fact.

There are undeniable weaknesses in the plot. The means by
which Pierce blackmails Strange to plant narcotics on Quince
seems implausible in its contrivance. Furthermore, judicial processes are shown at length when they are protecting the bad guys,
but these same processes are skipped entirely when the good guys
are being railroaded. The audience is being manipulated somewhat
to demand the impeachment of Warren or Fortas and the repeal
of the Magna Charta and the Bill of Rights. Thus the ritualistic
liberal can find sufficient cause to dismiss the film without a sociological hearing. Still, no police film from any country has ever
probed the raw paradoxes of law enforcement with so little sentimentality and self-righteousness.

What gives *The Strange Affair* its power to cause insomnia is its
honesty in presenting a condition without wrapping it up in a conclusion. The more I thought about the movie, the more I respected
it for not tipping off the audience with some reassuring moral.
Also, the movie is intellectually complex by "message" standards in
that it deals with two kinds of evil without subordinating one to
the other. If Stanley Kramer did a movie on police brutality, he
would show a brutal cop beating up an innocent man. If Kramer
did a film on organized crime, he would show an evil gangster
persecuting an idealistic cop. In either instance the audience could
pick sides, and even if the bad guy won in the permissive atmosphere of the post-Production Code era, the resultant immorality
could be rationalized for the audience as an exposé of current conditions.

As for Brecht and *The Three-Penny Opera* brand of cynicism,
the audience is merely tuned in to an updated version of Prou-
dhon's property-is-theft arguments. For the theater and cinema of
the Left, crime is a conveniently melodramatic metaphor for capitalism. Brechtian cynicism implies that a classless society will be
a crimeless society in theatrical terms.

The Strange Affair presumes to question the morality of means even when the ends are justified. ("Ends" and "means" seem to have disappeared from our language since the Trotskyists stopped splitting hairs with the Stalinists.) Jeremy Kemp gives such a persuasive performance as the persecuted plainclothesman turned paranoid that it takes a long time to realize that he is the real villain of the piece. The Quinces do horrible things with gay abandon, but they are less dangerous to the honest citizen than a policeman lusting for justice beyond the barriers of the law. This is a bitter pill for the average audience to swallow. The thought that organized criminals must be protected from honest policemen would be considered downright subversive in some quarters, but the fact remains, as Charlton Heston observes in *Touch of Evil* and Art Buchwald confirms from Moscow, that the problems of the police are permanently solved only in a police state.

However, we cannot expect policemen to do our dirty work without expecting them to be brutalized and corrupted by the process. Some of the violent rhetoric against police brutality suggests that the police have introduced evil to a peaceful pastoral paradise. Unfortunately, criminals are often monstrously inconsiderate to the point of depriving the honest citizen of his life as well as his ill-gotten gains, and even the most anarchistic householder may develop a sentimental attachment to his own possessions, which he expects the local Cossacks to defend from the rabble.

The Strange Affair does not indulge the specious sentimentality of arguing a theme with innocent protagonists, but neither does it ignore some of the more dubious activities of the police in the realms of "vice" and "morals." Also drugs. Is society protected by laws governing private behavior? And are not the police needlessly corrupted and alienated by having to enforce laws unpopular with large portions of their society? Again the movie does not answer these questions, but leaves them hanging as virtually unanswerable, which indeed they are. But there can be no compromise with the principle of restricting the powers of the police. Not that organized crime is an imaginary menace to our institutions, but rather that the individual even today is virtually at the mercy of the police and the courts, and the impoverished, friendless individual most of all. We must accept the muggings and the murders and the burglaries and the rapes as the price for an almost forgotten ideal of individual freedom. The virtue of *The Strange Affair* is that it does not shrink from showing us the high price we must pay for this ideal.

—*Village Voice*, August 8, 1968

■ 15. *THE BRIDE WORE BLACK;*
     TARGETS

François Truffaut's *The Bride Wore Black* has been reviewed as if it were a filmed sequel to Truffaut's book on Alfred Hitchcock. But it isn't. Whereas Hitchcock is basically a genre director, Truffaut's temperament is closer to the sprawling humanism of Renoir. Of course, no director can memorize the life's work of another director without picking up a few tricks and ideas along the way. When Charles Denner's pathologically lecherous artist delicately poses Jeanne Moreau in the white tunic of Diana the Huntress, the image of James Stewart adjusting Kim Novak's coiffure in Hitchcock's *Vertigo* comes immediately to mind with all its romantic reverberations. (The fact that Miss Moreau, like Miss Novak, is too substantial for the ethereal spirit of the illusion only heightens the resemblance.) Also, the mere fact that *The Bride Wore Black* is a violent melodrama with a soupçon of suspense is sufficient grounds for most critics to tag Truffaut with a Hitchcock label. However, even Renoir is not entirely a stranger to violent melodrama. The murders in *La Chienne, La Bête Humaine, The Crime of Monsieur Lange,* and *The Rules of the Game* are as memorable as any in the history of the cinema. But these murders do not make Renoir a genre director. Renoir's feeling for life flows over the violence like an inexhaustible torrent of tenderness. Whereas Renoir proudly sacrifices form (and art) for truth, Hitchcock salvages truth from an art that rigorously obeys the rules of the game. Truffaut breaks the rules of the genre without abandoning the genre, and thus teeters precariously between Hitchcock and Renoir without committing himself entirely to either.

Truffaut begins *The Bride Wore Black* by plunging into the action before its premises have been established. Thus the heroine has committed two murders and is well on her way to her third before the audience is informed of her motive. Truffaut's story-telling is consequently anti-Hitchcockian in that it sacrifices sus-pense for mystification. Once the audience is implicated in the lyricism of Moreau's murderousness, it is too late to measure her motivation. *The Bride Wore Black* succeeds therefore as a *fait accompli*. Truffaut manages even to get away with a big hole in the plot. We are told that the heroine is tracking down five men who were involved in the prankishly accidental murder of her hus-band as he was descending the steps of the church with his bride on his arm, an overwhelmingly Orphic piece of sexual imagery rem-iniscent of a similar incident in Sam Fuller's *Forty Guns*. We see the five men playing cards in the hotel room and then joking about the long-range capabilities of a hunting rifle. We see one man load it for fun, and another man fire it by accident. We see the bride-groom falling and falling and falling. We see the action in various speeds and colors until it is engraved on our minds with the reality of a recurring nightmare. But we are never told how the bride learned the identities of her bridegroom's murderers. By simply showing us the murderers, Truffaut discharges his obligations to the genre. If he had wanted us to think more seriously about the premise of the plot, he would have told us much sooner. As it is, the director's procrastination is justified by the wildly unconvincing casting of Jeanne Moreau as a vengeful bride turned into a true femme fatale. Truffaut conceived Moreau's character as a Hawks-ian heroine divested of her sexual sophistication for the sake of the severe intelligence her revenge demanded. The result is a per-formance from Moreau so dully deadpan that the interest shifts inevitably to her male victims, all of whom rise to the challenge with vivid glimpses of life and desire on the brink of death.

Consequently *The Bride Wore Black* derives its dramatic power from the irony of an illusion. The bride of vengeful death enters the life of five men as a temptress. She is unreal, unconvincing, and discouragingly uncooperative, but it doesn't matter. Her victims will grasp at any straw that promises even a moment of pleasure. Michel Bouquet's born loser is especially moving as an evocation of muddled middle-aged hopefulness in the presence of a sexual fantasy come to life. If Moreau's character were at all real, it would be impossible to forgive her for her mercilessness to this particularly pathetic child of woman. But because of the displaced sensibility of the film, the men are too real for the genre, and Moreau too fantastic.

Thus a second film emerges over the smudged design of the first, a film more interesting than the first because it is closer to Truffaut's true feelings. This second film concerns the obsession of men with the ever-receding realities of women. What Truffaut has taken from William Irish's action novel is the urgency of a melodramatic situation, the urgency without which Truffaut's feelings would spill out over the edges of his frames until more of him would be off-screen than on. What Truffaut has taken from Hitchcock is an adroitness in balancing abruptness of action with a drifting for meaning, so that every characterization can be enriched with an intimation of inevitability. The difference between Truffaut and Hitchcock is the difference between a life style and a dream world. Truffaut's males are derived from the director's sense of reality void of melodrama. If Hitchcock and Irish had not intervened, Truffaut's lecherous males would talk on night after night about all the women they'd laid and about all the women they wanted to lay until even their lechery would disintegrate in the lassitude of an uneventful life. By contrast, Hitchcock's characters are designed expressly for their genre functions in the sense that they correspond to conflicting impulses in the director's personality. Hitchcock is what he is, and Renoir is what he is, but Truffaut is still suspended between an art of meaningful forms and a world of changing appearances. Still, *The Bride Wore Black* is a film of undeniable if uncertain beauty by virtue of its director's critical intelligence in an era of mindless lyricism.

Peter Bogdanovich's *Targets* is considerably better than its gun-control selling point might indicate. Bogdanovich is known in film circles for his book-length interviews with Alfred Hitchcock, Howard Hawks, John Ford, and Fritz Lang, books that serve also as an index to a taste in film-making somewhat out of synch with the prevailing industry desire to do *The Son of the Graduate*. Bogdanovich and his wife, Polly Platt, turned out the script for *Targets* within certain commissioned guidelines involving the integration of Boris Karloff and one of his Roger Corman vehicles into the story line. The director doubled as an actor in what, aside from Mr. Karloff, could be described fairly as an economy cast. Time, as

THE QUEEN(S) 383

well as money, being in short supply, Bogdanovich had to fall back on intuitive responses to material that is relatively undeveloped by conventional message standards. For better or for worse, and I think better, the emphasis in *Targets* is not so much on why as what and how. There are no speeches on violence, only the spectacle of a clean-cut, blankly good-looking youth suddenly going berserk and shooting up his family and community. Bogdanovich is very strong on mechanical processes, and not only those connected with the loading and firing of guns. The act of projecting a film is rendered here more expressively and more dramatically than in any film I have ever seen. Also, the depiction of car culture achieves a casualness that represents the ultimate stage of corruption.

Bogdanovich uses the Los Angeles area to great advantage in showing the frightening impersonality of the social context without lecturing on it. The director has learned from Hitchcock how to implicate the audience in a crime by breaking the flow of the action in such a way that the audience subconsciously encourages the sniper out of an instinct for mechanical perfection. Bogdanovich is at times guilty of maintaining a contemplative distance from action lacking sufficient interest or information for that particular approach. Mizoguchi or Hawks can use a quiet camera because they have a noisy scenario, but such admirers of Mizoguchi and Hawks as Astruc and Rivette (and now Bogdanovich) have tended to misuse the contemplative calm of the camera by applying it to scenes requiring less the gaze of the camera than the beating heart of montage. All in all, however, Peter Bogdanovich has joined the ranks of promising directors with his very first feature, a movie to which such adjectives as gripping and compelling are appropriate.

—*Village Voice*, August 22, 1968

■ 16. *THE QUEEN(S)*

A reader recently complained that the print of *The Queens* shown in her locality lacked the episode dealing with a beauty contest in drag. The reader has apparently confused *The Queens*—an Italian four-part sex comedy—with *The Queen*—a documentary, more or less, of a beauty contest in drag. *The Queens* can be disposed of very quickly. Luciano Salce's episode with Monica Vitti is by far the best of the four episodes. The subsequent episodes with Claudia Cardinale, Raquel Welch, and Capucine can be skipped entirely by the discriminating anthology shopper.

Still, *The Queens*, for all its lack of inspiration is a movie. *The Queen* is more of a freak show, its rave notices notwithstanding. It's probably the only show of its kind you're ever likely to see, but its uniqueness does not excuse it for its uncertainties of form and viewpoint. Ever since *Nanook of the North*, a premium has been placed on getting a camera where no one else had ever gotten a camera before. That *Nanook* was personal art as well as scoop journalism seems almost superfluous to those who preach novelty merely for novelty's sake. Nonetheless Frank Simon's direction of *The Queen* can be severely criticized for not having done more with its outrageously original subject.

The Queen had several options it might have chosen, given the subject of transvestism on the stage of Town Hall two years ago. We might have been treated to one or more psychological sketches of the boys in the band. We might have been regaled by the metamorphosis of delicate masculinity into devastating femininity. We might have been roused by the sheer professionalism of the spectacle into a new chorus of "There's No Business Like Show Business." We might have been turned off forever from the demeaning exploitation of lechery in the Miss America contests. Instead, we were treated halfheartedly to a bit of everything, served up timidly as if the film-makers were afraid the material would burn up the screen if it were ever properly focused in any one direction.

Consequently we get glimpses of about a dozen or more drag queens, but no sustained exposure. We see some of the techniques of the metamorphosis, but not enough to satisfy our thirst for knowledge. Worst of all, we never get a well-staged view of the entertainment on the Town Hall stage. The production is, in a word, crude, the point of view confused, and the picture never takes off on the flights of fancy a true connoisseur of the subject might have achieved.

I suspect, however, that a more audacious treatment of *The Queen* would have been less successful than the semihumanist discretion of Frank Simon and his colleagues. What impresses me most about the tone of the critical consensus is its smugly urbane tolerance of these poor creatures who are after all human beings. It doesn't require an addiction to the sweaty smell of Ozone Park pastoral to feel that the subject of transvestism deserves some plain talk.

Liberal tolerance is dangerously double-edged in that it establishes social distinctions under the guise of facing social problems. Consequently one can at the same time bemoan the plight of the poor and yet be socially chilly to those poor wretches who make less than 50 thou a year. The charity balls that alone justify the existence of our plutocrats serve not only to reaffirm plutocratic virtue but also to reassure the plutocrats that there are still masses of rabble to be measured against favorably.

Similarly, liberal tolerance of transvestites and homosexuals contains the seeds of disdainful discrimination. Transvestism has been a proven laugh-getter since Aristophanes, and it has always been especially effective with bourgeois audiences, ostensibly secure in their sexual normality. Most of the classic comedians flaunted queer mannerisms in their repertoire, Chaplin's being the most elaborate and Stan Laurel's the most knowing. Every borscht-circuit comedian knows that his biggest laughs will come with lines like "Sitting out in the audience tonight is my wife Bruce." Zero Mostel is currently the most successful practitioner on stage of the heterosexual put-down of the homosexual through audience-involving mimicry.

The pattern of "fag-and-drag" humor is basically consistent. A certified heterosexual comedian—and he must be so certified to be comically effective—demonstrates to the audience how strange *they* are, and how normal *we* are. Never mind those hidden fears and insecurities. The comedian's fag-and-drag routines serve as religious rituals to exorcise the hidden fears and insecurities through laughter.

The Queen, I must hasten to add, does not arouse this kind of laughter. Much of the time the audience seems to be sucking in its collective breath as if it were on the edge of a precipice, and it is in a sense. Those are real queers up on the screen, baby, not Establishment queers. These are Hanoi Hannahs, not Saigon Sallies, and they are not so much interested in entertaining you as in expressing themselves. They are ridiculing your most sacred sexual feelings and fantasies, and if they ever came face to face with you, they'd size you up in a hurry and knock you off your high horse, darling. Fortunately, their director keeps them at a safe distance from the audience so that they can't do any real damage.

Nonetheless the drag-queen contestants are eminently likable in curiously peripheral ways. There is obviously less racial discrimination than there is in the lily-white Miss America contests. Also, there is something more appealing in the innocent corruption of the drag queens than in the corrupt innocence of the Miss Americas. Unfortunately, most of the drag queens emphasize the boisterous vulgarity of Ethel Merman and Maria Montez rather than the subtler transformations of the male and the female. Only an extraordinarily ambiguous creature called Harlow expresses the real message of the spectacle, that the difference between men and women is so slight and fragile that it is infinitely precious, and thus in their strange way the drag queens are quasi-religious figures.

—*Village Voice*, September 5, 1968

■ 17. THE SPAGHETTI WESTERNS

I

The spaghetti westerns are taken less and less seriously as the body counts approach the scale of moral genocide, Tony Anthony's *Stranger* in particular constituting a one-man extermination service. However, spaghetti westerns, particularly those of Sergio Leone, have managed to influence the genre in ways insufficiently discussed up to now. Those who bemoan the degeneration of the post-Leone western tend too often to pay attention to westerns only in periods of alleged degeneracy. The New York cultural scene, effetely feminized as it is, remains basically hostile to westerns even as precincts of camp. Relatively few westerns of the past forty years have been dignified with a review in *The New York Times*, and few urban moviegoing memories dwell on the mythology of the subject. Walker Percy's *The Moviegoer* might recall John Wayne's rifle showdown in *Stagecoach*, but *Stagecoach* was a John Ford–Dudley Nichols blue-ribbon special, not a bread-and-butter western. Curiously, the western is the one genre that is enriched by being debased. The western hero as a classical archetype possesses a certain nobility, but he is too solemn and simpleminded to deserve the majesty of his milieu. If I had a choice between the western before 1945 and the westerns after 1945, I would opt for the latter period without hesitation. The western, like water, gains flavor from its impurities, and westerns since 1945 have multiplied their options, obsessions, and neuroses many times over. Until very recently, however, the Hollywood western dominated the genre so completely that all its sociological and stylistic variations were derived from a common philosophical base. Even the antiwestern that came into prominence in 1943 with *The Ox-Bow Incident* managed to fit into a historical tradition. Whereas Owen Wister's *The Virginian* had sanctioned lynching as a penalty for stealing cattle, *The Ox-Bow Incident* condemned lynching, though with the sentimental proviso that the victims were innocent. Owen Wister and some of the earliest western writers had developed the western as a racist genre, a celebration of Manifest Destiny for the Wasps westward. One of William S. Hart's oaters was titled without irony *The Aryan*.

Needless to say, such sagas rendered the Negro invisible and the Indian expendable. A reaction of sorts in favor of the Indian materialized on the screen in the late twenties and early thirties in the form of pleas for justice from the Great White Father. Nowadays the Indian is almost invariably sentimentalized, and there are frequent attempts to integrate the Negro into a history from which he was deliberately excluded by earlier film-makers. Sydney Pollack's *The Scalphunters* fires both barrels at the audience by giving the Indians dignity and authority and Ossie Davis moral and physical parity with Burt Lancaster in the film's quest for black and white interchangeability. *The Scalphunters*, however, is not an antiwestern. Antiwesterns merely use the West as an allegorical device to denounce the East. *High Noon, The Big Country, The Unforgiven,* and *The Ox-Bow Incident* all express disgruntlement with some aspect of the human condition, be it cowardice, pugnacity, prejudice, or just plain mob hysteria. By contrast, *The Scalphunters* strives for open-ended adventure and an ambiguous attitude toward the evil represented by Telly Savalas and his scalphunters. There is an optimistic suggestion in the film that men can work off their prejudices through action. Lancaster and Davis, like Charlton Heston in *Will Penny*, like Henry Fonda and James Stewart in *Firecreek*, are transcendental figures fully conscious of their roles in American history. As Americans they are aware of their part in a process of time and space. Most often they are poignantly aware that they have come too soon or too late, too far or too near, but they never lose faith in the civilizing, pacifying force of the future. It may come when they are old or on the run or dead, but it will come and nothing can stop it. Consequently there is a moral serenity to the American western hero that can never be imitated from abroad.

When Sergio Leone released *A Fistful of Dollars* in 1964, connoisseurs of story lines immediately spotted the plagiarism of Akira Kurosawa's Toshiro Mifune samurai vehicle *Yojimbo*. Japan's samurai films have often been compared to American westerns, and Japan, like Italy and Germany, was a defeated nation in World War II. Consequently the heroes of samurai films, like the heroes of Italian and German westerns, are less transcendental heroes than existential heroes in that they lack faith in history as an orderly process in human affairs. What Kurosawa and Leone share is a sentimental nihilism that ranks survival above honor and revenge above morality. Hence the Kurosawa and Leone hero possesses and requires more guile than his American counterpart. Life is cheaper in the foreign western, and violence more prevalent.

Strangely, Leone has moved deeper into American history and politics in his subsequent films—*For a Few Dollars More* and *The Good, the Bad, and the Ugly*. I say "strangely" because an Italian director might be expected to stylize an alien genre with vague space-time coordinates, like the universal Mexico that can be filmed anywhere on the Mediterranean for any century from the sixteenth to the twentieth. Instead, Leone has dwelled obsessively on the ragged edges of the Civil War, an interlude treated in American westerns as an interruption to our Manifest Destiny. For Leone, however, the fratricidal fury of the Civil War is one of the keys to the rapacity and violence of the American West. The America of Sergio Leone is an America of rape and pillage, an America moving toward that nihilistic nowhere with which Europe has been so familiar for so long.

II

The spaghetti western is ultimately a lower-class entertainment, and, as such, functions as an epic of violent revenge. Only in the American West of legend can blood flow profusely enough to satisfy the thirst of the most meanly embittered for fantasy retribution. Leone's westerns add gruesome cemetery touches of their own together with the dark humor of implacable fatality. Leone's Italian imitators have augmented the unreality of the genre with new excesses in weaponry and sadism, but Leone's humor is relatively original. *The Good, the Bad, and the Ugly* could never have been made in America. For one thing, it is too long and plot-heavy for the generally single-point-of-view Hollywood westerns. Leone, far from being glossy, seems to revel in the texture of Death Valley dustiness. When Eli Wallach (the Ugly) drags Clint Eastwood (the Good) across a desert, the suffering becomes so intensely vivid and the framing so consciously poetic that the audience is subjected to a kind of Cactus Calvary. No American western would ever wallow so ecstatically in pain and privation worthy of the most masochistic Messiah. But Clint Eastwood is more a mercenary than a Messiah, and he will be rewarded in this world long before the next. Leone knows this, and Leone's audience knows this. Then, why is the mercenary's reward so long deferred? Simply because the sheer duration of the suffering makes Eastwood a plausible lower-class hero whose physical redemption is the contemporary correlative of Christ's spiritual redemption. Leone's longueurs are thus part of a ritual alien to the American's traditional confidence in his ability to conquer nature. Leone's characters require more than strength and determination to survive. They require also a guile and reason more European than American. That Eastwood does not kill Wallach at the final fade-out is due not so much to Eastwood's being moral as to his being civilized by an ancient code of resignation that is hardly the code of the West.

Unfortunately, the post-Leone western has already escalated violence and viciousness to the point of silly self-parody. Tony Anthony rides around in the *Stranger* series like a portable ammunition dump financed by the Warsaw pact, and just when American westerns had become reasonably frugal with firearms in the workaday West, celebrated most painstakingly by Sam Peckinpah in *Ride the High Country*. The old joke about firing twenty bullets from a six-shooter without reloading is irrelevant to a genre in which gunpowder seems as plentiful as dust. How do the spaghetti sharpshooters pay for their bang-bang? The screen is seldom quiet enough for the question even to be asked, much less answered, and, anyway, economics and sociology are always fuzzily focused in the mists of mythology.

The spaghetti western is not only flourishing on its own, however; it is slithering into Hollywood westerns as well. Henry Hathaway's *Five-Card Stud* is a peculiar blend of the director's leisurely classical pace of storytelling with a plot full of dark corners and unsavory violence. Killings have been replaced by murders, the vanity of villainy by an insane deviousness. I was laughing at German horse operas only a few years ago for imposing Jack-the-Ripper murder mysteries on an extroverted genre like the western, but the introverted loonies have now invaded the prairies, and we may be in for a long siege of stranglers with ten-gallon hats.

Indeed, strangulation is second only to the six-shooter as a preferred form of homicide in the post-Leone western. *Hang 'Em High* is concerned ostensibly with the moral ambiguities of a hanging judge (Pat Hingle) and his vengeful marshal (Clint Eastwood), himself a lynching victim with a brand on his throat. The script makes gestures toward the transcendental tradition of the Hollywood western with references to statehood and law and order, but the transcendentalism is pure rhetoric in this instance. The point of the spectacle is the elaborately staged hangings themselves, vivid and numerous beyond the demands of the debate, catering to the lowest instincts not of lynching hysteria, which is after all a temporary emotional state, but rather of a gruesomely cultivated expertise of spectators who have witnessed too many public executions as if they were Roman circuses.

The role of women in westerns has always been problematical, but never more so than in this era of giddy brutalization. The thin veneer of Madonna-worship has been scraped away in the spaghetti western to reveal an astonishing hatred of the female, a hatred never remotely approached even in the wildest of the Freudian Hollywood westerns beginning with the Vidor-Busch-Selznick *Duel in the Sun* in 1947 and continuing into Raoul Walsh's *Pursued*,

Nicholas Ray's *Johnny Guitar*, Anthony Mann's *Naked Spur* and *Man of the West*, Fritz Lang's *Rancho Notorious* and Sam Fuller's *Forty Guns*. For one thing, there was an awesome dramatic centrality in the sagebrush sirens incarnated by Jennifer Jones, Teresa Wright, Joan Crawford, Janet Leigh, Julie London, Marlene Dietrich, and Barbara Stanwyck. If most of these lovelies were perforated with bullet holes by the final fade-out, it was the outcome more of passion than contempt. The females of the spaghetti westerns are virtually anonymous and indistinguishable by comparison.

Actually, the *Duel in the Sun* divergence for the western heroine was long overdue in a genre that suffered traditionally from the dramatic anemia of school-marm gentility and evasion. The West, however, retained its freshness as an arena of adventure, with the competitive violence of males spilling over into the male-female confrontations, sometimes with the phallic obliqueness of an unsheathed six-shooter and sometimes with the more direct stimuli provided by Howard Hughes and Jane Russell in *The Outlaw*, the movie that enthroned the bosom at the expense of the limbs for almost an entire generation. In either case, the Freudian western amplified the mythology of the male by giving him a female partner. By contrast, the spaghetti western has reduced the female partner to a mindless, helpless victim, a mere detail in the bloody decor.

Yet the most "realistic" Italian films are relatively squeamish about abusing the Madonna principle lurking in even the boldest whore. Consequently the western provides the necessary distancing for Italian directors to abuse a species they at least subconsciously despise. The western for the Italian director is thus comparable to the French bedroom farce for the American director of yore in that only by the distancing represented by Gay Paree could adultery achieve the necessary lightness for an artist and audience of puritans. Even today a comedy of adultery like George Axelrod's *The Secret Life of an American Wife* turns off audiences with its uptight nuanced gravity that treats the subject neither as problem nor as fantasy but rather as a not too unusual reality.

Fortunately, Americans still retain a feeling for the dramatic integrity of women even in their post-Leone westerns. However, the tendency for the newest heroines, played most of the time either by Inger Stevens or Janice Rule, is to project a ruined past rather than a ruinous future. The Freudian heroines of the forties and the fifties burned brightly in the present tense; the Stevens-Rule syndrome expresses itself more as a burned-out case of lost love and remembered rapes. The post-Leone western here and abroad seems to be saying the same thing. We are a tired civilization with more of a past than a future, and now it is coming down to every man for himself.

—*Village Voice*, September 19 and 26, 1968

■ 18. *FUNNY GIRL*

Funny Girl is so much better than I thought it would be that I am almost tempted to recommend it. But a few words of warning may be in order at the outset. Musicals have never been everyone's cup of tea, but the Broadway bonanzas of recent years have become a veritable anathema to a new generation of intellectuals. I am certainly not defending the brainwashing procedures by which an overpriced hit show continues to sell out (literally and figuratively) long after Zero Mostel has been replaced by Eddie Bracken. Nor is it merely crotchety nostalgia to suggest that the Broadway musical stage has gained in vulgarity what it has lost in vitality over the past two decades. A minor writhe-rock frolic like *Hair* seems ten years ahead of its time because it is only two or three years behind while the rest of Broadway is twenty years behind. Meanwhile a childish charade like *Man of La Mancha* threatens to run forever on the whimsical behinds of its human horses. However, the musical is a genre like any other, and, as such, it continues to flourish for its friend even as it withers for its enemies. The point, dear reader, is that you either take musicals as they are or leave them alone—and if you're in the habit of leaving them alone, *Funny Girl* will seem like much ado about nothing.

Funny Girl is actually much ado about something, or more precisely, about someone—namely, the one and only Barbra Streisand. Indeed, *Funny Girl* is the ultimate expression of Barbra in all her barbaric solitude. The rest of the movie is a desert of destroyed egos. Omar Sharif's Nick Arnstein comes over as a two-legged

cocker spaniel with a ruffled shirtfront. Anne Francis seems harm-
lessly amiable as a blonde Follies girl, but most of her part reportedly found its way to the cutting-room floor. Walter Pidgeon's
Florenz Ziegfeld makes an embarrassingly passive patsy for Barbra's nervy version of Fanny Brice, and Kay Medford's Jewish
mother backstops Barbra with a shrewd stock imitation of Connie
Gilchrist. As for the "Ziegfeld Girls" on display in the film, let us
say simply that no effort seems to have been made to flank Barbra
with scene-stealing charm and pulchritude, even on the lurid level
of the old-time Goldwyn girls. Fortunately, Jule Styne's songs manage to rise above the occasion provided by Isobel Lennart's drool-
ingly derivative script.

That leaves us with Barbra and her archantagonist, director William Wyler, and despite their well-publicized brawls, they seem to
have struck the right sparks from each other. Wyler has not so
much directed Barbra as mounted her (figuratively of course, not
literally). Barbra slithers into the very first frame of the film
through a slightly overhead angle shot from the rear of a creature in
a leopard-skin coat. The camera follows her with portentous persistence and suddenly there is a mirror and Barbra-Fanny greets her
reflection with the sardonic salutation: "Hi, Gorgeous." Thus Barbra is allowed to capitalize on the laughter of self-mockery after
an ego-building entrance that would have been considered too
gaudy for Garbo in her prime. Moreover, the laughter gains a
cutting edge from the extraordinarily exaggerated Jewish intonation of Barbra's reading. But there is something overdone about
the effect, as if Barbra took too seriously her not taking herself
seriously. Barbra Streisand is ham on wry, and the ugliness that
lingers is less in her visage than in her vanity. And *Funny Girl* is
nothing if not a monument to Barbra's vanity. She sings all the
songs, dances all the dances, and dominates all the drama. The
world is a stooge, and Wyler little more than a glorified stage manager as he maneuvers bits and pieces of non-Barbra all the better
to enhance Barbra. A critic has suggested that Barbra possesses
authentic star quality. Perhaps. From the evidence of *Funny Girl*,
however, I would be inclined to credit Barbra more with star quan-
tity than star quality. A star generally emerges from out of a con-
stellation of heavenly bodies without any undue manipulation of
mise-en-scène. It is no trick for a star to hold an audience's atten-

tion when every lens and filter has been recruited in that star's service and all traces of otherness have been banished from the screen. Not that Barbra can't hold her own under more difficult circumstances. She probably can. The fact remains, however, that *Funny Girl* might have been more aptly titled "An Evening with Barbra Streisand."

In all fairness to Miss Streisand, she might have fallen flat on her face after all the buildup, and she didn't. Practically every song number elicits spontaneous applause from the paying customers, and even this certified Barbraphobe found himself stirred on occasion by La Streisand's talent and energy. And when it was all over, and Barbra had belted out the old Brice standard "My Man" against a black abstract background that put Barbra one on one on the audience, there was a ripple of electricity in the theater, but, curiously, no warmth. The power had been turned on, but the power source seemed to be a career battery rather than a beating heart. Also, too much of Barbra's effectiveness was derived from a peculiar trick of contrasting intonations between speech and song.

Barbra exploits her Jewishness in a way that seems to titillate non-Jews more than Jews. Barbra comes on stronger than the Yiddish Art Theatre and Borscht Circuit combined, but her strongest appeal is nonethnic in nature to the extent that Jewishness has been considered in and hip and Now for the past few years. So much for Barbra speaking. Barbra singing is about as close to Fanny Brice's Lower East Side as Peggy Lee or Ethel Merman. The contrast is as exciting as the flash of Rocky Marciano's sophisticated right hand used to be after rounds and rounds of clumsy footwork, crude stalking, and costly vulnerability. Barbra is similarly exciting and shocking in her shifts from crudity to sophistication. Shocking not only because of the aesthetics but also because of the sociology. Jewish entertainers have been making it in the Wasp world ever since any of us can remember, but there was always an aspect of assimilation in the process. A Fanny Brice, an Al Jolson, a John Garfield, a Danny Kaye, a Jack Benny, or a Judy Holliday were recognizably Jewish to the Jews, but sufficiently restrained in their mannerisms and intonations to pass as Wasps in national entertainments. Even the broader comedians retained a certain distance between themselves and their dialect creations. The actresses who played Molly Goldberg and Mrs. Nussbaum were hardly one and the same with their creations. Barbra Streisand's specialty is destroying the distance between herself and her tactless, boisterous stereotype. It is as if Stepin Fetchit could turn himself off to be Sidney Poitier and then turn himself back on again, or as if Butterfly McQueen could deliver a song as if she were Lena Horne and then return to being Butterfly McQueen. A *Look* magazine article describes Barbra Streisand as "tactless," precisely the adjective that Jean-Paul Sartre ascribes to Jews in the eyes of anti-Semites. Ironically, however, Barbra Streisand seems less typically Jewish than her talented predecessors precisely because she sounds more Jewish. The drama and trauma of Jews in America has been the painful assimilation into a hostile or indifferent society. The discerning eye could see the hidden pain of Jewishness in a Sylvia Sidney or a John Garfield or a Judy Holliday because these glorious sufferers carried their Jewishness like a cross. Barbra Streisand wears it like a badge. The Jews have been a great people because they have always wanted to transcend their Jewishness with a universal idealism. By appropriating the most parochial mannerisms of Jewishness as her personal trademark, Barbra Streisand has scored a stylistic coup on the surface at the expense of a deeper vision of life. *Funny Girl* is a stirring entertainment, but all the chill cannot be attributed to the air conditioning. Even the corny self-sacrifice of the backstage-and-gangster plot loses its pathos to Barbra's unyielding professionalism. Forget about Janet Gaynor and Judy Garland in two versions of *A Star Is Born*. Forget about Katharine Hepburn in *Morning Glory* and Andrea Leeds in *Stage Door* and even Gloria Swanson in *Sunset Boulevard*. *Funny Girl* reminded me most of Betty Hutton in *Incendiary Blonde*, with a year to live while her gangster boy friend is going up the river for two years, and Betty Hutton just accepting the horrible irony with a brave smile and no huge star treatment, and I don't think I'll ever forget it. Finally, admirers of William Wyler's staging of dramatic scenes might compare the visual lines of tension the director establishes in the sofa-and-I'll-see-you-to-the-door scene with the equivalent effect in *The Letter* back in 1940. Wyler has lost none of his impersonal expertness over the years. He and Barbra were well matched in their chilling professionalism.

—*Village Voice*, October 10, 1968

■ 19. *BEYOND THE LAW*

Norman Mailer's *Beyond the Law* represents an infinite improvement over *Wild 90*, Mailer's maiden effort in cinematographic expression. *Beyond the Law* is at least sittable-through and occasionally amusing. The photography and sound recording seem to have advanced from welfare to poverty row, and the acting from amateur night to charity benefit. There is more point to the profanity, more of a correlative for the noise and violence. George Plimpton's imitation of John Lindsay adds a new dimension to racial slander in this year of the waffled Wasp. And Mailer himself is more himself here than he was as the Gallo goon in *Wild 90*. Even in its weakest moments *Beyond the Law* benefits from the comic tension between corrupt authority and outraged criminality, a tension completely lacking in the Mafia masquerade of *Wild 90*.

Unfortunately, Mailer's brand of minimal movie-making remains more interesting to talk around than to talk about. It is not for me to tell him what to do with his time and money, but I can't help wishing aloud that he would stop making movies. It's not that I have any mystical feelings about who is or who is not worthy of working in the medium. It's just that whenever Mailer comes out with a movie, I have to see it and review it, not only—or not entirely—because Mr. Mailer is one of the stockholders of the *Village Voice* but also because Mailer has matured into an authentic culture hero for a generation that can still appreciate intellectual honesty expressed in muscular prose, and I derive no particular pleasure from panning his film-flams when I would much rather contemplate his amazing and heartening performance in the literary ring. Still, I know in my bones that he will never make a movie that I can enjoy, because in his totalitarian way he is determined to punish cultural derelicts like me for ever having been beguiled by Hollywood myths. That is to say if Norman Mailer ever got aholt of $100 million to make the movie of his dreams, he would only wind up 100 million miles away from the true cinephile's heart of darkness. Norman Mailer is no more of a movie-maker than Jean-Paul Sartre is Jean-Luc Godard in medium-message drag. But to explain why I would reject Mailer's ultimate screen vision requires a fuller statement of my personal feelings toward the artist, if only to balance out the bias elements. An existential entertainer like Mr. Mailer deserves no less.

Norman Mailer was born January 31, 1923, in Long Branch, New Jersey, and grew up in Brooklyn, New York. I was born October 31, 1928, in Brooklyn, New York, and never grew up, but I can always console myself with the fact that I will always have somewhat more than five years to catch up with Mailer—much like the tortoise racing Achilles with full confidence in an eternity disdainful of differential calculus and hence free of petty metaphysical malice toward the wing-footed warrior. Besides, my long years of deserved obscurity have conditioned me to identify more with late starters than with prodigal prodigies who managed to squander their literary inheritance on dubious psychological investments. As it happens, 1968 marks the twentieth anniversary of *The Naked and the Dead*, the novel that made Mailer not merely a literary celebrity but an accursed white hope of creation, endlessly tarnished through the dark ages of political fragmentation and demonically destructive criticism. Having missed World War II, I was still in Columbia in 1948, always sneaking off to movies, drifting imperceptibly from the rock-ribbed Republicanism of the campus Metternich Society to the doctrinaire populism of Harry Truman. (Mine had been the only relief family in Brooklyn to vote for Alf Landon in 1936.) Mailer, I think, was for Henry Wallace, and hence remote from my relatively timid traumas. My own reaction to *The Naked and the Dead* at the time was fogged up by my complete ignorance of the political context in which literary reputations were established. The Trotskyist formalism of the *Partisan Review*ers, for example, seemed needlessly polemical to a reader for whom Stalinist strictures had been not merely absurd but anathema in the most reactionary sense. Somewhat later I wrote off *The Naked and the Dead* as warmed-over Dos Passos, almost an updated remake of *Manhattan Transfer* and *U.S.A.*, though whereas Dos Passos stacked Marxist maxims atop the fugging corpses of Flanders Fields and psychopathic Wilsonian idealism and vampirish American capitalism, Mailer repudiated the American dream of Uncle Franklin and Aunt Eleanor in the name of a radicalism that was to be defined in the next twenty years out of the fevered impressions and expressions of a world gone mad.

Mailer has been a name for twenty years, a name not entirely free of notoriety, but a name nonetheless. At times the progression of a personality took precedence over the course of a career. *Barbary Shore* and *The Deer Park* were treated more like the scandals of a shameless exhibitionist than the spiritual testaments they seem like today. Mailer's addled agit-prop exploded every form he attempted, but the literary Establishment only mourned his failure to conform to the contours of the Great American Novel. More successful was the Mailer of the magazine pieces, the ambassador without portfolio from the Old Left at the summit with the beats, the blacks, the hipsters, and, always, the beautiful people. This was the Mailer whom Robert Lowell and his wife insulted as the "greatest journalist in America." Even now that Mailer has virtually invented new fictional forms on the steps of the Pentagon and in the streets of Chicago, he still seems to feel cut off from his proper constituency, the ever-yearning youth of America. So much hard work, so many polished paragraphs, so many scintillating similes, so many incisive insights gouged out of his guts, and all for the applause of middle-aged intellectuals who have forgiven him all his follies and hang-ups, and all the while the Beatles and Dylan go *mmmmmm* and unleash all the magic and fantasy that mere intellect and intelligence can never inspire. And what better shortcut to the senses than movies, that lucrative profession of mediocre manipulators, perverts, and imbeciles? Mailer has never been prudent in the projection of his personality, and too often the attempted magnification of his image has only diminished it in the compulsive descent from strength to weakness.

Mailer credits himself with some witty ripostes to Eugene McCarthy's Jesuitical jests, and I believe Mailer in the painfully honest context of his *Harper's* piece on the Chicago convention. Mailer doesn't need to rewrite his personal history with staircase wit, because the one talent he does possess is the ability to rise to the moment of immediate intimacy. If you stand five feet from Mailer at a moment when he is not aware of being on display, you get the exhilarating sensation of a brilliant quarterback changing to an automatic to counter a charging linebacker. Mailer's is a mind in motion to the very moment of its contact with reality, and is this not the mark of the journalist rather than the novelist, the conversationalist rather than the orator?

It is only when Mailer tries to ritualize his persona that he becomes ridiculous. Hence I would rather read all of Mailer's insightful perceptions of policemen in the pages of *Harper's* than see these same perceptions enacted piecemeal on the screen. Similarly, I would rather look at Steve McQueen's cop in *Bullitt* and Clint Eastwood's in *Coogan's Bluff* than read their rambling ruminations on law and order. McQueen and Eastwood are interesting screen personalities because their essence is more interesting than their existence. Mailer is uninteresting on the screen because his essence is less interesting than his existence. The screen functions to freeze life styles into myth rather than to adjust life forces to art. The beauty of actors is that they are basically vain enough and stupid enough to allow themselves to be embalmed for the edification of their audience. By contrast, intellectuals are always undercutting their personae with their anxieties and analyses. Besides, Mailer is a lousy lecturer, a lousy actor, and a lousy TV panelist. (To be chewed up by Buckley is no disgrace, but to be chewed up by Truman Capote!) Of course, a brilliant writer like Mailer can dismiss lecturing, acting, and TV paneling as the most minor of art forms, but to persist in these activities is merely to indulge in prolonged Plimptonism.

Mailer is quoted in *Variety* as complaining that some of the critiques of *Wild 90* failed to take into consideration that he was a beginner in his craft; seemingly, first novelists are given greater leeway than first film-makers. We will not go into the comparative generosity of book and movie reviewers, except insofar as certain writers are pampered and others ignored and certain lines are upheld, not to mention Mailer's singularly ungenerous critique of Mary McCarthy's *The Group* in the *New York Review of Books*—and she no mere beginner. Also, movie reviewers are under greater pressure from their readers, because people see movies almost as fast as they are reviewed, and they have strong opinions about them, whereas no one reads books anymore if a comprehensive review is available.

When Mailer talks about "craft" in movie-making, he seems to be confusing a medium with an art form. No one expects Mailer to start taking film courses in his mid-forties so that he can mouth the technical mumbo jumbo. People hate *Wild 90* because the dialogue is almost inaudible, and this has nothing to do with "craft." The production is simply too cheap to afford the proper facilities, and this is a problem of money. Would Mailer's articles be admired as much if they were circulated clandestinely on smudged-up mimeograph sheets with innumerable typos? Mailer himself used to complain about the typos in his *Village Voice* articles, and he finally stopped writing for this periodical because of his bruised sensibilities. Moviegoers prefer glossy screens the way readers prefer glossy pages, and there is nothing to be done about it. If anything, the screen as a window to dreams and realities demands more technological care than the printed page. If Norman Mailer wants to win over audiences, he doesn't have to learn his craft. He can buy it on the open market, but it will cost a great deal more than he has been willing to invest thus far, and I don't think it will be worth it.

—*Village Voice*, October 24, 1968

■ 20. *WEEKEND*

Weekend consolidates Jean-Luc Godard's position as the most disconcerting of all contemporary directors, a veritable paragon of paradoxes, violent and yet vulnerable, the most elegant stylist and the most vulgar polemicist, the most remorseful classicist and the most relentless modernist, the man of the moment and the artist for the ages. When I bore witness to *Weekend* at the Berlin Film Festival back in June, Godard seemed to be tuned in to the youthful frequency of the future. He lost me somewhere between the garbage truck of the Third World and the slaughtered pig of the new breed, but I did feel the film unwinding with all the clattering contemporaneity of a ticker tape, and the reading for Western Civilization was down, down, and out. Seeing *Weekend* again on a chill Nixonish November in New York, I am struck more by Godard's melancholy than by his message. As much as Godard indulges in the rhetoric of rebellion, his deepest feelings seem to be situated before the revolution. He was born, he implies, too soon and too late—too soon to forget the sweetness of the past and too late to perpetuate that same sweetness, particularly in the remembered realm of movies with subjects not yet swallowed up by the subjective. Gosta Berling calling Johnny Guitar, Godard's puppets prattle into their walkie-talkies. Potemkin calling Prisoner of the Desert (the French title for John Ford's *The Searchers*). And there are still meaningful responses from the alumni federation of the first row of the Paris Cinémathèque. Johnny Guitar to Gosta Berling. Prisoner of the Desert to Potemkin. Communication confirmed.

But for how much longer? Can there be as much fun in the future with Jean-Luc Godard calling Bernardo Bertolucci and Bernardo Bertolucci calling Alexander Kluge and Alexander Kluge calling Andy Warhol atop the last scrap heap of waste in the West? (We must try not to anticipate Antonioni's pilgrimage to Zabriskie Point.) Godard seems to want it both ways as the prime prophet of the first-person film and the lead mourner of the third-person movie. Indeed, Godard has been bemoaning the death of movies ever since *Breathless,* a period of almost a full decade, long enough to turn the tears of a meaningful prophet into the tears of a professional mourner. With *Weekend* Jean-Luc has been to the wailing wall once too often. Godard's weeping over the past is now merely one of his regular routines, a means of rationalizing his own increasing fragmentation in terms of the alleged chaos of his time. Hence the opening credits of *Weekend* proclaim that what we are about to witness is more a relic of our reality than an interpretation of that reality. Godard's whimsically apocalyptic context for his films enables him to peruse newspapers as if they were ancient tablets—and why not? Who is to say that future civilizations might not be more intrigued by the casual observation that Frenchmen had become so Americanized by 1967 that they were driving Japanese cars than by any of the antimemoirs of Malraux? Godard's compulsive tendency to juggle cultural references from brassiere-ad copy to Brecht leaves him vulnerable to the charge of intellectual superficiality, a charge balanced off by the simple fact that Godard, like the subject of the brassiere-ad copy, looks better than he reads, and a visual flair still counts for something even in the most modern cinema.

Godard's strengths and weaknesses are immediately apparent in the opening shots of *Weekend.* Husband, wife, and wife's lover-analyst sit on a leafy terrace. Phone rings and intrigues commence. Wife is cheating on husband and husband on wife, talk of poisons and inheritances, lust and avarice, on the Jeeter Lester level of characterization, barnyard-animal dramaturgy out of the nastiest comic-strip capitalism imaginable. But Raoul Coutard's fully textured, subtly shadowed color cinematography undercuts the calculating crudity of the dialogue. The dissociation of the visual from the verbal is no accident, however. Within the same sequence Godard demonstrates the formal mastery of his material. The three bourgeois characters look down from their balcony at a street accident culminating in a violent brawl between the two drivers involved. Godard stages the brawl from such an insistently overhead viewpoint that he creates a metaphor for bourgeois detachment from social turmoil. The verticality of the viewpoint is sustained long enough to remind the educated moviegoer of a similar metaphor in Luis Buñuel's and Salvador Dali's more overtly surrealist classic, *Un Chien Andalou*. Whereas Buñuel and Dali treated apparent moral indifference as actual metaphysical liberation, Godard treats idle curiosity as immoral complicity. The difference between Buñuel-Dali and Godard is therefore the difference between irony and allegory. Furthermore, Godard's brawl is staged so elaborately that its violence is more rhetorical than real, more for the sake of a voyeuristic spectacle than for the release of psychic tensions. Hence—and this is true throughout *Weekend*—Godard's violence is more cerebral than visceral.

The bourgeois couple impersonated by Mireille Darc and Jean Yanne are less the involved subjects of *Weekend* than its detached objects. Never before has Godard been so far outside a pair of protagonists. Never before has he shown so little concern for their fate and so few close-ups of their features. After my first viewing of *Weekend* I could barely remember what Darc and Yanne looked like, a sure sign that the closest bond between Godard and his characters is one of contempt. Even the *voyous* of Jean-Paul Belmondo in *Breathless* and Claude Brasseur in *Band of Outsiders* have hitherto been infiltrated by Godard's sensibility. By contrast, the bourgeois yahoos of Darc and Yanne are repeatedly harangued by Godard from the outside. Far from being treated as the victims of bourgeois society, they emerge as its arch villains. Symptomatic of Godard's intransigent indifference toward this despised duo is the fact that the death of the husband and the desecration of the wife transpire offscreen with the most callous casualness.

Nonetheless Mireille Darc does manage to dominate a curiously sacramental scene in which her flesh is offered up to a Godardian fantasy reminiscent of the bare-buttocked Bardolatry of *Contempt*. This is the scene in which Darc describes an orgy in extravagant detail to her lover-analyst. When I saw *Weekend* in Berlin, most of Darc's descriptive dialogue was inaudible on the sound track, as if Godard were holding back on the lurid details to create a more ritualistic effect. In the version now on view in New York, the Grove Press subtitles come over lewd and clear, and the effect is therefore more sensually insinuating.

Darc's confessional has been compared to Bibi Andersson's in *Persona*, the latter hailed by many critics as supremely erotic. (I have never understood whether the existence of eroticism was established by the empirical evidence of erection or by a logical analysis of visual and verbal expression. Admittedly, even Wittgenstein would wander far afield in this region of research.) The erotic element in Andersson's account is not so much the actual experience she is describing as the emotional vulnerability that she exposes in telling the story to Liv Ullmann, she of the vampirish eyes and seductive proximity. Bergman's sense of camera space is fundamentally bas-relief, with an occasional interchange of foreground and background for his eloquently expressive faces. Space itself does not really function for him as a stylistic figure. By contrast, Godard has inherited Murnau's mysticism about space on the screen, and his use of the camera in *Weekend* is therefore more dynamic than Bergman's in *Persona*, particularly as regards their respective oblique sex scenes. If I would argue that Godard is more erotic than Bergman on this occasion, it would amount virtually to a paradox. Normally Bergman is much more erotic than Godard, and there is simply no contest between Bibi Andersson (especially in *Le Viol*) and Mireille Darc. The difference is in the marvelously ceremonial indecorum with which Godard stages Darc's confessional. Seated on a sacrificial table with her legs drawn up, down to her bra and panties, deliberately shifting her position with each new climax to her confession, talking in a singsong monotone that emphasizes her emotional detachment from her outrageous complicity in the most bizarre perversions, Mireille Darc awakens a fantasy response through Godard's reflective ritual, the same ritual that ultimately delivers her body to her ambivalent lover-analyst. If Bibi Andersson misses out on this fantasy response, it is because she is too encumbered by Bergman's psychological mysteries, which generate too much suspense for erotic ritual.

Eroticism aside, Weekend is most likely to be remembered for the sustained tracking shot of a traffic tie-up extending for miles across the dull French landscape. The first time I saw Weekend I was struck most forcibly by Godard's lack of comic inventiveness in the description of the delay. By the standards of classical slapstick —Chaplin, Keaton, Lloyd, and Laurel and Hardy, the latter particularly for Two Tars—Godard runs out of inspiration about a third of the way along or at about the time he repeats the gag about the two motorists playing chess. I wasn't impressed even when Godard sought to implicate the audience in the discovery of the bloody bodies that, once discovered and passed, enabled our stalled motorists to speed away with a lyrical vavoom to liberty and grace. Still, I recognized that old familiar feeling of survival of the fittest (or luckiest) on the open road. I just happened to be one or two beats ahead of Godard in anticipating his moralistic tag shot, and so I wrote off the scene as failed shaggy dog story. This time around in New York I was struck more by the insanely insistent honking of horns for minutes upon minutes until the bloody bodies became a blessed relief even to this forewarned spectator. Again, the morbid beauty of the camera movement convinced me that this was indeed no time for comedy or even satire. There was something too deterministic about that inexorably moving camera across the intransigently neutral landscape. Mere litterateurs can never appreciate the intoxicating quality of a meaningful camera movement as it obliterates the formal boundaries of the picture frame. Toward the end of the film Godard stages an orgiastic Ode to the Ocean performed by cannibalistic French hippies, but the scene doesn't really work because Godard doesn't seem to feel the ode very deeply, or the communal mysticism the ode is supposed to express. Also, there is much more of the "oceanic" feeling Romain Rolland described to Sigmund Freud in Godard's tracking shot of the traffic jam than in the Ode to the Ocean.

The high point of Weekend is the culmination of the second circular camera movement around a pastoral, even rural, agricultural, barnyard performance of Mozart's Piano Sonata, K. 576. Paul Gégauff is one of Chabrol's wilder scriptwriters. Gégauff's argument, perhaps Godard's also, is that so-called serious modern composers have less to offer the modern listener than do such genuinely Mozartian descendants as the Beatles and the Rolling Stones. Godard would seem to be establishing a different critical line for music (his avocation) than for cinema (his vocation). It doesn't matter. Godard is interesting less for his attitude toward ideas than for his aptness for images together with the feelings these images express. Godard's concert is the most beautiful expression of the rapport between art and nature I have ever seen on the screen. The beauty may be attributable to the fact that Godard is somewhat ill at ease with both nature and art, and thus emotionally responsive to both.

Apart from its admirable set pieces, *Weekend* tends to disintegrate into witless bourgeois-baiting and coy Pirandellianism. Godard has destroyed the notion of beginning, middle, and end by shooting everything in existential sequence, so that his films do not so much end as stop. The disadvantage of this approach even for Godard is becoming increasingly apparent. Godard seldom has any kick left for the last lap. His best scenes are likely to be in the middle or the beginning or whatever day of shooting he felt up to it. By contrast, a brash entertainer like Fellini always saves something extra for his endings, so that his audience can go dancing or crying out of the theater to Nino Rota's moodily Chaplinesque melodies. Fellini's instinct for showmanship is sounder and more appealing than Godard's instinct for audience alienation through calculating abruptness. But there is always something that lingers in a Godard film, perhaps a disturbing ambivalence or a morbid streak of style, but most often a uniquely cinematic intelligence that verges on artistic brilliance by any standard. The way Godard is able to deliver an impromptu essay on the point of view of an unmanipulated stone makes up for any number of embarrassingly inside "asides." One such outrage is the embarrassing tramp character right out of Bresson's *Mouchette* who proceeds to rape Mireille Darc out of sight in a deep hole, and then rises out of the hole, glances at his victim's husband, the camera moving with his glance past the husband to a meaningless distance down the road solely to give time for Mireille Darc to climb out of the hole and rejoin her husband

—all this in one shot, and that the most gratuitous in the history of the cinema. And yet there is the orgy and the traffic jam and the rock and the concert and, as always with Jean-Luc Godard, the promise of a fascinating future.

—*Village Voice*, November 21, 1968

■ 21. *FACES*

I would like to recommend *Faces* without restructuring the reader's aesthetic expectations, but I know by now that I can't escape the consequences of my criticism. *Faces*, if seen at all, should be seen with a degree of tolerance for its rough edges and raw nerve endings. Indeed, the first half hour strains so hard for its strained conviviality that the movie becomes a bad bet to last two hours without bursting a blood vessel. Writer-director (but here not actor) John Cassavetes begins the proceedings with a framing scene that is recalled in retrospect as a half-baked Brechtian distancing device. It doesn't really belong to the picture, but, curiously, it works on its own terms. A comically hard-boiled TV producer (John Marley) grumpily sips his early-morning-dawn's-ugly-light coffee in a screening room consecrated by his staff to the exhibition of a slice of real life in which Mr. Marley himself is to be reincarnated as one of the pathetic protagonists. Already we are being treated to the ear-shorn, nose-heavy facial distortions of *caméra vérité*, not to mention the serpentine person-to-person and room-to-room camera movements with which we have become so familiar on television's more realistic spectacles, such as the "When is Mr. Nixon coming down, Herb?" show on election night. Look at me! the camera screams too stridently. Look how honest and real and true I am! This viewer, I must confess, braced himself at this point for a strenuous session of formlessness masquerading as fearlessness. And who are all these strangely worn unknowns? The only familiar face among the players is Gena Rowlands' (Mrs. John Cassavetes), and even she has hardly been victimized by overexposure these past few years. The whole project smells so strongly of poverty row that the more cautious critic may beware the thin line between inspired naturalism and nagging indigence. Exterior shots, for example, are rarer in *Faces* than in the raunchiest sexploitation films. Scenes go on and on with Warholian exhaustiveness (though not exhaustion). And Cassavetes lets all the players laugh their heads off to the point that nervousness is transformed into purgation. Strange, different— but is it good? The notion of art as selection and compression gets short shrift in *Faces*. All in all, there are only seven master scenes with three very brief transitions and virtually no parallel editing for contrast or irony. No one seems to be cut off and nothing seems to be cut. Even at its best, *Faces* cannot be considered a triumph of cinematic form, and the formalist in me has been resisting the sloppy eccentricities of Cassavetes ever since *Shadows* a decade or so ago.

Ultimately, however, *Faces* emerges for me as the revelation of 1968, not the best movie to be sure, but certainly the most surprising. (Buñuel's *Belle de Jour* merely caps a career that has crested many times before.) After its somewhat strained beginning, *Faces* not only works, it soars. The turning point is the first desperately domestic conversation between John Marley and Lynn Carlin, a conversation swept along on its banal course by gales of nervous laughter, a conversation accompanied by physical withdrawal behind the luxurious barriers of space, walls, doors, and furniture, a conversation that in its lack of topical details and symbolic overtones is perhaps closer to aimless soap opera than to deliberate drama. But it works in ways that are mysterious to behold, as if for once a soap opera was allowed to unfold out of its own limited logic for two hours without interruption for commercials or station identification. What we have in *Faces*, therefore, is not only a failure to communicate but a reluctance to terminate, and this reluctance is one of the reasons *Faces* achieves an otherwise inexplicable intensity of feeling that transcends the too easily satirized milieu of affluently superficial Southern California. Although it is concerned almost exclusively with the lecherous delusions of pickups and pick-me-ups, *Faces* is never sordid or squalid. Cassavetes stays with his tormented, alienated characters until they break through the other side of slice-of-life naturalism into emotional and artistic truth.

Faces works even if we question its creator's original intentions.

Who can ever say for sure that *Faces* is not a kind of serendipity cinema, that is, a movie that started out as a dull diatribe against American life and ended up as a heroic saga of emotional survival through an endless night of loneliness and shattered defenses? *Faces* is certainly more interesting in itself than for all the things that can be said about it, a mark of merit more intrinsic than extrinsic. Still, Cassavetes deserves full credit for the inspired idea (possibly intuitive) of developing characters objectively in odd-numbered relationships before exploring them intimately in even-numbered couplings. Hence the first scene features two men competing in the apartment of the girl they've picked up in a bar. The infernal triangle brings out all the self-hatred of the errant husbands and takes us quite logically into a scene of domestic coupling through which self-hatred takes on new dimensions. The husband tells the wife he wants a divorce, and thus two become one and one, but when he calls the girl he picked up earlier in the evening, it turns out that she is occupied with a double date. No matter. The tormented husband bursts in on the party of four to make an unwelcome fifth, scuffles grotesquely with an equally aging, equally affluent philanderer, but then everyone makes up as a sixth girl is recruited to restore the original double coupling of the evening and leave the husband alone with his original date. The arithmetical progression proceeds four to five by intrusion, five to six by augmentation, and finally two and four by division. Meanwhile the deserted wife and three of her more domestically disaffected girl friends visit a go-go dance joint, where they allow themselves to be picked up by a swaggering but thirtyish hippie. (The movie was shot at least two years ago, and thus the skirts look curiously long and the dances relatively coherent, a good sic-transit-go-go-gloria argument against ever trying to be too timely.) The circle of five disintegrates into a series of jealous explosions until wife and hippie are left alone in illusory togetherness, a dubious coupling that leads the wife to the medicine cabinet in search of the ultimate number —zero.

All through the movie, people are intimating that they want to be alone with each other even though they have been conditioned to function only in a crowd. They are driven to sex not by desire but by adolescent bravado that they know instinctively is spiritually futile, but still they pay lip service to the ideal of intimacy, the

very ideal their society has degraded with its dirty jokes and infantile inhibitions. The characters in *Faces* start off as a lineup of
emotional cripples, but somehow they all make it to the finish line
with their souls intact. Among the players I would single out Lynn
Carlin, John Marley, Seymour Cassel, and Gena Rowlands for
special praise out of a virtually flawless ensemble. And if this be
actor's cinema, long may it flourish. At the very least, Cassavetes
deserves full credit for staging the spectacle with both conviction
and compassion.

—*Village Voice*, December 5, 1968

■ 22. *THE BIRTHDAY PARTY*

The Birthday Party is fundamentally faithful to Harold Pinter's
fragmented vision of the world, so much so, in fact, that many
viewers may resent being forced to accept the film on faith in the
name of high art. The plot, such as it is, moves from unexplained
eccentricity to undefined menace without any stops along the way
for motives or morals. An unkempt young piano player named
Stanley (Robert Shaw) boards at the seedy, seaside cottage of two
pseudoparental figures nicknamed Meg (Dandy Nichols) and
Petey (Moultrie Kelsall). Stanley may or may not have given a
concert once before the destructive "They" of Edward Lear's anti-
conformist limericks closed out his career. Meg can't afford a piano
for Stanley, but she has bought him a drum to beat on what may
or may not be the occasion of his birthday. Meg's comically surreal
breakfasts—corn flakes in spoiled milk followed with a flourish by
fried bread—are patiently endured by the passively living Petey,
but the spoiled Stanley sputters, snorts, and cackles over every last
culinary indignity of his existence. A saucy girl next door named
Lulu (Helen Fraser) rounds out the expositional environment, but
this creature of fantasy accessibility counts for even less in the
movie than she did in the play. (Harold Pinter's world seems to
focus almost invariably on the male in malevolence.) Into the
comfortable disorder of Stanley's navel-scratching existence come

two strangers lacking logical reasons for either arriving or existing. Petey tells Meg that the two men are looking for a place to stay, and Meg finds their request perfectly reasonable. Stanley, however, immediately suspects a sinister purpose in their arrival. Thus domestic farce of an insane intensity is mixed with the suspenseful paranoia of melodrama.

Robert Shaw's Stanley combines some of the table-swiping gusto of Marlon Brando's Stanley Kowalski in A *Streetcar Named Desire* with some of Joseph Cotten's feline apprehensiveness in *Shadow of a Doubt* whenever the presence of two strange men is reported. Detectives, hired killers, salesmen, and other depredators of capitalistic fact and genre fiction travel traditionally in pairs. Many of the nightmarish images of William S. Burroughs were undoubtedly inspired by the mythic presence of a team of narcotics agents in every two strange faces on a street corner. Pinter's pairing, however, is more eccentric than most. Goldberg (Sydney Tafler) and McCann (Patrick Magee) resemble at first glance a cartoonist's conception of brains and brawn except that they seem to understand each other better than the audience understands either of them. The most striking incongruity in their relationship is not so much that Goldberg is Jewish and McCann Irish as that both Goldberg's Jewishness and McCann's Irishness are too exaggerated for the normal ecumenical demands of dramatic realism. They are less types than archetypes, and, as such, contribute to the allegorical spell of their scenes.

Stanley's worst fears are soon justified. Goldberg and McCann have in fact come for Stanley in the name of Monty, apparently Pinter's code name for some metaphysical syndicate. But with a true *Darkness at Noon* deviousness, Goldberg and McCann do not hustle their victim to his destination until he has understood the inevitability of his fate through a series of rituals—a garbled third-degree inquisition, a traumatic birthday party complete with a game of blindman's buff, and a sexual initiation culminating in a nervous breakdown.

The next morning Stanley has been reduced to stammering inarticulateness, and despite Petey's kindly paternal protests, he walks off with his captors to an unknown fate. Meg comes back and asks if Stanley is awake yet, and Petey advises her to let Stanley sleep for once, especially on this morning of mornings, and Meg accepts this unaccustomed advice because she is still basking in the glow of the birthday party the night before, when her feelings and femininity were appreciated for what seemed like the very first time.

What does it all mean? Some people would argue that it is all meaningless mystification and that you can't prove that it means anything. Pinter himself discourages any elaborate analysis of his writing by asking rhetorically, "What does 'mean' mean?" He pulled this line on a panel I moderated with him and Losey last year, and the line pops up again in the mouth of a child onstage in Pinter's *The Tea Party*. But what *does* "mean" mean? This is a problem that is especially pertinent to modern culture, with its built-in defenses and disclaimers. The critic proceeds, of course, at his own peril, but he has no choice if he is to be called a critic.

The first time I ever worried about what a work of art meant was when I read *Moby Dick* in high-school freshman English after my teacher had warned me I wouldn't understand it. But I did. As Rosalind Russell once observed in *Wonderful Town*, Melville's book is about this whale . . . Unfortunately, there is no whale in the plays of Harold Pinter, no apparent subject with which to placate the audience. That does not mean that Pinter is deeper or more profound than Melville or Shakespeare. It means simply that Pinter operates with one less layer of meaning than did his classical predecessors and is hence more obscure on the surface. Of all the books I read when I was in high school, and my uneducated tastes ranged from Marcel Proust to Percival Wren, the only book that baffled me completely was Laurence Sterne's *Tristram Shandy*, and only now have I come to realize that what I couldn't understand was Sterne's penchant, like Godard's, for sacrificing form for fact. What I didn't understand at the time at all was that a work of art may be analyzed for centuries and never yield up all its possible meanings. *Moby Dick* was more than material for one reading; it was the testament of a man in his time, at once a projection and a reflection of ideas and feelings externalized through images and fictions. At the very least, a reading of *King Lear* might help explain some of the stormy mise-en-scène of *Moby Dick*. It would help also to trace Melville's life into the innards of his art.

Since art need not be obscure to be profound, or profound to be obscure, Pinter doesn't get any points automatically for being dif-

ficult to decipher. Indeed, obscurantism is becoming increasingly
unfashionable. Why, then, does Pinter get generally good reviews?
Partly, I suppose, because he fits conveniently into the Kafka bag,
a context of sentimental pessimism for disaffected intellectuals the
world over. Partly also because he has become required reading in
the curriculum of the absurd with Beckett and Ionesco, though I
find him neither absurd like Beckett nor grotesque like Ionesco,
but instead eccentric in the tradition of Oscar Wilde's *The Importance of Being Earnest*. Usually, however, Pinter is praised
more for his small talents than his large meanings, and these small
talents are considerable indeed. Pinter has the best ear for spoken
English of any living playwright. (Beckett may have the edge on
the basis of an inner ear, but the modes of thought are those of the
expatriate.) Pinter's dialogue can be deeply, darkly funny to the
point of a too tempting facility. And he has an actor's ability to
milk a bit of business till the cows come home. McCann's obsessive paper-tearing, for example, turns a prop into a brutally hypnotic piece of characterization. Stanley's toy drum is turned virtually
inside out from prop to symbol to sacrament until it reverberates
with all sorts of emotional echoes.

But what of his large meanings, if any? I find it significant that
critics concentrate on the malevolence in his work at the expense
of the pathos, and yet I find *The Birthday Party* more sad than
menacing, even in William Friedkin's badly directed film version
with its stately, pretentious, positively funereal pacing. However,
Pinter himself is a man for all media, and it seems that he had
much to do with Friedkin's folly of piling cinematic eccentricities
atop theatrical eccentricities with an affectation of austerity—eccentricities, moreover, in their most literal sense of approaching
reality from an angle somewhat off-center. Thus though the movie
is blessed with a dream cast, it is considerably less affecting than
the American stage production I saw in 1966. For one thing, Friedkin kills the emotional curtain effects of the first and second acts
by muffling the climaxes with visual indirection. Thus we never see
the interplay of defiance and dependence in Stanley's beating on
the drum until, unable to bear his lonely liberty, he seeks to bury
his head in the womb of his figurative mother. Worse still, the
whole point of the birthday party itself is lost in a devious darkness that makes it impossible for us to see Stanley's fatal sexual ini-

tiation that leaves him a cringing figure of guilt and shame, and hence, in the eyes of the world, a fully mature adult. (Indeed, *The Birthday Party* could be subtitled *Growing Up Absurd*.)

Pinter exploits another artistic alibi apart from the Kafka bag, and that is, quite simply, that his protagonists are crackers in the most clinical way, and so what seems like stylized fragmentation is a kind of Caligari realism that reveals the world from the point of view of a nervous breakdown. What it pays Pinter to mean, however, may be quite different from what he really means, and though it may take centuries to be reasonably sure, I would like to take a stab at Pinter's real meaning.

Actually, *The Birthday Party* was first produced back in 1958, and was Pinter's second play, *The Room*, I believe, being his first. We know that Pinter's father was a Jewish tailor in East London, and it is reasonable to trace the knowingly patriarchical intonations of Goldberg back to the echoes of the playwright's childhood. Pinter did not have much formal schooling, left home at an early age to become an actor, and toured Ireland (McCann?) in classical repertory under the name of David Baron. For a time he was actually a caretaker in a basement apartment, a striking indication of Pinter's reliance on his own raw experience to flesh out his supposedly stylized plays. If we lump all of Pinter's writings into one pile, we are left with two overwhelmingly obvious impressions: First, Pinter's plays are generally constructed meaningfully around or within architectural enclosures—*The Room, The Basement, The Dumb Waiter, The Caretaker*—or family occasions—*The Birthday Party, The Homecoming, The Tea Party*. Thus Pinter's locus, unlike Beckett's, is domestic rather than cosmic. Second, Pinter's plays are dominated by essentially male rivalries in which women figure only as creatures of fantasy and desire. The obsessive repetitiveness of this latter plot formula suggests some strong sibling rivalry either in his own family or in the professional family of actors, intellectuals in the rough, collaborators, or the like. Born in 1930, Pinter was a child of the mass media—in his time mainly movies and radio. Drenched in popular culture, and yet drawn to the temple of high art (*vide* Goldberg's adult-education affectations that make him sound at times like a homegrown Spinoza), Pinter resists intellectual corruption by recording it in stylized spectacles. Thus on one level *The Birthday Party* is a gangster movie with realistic overtones, or rather a recollection of one of life's bitterest experiences disguised at the time as a bad movie. When Pinter complains that conversations do not yield up all the emotional meanings of relationships, what he may really be saying is that his earliest conversations never came close to expressing the feelings he was to remember much later when it was too late.

What has happened to Pinter and to all of us is a psychological displacement brought about through an instinctive mimicry of the life styles of stars and other celebrities, a rhetorical indirection of expression by which modern families conceal their deepest emotions in the false camaraderie of a shared culture. Thus what is most irritating about Pinter as an artist is also most meaningful. He plays too much to his proven strengths and seldom ventures forth into the unexplored terrain of explicit emotions, but it is reasonable to assume that if he regrets indirection of expression, he was also somewhat victimized by it in his emotionally formative years and now finds it difficult to release his feelings in his art. He never seems to follow through on characterizations to a decisive definition of identity. Stanley disappears from view in *The Birthday Party* for so long a time that both play and film become emotionally disoriented. Again a meaningful flaw, since it suggests the idea of interchangeability that runs through all of Pinter's work and some of Godard's as well. Hence the tendency of Pinter's characters to use each other's lines, at times to speak with one voice, defines the crisis of cultural identity in a mass culture. Ultimately, Pinter is telling his audience not to ask him what his art means because it means too much to him. Also, if his metaphysically menacing melodramas were unveiled as nostalgic family chronicles, the culture vultures would abandon him for ventures more satisfyingly misanthropic. Whatever anyone may say, I don't believe that Stanley is going to his death at the end of *The Birthday Party*, or that Goldberg and McCann mean him any harm in the luridly melodramatic sense. Stanley has simply grown up, and he can't stand it because he has left too much unfinished emotional business behind, but he must go out in the world, supposedly to find himself, but actually to find himself, like Pinter, lost irrevocably to the echoes of many voices chattering in endless, unrelated conversations.

—*Village Voice*, December 19, 1968

■ 23. *THE BLISS OF MRS. BLOSSOM; THE KILLING OF SISTER GEORGE*

The Bliss of Mrs. Blossom is so much the sleeper of the year that not only has it virtually disappeared from view amid the holiday rush but I almost missed it myself. Indeed, were it not for the eloquent exhortations of such certified sleeper-spotters as Michael McKegney and David Ehrenstein, I might have postponed the pleasure of seeing it until sometime in 1969. Around twenty-five movies have opened this month, and it is simply impossible for a single pair of professional eyes to catch them all. Also, a coy title like *The Bliss of Mrs. Blossom* is calculated to keep audiences away, particularly in this era of raw meat. Whatever they may say, people are not that interested in mere wit and charm. As much as they deplore sensationalism, they rush off to see *The Killing of Sister George, The Boston Strangler, Candy, et al.* Simply for the box office the title of the movie should have been changed from *The Bliss of Mrs. Blossom* to *Adultery in the Attic.* A bit sensational, I would be the first to admit, but that's just to get the suckers into the tent. Once inside, they would be treated to a bubbling, sparkling, civilized comedy of marital and extramarital manners, an exercise in stylistic sublimation that elevates Joseph McGrath (*Casino Royale, 30 Is a Dangerous Age, Cynthia*) to the top of the class, ahead of Lester, Donner, Donen, Sarne, and others. Alec Coppel and Dennis Norden wrote the screenplay from a play by Coppel based in turn on a story by producer Josef Shaftel, but I don't want to go too much into the plot, because, with all the good will in the world, it doesn't sound like very much. Shirley MacLaine, Richard Attenborough, and James Boothe are deftly directed in their daft roles, and Freddie Jones does a swishy Scotland Yard inspector to a fare-thee-well. However, Shirley MacLaine is the biggest revelation in the most restrained performance of her career. All in all, *The Bliss of Mrs. Blossom* belongs neither on Forty-second Street nor Eighth Street, but in the Radio City Music Hall with all the gaudy gauze of the Christmas show. It would have been a better choice than the obscene family spectacle of *The Impossible Years.*

viii

1969

■ 1. *THE SEA GULL; OLIVER!*

The Sea Gull sighs and flutters with every step it takes into a forest of feelings. Sidney Lumet's tactful, tasteful direction serves Anton Chekhov admirably, but at one remove from the original inspiration, so that what was once tragicomic is now bittersweet. Lumet is too often dismissed as an expressive embalmer of theater pieces, as if expressive embalming were not an art in its own right. The fact remains that Lumet has understood Chekhov's subtler nuances sufficiently to render them more naturally than they could ever be rendered on the stage. Comparing Moura Budberg's new adaptation from memory with a dog-eared copy of my old Constance Garnett translation, I must give an edge to the Budberg version, if only for the deletion of Chekhov's clumsy asides, which, if transferred intact to the screen in the form of inner monologues, would have turned *The Sea Gull* into a Slavic *Strange Interlude*. Otherwise, Budberg's "gynecologist" seems preferable to Garnett's "accoucheur," and Trigorin's candid critique of Treplev's art is more sharply expressed by "he never strikes the right note" (Budberg) than by "he never quite comes off" (Garnett). Occasionally the Budberg adaptation strains too hard for contemporaneity, as in Treplev's somewhat improbable if not downright anachronistic reference to Trigorin's prominence in the "gossip columns," the latter a strictly American innovation.

The cast has an odd sort of Lumet stamp—James Mason, Simone Signoret, David Warner, and Harry Andrews having ap-

419

peared previously in Lumet's *The Deadly Affair*, and Kathleen Widdoes having sprung from *The Group*. Lumet is well served by all his players but one, and she is the intransigently indecipherable Simone Signoret, a veritable mélange of mispronunciation and miscasting as Irina Nikolayevna Arkadin, allegedly an actress in the grand manner, vain, selfish, self-absorbed, everything Signoret is not and never could be and never could play. When Signoret's Arkadina says in effect, "Look how I take care of myself and my looks," we look past Chekhov's dramatic persona to Signoret's iconographic incarnation of the neurotically modern performer who lets herself go to prove somehow that she is superior to the narcissism of her profession. Whereas Arkadina is supposed to look at least ten years younger than she is, Signoret has spread out to look ten years older than she is. Also, the rugged somnolence of Signoret's features hardly befits the fussy volatility of Arkadina's character. Mother Courage simply has no place in Chekhov.

Far from playing around Signoret, Lumet has paused to pose her in a shimmeringly ultra-Chekhovian composition of lyrical lethargy, with Signoret's Arkadina and Vanessa Redgrave's Nina swinging gently from opposite ends of a hammock. The only trouble with the composition is the feeling it evokes that Signoret would rather be out ploughing the fields. More's the pity, because Vanessa Redgrave plays this and every other scene as if she were to the manor born, a high-flying swan deflected from her flight of passion by reality and turned into a wounded sea gull, not so much destroyed as defined by her suffering. The sea gull is of course a metaphor for the muse of art, freshly bloodied by the willful, intuitive, fanciful Treplev, eventually stuffed for the deliberate, intelligent, precise Trigorin. As the two sides of art, or at least of Chekhov's art, Treplev and Trigorin are irresistible characters for anyone who has ever stood poised for even an instant for the leap from the shadow of an awesome antiquity into the blinding uncertainty of posterity. "And when I die," Trigorin tells the awestruck Nina, "my friends, passing by my tomb, will say, 'Here lies Trigorin. He was a good writer, but inferior to Turgenev' " (in the Garnett version—Tolstoy in the Budberg).

Treplev might have materialized from an off-off-Broadway stage when he rages against the theatrical first lady who happens to be his mother: "You, with your hackneyed conventions, have usurped the supremacy in art and consider nothing real and legitimate but what you do yourselves; everything else you stifle and suppress." Trigorin's art is form without life, detail without passion; Treplev's is life without order, passion without purpose. And *The Sea Gull* is a dramatization of failed lives passing momentarily through the prism of art.

Lumet has chosen to enhance Chekhov without either extending or expanding him. Visually, this means employing cinema's greater accessibility to nature in the service of stagecraft. From a cramped-up garden on the stage we move deeper into the countryside, spreading out the characters so that Chekhov's slowness of mood can be justified by the new logistics. But Lumet is careful never to act out anything that Chekhov merely describes, nothing, that is, except the ultimate onscreen discovery of Treplev's offstage suicide. Thus the two years that pass between the third and fourth acts are indicated on the screen by a title, and these are years in which Nina comes to Moscow in pursuit of Trigorin, and Treplev comes in pursuit of Nina, and all ends badly. It requires a director of great cultural chastity to resist the temptations of actually showing Vanessa Redgrave's Nina, James Mason's Trigorin, and David Warner's Treplev in such a romantic roundelay, particularly when the players themselves exude charm and feeling of such an order that at times they seem to be singing their parts rather than playing them.

If Vanessa Redgrave, James Mason, and David Warner are ideally cast, Kathleen Widdoes as the morbid Masha, Denholm Elliott as the discerning Doctor Dorn, and Harry Andrews as the self-pitying Sorin all manage to triumph over subtle incongruities in their casting. I was particularly concerned about the too lightly ironic long-shot reading of Masha's first line by Kathleen Widdoes when asked by Alfred Lynch's too sensitive Medvedenko why she always wore black: "I am in mourning for my life. I am unhappy." More pragmatically American than passionately Russian, I feared, but Miss Widdoes turns out to be starting off in low gear and then emotionally accelerating the rest of the way until she is quite overpowering at the final card game, in which, through Chekhov's alchemy and Lumet's affinity, words are sublimated into numbers.

Eileen Herlie and Ronald Radd round out the cast and the countryside with colorless performances in the colorless roles of a love-starved wife and her self-sufficient steward husband, but they, too, have their moments of merciless illumination in Lumet's *tableau vivant*. But although Lumet has fully indulged Chekhov's sentimental longueurs, so, too, has he understood the moments of dramatic rigor when weak wills are snapped by the vagaries of domestic decisions, as when Nina and Trigorin allow their lives to be decided by the offscreen whim of Arkadina on whether to stay in the country or return to the city.

Lumet is even more successful in evoking the conflict between domesticity and destiny with a stunning, lunging shot of the distraught Treplev pushing his head out the window to gulp in air that might still his too turbulent heart and saying to himself, "How dark it is! I don't know why I feel so uneasy." At which point his mother, the aforesaid Arkadina, calls out from the card table, "Kostya, shut the window, there's a draft." Chekhov's genius as a dramatist can be measured by the chasm he creates between an unloved son and an unfeeling mother, between an illusion of life and an imperative of living, between what we like to think we are and what we are compelled to become. Treplev is dead the moment he shuts the window. And all it has taken is one line of unfeeling but irreproachable comfort-seeking. Lumet may not be the most inspired director in the world, but his intelligence coupled with Chekhov's genius make *The Sea Gull* one of the most edifying entertainments of the year now past in all but its still unseen and unreviewed productions.

Oliver! is not merely unfaithful to Dickens but completely inappropriate as well. First of all, Lionel Bart seems to belong to that Broadway-West End school of thought that believes a musical can be made of anything from *The Decameron* to *Das Kapital*. (Why not a musical of *Oblomov*, if only for a rousing Thousand Beds number a la Busby Berkeley?) I've never much liked *Oliver Twist* either as a novel or as a straight movie, and I've seen two of the four film versions, namely the ones of 1934 and 1951. I don't like any of Lionel Bart's songs or any of the singers, and I don't appreciate the rather disquieting spectacle of a horde of pint-sized chorus boys doing Jerome Robbins imitations in the midst of fustian melodramatics. As for Ron Moody's fey Fagin, his school-of-hard-knocks song spiels remind me of nothing so much as Zorba the

Fiddler from La Mancha, that all-purpose monster of middle-class, middle-aged, middlebrow metaphysics. Carol Reed's impersonal direction is expert enough, particularly when he is personalizing a dog and an owl with some of the flair he displayed years ago with the tracking cats of *Bank Holiday* and *The Third Man*. But I can't understand the raves for the film.

Oliver Twist is a story of one boy's exposure to evil and depravity while seeking his actual identity. Oliver himself is a fantasy David Copperfield, a snobbish little boy who inspires an upper-class lynch mob to rescue him from Jews (Fagin and his ilk) and Cockneys (Bill Sykes and his). Dickens indulges every child's fantasy of being so loved and desired that adults will fight and die for the privilege of possessing him, and it was only right that the upper-class people should win out in the end. Interestingly enough, each succeeding adaption of *Oliver Twist* has tended to reduce the warm glow of satisfaction felt by the child when he is finally rescued. David Lean's otherwise tasteful production was relatively cold in comparison with an affectingly artless Monogram production back in 1934, and now Carol Reed's production carries us to the point where the emotional displacement is so complete that Oliver is less the protagonist than the sentimental foil for the affectionate father-and-son team of Fagin and the Artful Dodger. For all his snobbery, Dickens was at least honest enough to despise the vice and criminality of the slums as he exploited them for melodrama. By contrast, Lionel Bart sentimentalizes the grime and crime with his ludicrous lyrics. Worse still, the group numbers of lower-class Londoners destroy the Dickensian literary heritage of individuality and grotesque contrast.

—*Village Voice*, January 9, 1969

■ 2. *PIERROT LE FOU*

Pierrot le Fou is the first Godard film I have ever had to stand on line to see, and thus another coterie taste has been engulfed by the crowd. But I wonder what the crowds make of Godard now that he has become popular as well as fashionable, particularly in a four-year-old film that actually preceded such earlier American Godard releases as *Masculine Feminine, La Chinoise,* and *Weekend,* and the still unreleased *Made in USA* and *Two or Three Things I Know About Her.* There are at least two more Godard films in the can, so that *Pierrot le Fou* is at least seven films ago in Godard's compulsive career. Since my own feelings toward Godard and his alter ego Pierrot have been changing over the years, it might be well to keep the emotional chronology of the film in mind.

I first heard about *Pierrot le Fou* in the fall of 1965, at which time it was unveiled at the Venice Film Festival to less than universal acclaim. I finally caught the film in Paris in the summer of 1966 while on a scouting expedition for the New York Film Festival, and in the fall of 1966 *Pierrot* graced the New York Film Festival along with Godard's *Masculine Feminine,* which on the whole was better received. In those days Godard films, if released at all, never had much of a first run. The Godardians were full of sound and fury, and they wrote in the most prestigious publications, but there were never too many of them at the box office. Year after year the New York Film Festival would be denounced by the *Times* and *Trib* for indulging the hard-core Godardians with two films from their favorite instead of making do with the more prudent single entry. But Godard was a very special case. He seemed to drive himself every year to make one film for the Berlin Festival and another for Venice, and more often than not he would land miraculously on his feet after a triple somersault through the most dubious improvisations. The pattern was always the same. Each new film would be assailed by his detractors as his biggest mess yet, and even his friends would look a little uncomfortable. A year later the same film would look like a modern masterpiece, and two years later like the last full-bodied flowering of classicism.

Pierrot le Fou, however, was something very different. It was the kind of last film a director can make only once in his career. It reminded me of Murnau's *Tabu,* Welles's *Lady from Shanghai,* and even Chaplin's *Limelight.* Where could Godard go from here, I wondered, and Godard has answered my wonderment with increasing violence and fragmentation, most of which I like less than I did *Pierrot le Fou,* the last local stop for Godard's express train of history. If I prefer *Pierrot le Fou* to, say, *Weekend,* it is because

I find the end of an affair an infinitely more interesting subject than the beginning of a revolution, and *Pierrot* is nothing if not a lament for a lost love.

Under the circumstances, the only decently romantic gesture Godard could perform after the suicidal ecstasy of *Pierrot le Fou* would be to blow his brains out. But no artist, least of all a French artist, ever dies for love. Godard had blown his brains out metaphorically, that is, he had blown his mind, and that's all that Anna Karina or any woman deserved. But still, *Pierrot le Fou* cannot possibly seem as emotionally painful seven pictures later as it did at the time. Hence, though I see *Pierrot* more clearly than I did at the time, I feel it less deeply. And yet, though I like Godard less, I admire the film more. Time has sweetened the song as it has soured the singer. Why? The main reason is Jean-Paul Belmondo. He gives Pierrot more charm, dignity, and resignation than Godard himself alone is capable of, and the jokes that worked in *Breathless*, those churlish jests that haven't worked since, work once more.

Without Belmondo's too-many-drinks-and-cigarettes-the-night-before-this-morning-face to serve as ballast, Godard's giddiness becomes too flighty for the gravity required of any effective humor. Belmondo's appeal, like Bogart's, lies not in the actor's insolence but in the weary gallantry the actor's insolence never quite conceals. Also, Belmondo, again like Bogart, testifies with his face to a life lived to the hilt. Hence there are authentic chuckles when Belmondo's Ferdinand/Pierrot is accosted by an old acquaintance he can't quite place, and the acquaintance proceeds to jog his memory in a very friendly way with reminders of money and a wife borrowed from the acquaintance, the debt still unpaid and the cuckoldry still unavenged, but neither social outrage capable of causing hard feelings now that the mere familiarity of a face is the last shred of evidence that anything at all has ever happened. Belmondo doesn't embellish this embarrassing situation as much as he endures it. We laugh both at Belmondo's deadpan arrogance and his deathly discomfiture. Ultimately, we can be moved by Belmondo's renunciation of the world simply because we can believe that Belmondo once resided in it. He was married, had children, affairs, held a job, many jobs, bought furniture, felt pleasure and pain, and then one night, while he was reading a book on Velasquez to his lyrical-susceptible daughter, he was rudely interrupted by his literal-repressive wife and told to dress for a starchy status-seeking party, complete with topless diversions. And when he had had enough of the party and its unending television-commercial conversation, he returned home and ran off with the babysitter, who just happened to be an old flame named Marianne Renoir. Not the most convincing plot in the world certainly, and every time Godard picks up the plot he lets it fall to pieces, but it rings emotionally true nonetheless because of the beautiful visual aspect of Belmondo's nihilistic personality.

Still, *Pierrot le Fou* makes no sense either as drama or as documentary, and Belmondo's Ferdinand/Pierrot le Fou is hardly the hero of a well-made fictional film. Godard's very unique sensibility spills over every frame of the film from the first illustrations of the Velasquez aesthetic—white tennis tunics against pink flesh, Paris as a night landscape against the blue-green Seine, Belmondo gazing at the sensuous stream of colors on a bookstall—to the last shot of the sea that reconciles the doomed lovers after death to the recited lines from Rimbaud: "Elle est retrouvée / Quoi? / L' Éternité/Non, c'est la mer allée avec le soleil . . ."

Pierrot le Fou is a film of fireworks and water, of explosion and immersion, the metaphorical expression of passion being cooled by existence, the visual equivalent of feelings being chilled by words. The influence of Renoir, Jean even more than Auguste, is everywhere, even in Belmondo's hilarious imitation of Michel Simon, but especially in the pervasive wetness of *Pierrot le Fou*, itself at least partly an ode to liquid pastoral à la Lautréamont in *Weekend*. It is of course no accident that Anna Karina's alter ego is an Auguste Renoir print plastered on the screen in Godard's peculiar montage-collage style that seems less peculiar with each increasingly fragmented year. Even the "inside" cinematic jokes—Sam Fuller in person describing the cinema as a battleground of emotions, the umpteenth joke about Nicholas Ray's *Johnny Guitar*, a reverent reference to Jean Renoir's *La Chienne*—seem to slide into the stream of sensibility without any bumps.

Audiences may still be jarred somewhat by the violent clash between blood-red melodrama and sky-blue contemplation, by the contradictory rhetoric of musicals and metaphysics, and by the director's lingering affection for what he considers to be dying genres, but that is precisely what I love about *Pierrot le Fou*. Belmondo and Karina and Coutard and Antoine Duhamel (music) translate Godard's most tentative ideas into sensuous spectacle, so that what is actually on the screen is usually more interesting than anything that can be said about it. Interestingly enough, none of the topical satire has dated in the slightest, not Godard's first tentative comments about Vietnam, or his relatively gentle gibes at car culture, or even a breathtakingly romantic defense of the lovestruck moon against the calculating Cold War onslaughts of American and Russian astronauts.

One reviewer complained about the film's physical chastity, presumably in a reflex reaction to the prevailing permissiveness by which love and nudity walk hand in hand, and truth to tell, there is not the slightest intimation of sexual intercourse in *Pierrot le Fou*. And yet, time and again, I felt the chilling sublimation of love into art and then the warming translation of art back into love. As a genuinely lyrical expression of love, Godard's *Pierrot le Fou* is worth a thousand anemically academic *Elvira Madigans* and a million mendaciously swirling and swishing *Romeo and Juliets*. Nevertheless I'd hate to imagine *Pierrot le Fou* without Belmondo, if only because Belmondo magnifies Godard's soul on the screen, much as Mastroianni magnified Fellini's in 8½, and Chaplin the inspired actor always magnified Chaplin the ignoble self-pitier. The cinema is, as always, a director's art, and feelings are expressed *through* actors rather than *by* them, but the point is still to see what is felt rather than to figure out what is meant, and in this respect the bleary-eyed Belmondo undoubtedly looks the way Godard felt when Godard was making *Pierrot le Fou*, and the resultant unity of features and feelings is beautiful to behold.

—*Village Voice*, January 23, 1969

■ 3. *STOLEN KISSES*

François Truffaut's *Stolen Kisses* reminds us once more that the French at their most felicitous are still the most civilized observers of the obsessiveness of love. Paris may no longer be the ooh-lah-lah capital of the world, if indeed it ever was, and the Eiffel Tower may no longer communicate as the world's most explicit erection, Truffaut's corny visual gag to the contrary nothwithstanding. But somewhere in the streets of Paris the idealism of love still shines, even though the illusion of love is somewhat tarnished. At least in the slyly sentimental world of François Truffaut, that poet of love's sweet pain and excruciating embarrassment. There have been occasions in the past when I felt that Truffaut exploited his emotions more than he expressed them, and I feared the worst when I heard advance reports of the improvisatory looseness of *Stolen Kisses*. Happily, my fears were unfounded, and *Stolen Kisses* emerges as the most genuinely enjoyable movie, for squares as well as hipsters, in many a moon.

Truffaut's over-all career seems to alternate quite deliberately between the open, life-size lyricism of Renoir and Vigo (*Les Mistons, The 400 Blows, Jules and Jim,* "Antoine and Colette" from *Love at 20*) and the closed, genre-shaped fantasies of Hitchcock and Hawks (*Shoot the Piano Player, The Soft Skin, Fahrenheit 451, The Bride Wore Black,* and, I suppose, the forthcoming *The Siren of Mississippi*). *Stolen Kisses* is closer to the Renoir-Vigo influence than to the Hitchcock-Hawks, that is, more direct in its feelings and less inventive in its fictions. Actually, Jean-Pierre Léaud's Antoine Doinel exists as a biological continuation of the same character from tortured childhood in *The 400 Blows* through anguished adolescence in *Antoine and Colette* and now through muddled manhood in *Stolen Kisses*. As Léaud's (and Truffaut's) alter ego has matured, so has Truffaut. The director's canvas has expanded with the range of his sympathies to embrace more of humanity than ever before, and with emotional growth has come aesthetic distance. Truffaut can even confront his traumatic experience with the Army as multifaceted irony flickering across Léaud's volatile features. It is startling to observe how meaningfully different a persona Léaud projects for Truffaut than for Godard in *Masculine Feminine* and *La Chinoise* and for Skolimowski in *Le Départ*. Curiously, I have met all three directors, but I have never met Léaud himself. He exists for me purely as a figment of their imaginations, and I can never help seeing them through him, rather than vice versa. Truffaut's Léaud starts out seeming more vulnerable than the other two, but somehow winds up being more complacent both sensually and emotionally. Life cradles him more with its sentimental education. Whereas Godard's Léaud never understands even himself, Truffaut's Léaud comes to understand himself and everyone around him.

Fortunately, Truffaut's knowingness is tempered with observant humor. Antoine Doinel still has more luck with a girl's parents than with the girl herself (as in *Antoine and Colette*), but now this self-mocking gag is amplified to include Léaud's (and Truffaut's) alienation from revolting upper-middle-class students, who can never understand the quiet desperation of lower-class necessity. Truffaut expresses this alienation most economically by Léaud's blank expression when he is told that his girl has gone skiing while the student body is on strike. Léaud's reaction is a candid-camera miracle of instinctive incomprehension. Later when the girl (Claude Jade) complains that he mauls her in the movies, Léaud turns around with an anxious look at the girl's imperturbable parents, an instantaneous reflex of drugstore-candy courtliness that defines the decency of a class and a period.

The scenario of *Stolen Kisses* (by Truffaut, Claude de Givray, and Bernard Revon) is a perpetual juggling act by which harsh truths are disguised as light jokes. The sheer horror and inanity of competing in the open market for a routine job is hilariously summed up in a straight-faced shoe-wrapping contest, the outcome of which, to add to life's injustices, has been fixed in advance. Antoine's other jobs—hotel night clerk, private detective, TV repairman—mark him as a disreputable drifter capable, like Truffaut and his breed of break-out artists, of sinking all the way to the bottom in order to rise to the top. One day, we presume, Antoine will have learned so much about the human condition that he won't be able to keep himself from becoming an artist.

Amid all his careful calculations designed to suggest careless rapture, Truffaut does indulge himself in genuinely privileged moments worthy of Renoir and Vigo. The opening moments, for example, in which the delicate task of mine detection becomes a military metaphor for the equally delicate seduction of a woman, might have amused Renoir as a revelation of the French race. Antoine, released from the stockade, promises his comrades that he will make it with a Pigalle prostitute at five o'clock so that they can participate vicariously. Renoiresque camaraderie and all that, but in his haste Léaud-Truffaut betrays a contempt for prostitutes that keeps popping up in his most lyrical essays on love (vide *Jules and Jim*). Godard, by contrast, sees prostitution as a morbid, sordid metaphor for all human existence, a torture chamber in which feelings are broken on the wheel of economics. Hence Godard is completely antierotic, by virtue of treating eroticism itself as a capitalistic commodity. Truffaut retains his commitment to the elective affinities, but redeems all sexuality, even the most sordid, as an affirmation of the life force. Thus when a sort of father-figure to Antoine is buried, the distraught young man goes straight from the funeral to a streetwalker, almost as if the transition from the morbid to the sordid were prescribed as part of a religious ritual.

While stalking a homosexual's straying lover for his detective agency, Antoine participates in a Vigoesque privileged moment with a lyrical magician right out of *L'Atalante*. That Truffaut should pause to savor this rhapsody of colored fabrics and tinkling melodies suggests the furtive manner in which the director worships beauty for beauty's sake. Later when the distraught homosexual client goes berserk upon discovering that his lover is married, the magic act becomes the aesthetic correlative for a fit of madness. Gradually one obsession piles upon another until all Paris seems drenched with desire. Antoine's highest moment of civilized acceptance comes quite naturally with the spectacular entrance of Delphine Seyrig's not-too-married woman, a model of taste and discretion, with perhaps a dash too much of makeup and mannerism and literary sensibility, but delectably accessible withal in a way Alain Resnais never quite suggested in the icy realms of *Marienbad* and *Muriel*. Finally, we are treated to our last madman, a persistent pursuer of Antoine's at-last-compliant Christine. The madman walks up to the two lovers and speaks of a more consuming love to Christine. The camera stays on the backs of the two lovers looking full-face at the madman. The shot is held long enough for the viewer to feel Antoine's hair on the back of his neck tingling with embarrassed identification. The madman departs. Antoine and Christine rise from the park bench. We see their faces. "He's crazy," Christine exclaims. "Yes, he is," Antoine answers with that quiet, almost reverent blankness on his face that reveals to us that we are all crazy, that all love is crazy. Crazy and divine. Godard makes the same point in *Pierrot le Fou* in perhaps one-tenth the time and with ten times the force, but he doesn't let us linger over it with any feeling of lyrical contemplation. He doesn't point it up with reaction shots and intersecting plot elements. Godard almost punishes us with his insights; Truffaut persists in pleasing us. And I am no longer sure which course requires more strength of character.

—*Village Voice*, February 27, 1969

■ 4. *GOODBYE, COLUMBUS*

Goodbye, Columbus has been filmed about ten years too late for its assorted audacities to create much stir. But, then, ten years ago Philip Roth's novella would have been considered too hot to handle, not only for the daring derelictions of its college kids but also for its savage satire of the Jewish nouveau riche. As it is, Arnold Schulman's screenplay is reasonably faithful to the spirit of Roth's Portrait of the Artist as a Young Creep, and the casting comes out better than anyone had any right to expect. Ali McGraw's Brenda makes up for all the fashion models over the years that have fizzled after their first fizz on the screen. Heaven knows the Radcliffe Jewish intonation is child's play by now, and even Roth's ambiguously nice girl may represent type casting for Miss McGraw. The fact remains that she seems fully capable of transcending the gilded ghetto of *Goodbye, Columbus*. Not so Richard Benjamin, making his screen debut as Neil. Mr. Benjamin is so ideally cast as Philip Roth that it is almost frightening to think of his ever playing anything else. And who wants to *look* at Philip Roth as a figure of fantasy? Whereas Dustin Hoffman is what clumsy intellectuals would like to be on a blind date, Richard Benjamin (alas!) is what they actually are. It's not Benjamin's fault that he looks like a creep in the never-never land of the screen. It may turn out to make his fortune in this antiheroic period. For the nonce, he serves to place Roth's tortured sensibility in clearer focus simply by functioning on the screen as Roth's visible, if not visual, alter ego.

Before blaming Roth for everything mean-spirited and malicious in the film version of *Goodbye, Columbus*, note must be taken of the updating and relocating of Schulman's adaptation. *Goodbye, Columbus* was published in book form in May 1959, after appearing in the *Paris Review*, and the events in the book are clearly dated in the late fifties. Ronald Patimkin, Ohio State's great basketball player from Short Hills, New Jersey, plays his "Goodbye, Columbus" record as a dim-witted alumnus of the class of '57. We get the distinct impression that Ronald Patimkin's monstrous marriage ceremony with Harriet Ehrlich takes place in 1958, or 1959 at the very latest. Schulman can hardly be criticized for casually updating the action to the present. The recent past is the hardest period to reproduce, and it hardly seems worth all the trouble researching skirt lengths and dance steps merely to return to a novelist's starting point in time and space. In the unlikely event that *Goodbye, Columbus* took off commercially like *The Graduate*, we might expect double-domed think pieces in the quality magazines to complain that Neil Klugman doesn't worry enough about Vietnam and that Ronald Patimkin doesn't express enough concern about the draft. But Roth can hardly be blamed for not anticipating 1969 in 1959, and Schulman can hardly be criticized for not rewriting Roth's historical awareness to fit Schulman's specifications. Nonetheless *Goodbye, Columbus* is somewhat lost in the limbo of 1969's plasticity describing 1959's sensibility.

If the time during which the film takes place is double-focused, the place itself is dislocated from Roth's exotically personal Newark (for the nebbishes) and Short Hills (for the *nouveau riche*) to Schulman's more conventional Bronx-to-Westchester upward mobility. With reorientation comes a certain dissociation between the novella and the movie, but also a sudden recognition of Roth's reliance on stock characters to illustrate his personal complaints. Roth is especially skillful at suggesting his own exquisite taste (and my-son-the-novelist snobbery) by a deadpan description of other people's awful taste. Hence Ron Patimkin must guilelessly express his enthusiasm not only for André Kostelanetz but for Mantovani as well, and, to rub it in for the benefit of the most fatuously culture-climbing reader, Ron must actually say, "I like semiclassical a lot." Goodbye, Mozart, and all that.

But a curious thing has happened in the treatment of the sexual scenes between novel and film. It used to be that novels would be toned down in adaptation. By contrast, *Goodbye, Columbus* is turned up to a point that reflects Roth's own increasingly clinical frankness between *Goodbye, Columbus* in 1959 and *Portnoy's Complaint* in 1969. And as for movies, forget it. We've come so far from Andy Hardy and Dobie Gillis that we may be coming out the other side into a New Naïvete. Still, I don't recall offhand the last time two movie characters, domestic or foreign, discussed the comparative merits of the Pill and the Diaphragm. Roth's novella is keyed to discussions of diaphragms with Mary McCarthy's confessional story on the subject as the cultural jumping-off point. The movie omits Roth's mention of Mary McCarthy, possibly so as not to remind movie audiences that the Joan Hackett character in *The Group* dabbled with a diaphragm as a McCarthyesque mechanism signifying the servitude of the New Woman to the Old Adam. (If the rights could be cleared, what a movie could be made out of the meeting of a Philip Roth hero and a Mary McCarthy heroine! Hieronymus Bosch, make way for a new vision of hell on earth!) However, the most interesting difference between Roth's novella and Schulman's screenplay is to be found in Roth's relative reticence *vis-à-vis Portnoy's Complaint* and Schulman's relative frankness in devising situations involving male "hard-on" humor that not even Roth indulged in back in 1959. Neil's initial seduction of Brenda on the living room couch comes rather easily and casually in the novella, but in the movie there is an added, preliminary scene in which Neil tries to make it with Brenda in the convertible, and she says no, and he manages to suggest that it would not be safe for him to be seen in public in his frustrated condition, and she laughs understandingly, and he smiles, and they talk to each other on the phone later that night, and they know it will happen the next time, and it is all rather nice and possibly more realistic than the freer and easier Roth version.

Naturally it doesn't work out, because if it had, Roth would not be psychologically primed to write *Portnoy's Complaint* ten years later. The movie doesn't work out either. Actually, it made me a little sick. Larry Peerce's dreadfully derivative gimmicks of direction make *Goodbye, Columbus* look undergraduate and sub-*Graduate*, and his inability to establish individuals in crowd scenes makes more of a shambles of the climactic Jewish wedding than even Roth ever dreamed of in his peculiarly masochistic philosophy.

Ultimately, however, it is Roth's vision of life that is at issue here, and it just won't do for movies where journalistic nuances are inevitably sacrificed to mythic configurations. When Brenda tells Neil (in the movie) that he looks down his nose at everyone, she is perfectly right about Roth as well as about Neil. It is not that Roth is unfair or inaccurate, but merely incomplete. His literary works lack even the momentary perspective of the overhead shot through which we all find ourselves strangers Down Here. The spectacle of Ronald Patimkin listening to the record of "Goodbye, Columbus" should make us cry. Larry Peerce directs it to make us giggle a bit at our own cultural superiority. Awful direction. I reread *Goodbye, Columbus* to see if Roth meant to make us cry. He didn't. Instead he had Neil conclude the scene with the inner chill and ingrained intellectual snobbery of "Thee! I thought, my brother-in-law." Honest? Perhaps. But so is the self-concern of a cockroach.

—*Village Voice*, April 3, 1969

■ 5. TRULY TO BE A MAN:
   REVIEWS OF *SPENCER TRACY*,
   BY LARRY SWINDELL, AND
   THE FILMS OF SPENCER TRACY,
   BY DONALD DESCHNER

Larry Swindell's remarkably knowledgeable biography of the late Spencer Tracy (*Spencer Tracy*, New American Library/World) deserves the attention not only of the actor's admirers in particular but also of film scholars and historians in general. The author skillfully threads his way through a maze of Hollywood gossip, scandal, ego thrust, and power politics without losing sight of the myth and magic and even art of the movies. By contrast, Donald Deschner's book on the actor's career (*The Films of Spencer Tracy*, Citadel Press) is strictly a paste-up of newspaper clippings and pallbearing testimonials dedicated to the overfamiliar proposition that Spence was a nice guy who tended to underplay all his roles both on and off the screen, a far cry from the madcap Irish whirlwind Swindell describes in much breezier fashion.

Nevertheless the Deschner picture book could conceivably supplement the more literate and linear Swindell version, because it provides stills, credits, and synopses, all very useful, for the 74 feature-length films in which Tracy appeared. It was a career that began almost concurrently with the talkies in 1930 and ended with his death on June 11, 1967, only ten days after he had finished reading a consciously valedictory remembrance speech in *Guess Who's Coming to Dinner* while Katharine Hepburn's eyes sparkled tearfully in the background, for the man even more than for the character.

Tracy, a child of the century (born Spencer Bonaventure Tracy in Milwaukee, Wisconsin, April 5, 1900), was well into his thirties before he became an Oscar-worthy adornment at Metro. Swindell's book is especially useful for its rediscovery of Tracy's young, lost years (for the mythmakers) between 1930 and 1936, when he was grinding out the kind of program pictures from which posthumous cults are conceived. Justice Douglas (in the Deschner book) likens Tracy's "American" quality to that of Thoreau, Emerson, Frost, but this again is an image of the elder Tracy, in whose reformed features the indomitable granite jaw firmed up the sensual leprechaun lips and steadied the guileful Irish eyes of the rascals he played in such undeservedly neglected early-thirties movies as John Ford's *Up the River*, Rowland Brown's *Quick Millions*, Michael Curtiz' *20,000 Years in Sing Sing*, William K. Howard's *The Power and the Glory*, and Frank Borzage's *A Man's Castle*, one of the very few films that ever captured the emotional nuances of the Depression.

Tracy never really made it on his own as a screen personality. He was not considered sexy enough to compete with the Coopers and the Gables, or even with mere pretty boys like Robert Taylor and Tyrone Power. He was not anarchic enough to fill the gangster slots of the Cagneys and the Robinsons, or earthy enough to swagger in character leads like the Laughtons and the Beerys. In his younger days he never successfully projected either the rural idealism of James Stewart and Henry Fonda or the urban nonconformism of Humphrey Bogart and John Garfield. At Metro he fell into the somewhat demeaning best-friend-who-never-gets-the-girl relationship to Clark Gable that Tracy's erstwhile New York roommate Pat O'Brien had fallen into at Warners with James Cagney.

Significantly, he won his first Oscar in a film (*Captains Coura-geous*) in which he had second billing to Freddie Bartholomew, and his second in a film (*Boys' Town*) in which he played second fiddle to a little hamster named Mickey Rooney. He played, albeit reluctantly, too many priests and too many men of dull distinction. Insult was added to indignity in 1943 when Tracy was forced to die in *A Guy Named Joe* so that he could lose his sweetheart (Irene Dunne) to Van Johnson for the sake of teen-age audiences. Tracy's presence onscreen as a ghost egging on Dunne and John-son is as embarrassing today as his quiet contemplation of Irene Dunne serenading him by the fire with "I'll Get By" is enchanting.

Unfortunately, Tracy's habitual superiority to his material tended to limit the range of material offered to him. In later years, particularly, he tended to appear in sermons rather than movies. Still, there were the nine stylish Adam's-rib adventures in which he played a puckish Petruchio to Hepburn's luminous Kate, and those unforgettably mortal moments in *Captains Courageous*, *Bad Day at Black Rock* and *The People Against O'Hara* when Spencer Tracy gazed at the angel of death and showed the world through the art of acting what it meant truly to be a man.

—*Book World*, April 20, 1969

■ 6. *LAUGHTER IN THE DARK*

The film version of *Laughter in the Dark* transplants Vladimir Nabokov's eerie novel from the early thirties' Weimar Berlin to mod, mad London. I can't say I entirely blame director Tony Rich-ardson and scenarist Edward Bond for trying to update Nabokov's dreamlike milieu, and it is a good try, full of intelligent modifica-tions and economical equivalences, many of which can be fully ap-preciated only by someone who has read the book. Unfortunately, the ingenuity of Richardson and Bond is never equal to the inspi-ration of Nabokov, and the movie fails, as the novel succeeds, on that mysterious meeting ground of story and style. And so the reader of this column is advised to read the novel, see the movie, and then, and only then, return to this review, which is now prepared to unravel the tangled plot in order to trace the downward trajectory of novel into film.

The basic anecdotal material is the same in both media. A dull, repressed, wealthy art collector, more boring than bored, allows his infatuation for a vulgar movie usherette to divest him of his wife, his little girl, most of his friends, and much of his place in society. Subsequently, his sly mistress decides to deceive him with a former lover, a satanic opportunist on the fringe of the art world. The already ridiculous love nest becomes a grotesque *ménage à trois* when the usherette's secret lover not only ingratiates himself with the unsuspecting collector but proceeds to pass himself off as a harmless homosexual, thus wickedly throwing himself upon the mercy of the collector's sophisticated tolerance. Always the prisoner of events rather than their master, the thereby doomed protagonist is unable to cope with a series of interrelated catastrophes—the death of his daughter, the discovery of his mistress' deception, an automobile accident that leaves him blind and helpless in the care of his mistress at a Swiss chalet, ideal in its isolation for a more morbid variation of the original *menage à trois*. Now the collector is optically as well as metaphorically blind, and the teasing and the taunting increase in intensity until the mise-en-scène, Nabokov's more than Richardson's, becomes a paranoiac's nightmare. In the most bizarre version of blindman's buff ever devised in a novel, the girl and her lover improvise all sorts of delicate dares, which the blind man, unaware of the lover's presence at the chalet, is unable either to ignore or to confirm. Only the unexpected arrival of an old family friend allows him to escape the fiendish trap, but only long enough to set the stage for his final destruction in a violent confrontation with his faithless mistress.

So much for the bare bones of the plot. It is easy enough to see why Richardson would be tempted by this sort of material, with its apparent sourness and cynicism, its modishly sick humor, and its intellectually certifiable melodrama. Nabokov's novels are often slighted with the snap judgment that they possess style without feeling, as if style could ever be conceived without feeling. Indeed, no feeling is more profound than that of the artist's form attempting to apprehend the universe's formlessness. On the day of the accident, Nabokov writes, "the cheek of the earth from Gibraltar to Stockholm was painted with mellow sunshine." Richardson's

best visual effect—the convergence of the victim's car and a cluster
of cyclists from opposite directions on a winding mountain road—
is taken directly from the novelist's extraordinarily outer-spatial description. But the resemblance of novel to film is only on the surface. The psychological links from beneath the surface have been
neatly severed by the adaptation.

I haven't read too much secondary literature on Nabokov, and
I don't know for sure where he got the plot for Laughter in the
Dark, but I strongly suspect that he was familiar with some of the
German UFA triangle dramas of the late twenties and early thirties
and that he had probably seen Emil Jannings in The Blue Angel.
(At one time my impossible dream cast for Laughter in the Dark
consisted of Emil Jannings as the collector, Conrad Veidt as the
poltergeist, and Louise Brooks as the temptress.) Curiously, the
book is more overtly movie-oriented than the movie. The collector
(named Albinus in the novel and Sir Edward More in the film)
even mentions Veidt at one point in making a facial comparison,
and there are long discussions about animating classical paintings,
so that a painter's world, Breughel's for example, could spring to
life from the canvas to the screen. The poltergeist (named Axel
Rex in the book and Herve Tourace in the movie) is first described
by Nabokov as a "wonderful hand at freaks—had, as a matter of
fact, designed a Persian fairy tale which had delighted highbrows
in Paris and ruined the man who had financed the venture." But
most important of all, Albinus actually produces a film for his pro-
tégé (Margot in both book and movie), and she is awful in it,
easily outclassed by the Dietrich-like star, Dorianna Karenina, the
occasion of a Nabokovian pun on Doll's Toy and Tolstoy.

There is no mention of movies in the Richardson-Bond adaptation, and very little professional concern with art at any level. Nicol
Williamson's collector is presented as an authority figure in the art
world, but more in terms of his swank and power than in the plod-
ding pedantry of the character in the novel. Hence Williamson's
initial movements, much less his motivations, are never plausible.
We can believe Nabokov's Albinus sneaking into a movie house
because of his obsession with a movie usherette. This kind of fall
is appropriate for the old UFA myths of bourgeois Berliners straying from the straight and narrow, but Nicol Williamson's poised
Londoner seems curiously dislocated in the darkness of a dingy

movie house, and the miniskirted world around him seems more accessible to his slumbering sensual appetites than his fumbling gestures of frustration would indicate.

In the space of about 60,000 words Nabokov tells us more about his bizarre characters than lesser novelists could tell us in 600,000 words. Even the occasionally elliptical coyness of the sexual descriptions serves to place the reader in the mind of the character to the extent of lovingly implicating him in the character's lack of insight. And who are Albinus and Axel Rex really but the two sides of Nabokov and the two aspects (pedantry and trickery) of his art? This, then, is the source of Nabokov's dark, deep humor: nothing more or less than the ability to see all his dimensions with cruel lucidity and the will to disguise his deepest feelings with the most frightful fictions at his command. Hence the sexual pathology of the situation is merely the means by which the failed artist-protagonist finds the dazzling self-illumination that was denied him until he dared live life to its fullest. When Albinus is first blinded, he realizes that he never fully perceived all the sensuous surfaces he so expertly appraised in the days before his blindness. Thus he had always been artistically blind even when his eyes were working, but at the moment that the fatal bullet enters his body, "there came a stab in his side which filled his eyes with a dazzling glory. 'So that's all,' he thought quite softly, as if he were lying in bed. 'Must keep quiet for a little space and then walk very slowly along that bright sand of pain, toward that blue, blue wave. What bliss there is in blueness. I never knew how blue blueness could be. What a mess life has been. Now I know everything. Coming, coming, coming to drown me. There it is. How it hurts. I can't breathe . . .'"

Nabokov chooses not to end the novel at this moment of unbearable intensity and self-revelation, but instead to distance death itself through the swirling moonbeams of a silent movie projector: "Stage directions for last silent scene: Door—wide open. Table—thrust away from it. Carpet—bulging up at table foot in a frozen wave. Chair—lying close by dead body of man in a purplish-brown suit and felt slippers. Automatic pistol not visible. It is under him. Cabinet where the miniatures had been—empty. On the other (small) table, on which ages ago a porcelain ballet-dancer stood (later transferred to another room) lies a woman's glove, black outside, white inside. By the striped sofa stands a smart little trunk,

with a colored label still adhering to it: 'Rouginard, Hotel Britannia.' The door leading from the hall to the landing is wide open,
too."

By contrast, Tony Richardson turns the protagonist's ordeal into
a pseudoreligious Passion Play à la Pasolini with the aid of the insistently Bressonian "L'Incoronazione di Poppea" of Monteverdi
on the sound track. Unfortunately, where Pasolini and Richardson
merely graft the spiritual grandeur of music to the grotesque profanity of their images, Bresson matches the moral severity of the
most implacable music with the moral severity of his frames. As it
is, Richardson's version of Nabokov's tortures soon degenerates
into ludicrously phallic self-indulgence reminiscent of Moreau's
silly snake routines in *Mademoiselle* and indicative of the director's
debased interpretation of the novelist.

This is the movie for which Richardson hired Williamson after
firing Richard Burton, and it is interesting to speculate what Burton would have been like in the role. More charm and more guts,
probably, at the price of less skill and less subtlety. Williamson's
best scene is his discovery of his own blindness, and I can't think of
an actor alive who could do it as well. But he always seems to be
skipping a beat in his heart, and he seems dead from the waist
down. His weakest scene occurs when he learns that his daughter
is dead. Williamson is curiously detached from other people without the usual compensatory narcissism taking up the psychic slack.
He was ideally cast in Osborne's *Inadmissable Evidence* because
he was incapable of feeling anything even about his own lack of
feelings. He simply disintegrated before our eyes from some mysterious internal pressure. Actually, James Mason might have been
better casting in *Laughter in the Dark* because his suffering would
seem less mysteriously cerebral.

The casting of Anna Karina is indefensible on any count. She is
completely unreal in all the stages of her frantic Franco-Cockney
coquettishness, and much more diabolically devious than Nabokov
ever imagined when he raised her from the foxy-sly working-class
warrens of Berlin. For example, she herself invents her lover's
homosexuality as a cover for her infidelity in the movie, whereas in
the book it is all Axel Rex's idea. Jean-Claude Drouot comes over
as a more ambiguously depraved French lover than Louis Jourdan,
but I suspect he was cast more for physical type than psychological

temperament. All in all, not a bad movie. And after *Charge of the Light Brigade* and *Laughter in the Dark*, Richardson can be said to have reached at long last the level of mere competence, a far cry from what was required for a Nabokov novel—namely, the lost magical talents and mise-en-scène of the late F. W. Murnau.

—*Village Voice*, May 15, 1969

■ 7. *MIDNIGHT COWBOY*

Midnight Cowboy might be considered a homosexual fantasy in which Jon Voight's Joe Buck and Dustin Hoffman's Ratso Rizzo lend their luminous eyes to a composite reflection of Camille— Voight supplying the cowboyish coquettishness for the fate worse than death, Hoffman the midnight cough for death itself. I begin with the actors simply because the performances and presences of Voight and Hoffman are so extraordinarily affecting that their scenes together generate more emotional power than the dramatic wiring of their relationship deserves. By skillfully shifting back and forth between the keys of tough and tender on the theme of lonely vulnerability, Voight and Hoffman draw a few furtive tears from even the most dry-eyed sensibility. But as befits the hustlers they play, they haven't really earned the tears on traits of characterization as much as they've stolen them with tricks of acting. Fortunately, the tricks are enjoyable enough to justify the emotional larceny involved. By following up the glamorous *Graduate* with the dregsiest dropout imaginable, Dustin Hoffman has achieved his aim of not becoming the Andy Hardy of the sixties and seventies. With a dragging limp, a perpetually preserved five-o'clock shadow, a funguslike feverishness of expression, and a way of smoking a squashed cigarette as if he were inhaling oxygen under water, Hoffman will not only preserve all his old following of adoring females but should even add a few more masochistic maidens to his fan club. Still, by any reasonable standard of dramatic dominance, Hoffman's Ratso Rizzo is clearly overshadowed by Jon Voight's Joe Buck, who is, after all, the title character of *Midnight Cowboy*, traveling (out of James Leo Herlihy's novel into Waldo Salt's screenplay under John Schlesinger's direction) from Texas to Times Square in search of rich, neglected women, starving for a stud at any price. But something goes wrong with this heterosexual American dream, and God's gift to women is reduced to being felt up by Forty-second Street fairies in darkened movie theaters and dingy hotel rooms, and yet, even at the moment of unwanted ecstasy, all the sentimentally corrupted innocent can think of is a fleshly adolescent romance with a Texas tramp, and the destructive but oh how typically American gang-bang that sends her into an insane asylum. Voight projects Joe Buck's heartbreakingly stupid male beauty and inarticulate sensitivity with such force and grace that he almost gets away with one of the most horrible scenes of unconsciously sadomasochistic violence ever simulated on the screen. Almost, but not quite. Something unpleasant and dishonest lingers on the screen despite the undeniable virtuosity of the two leads.

Hence, though *Midnight Cowboy* is a film everyone should see once with or without critical encouragement, I seriously doubt that a second viewing or even second thought will seem mandatory. As with *Darling*, there are many things I like about the movie so much more than John Schlesinger's over-all wheezingly breezy direction that I am almost tempted to overlook formal deficiencies for the sake of nuances and novelties and new directions on the content level. And to be fair, Schlesinger deserves much of the credit for the almost invariably intelligent performances of his players (Bates, Courtenay, Bogarde, Christie, Harvey, Finch, Stamp, and now Voight and Hoffman) even when his mise-en-scène is at its messiest. Besides, I'll take Schlesinger's slick speciousness in *Midnight Cowboy* anytime over Richardson's tortured, tawdry ambitiousness in *Laughter in the Dark*. But somehow I am not as favorably disposed to *Midnight Cowboy* as I was to *Darling*, possibly because the implied social criticism common to both films seems today less fresh than facile, less analysis than alibi. I say "implied" social criticism because movies can make world-weary statements without even trying very hard. A director can suggest all sorts of problems simply by letting his camera stare at almost any urban street scene, and Schlesinger has gone to even greater lengths (almost, in fact, to the last dregs of La Dolce Vita-ism) to make modernity seem meaningfully meaningless. All the luridly neonized flora and fauna on Forty-second Street don't necessarily foreshadow the decline and fall of American Civilization. Nor does the mere existence of this freak show indict Mom, media, and the other manipulators of evangelical capitalism for lack of love and truth and understanding. Indeed, *Midnight Cowboy* is at its most mendacious when it inserts Viva and other Votaries of the Velvet Underground into a party-bopping-and-popping interlude that strikes the same kind of false note that the slow-reflex pot-party sequence struck in *Blow-Up*. The fictionalized hustler myths incarnated in Voight and Hoffman have no business mixing with the self-consciously garish gossip-column items incarnated in Viva and similarly exhibitionist publicity vultures.

Once more, the book is more illuminating than the movie, though not so much because Herlihy is too lavishly literary for the screen as because his greatest strengths of expression require more verbalization than most movies can afford. Like Pinter, Osborne, Godard, Albee, and other modishly alienated modernists, Herlihy tends to drown out the dialogues of his characters with his own very compulsive monologues. (The unfortunately underrated trio of Herlihy playlets collectively entitled *Stop, You're Killing Me* were on the whole more effective expressions of Herlihy's explosive nightmare visions of sexual *qua* spiritual vulnerability than is the relatively muddled movie version of *Midnight Cowboy*.) Movies, unfortunately, tend to undermine monologues with the most obvious manifestations of otherness, but Herlihy, astute man for all media that he is, has anticipated this problem with the very brilliant cinematic device of designing a character who can communicate only with his own reflection in the mirror.

Hence Jon Voight's self-contemplative and self-deluding Joe Buck is a poetic extension of the myth of Narcissus, an extension, moreover, that in its dramatic force and symbolic elaboration is worthy of the mirrored chambers of Jean Cocteau. But onscreen we never really find out why Joe Buck converses with his own reflection. We are merely encouraged to laugh lightly at the satiric implications of the spectacle of a grown-up man still taking the western myths of manhood seriously. In fact, the movie opens on its own darkness with a sound of horses' hooves on the sound track dying out as the screen illuminates a blank drive-in screen by the gray light of dawn.

And thus do John Schlesinger and Waldo Salt set the stage for a satiric interpretation of the protagonist with their precredit metaphor for mythic manipulation. Thus the first key to the character is manifestly cultural rather than psychological, more a group campfire of condescension than a personal beacon of concern. Thus we have to take Joe Buck's loneliness and stupidity and vulnerability on faith, and I for one never really believed his Texas past as it was presented piecemeal in the movie. Nor did I believe the traumatic gang-bang and the persistence of heterosexual idealism in the midst of homosexual experience, as if there is a distinction in sexual behavior between what we are and what we do. Nor does the movie make clear the signification of the steady stream of bleached-blonde defense-plant victory-girl "mothers" and "grand-mothers" who presumably spawned, among other mutations, a whole generation of restless, fatherless, superegoless bastards doomed to hit the open road in every conceivable direction and into every forbidden orifice.

Herlihy is more precise than any movie could manage to be with such stylishly nuanced self-hatred, and the parts of Joe Buck's experience that ring true tell an interesting story of mythic decadence. At one point in the movie, the most terrifying point actually, Joe Buck begins beating up a whimpering, guilt-ridden, middle-aged midwestern queer. What the movie never makes clear is that the victim is the loving, doting son of a ninety-nine-year-old woman who, once long ago, went west on a covered wagon so that her son might someday come east to celebrate her epic journey by seducing a pseudocowboy. One lost monologue from the book cost one mythic reverberation in the movie.

Even so, the saga of Joe Buck and Ratso Rizzo is deeply enough felt on the screen to suggest a reality basic enough to sustain Marxian, Freudian, and Christian interpretations of the story, and *Midnight Cowboy* is, above all, a story with its mythic roots, if not its flowery sentiments, in the rich soil of American life. The Marxist view of Joe Buck would focus on his lack of economic power in a society that shamelessly conceals its inequities of inherited wealth behind an egalitarian facade of shared tastes and customs. Joe Buck is deceived by the self-serving myths of the manipulators to affect a style of dress and manner that emphasizes his masculinity and individualism and aesthetic attractiveness, as if these qualities, deified in capitalist advertising, would somehow enable him to exploit the exploiters by converting his own sexual potency into the socially acceptable currency of the realm. He journeys to New York, that most corrupt citadel of world capitalism, and finds that New York women are more interested in supplementing their money and power through sexual congress than in making any mutually pleasurable exchange with a lower-caste outsider. Joe Buck must pervert his natural instincts in order to compete in the only marketplace available to a man of his limited guile. But he is cheated even in his perverted pursuits by the quasi-criminal instincts of his guilt-ridden customers. He finds his own identity only when he allies himself with a man of his own deprived class, and thus learns to pool his talents in a collective effort.

The Freudian would look at the essentially fatherless Joe Buck in search of superego through a continuing confrontation of his own reflection and conclude that the progression from Joe's narcissism (an adoration of his own maleness) to homosexuality (an adoration of another's maleness) would seem a pronounced possibility. The Christian would perceive that Joe Buck achieved spiritual redemption even in a diabolically sensual world by subordinating his own will to the love of another, and through this conversion to altruism, to the love of God. Marxist, Freudian, Christian alike could not help but be moved by the spiritual addition of two deprived and depraved individuals into a collective union of love and self-sacrifice; and there is even more to be considered in this latest misadventure of America's Manifest Destiny. So there is truth of a sort in *Midnight Cowboy*, but it is ultimately subverted by the devious sentimentality of the characterizations and the calculating dishonesty about the real feelings that gave birth to the homosexual sensibility with which the pseudoreligious stigmata of *Midnight Cowboy* are ultimately concerned. So much pain, so much suffering, so much dirt, and so much death is too much to be borne merely by Christ. On the whole, I prefer Kenneth Anger's directness in *Scorpio Rising* on this most delicate of all impostures.

—*Village Voice*, May 29, 1969

■ 8. *EASY RIDER*

When the Cannes Film Festival hailed *Easy Rider* as a poetic and perceptive vision of American life, I didn't exactly hold my breath with anticipation. Motorcycles, materialism, misanthropy, and murder have long served as adequate cinematic correlatives of American life for Europeans, and never more so than in this year of law and order on Hamburger Hill. That the American Dream has come to resemble a quickie production out of American-International does not in and of itself transform every vavoom on the screen into a meaningful statement.

As it turns out, however, *Easy Rider* displays an assortment of excellences that lift it above the run and ruck of its genre. First and foremost is the sterling performance of Jack Nicholson as George Hanson, a refreshingly civilized creature of Southern Comfort and interplanetary fantasies. *Easy Rider* comes to life with Nicholson's first hung-over entrance in a Deep South dungeon.

We have been traversing the open road with Peter Fonda and Dennis Hopper on their defiantly nonconformist bikes, and we have been treated to some wide-angle distortions of drug-trafficking, some cut-rate spirituality in a hippie commune, some cryptic conversation on the sanctity of living off the soil, and an endless array of roadside traveling shots lyrically photographed by Laszlo Kovacs. Nothing too extreme, mind you, just little bits and pieces of sociological petit point interspersed with musical strands fashioned by Steppenwolf, the Byrds, the Band, the Holy Modal Rounders, Fraternity of Man, the Jimi Hendrix Experience, Little Eva, the Electric Prunes, the Electric Flag, an American Music Band, and Roger McGuinn from compositions by Hoyt Axton, Mars Bonfire, Gerry Goffin and Carole King, Jaime Robbie Robertson, Antonia Duren, Elliott Ingber and Larry Wagner, Jack Keller, David Axelrod, Mike Bloomfield, Bob Dylan, and Roger McGuinn, or Richard Goldstein, where art thou with thy Pop Eye and Folk and Rock Ear? With all the rousingly rhythmic revelry and splendiferously scenic motorcycling, *Easy Rider* comes to resemble a perpetual precredit sequence, but reasonably pleasant withal.

Unfortunately, there is something depressingly *déja vu* about the moralistic view of America from a motorcycle. And after about the twentieth man-cool mumble, the equation of anticonformity with anticonversation seems too facile by far. Also, Peter Fonda and Dennis Hopper leave a great deal to be desired as allegedly affecting figures of alienation, Fonda being as irritatingly inert as ever and Hopper annoyingly mannered behind the bushy mustache of a character performance. Along the way, Warren Finnerty's fecund farmer and Luke Askew's hirsute hitchhiker play off to advantage against the self-righteous taciturnity of Fonda and Hopper, but not until Jack Nicholson enters the picture with his drawling delivery of good lines can we get involved beyond the level of lethargic lyricism, Peter Fonda, Dennis Hopper, and Terry Southern are credited with the script, and Dennis Hopper with the direction, but see *Easy Rider* for Nicholson's performance, easily the best of the year so far, and leave the LSD trips and such to the collectors of mod mannerisms.

I don't want to draw any aesthetically conservative point from Nicholson's preeminence in *Easy Rider*. It is too easy to say that camera tricks and dazzling cuts are no substitute for full-bodied characterizations. Too easy and too misleading. We are simply too close to the popular cinema of today to read it correctly. If American movies seem today too eclectic, too derivative, and too mannered, so did they seem back in the twenties, the thirties, the forties, and the fifties. The *nouvelle vague* tricks and Bergman-Fellini-Antonioni mannerisms are no more voguish today than the UFA German expressionist and Soviet montage tricks were in the late twenties and early thirties. But out of all the mimicry of earlier times emerged very personal styles, and there is no reason to believe that the same thing will not happen again and again. Hence beware of all generalizations, including this one, perhaps especially this one, because it is just remotely possible that after all the false cries of doom, the cinema might actually be racing to the creative standstill so long predicted for it. But I doubt it. It is not the medium that is most likely to get old, tired, and cynical, but its aging and metaphysically confused critics. This particular critic has never felt younger in his life.

—*Village Voice*, July 3, 1969

■ *9. THE WILD BUNCH; LAST SUMMER*

Sam Peckinpah's *The Wild Bunch* is the work of a distinctive talent—warts, cuts, flaws, lags, and all. Even in its currently mutilated version, the picture is too long, the plot too lumpy, the acting

with more pointedly political rhetoric in Richard Brooks's *The Professionals*. Above all, Peckinpah has put together the divergent classical themes of his own *Ride the High Country* and *Major Dundee*—the first film demonstrating through heroic angles of Randolph Scott and Joel McCrea the moral and physical courage of the Western Gunfighter, and the latter demonstrating through blood-red rivers that war is hellishly beautiful. Even the opening slaughter in *The Wild Bunch* in which civilians are massacred in the crossfire between the Wild Bunch and the law-and-order bounty hunters working and killing for the railroad, the obvious parallel with Vietnam is clouded by the subtler ambiguities that creep into any violent confrontation. And well-meaning, moral-priority humanists to the contrary notwithstanding, there is infinitely more poetry in Peckinpah's shooting scenes than in his sex scenes. It is good to see William Holden and Robert Ryan, those tortured presences of the fifties, in roles with some moral tension. Good but not great. Ernest Borgnine is more restrained than usual, and Edmond O'Brien much less restrained than usual, and almost unrecognizable to boot. The late Albert Dekker's last screen performance closed out a career that was more than a footnote and less than a lead.

Frank Perry's *Last Summer* takes place mostly on a deserted beach on Fire Island, but the way the people in the picture talk about the "mainland," I'm not sure that the story is meant to unfold anywhere as specific as Fire Island, with its very precise sociological spectrum. There is a vague, vacant universality to the goings-on that strikes me as an abstractly literary approach to the Problems of Young People Today. For one thing, the Generation Gap is treated as if it were Grand Canyon. Oldsters (anyone over thirty) are seldom even shown, and parents are invariably described in the most unflattering terms of adult addiction to drink, deceit, divorce, and debauchery. That leaves the kids to roam around the beach in search of their own values, and here the plot thickens. Two very blond boys (Richard Thomas and Bruce Davison) pick up a teen-age siren (Barbara Hershey), who in turn has picked up a wounded sea gull with a swallowed fishhook in its throat. The boys help her bring the sea gull back to health, and she teases the boys' giggly-sensual instincts by going topless now and then and letting them feel her up when the three of them patronize a movie on the "mainland," where three toughs lurk throughout the film like a Greek chorus of ceremonial menace. A series of set pieces moves the plot forward without ever getting too deep into the characters. The gull bites the girl, and as the boys discover later, she kills the gull, because it has turned on her after she has given it her love and affection. The boys scold her for lying to them and sending them off on a wild-gull chase in search of her missing pet when all the time the gull was lying dead in a thicket where the girl had killed it. Already there is enough anecdotal material for a full-length play by Chekhov or a novella by Turgenev, but Frank Perry skips off into new views of the beach and a whole brand-new character (Cathy Burns), a sensitive ugly duckling with a head-shrinker's sensibility. At first she seems even more square and backward and inhibited than the two boys, who seem like repressed infants next to the manipulative glamour girl they lech after. Perry has scored a coup in the contrasting casting of the two girls *vis-à-vis* the relative uniformity of the two boys, but he tends to keep safely on the outside of the dramatic conflict at all times. Finally, even the ugly duckling is compromised by a dramatic soliloquy on the accidental drowning of her mother, a soliloquy so dripping with analytical self-awareness that the rest of the character makes little sense. Also, the lechery in the film seems to oscillate between both sides of the generation gap, between the forties, when nobody in high school got laid, and the sixties, when everybody in high school gets laid, between a generation that was supposedly hot and bothered and frustrated and a generation that is supposedly cool and collected and complacent, between a generation that twisted around sex and a generation that floats beyond it. Perry's young people seem to be caught in the gap, because the script (by Eleanor Perry) persists in asking forties moral questions with the institutionalized jargon of the sixties. Hence when the two boys are goaded by the glamour girl into raping the ugly duckling, Perry retreats from the carnal carnage before him with a lofty overhead shot typical of a style that prefers symbolic evocation to psychological exploration. That much of *Last Summer* is fascinating without being convincing can be attributed to the current tendency to freeze youth into moral and political patterns fashioned out of adult fantasies gone sour.

—*Village* Voice, July 31, 1969

■ 10. MARILYN MONROE:
A REVIEW OF *NORMA JEAN*,
BY FRED LAWRENCE GUILES

The very title of this latest biography of Marilyn Monroe suggests a concern with facts rather than myths, substantiated testimony rather than lurid gossip, the crude beginnings as well as the cruel end. Unfortunately, the facts (at least, those unearthed here by Fred Lawrence Guiles) are considerably less interesting than the fantasies evoked by any one picture of Marilyn Monroe in her familiar pose of sensual supplication.

Guiles has apparently tried hard to be fair and objective—but his cool tone manages to freeze all the feelings out of his material, and what starts out being dispassionate ends up being dull. Worst of all, he seems so unmoved and unimpressed by the Monroe movie iconography (and movies generally) that his motivation for writing this biography becomes one of its biggest mysteries. Indeed, he seems only dimly aware of the sense of loss his subject's death aroused even among many who had never been overwhelmed by her presence in the midst of life.

Marilyn Monroe, who died of an overdose of sleeping pills during a lost August weekend in 1962, was born Norma Jean Mortenson on June 1, 1926, not far from where she was to be eventually incarnated and ultimately entombed as the American sex goddess of her era. Her mother actually lived for a time in Hollywood and worked at the processing laboratories of Consolidated Film Industries. The identity of her father always remained a speculative question, and Norma Jean ran the gamut of orphanages, foster homes, madness in the family, and the savage, rootless religiosity, then as now, of Southern California.

The author resists the temptation to turn Norma Jean's childhood into a Freudian horror story. Indeed, he makes it quite clear that she was likable enough to obtain more than her share of affectionate treatment. She was far above average in looks, wit, intelligence, and emotional manipulativeness—all requisites for the rise of a lower-class nobody to the status of an instantly identifiable

Beautiful Person. Even her three marriages could be said to represent a calculated climb in her career on the successive rungs of
private anonymity (James Dougherty), crowd-pleasing myth (Joe
DiMaggio) and coterie art (Arthur Miller).

Guiles received considerable cooperation from Dougherty and
Miller, but apparently none from DiMaggio. So there is an inevitable imbalance of accounts that comes close to bias against the
Yankee Clipper—but that, of course, is one of the hazards of editorial enterprises of this kind. The cooperative take their revenge
on the uncooperative, the solvent (who can sue) on the insolvent
(who can't), and the living (who are allowed afterthoughts) on
the dead (who aren't). Hence when Jim Dougherty received a
Dear John letter from Norma Jean in 1946 while his merchant
ship was docked in Shanghai, "he lay back in his bunk," as the author would have it, "his eyes squeezed shut, hot with anger and the
conviction that he was a damned fool; but he remembers, too, that
he was full of anxiety for the future of Norma Jean."

The reasonably disinterested reader may find it difficult to be-
live that a rejected husband would be so solicitous of his wife's
future at that precise moment in their relationship. It is more likely
that Dougherty, like the rest of us, felt vaguely guilty when Marilyn's life was snuffed out, and this guilt has colored and softened
his recollection. In fact, most of the recollections in the book are
reported in a muffled manner, as if the witnesses were treading
softly in a funeral parlor and did not wish to show disrespect to the
corpse in the coffin. The book is gradually stifled by sanctimonious-
ness, if not downright hypocrisy, and there are not enough compensations of anecdote or analysis.

Part of the problem may be that Guiles has researched his subject almost entirely from the outside. There are few resonances
and echoes of the Marilyn who exploded on the American landscape during the dully repressed Eisenhower years. The impact of
her image was something more than the sum total of her movies,
photos, nude calendars, and publicity. She was simply there, both
flaunted and frightened, trapped, as we all were, in a puritanical
society in the throes of a painful transition.

Guiles never examines the paradox of Marilyn's being fired by
Fox for behavior much less outrageous than Liz Taylor's on the set
of *Cleopatra* at the same time. Indeed, it was said then that Fox

revenged itself on Miss Taylor by firing Miss Monroe, the difference being, of course, that Marilyn was not as strong as Liz at the
box office, largely because Marilyn expressed an emotional generosity to men that turned most women against her even on the most
mythic level.

Also, Middle America may have chosen to revenge itself on a
creature who had abandoned her Hollywood goldfish bowl for that
section of the eastern elitist swamp inhabited by the Miller-Stras-
berg culture vultures. Try as he may, Fred Guiles never conveys
the magical magnification of a little blonde girl with a large head,
an often dumpy body, a stammering breathlessness, and a warm,
muddled mind into the stuff that so many dreams were made of.

—*New York Times Book Review*, August 3, 1969

■ 11. *TRUE GRIT;*
   TAKE THE MONEY AND RUN

True Grit has apparently accomplished the difficult feat of making
John Wayne a respectable culture hero east of the Mississippi and
left of the ABM bomb-shelter belt. Even Abbie Hoffman and Paul
Krassner seem to have come to terms with the apparent indestructibility of the Duke. And there is talk of an Oscar for Wayne after
forty years of movie acting and after thirty years of damn good
movie acting. Wayne's performances for John Ford alone are
worth all the Oscars passed out to the likes of George Arliss, Warner Baxter, Lionel Barrymore, Paul Lukas, Broderick Crawford,
José Ferrer, Ernest Borgnine, Yul Brynner, and David Niven. Indeed, Wayne's performances in *The Searchers, Wings of Eagles,*
and *The Man Who Shot Liberty Valance* are among the most
full-bodied and large-souled creations of the cinema; and not too
far behind are the characterizations in *She Wore a Yellow Ribbon,*
They Were Expendable, Fort Apache, Rio Grande, Three God-
fathers, The Quiet Man, The Horse Soldiers, Donovan's Reef,
Stagecoach, and *The Long Voyage Home.* And that is only the
Ford oeuvre. *Rio Bravo, El Dorado,* and *Red River,* for Hawks, are
almost on the same level as the Fords, and *Hatari!* is not too far

behind. Then there are the merely nice movies like *Reap the Wild Wind* (with Paulette Goddard), *The Spoilers* (with Marlene Dietrich), *The Lady Takes a Chance* (with Jean Arthur), *Tall in the Saddle* (with Ella Raines), *Wake of the Red Witch* (with Gail Russell), *The High and the Mighty*. Finally there are the leisurely Hathaway movies—*Shepherd of the Hills* (with the curiously grim Betty Field), *North to Alaska, The Sons of Katie Elder*—and now *True Grit*.

Wayne has had his share of disasters like everyone else in Hollywood, and no one has suggested that his acting range extends to Restoration fops and Elizabethan fools. But it would be a mistake to assume that all he can play or has played is the conventional western gunfighter. There is more of Christian submission than pagan hubris in the Duke's western persona. Relatively "liberal" types like Henry Fonda and Paul Newman have been considerably more conspicuous than Wayne in the matter of flaunting virility and swaggering about with six-shooters at the ready. Newman, in particular, exploits the western to express his own anarchic spirit. Wayne embodies the brutal, implacable order of the West less with personal flair than with archetypal endurance. He is more likely to outlast his opponents than to outdraw them, and ever since *Stagecoach* he has never hesitated to use the rifle, an instrument more efficient, if less phallic, than the six-shooter.

Ironically, Wayne has become a legend by not being legendary. He has dominated the screen even when he has not been written in as the dominant character. Thus I can understand why some of Wayne's more knowledgeable admirers have been disconcerted by his first scenes in *True Grit*, the actor colorful as all get-out with an eye patch over his left eye, all restraints released from his aging, sagging frame, and little bits of old Wallace Beery booziness seeping around the edges of the performance. I suppose his erstwhile detractors assumed that Wayne had earned their tolerance by lapsing into self-parody, as if to prove that the only good western nowadays is a camped-up western. If Wayne should obtain his long-deferred Oscar, it will be due to the same principle of emasculation that denied Cagney, Bogart, and Muni awards for their more virile, anarchic parts in *Public Enemy, Casablanca,* and *Scarface*. Cagney did get his award finally, but only after wrapping himself up inside an American flag as George M. Cohan in *Yankee Doo-*

dle Dandy, Bogart only after letting his whiskers grow and acting like a monkey in The African Queen, and Muni only after growing a beard and impersonating Louis Pasteur and Emile Zola. A trick accent, a beard, an eye patch, old-age makeup—these are the accoutrements of acting to many people. And that is why the worst acting is so often mistaken for the best, particularly on the screen, where being is more important than pretending, and just standing there often more impressive than doing something.

Fortunately, Wayne settles down in True Grit and proceeds to dominate the action. The focus shifts from the pseudospinsterish-folklorish point of view of the Charles Portis novel to the distanced-small-epic-small-movie style of Henry Hathaway, who directs the actors somewhat against the consciously literary dialogue of the Portis novel and the Marguerite Roberts screenplay. The charm of the novel is derived from the author's skill in intertwining the strands of a wild yarn into the tapestry of Arkansas-Oklahoma frontier history, complete with details on the cotton-cattle economy, racially segregated society, partisan politics, outlaw celebrity, and vengeful uses of law and order. The movie is reasonably faithful to the action of the novel, but it stops at the point where the novel sets out to embalm the action in pastness. The plot is switched slightly, partly to keep Wayne's character in the forefront and partly to tidy up the emotional loose ends. I rather liked Kim Darby as the fourteen-year-old girl who sets the plot in motion, and I didn't mind Glen Campbell as the callow Texas Ranger, but I thought the outlaws were especially appealing in their ambiguity. The climactic gunfight in which Wayne flips his weapons ostentatiously as he rides toward his four antagonists is more moving to a spectator who knows Wayne's total career than to one who does not. Wayne has never been ostentatious in the past. It is only now that he is so near the end that he will give the dudes one last show with the broad, vulgar gestures of mesa machismo so alien to the true spirit of the actor and the genre. True Grit is well worth seeing, but it is hardly a monument either to Wayne or to the western. But if Wayne should get an Oscar for True Grit, perhaps next year Cary Grant might be induced to grow a beard and pose as a Bowery bum, and he could win his Oscar too. That would still leave Chaplin and Garbo without competitive Oscars, but you can't have everything.

Woody Allen's *Take the Money and Run* manages to satirize a wide variety of movies from *Citizen Kane* to *Cool Hand Luke* without ever losing its own cool. As a movie-maker, Allen remains a monologist. He never really responds to other people. At best, he merely retorts to them, but more often he is not tuned in to any other wavelength but his own. Deep down, Lenny Bruce, Nichols and May, Jules Feiffer, and most of our other contemporary satirists want to save the world. At times they are inhibited by their own idealism from the satiric savagery of which they are capable. But Allen gives the impression that he is not so much interested in saving the world as in salvaging something for himself from the wreckage. This is his strength as a humorist and his weakness as an artist. But it has long been obvious that Allen was not going to replace Proust and Pirandello. Nonetheless I still find him funny and even congenial as an astute critic of film forms. *Take the Money and Run* is at the very least the definitive take-off on the *cinéma vérité* interview. Allen has exploited what I think is a very justifiable conclusion about the abuse of *cinéma vérité* to the point that everyone in the world is encouraged to talk to himself or herself (via the camera) without regard for the point of view of any other human being. Self-expression has subverted communication, and release has destroyed rapport. Perhaps the time has come in film as well as in life for people to stop talking to themselves and start talking to each other. Until that time comes, Woody Allen will be making a comfortable living expressing his own paranoid vision of existence and describing the guerrilla tactics he had devised to extend his ego from out of the ghetto of his soul.

—*Village Voice*, August 21, 1969

■ 12. *ALICE'S RESTAURANT*

Alice's Restaurant is about as likable in a limited way as Arlo Guthrie, a curiously coquettish folk-something unlike anything else. Peeping out from under his lanky locks with passively blank eyes and stubbornly pursed lips, he resembles nothing so much as a perverse tomboy determined not to wear a party dress ever. He's not a great artist, even by the instant immortality standards of the pop scene, and I can't say his talk-sing ballads ever turn me on, but he does have something; charm, perhaps, more than talent; now-ness more than newness. I feel also that he is psychically and sex-ually healthier than those of his elders who choose (unwisely) to question his manhood. Even though he does not yet fully know himself, Arlo Guthrie is fully content to be himself with all the hard knocks that go with being first person singular in a world pro-grammed for third person plural. But unlike other hippie artifacts, *Alice's Restaurant* does not insist on confusing the first person sin-gular with the first person plural. Guthrie, writer-director Arthur Penn, and coscenarist Venable Herndon are to be commended for not extending the small world encompassed in Guthrie's ballad "The Alice's Restaurant Massacree" to an entire generation. Hence there is not in *Alice's Restaurant* any of the peevish paranoia to be found in almost every reel of *Easy Rider*.

Arthur Penn's career has consisted mostly of ballads of one form or another; at worst, exercises in muddled allegory (*Mickey One* and *The Chase*) and even at best a tendency toward mindless lyri-cism (*The Left-Handed Gun and Bonnie and Clyde*)—all in all, a cinema considerably stronger in feelings than in forms, a cinema concerned more with images than with ideas. Significantly, Penn's best films (and *Alice's Restaurant* is one of his better ones) deal with characters at least partly biographical rather than completely fictional. Penn's personality as a director manifests itself therefore through a flair for adding a poetic dimension to reality and a lyrical refrain to biography. The exuberant humor in Penn's films serves to intensify the sadness and loneliness of his characters. It is as if he were staging pillow fights in funeral parlors. Penn does not so much switch from mood to mood as express through each mood the nerve-wracking instability of existence. But his films, unlike those of the Perrys, never give the impression that he knows where it is all going to end. Life is hard and uncertain and virtually hope-less, but it can be fun if you don't think too far ahead. Indeed, Penn's instincts are so contemporaneous that it strikes this neu-tral, disenchanted observer that if Arlo Guthrie had not met Ar-thur Penn, they would have had to invent each other to get *Alice's Restaurant* out of the kitchen and onto the screen.

The movie is well served by a real-life-looking cast headed by

Guthrie, Pat Quinn's remarkably reasonable facsimile of Alice, complete with her roosterish Ray, played by James Broderick—a dead ringer for Norman Mailer and, I am told, the late James Agee; and, of the real-real players, an extraordinarily genial and expansive incarnation of Officer Obie by the officer himself, William Obanheim. Except for some ugly encounters in the beginning between Ultra-America and Un-America, *Alice's Restaurant* is mercifully free of gratuitous malice. The sexual intrigue involving Alice and the mixed-up male moths fluttering around her libidinous light erupts on the screen like an ancient melodrama out of the Garden of Eden. The human animal is not capable of sustaining the psychic generosity required for universal brotherhood and love, and new forms, as Antonioni has told us so many times, cannot entirely obliterate ancient feelings. And so *Alice's Restaurant* ends sadly, if not badly, with little hope and less joy and a curiously generalized camera viewpoint, as if Penn, Guthrie, and especially Alice didn't have the foggiest idea of who was to blame for the end of a dream and the death of a community. Still, it was fun while it lasted, especially when Arlo Guthrie was sidestepping the draft board, the long arm of the law, and the siren squeak of Shelley Plimpton's pop-bop-and-sniffle courtesan.

—*Village Voice*, August 28, 1969

■ 13. *SPIRITS OF THE DEAD*

Spirits of the Dead is so much more a producer's package than a director's dream that the individual ingredients deserve more attention than the total concoction. Take three anomalous stories by Edgar Allan Poe, the first broodingly atmospheric (*Metzengerstein*), the second psychologically incisive (*William Wilson*), and the third mockingly moralistic (*Never Bet the Devil Your Head*), add meaty chunks of Jane Fonda, Peter Fonda, Alain Delon, Brigitte Bardot, and Terence Stamp, and whip with Roger Vadim, Louis Malle, and Federico Fellini. If this artistic recipe results merely in a kind of Gothic goulash, who really cares? At the very least, it's good to see Fellini gainfully employed again after nearly

five years of mysteriously aborted activity. Vadim's zestfully lecherous exploitation of Jane Fonda is worth a few chuckles, and Terence Stamp is always worth catching even in interlinguistic interludes of suspended animation. But the film as a whole turns out as
useless and as pointless as it figured to be in advance. Poe's poetics,
such as they are, both anticipate and defeat the cinema they are
supposed to serve. The dreamlike logic of his narratives is driven
by the same conviction we find in the best movies, and directors as
disparate as D. W. Griffith and Jean Epstein have been drawn to
the Poe oeuvre without adding appreciably to their laurels or his.
Poe's adaptability to the screen is more often than not as illusory
as his grasp on reality. His prose style runs parallel to the ghostliest
mise-en-scène, and hence never intersects it at a point of mutual
expressiveness. Of course, Poe's name on a marquee is merely a pretext for hammy theatrics against a garish setting of supernatural
horror. That Poe was a poetical poet as well as a specialist in many
culturally disreputable genres merely provides movies made in his
name with that vague sense of uplift the movie industry cannot
seem to function without. At that, the Roger Corman specials provide more interesting variations on Poe than are to be found in the
more consciously arty *Spirits of the Dead*.

Curiously, Roger Vadim's episode with Jane and Peter Fonda—
Freudian flames, the metempsychosis of a gloomy rider returning
as a black horse to be ridden by his mistress through the ultimate
ecstasy of fiery destruction, unearthly art, and earthly lust—is both
the silliest and most sympathetic of the three episodes. Vadim's
erotic fetishism has never been more laughably grotesque and ludicrously anachronistic, but the lyrical force of the riding sequences
is closer to the gratuitousness of Poe's art than anything in the
Malle or Fellini episodes. Vadim's talent is minuscule next to Fellini's, but Vadim is at least trying to tell a story, whereas Fellini
is content merely to flourish his own very formidable style to the
point of self-parody. (We can charitably skip Louis Malle's dull
misdirection of *William Wilson* and the badly dubbed, monoto-
nously somnambulist performances of Alain Delon and Brigitte
Bardot.)

It is perhaps no accident that the Fellini episode is loosely based
on the most trifling of Poe stories, a spoof of his morally captious
critics, indeed a spoof with about as much anecdotal matter and

dramatic substance as an Art Buchwald column. I don't know whether this story (*Never Bet the Devil Your Head*) was imposed upon Fellini or whether he chose it for himself. In either case, Fellini makes it completely his own in that baroque manner he has developed ever since *La Dolce Vita*. What little the Poe story may have meant originally is swept aside in a flood of Felliniana. All the doubt and self-hatred of 8½ reappears in Terence Stamp's Toby Dammit, a dubbed English actor who has come to Italy to make the first Christian western, something, a priest tells us, that will combine Carl Dreyer and John Ford, Fra Angelico and Fred Zinnemann. Fellini's grotesque gargoyles grimace frantically into the camera as if they had just been resurrected from the out-takes of *Juliet of the Spirits*. Whatever else he is, Fellini is undeniably the Busby Berkeley of metaphysics. No other director in the past twenty years has tried so strenuously to dance his way through the complexities of the modern world with the same chorus line of brutalized flesh. Once more we are treated to the spectacle of media-manacled man blinded by the glare of modern publicity, and now there is not even the innocence of a little girl to serve as a moral beacon. Fellini's little girl seems to have taken a postgraduate course with Luis Buñuel so that she may double as the devil that wins Toby Dammit's severed head. Most critics seem impressed by the Fellini episode. I was appalled. If Fellini can trot out the same old satirical routines at the drop of a hat or an option, what possible meaning could they ever have had? At what point, therefore, does a personal cinematic language become a tired cliché. I ask this question of a Fellini film as I would of a Ford or a Hitchcock or an Ophuls or a Renoir film because it is the ultimate question of film criticism and a question that is still under debate. For myself, I feel that Fellini's ironies have become too facile by far as they have degenerated from creative responses to conditioned reflexes. Critics and audiences may continue to eat them up nevertheless simply because Fellini allows us all to feel smugly superior to the bright lights of showbiz. But Fellini has spent a whole decade on this theme, and we are now moving into the seventies. Perhaps his *Satyricon* will be a source of artistic renewal or, in some ultimate way, an occasion for artistic release of his more repetitious mannerisms.

—*Village Voice*, September 11, 1969

INDEX